THE MALADAPTED MIND

The Maladapted Mind
Classic Readings in
Evolutionary Psychopathology

edited by
Simon Baron-Cohen
University of Cambridge

Psychology Press
a member of the Taylor & Francis group

Copyright © 1997 by Psychology Press
an imprint of Erlbaum (UK) Taylor & Francis Ltd.

Psychology Press, Publishers
27 Church Road
Hove
East Sussex BN3 2FA
UK

British Library Cataloguing in Publication Data
A catalogue record for this book is available from the British Library

ISBN: 0-86377-460-1
ISBN: 0-86377-461-X (pbk)

Typeset by GCS, Bedfordshire, UK
Printed and bound in the United Kingdom by T.J. International Ltd, Padstow, Cornwall

Contents

Acknowledgements

I am indebted to several people who have helped shape this book. First, the contributors each made useful suggestions about readings that should be considered for inclusion. Secondly, Helena Cronin, through her organisation of the conference on Evolution and the Human Sciences (LSE, 1993) and the Darwin Seminars (LSE, 1994 onwards), has inspired many behavioural scientists (including me) to consider their work in the larger, evolutionary picture. Helena Cronin, Steve Pinker, Leda Cosmides, and John Tooby also suggested readings for this book that I might otherwise have overlooked. Thirdly, the editors at Psychology Press, and Shelagh Eggo, have made my job far smoother by their help. Finally, I want to thank Bridget Lindley for her invaluable advice on aspects of the production of the book, and her support throughout. My children, Sam, Kate, and Robin, have also helped me rethink evolutionary issues by asking refreshingly original questions in our discussions.

I am grateful to the authors and publishers of chapters 1–12 for allowing this material to be republished in this collection, as follows:

Chapter 1: *Evolution and healing.* Publisher: Weidenfeld and Nicolson (1995).

Chapter 2: *Acta Psychiatrica Scandinavica* (1992), *86*, 89–96. Publisher: Munksgaard International Publishers Ltd.

Chapter 3: *Acta Biotheoretica* (1993), *41*, 205–218. Publisher: Kluwer Academic Publishers.

Chapter 4: *Ethology and Sociobiology* (1994), *15*, 247–261. Publisher: Elsevier Science Publishing Co. Inc.

Chapter 5: *Ethology and Sociobiology* (1987), *8*, 73S–83S. Publisher: Elsevier Science Publishing Co. Inc.

Chapter 6: *Cognition* (1995), *57*, 1–29. Publisher: Elsevier Science B.V.

Chapter 7: *Science* (1988), *242*, 519–524. Publisher: American Association for the Advancement of Science.

Chapter 8: *Behavioral and Brain Sciences* (1995), *18*, 523–541. Publisher: Cambridge University Press.

Chapter 9: *Ethology and Sociobiology* (1992), *13*, 3–18. Publisher: Elsevier Science Publishing Co. Inc.

Chapter 10: *Cahiers de Psychologie Cognitive/Current Psychology of Cognition* (1994), *13*, 513–552. Publisher: Association pour la Diffusion des Recherches en Sciences Cognitives de Langue Française.

Chapter 11: *British Journal of Psychiatry* (1994), *164*, 309–315. Publisher: Royal College of Psychiatrists.

Simon Baron-Cohen
Cambridge

Preface

Why evolutionary psychopathology?

Simon Baron-Cohen
Departments of Experimental Psychology and Psychiatry,
University of Cambridge, Downing St, Cambridge, CB2 3EB, UK.

Why a book on evolutionary psychopathology? Indeed, what is evolutionary psychopathology?

Let us briefly sweep definitional issues out of the way. First, since pathology is the study of illness, psychopathology is therefore the study of mental illness. This encompasses both psychiatric and psychological approaches. Psychopathology usually considers a wide range of causal factors for different mental conditions. These typically include social factors, cognitive factors, developmental factors, structural brain damage, neurotransmitter imbalance, and genetic factors. But rarely is psychopathology considered within an *evolutionary* framework. Hence the need for this book, which aims to bring together readings that exemplify this new approach. Hence also its subtitle: "Essays in Evolutionary Psychopathology".

Leda Cosmides and John Tooby, in their book *The Adapted Mind* (Barkow, Cosmides, & Tooby, 1990), argue persuasively for considering evolutionary factors in psychology, the study of the normal mind. Their book stands as something of a manifesto for the new area of "evolutionary psychology". The title of the present book—*The Maladapted Mind*—explicitly echoes theirs, for it shows how evolutionary considerations can be applied to psychopathology. We hope this book may help set the scene for the area of "evolutionary psychopathology".

The neglect of evolutionary considerations in psychopathology is somewhat surprising, though there may be historical reasons for it (which I touch upon later). It is surprising because mental illness is ultimately a product of brain function, and the brain is obviously a biological organ. It is taken for granted in all other areas of biology that to understand biological phenomena, evolutionary factors must be considered. It is time to redress this neglect in psychopathology. If this book does nothing more than rekindle the debates about the links between evolution and psychopathology, it will have done its job. Hopefully it will also spark more research in this important area.

WHY EVOLUTIONARY PSYCHOLOGY?

Evolutionary psychology encourages researchers to consider the universal aspects of the human mind, since these aspects of our make-up are most likely to be the result of our biology rather than our specific culture. Some universals are more obvious than others: They just jump out at you. Language is one (Pinker, 1994); colour vision is another (Zeki, 1995). Other universals are less obvious, or at least seem obvious only once someone has pointed them out. Cheater-detection is one such universal (Cosmides, 1989), and gaze-monitoring is another (Scaife & Bruner, 1975).

Having identified a universal aspect of behaviour or cognition, evolutionary psychology then encourages the researcher to consider its adaptive significance: What advantages does this behaviour or cognitive process confer on survival and reproduction? How might this behaviour or cognitive process have been shaped by natural selection in our ancestral landscape?

Such universals also need to be explained in terms of the neural mechanisms that control them—here, evidence from neuropsychological, neuroimaging, and neurophysiological methods needs to be considered. Ultimately, the genes that code for specific universal neurocognitive mechanisms will need to be identified. Both behavioural and molecular genetic techniques need to feature in such accounts.

Note that evolutionary psychology did not come out of the blue. There had been more than a century of "comparative psychology"—the psychological study of different species—the ultimate aim of which was to understand the human mind better. But in the course of comparative psychology, much research lost sight of this aim and of the importance of situating such work in an evolutionary framework. For example, it was not uncommon to see research programmes investigating maze-learning in the rat, *for its own sake*. This is perfectly valid, but its relevance to the human case is often left undiscussed. Evolutionary psychology refocuses research on to the important goal of attempting to understand the evolution of the human mind.

WHY EVOLUTIONARY PSYCHOPATHOLOGY?

If universal aspects of the mind, together with their neural mechanisms, are adaptive, then the breakdown of such mechanisms should be maladaptive.

Evolutionary psychopathology investigates the breakdown of such mechanisms, and their consequences for cognition and behaviour.

That might suggest that evolutionary psychopathology is strictly dependent on evolutionary psychology. First the universal, adaptive, neurocognitive mechanism must be identified in its healthy state, and only then can its breakdown be studied and its link to pathology explored. Examples abound: Language is identified as a universal, and the breakdown in its control mechanisms is then explored in studies of language impairment. Colour vision is identified as a universal, and the breakdown in its control mechanisms is explored in studies of colour blindness.

However, the relation between evolutionary psychology and psychopathology is not always one-way. It also sometimes happens that a universal, adaptive, neurocognitive mechanism is first revealed by its breakdown. That is, the mechanism might be overlooked when we observe the mind/brain functioning normally; but the existence of the pathology sounds the alarm that there must be a crucial mechanism at work, hidden until that point. Two examples will suffice to illustrate how evolutionary psychopathology can inform evolutionary psychology.

First, Frith (1992) suggests that the presence of auditory hallucinations in schizophrenia arises as a result of a breakdown in a monitor that identifies whether an action was produced by the self or by another. Previously it was taken for granted that we can distinguish between our own actions (including our thoughts, speech, and movement) and those of someone else. It is only the breakdown of this proposed mechanism that reveals how enormously important and adaptive such a mechanism must be. Was that my own thought (in my head) or someone else's voice (in the room)? The disturbing confusion that would follow from an inability to make such a distinction reliably is terrifying. Postulating the existence of a mechanism that monitors whether actions (in the broadest sense) are generated by self or by other helps us not only to answer the question "Why do patients with schizophrenia experience hallucinations?", but also to consider "Why do the rest of us not experience hallucinations?"

A second example of evolutionary psychopathology informing evolutionary psychology may be useful. My colleagues and I have suggested that abnormal social and communication development in children with autism arises as a result of a breakdown in the development of the capacity for mindreading (Baron-Cohen, 1995, and Chapter 10 in this volume). Earlier work had taken it for granted that actions, and social interactions, are interpreted in terms of people's mental states, and that attributing mental states to others is involved in predicting their behaviour. But there was little if any consideration that this "mentalizing" ability (as John Morton calls it) might be a universal (Morton, Frith, & Leslie, 1990). Again, it is only the breakdown of the control mechanisms for mindreading that reveals how enormously important and adaptive such mechanisms must be. Such mechanisms allow us to interpret effortlessly why, for example, that person said one thing but then did another. Interpreting the subtleties of social behaviour is a major puzzle for people with autism, who suffer from degrees of "mindblindness".

THE SCOPE OF EVOLUTIONARY PSYCHOPATHOLOGY

As will be seen, this book contains examples of work that illustrate evolutionary psychopathology, encompassing anxiety disorders, psychopaths, depression, and autism. These readings are just some examples that fall within the scope of evolutionary psychopathology. This raises the following questions: What are the limits of this approach? Can *any* psychiatric condition benefit from an explanation involving evolutionary considerations?

The answers to these questions are not straightforward. We might be tempted to think that this approach is only useful for those psychiatric conditions in which a genetic factor is implicated in their aetiology, since natural selection ultimately works on genes, via differential reproduction rates. On this argument, a condition like Post Traumatic Stress Disorder (PTSD), which by definition only occurs following a major environmental stressor (assault, witnessing or experiencing a terrible accident, and so on), is not the sort of phenomenon that should be brought into the framework of evolutionary psychopathology. What could evolutionary factors possibly have to do with current environmental causal factors?

But excluding such conditions from this framework might prove to be a mistake. It is by no means clear that just because the immediate causal event triggering PTSD lies in the person's environment, his or her specific *response* to it was not shaped by evolved neurocognitive mechanisms. This mirrors arguments explored in relation to depression (see Chapter 12, this volume). In sum, we do not yet know if there are psychiatric conditions that do not fit an explanation in terms of evolutionary psychopathology. It is part of the research programme for scientists in this area to identify which conditions do fit this framework, and which do not.

THE BENEFITS OF EVOLUTIONARY PSYCHOPATHOLOGY, AND ITS DANGERS

In the past, some writers have proposed the morally offensive (and scientifically nonsensical) argument that psychiatric patients are "throwbacks" in evolutionary terms. Such a notion was part of the eugenics movement in the 1930s, and was taken to tragic extremes in Nazi Germany, with the systematic extermination of people with intellectual and psychiatric disabilities and the legalised genocide of Jews and Gypsies, who were also perceived as being of a "lower order" in phylogenetic terms. The eugenics movement in the USA in the same period also led to systematic, legalised, compulsory sterilisation programmes of tens of thousands of people with so-called "mental retardation". In fact, such policies did not have the first thing to do with evolutionary biology, and this sinister history of *apparent* application of evolutionary considerations in psychiatry should not lead us to ignore their *actual* relevance in psychopathology. This history may, however, help us understand the relative neglect of evolutionary approaches in modern psychiatry, mentioned earlier.

It is for us to look to the potential of evolutionary psychopathology. What does this approach give us that other approaches do not? Studying the breakdown of neurocognitive mechanisms frequently throws additional light on their workings that would not be available by studying "normality" alone. All approaches to psychopathology acknowledge that we learn about the normal by studying the abnormal. But by definition, evolutionary psychopathology gives us a larger, more comprehensive picture: not just of behaviour and its control mechanisms in modern humans, but of the evolution of such mechanisms across hominid ancestral history. Ultimately, of course, the value of evolutionary psychopathology will lie in its generating new, testable predictions and discoveries; if some of these lead to a fuller understanding of psychiatric conditions, or to improved diagnostic and treatment methods, it will have proven its value.

REFERENCES

Barkow, J., Cosmides, L., & Tooby, J. (1990). *The adapted mind*. New York: Oxford University Press.

Baron-Cohen, S. (1995). *Mindblindness: An essay on autism and theory of mind*. Cambridge, MA: MIT Press/Bradford Books.

Cosmides, L. (1989). The logic of social exchange: Has natural selection shaped how humans reason? Studies with the Wason selection task. *Cognition, 31*, 187–276.

Frith, C. (1992). *The cognitive neuropsychology of schizophrenia*. Hillsdale, NJ: Lawrence Erlbaum Associates Inc.

Morton, J., Frith, U., & Leslie, A. (1990). The cognitive basis of a biological disorder: Autism. *Trends in Neurosciences, 14*, 434–438.

Pinker, S. (1994). *The language instinct*. Harmondsworth, UK: Penguin Press.

Scaife, M., & Bruner, I. (1975). The capacity for joint visual attention in the infant. *Nature, 253*, 265–266.

Zeki, S. (1995). *A vision of the brain*. Oxford: Blackwell Scientific.

1 Are Mental Disorders Diseases?

Randolph Nesse[1] and George Williams[2]
[1]*University of Michigan.* [2]*State University of New York*

I sometimes hold it half a sin
   To put in words the grief I feel:
   For words, like Nature, half reveal
And half conceal the Soul within.

But, for the unquiet heart and brain,
   A use in measured language lies;
   The sad mechanic exercise,
Like dull narcotics, numbing pain.

              —Alfred, Lord Tennyson,
              In Memoriam, canto V

A young woman recently came to the Anxiety Disorders Clinic at the University of Michigan, complaining of attacks of overwhelming fear that had come out of the blue several times each week for the past ten months. During these attacks, she experienced a sudden onset of rapid pounding heartbeats, shortness of breath, a feeling that she might faint, trembling, and an overwhelming sense of doom, as if she were about to die. A few years ago, such people usually insisted that they had heart disease, but this person, like so many now, had read about her symptoms and knew that they were typical of panic disorder. In the course of the evaluation it came out that she had experienced her first panic attacks at about the same time as she had begun an extramarital affair. When the doctor asked if there might be a connection, she said, "I don't see what that has to do with it. Everything I read says that panic disorder is a

1

disease caused by genes and abnormal brain chemicals. I just want the medicine that will normalize my brain chemicals and stop these panic attacks, that's all."

How times change! Twenty years ago, people who insisted that their anxiety was "physical" were often told that they were denying the truth in order to avoid painful unconscious memories. Now many psychiatrists would readily agree that depression or anxiety can be a symptom of a biological disease caused by brain abnormalities that need drug treatment. Some people, like the woman described above, so embrace this view that they are offended if the psychiatrist insists on attending to their emotional life. The opening lines of an influential review article summarize these changes:

> The field of psychiatry has undergone a profound transformation in recent years. The focus of research has shifted from the mind to the brain . . . at the same time the profession has shifted from a model of psychiatric disorders based on maladaptive psychological processes to one based on medical diseases.

Strong forces have pushed the field of psychiatry to adopt this "medical model" for psychiatric disorders. The change began in the 1950s and 1960s with discoveries of effective drug treatments for depression, anxiety, and the symptoms of schizophrenia. These discoveries spurred the government and pharmaceutical companies to fund research on the genetic and physiological correlates of psychiatric disorders. In order to define these disorders so research findings from different studies could be compared, a new approach to psychiatric diagnosis was created, one that emphasizes sharp boundaries around clusters of current symptoms instead of continuous gradations of emotions caused by psychological factors, past events, and life situations. Academic psychiatrists focus increasingly on the neurophysiological causes of mental disorders. Their views are transmitted to residents in training programs and to practitioners via postgraduate medical seminars. Finally, with the rise of insurance funding for medical care during recent decades and the possibility of federal funding for universal medical coverage in the United States, organizations of psychiatrists have become insistent that the disorders they treat are medical diseases like all others and therefore deserve equal insurance coverage.

Are panic disorder, depression, and schizophrenia medical diseases just like pneumonia, leukemia, and congestive heart failure? In our opinion mental disorders are indeed medical disorders, but *not* because they are all distinct diseases that have identifiable physical causes or because they are necessarily best treated with drugs. Instead, mental disorders can be recognized as medical disorders when they are viewed in an evolutionary framework. As is the case for the rest of medicine, many psychiatric symptoms turn out not to be diseases themselves but defenses akin to fever and cough. Furthermore, many of the genes that predispose to mental disorders are likely to have fitness benefits, many of the environmental factors that cause mental disorders are likely to be novel aspects of modern life, and many of the more unfortunate aspects of human psychology are not flaws but design compromises.

EMOTIONS

Unpleasant emotions can be thought of as defenses akin to pain or vomiting. Just as the capacity for physical pain has evolved to protect us from immediate and future tissue damage, the capacity for anxiety has evolved to protect us against future dangers and other kinds of threats. Just as the capacity for experiencing fatigue has evolved to protect us from overexertion, the capacity for sadness may have evolved to prevent additional losses. Maladaptive extremes of anxiety, sadness, and other emotions make more sense when we understand their evolutionary origins and normal, adaptive functions. We also need proximate explanations of both the psychological and brain mechanisms that regulate and express these emotions. If we find what look like abnormalities in the brains of people who are anxious or sad we cannot conclude that these brain changes cause the disorder in any but the most simplistic sense. Brain changes associated with anxiety or sadness may merely reflect the normal operation of normal mechanisms.

Knowledge about the normal functions of the emotions would provide, for psychiatry, something like what physiology provides for the rest of medicine. Most mental disorders are emotional disorders, so you might think that psychiatrists are well versed in the relevant scientific research, but no psychiatric training program systematically teaches the psychology of the emotions. This is not as unfortunate as it seems, since research on the emotions has been as fragmented and confused as psychiatry itself. In the midst of ongoing technical debates, however, many emotions researchers are reaching consensus on a crucial point: *our emotions are adaptations shaped by natural selection*. This principle holds substantial promise for psychiatry. If our emotions are subunits of the mind, they can be understood, just like any other biological trait, in terms of their functions. Doctors of internal medicine base their work on understanding the functions of cough and vomiting and the liver and the kidneys. An understanding of the evolutionary origins and functions of the emotions would begin to provide something similar for psychiatrists.

Many scientists have studied the functions of the emotions. Some have emphasized communication, especially University of California psychologist Paul Ekman, whose studies of the human face demonstrate the cross-cultural universality of emotions. Others emphasize the utility of emotions for motivation or other internal regulation, but emotions have not been shaped to perform one or even several functions. Instead, each emotion is a specialized state that simultaneously adjusts cognition, physiology, subjective experience, and behavior, so that the organism can respond effectively in a particular kind of situation. In this sense, an emotion is like a computer program that adjusts many aspects of the machine to cope efficiently with the challenges that arise in a particular kind of situation. Emotions are, in the felicitous phrase coined by University of California psychologists Leda Cosmides and John Tooby, "Darwinian algorithms of the mind."

Emotional capacities are shaped by situations that occurred repeatedly in the course of evolution and that were important to fitness. Attacks by predators, threats of exclusion from the group, and opportunities for mating were frequent and important enough to have shaped special patterns of preparedness, such as panic, social fear, and sexual arousal. Situations that are best avoided shape aversive emotions, while situations that involve opportunity shape positive emotions. Our ancestors seem to have faced many more kinds of threats than opportunities, as reflected by the fact that twice as many words describe negative as positive emotions. This perspective gives the boot to the modern idea that "normal" life is free of pain. Emotional pain is not only unavoidable, it is normal and can be useful. As E.O. Wilson put it,

> Love joins hate; aggression, fear; expansiveness, withdrawal; and so on; in blends designed not to promote the happiness and survival of the individual, but to favor the maximum transmission of the controlling genes.

But much emotional pain is not useful. Some useless anxiety and depression arise from normal brain mechanisms, others from brain abnormalities. Major genetic factors contribute to the causation of anxiety disorders, depression, and schizophrenia. In the next decade, specific genes will no doubt be found responsible for certain kinds of mental disorders. Physiological correlates have been found for all of these disorders, and neuroscientists are hard at work unraveling the responsible proximate mechanisms. The resulting knowledge has already improved the utility of drug treatments and offers the possibility of prevention. This is a bright time for psychiatry and for people with mental disorders. The advances in pharmacologic treatment have come so fast that many people remain unaware of their safety and effectiveness. Treatment is now more effective than the wildest hopes of psychiatrists who went into practice just thirty years ago.

Much confusion attends these advances. The human mind tends to oversimplify this issue by attributing most bad feelings either to genes and hormones or to psychological and social events. The messy truth is that most mental problems result from complex interactions of genetic predispositions, early life events, drugs and other physical effects on the brain, current relationships, life situations, cognitive habits, and psychodynamics. Paradoxically, it now is much easier to treat many mental disorders than it is to understand them.

Just as there are several components of the immune system, each of which protects us against particular kinds of invasions, there are subtypes of emotion that protect us against a variety of particular kinds of threats. Just as arousal of the immune system usually occurs for a good reason, not because of an abnormality in its regulation mechanism, we can expect that most incidents of anxiety and sadness are precipitated by some cause, even if we cannot identify it. On the other hand, the regulation of the immune system can be abnormal. The immune system can be too active and attack tissues it shouldn't, causing autoimmune disorders such as rheumatoid arthritis. Comparable abnormalities in the anxiety system cause anxiety disorders. The immune system can also fail to act when it should, causing deficiencies in immune function. Might there be anxiety disorders that result from too little anxiety?

ANXIETY

Everyone must realize that anxiety can be useful. We know what happens to the berry picker who does not flee a grizzly bear, the fisherman who sails off alone into a winter storm, or the student who does not shift into high gear as a term-paper deadline approaches. In the face of threat, anxiety alters our thinking, behavior, and physiology in advantageous ways. If the threat is immediate, say from the imminent charge of a bull elephant, a person who flees will be more likely to escape injury than one who goes on chatting nonchalantly. During flight, our survivor experiences a rapid heartbeat, deep breathing, sweating, and an increase in blood glucose and epinephrine levels. Physiologist Walter Cannon accurately described the functions of these components of the "fight or flight" reaction back in 1929. It is curious that his adaptationist perspective has never been extended to other kinds of anxiety.

While anxiety can be useful, it usually seems excessive and unnecessary. We worry that it will rain at the wedding next June, we lose our concentration during exams, we refuse to fly on airplanes, and we tremble and stumble over our words when speaking in front of a group. Fifteen percent of the U.S. population has had a clinical anxiety disorder; many of the rest of us are just nervous. How can we explain the apparent excess of anxiety? In order to determine when it is useful and when it is not, we need to ask how the mechanisms that regulate anxiety were shaped by the forces of natural selection.

Because anxiety can be useful, it might seem optimal to adjust the mechanism so that we are always anxious. This would be distressing, but natural selection cares only about our fitness, not our comfort. The reason we are sometimes calm is not because discomfort is maladaptive but because anxiety uses extra calories, makes us less fit for many everyday activities, and damages tissues. Why does stress damage tissues? Imagine a host of bodily responses that offer protection against danger. Those that are "inexpensive" and safe can be expressed continually, but those that are "expensive" or dangerous cannot. Instead, they are bundled into an emergency kit that is opened only when the benefits of using the tools are likely to exceed the costs. Some components are kept sealed in the emergency kit precisely because they cause bodily damage. Thus, the damage associated with chronic stress should be no cause for surprise and certainly no basis for criticizing the design of the organism. In fact, recent work has suggested that the "stress hormone" cortisol may not defend against outside dangers at all but instead may mainly protect the body from the effects of other parts of the stress response.

If anxiety can be costly and dangerous, why isn't the regulatory mechanism adjusted so that it is expressed only when danger is actually present? Unfortunately, in many situations it is not clear whether or not anxiety is needed. The smoke-detector principle, described previously, applies here as well. The cost of getting killed even once is enormously higher than the cost of responding to a hundred false alarms. This was demonstrated by an experiment in which guppies were separated into timid, ordinary, and bold groups on the basis of their reactions when confronted by a smallmouth bass: hiding, swimming away, or eyeing the intruder. Each group of guppies was then left in a tank with a bass. After sixty hours, 40 percent of the timid guppies and 15 percent of the ordinary guppies were still there, but none of the bold guppies had survived.

The psychiatrist's attempt to understand how natural selection has shaped the mechanism that regulates anxiety is conceptually the same as the electronics engineer's problem of determining if a signal on a noisy telephone line is actually information or just static. Signal detection theory provides a way to analyze such situations. With an electronic signal, the decision about whether to call a given click a signal or noise depends on four things: (1) the loudness of the signal, (2) the ratio of signals to noise, (3) the cost of mistakenly thinking that a noise is actually a signal (false alarm), and (4) the cost of mistakenly thinking that a signal is actually a noise (false negative response).

Imagine that you are alone in the jungle and you hear a branch break behind a bush. It could be a tiger, or it could be a monkey. You could flee, or you could stay where you are. To determine the best course of action, you need to know: (1) the relative likelihood that a sound of this magnitude would come from a tiger (as opposed to a monkey), (2) the relative frequency of tigers and monkeys in this location, (3) the cost of fleeing (the cost of a false alarm), and (4) the cost of not fleeing if it really is a tiger (the cost of a false negative response). What if you hear the sound of a medium-sized stick breaking behind that bush? The individual whose anxiety level is adjusted by an intuitive, quick, and accurate signal detection analysis will have a survival advantage.

The analogy with the immune disorders suggests that there might be a whole category of people with unrecognized anxiety disorders, namely those who have too little anxiety. Isaac Marks, the anxiety expert at the University of London, has coined the term "hypophobics" for such people. They don't complain and don't seek psychiatric treatment but instead end up in emergency rooms or fired from their jobs. As psychiatrists prescribe new antianxiety drugs with few side effects, we may create such conditions. For instance, one patient, shortly after starting on an antianxiety medication, impulsively told her husband that she wanted him to leave. He was very surprised but did. A week later she realized that she had three small children, a mortgage, no income, and no helpful relatives. A bit more anxiety would have inhibited such hasty action. Of course, no case is simple. This particular woman had long-standing marital dissatisfactions and her emotional outburst might, in the long run, have left her better off. Her story illustrates one possible function of passions, as distinct from rational decisions. As suggested by Cornell economist Robert Frank, passions motivate actions that seem impulsive but may actually benefit the person in the long run.

NOVEL DANGERS

In the chapter on injuries, we described experiments that showed how monkeys' fear of snakes is "prepared." Most of our excessive fears are related to prepared fears of ancient dangers. Darkness, being away from home, and being the focus of a group's attention were once associated with dangers but now mainly cause unwanted fears. Agoraphobia, the fear of leaving home, develops in half of people who experience repeated panic attacks. Staying home seems senseless until you realize that most episodes of panic in the ancestral environment were probably caused by close encounters with predators or dangerous people. After a few such close calls, a wise person would try to stay home when possible, would venture out only with companions, and be ready to flee in panic at the least provocation: the exact symptoms of agoraphobia.

Do anxiety disorders, like many other diseases, result from novel stimuli not found in our ancestral environment? Not often. New dangers such as guns, drugs, radioactivity, and high-fat meals cause too little fear, not too much. In this sense we all have maladaptive hypophobias, but few of us seek psychiatric treatment to increase our fear. Some novel situations, especially flying and driving, do often cause phobias. In both cases, the fear has been prepared by eons of exposure to other dangers. Fear of flying has been prepared by the dangers associated with heights, dropping suddenly, loud noises, and being trapped in a small, enclosed place. The stimuli encountered in an automobile zooming along at sixty miles an hour are novel, but they too hark back to ancestral dangers associated with rapid movement, such as the rushing attack of a predator. Automobile accidents are so common and so dangerous that it is hard to say if fear of driving is beneficial or harmful.

The genetic contributions to anxiety disorders are substantial. Most people with panic disorders have a blood relative who has the same problem, and the search is on for the responsible genes. Will these genes turn out to result from mutant genes that have not been entirely selected out? Will they turn out to have other benefits? Or will we discover that genetic susceptibility to panic is simply one end of a normal distribution, like a tendency to develop a high fever with a cold or a tendency to vomit readily? When we find specific genes that predispose to panic and other anxiety disorders, we will still need to find out why those genes exist and persist.

SADNESS AND DEPRESSION

Depression sometimes seems like a modern plague. After motor vehicle accidents, suicide is the second leading cause of death of young adults in North America. Nearly 10 percent of young adults in the United States have experienced an episode of serious depression. Furthermore the rates seem to have increased steadily in the past few decades, doubling every ten years in many industrial countries.

Depression may seem completely useless. Even apart from the risk of suicide, sitting all day morosely staring at the wall can't get you very far. A person with severe depression typically loses interest in everything—work, friends, food, even sex. It is as if the capacities for pleasure and initiative have been turned off. Some people cry spontaneously, but others are beyond tears. Some wake every morning at 4 a.m. and can't get back to sleep; others sleep for twelve or fourteen hours per day. Some have delusions that they are impoverished, stupid, ugly, or dying of cancer. Almost all have low self-esteem. It seems preposterous even to consider that there should be anything adaptive associated with such symptoms. And yet depression is so frequent, and so closely related to ordinary sadness, that we must begin by asking if depression arises from a basic abnormality or if it is a dysregulation of a normal capacity.

There are many reasons to think that the capacity for sadness is an adaptive trait. A universal capacity, it is reliably elicited by certain cues, notably those that indicate a loss. The characteristics of sadness are relatively consistent across diverse cultures. The hard part is figuring out how these characteristics can be useful. The utility of happiness is not difficult to understand. Happiness makes us outgoing and gives us initiative and perseverance. But sadness? Wouldn't we be better off without it? One test would be to find people who do not experience sadness and see if they experience any disadvantages. Or an investigator could use a drug that blocks normal sadness, a study that we fear may soon be conducted inadvertently on a massive scale as more and more people take the new psychoactive drugs. While we wait for such studies to be done, the characteristics of sadness and the situations that arouse it provide clues that may help us to discover its functions.

The losses that cause sadness are losses of reproductive resources. Whether of money, a mate, reputation, health, relatives, or friends, the loss is always of some resource that would have increased reproductive success through most of human evolution. How can a loss be an adaptive challenge, a situation that would benefit from a special state of preparation? A loss signals that you may have been doing something maladaptive. If sadness somehow changes our behavior so as to stop current losses or prevent future ones, this would be helpful indeed.

How can people behave differently after a loss in a way that increases fitness? First, you should stop what you are doing. Just as pain can make us let go of a hot potato, sadness motivates us to stop current activities that may be causing losses. Second, it would be wise to set aside the usual human tendency to optimism. Recent studies have found that most of us consistently over-estimate our abilities and our effectiveness. This tendency to optimism helps us to succeed in social competition, where bluffing is routine, and also keeps us pursuing important strategies and relationships even at times when they are not paying off. After a loss, however, we must take off the rose-colored glasses in order to reassess our goals and strategies more objectively.

In addition to sudden losses, there are situations in which an essential resource is simply not available despite major expenditures and our best plans and efforts. Jobs end, friendships fade, marriages sour, and goals must be abandoned. At some point one must give up on a major life project in order to use the resources to start something else. Such giving up should not be done lightly. Quitting one's job shouldn't be done impulsively, because there are costs involved in retraining and starting at the bottom of another hierarchy. Likewise, it is foolish to casually give up any important relationship or life goal in which a major investment has already been made. So we don't usually make major life changes quickly. "Low mood" keeps us from jumping precipitously to escape temporary difficulties, but as difficulties continue and grow and our life's energies are progressively wasted, this emotion helps to disengage us from a hopeless enterprise so that we can consider alternatives. Therapists have long known that many depressions go away only after a person finally gives up some long-sought goal and turns his or her energies in another direction.

The capacity for high and low mood seems to be a mechanism for adjusting the allocation of resources as a function of the propitiousness of current opportunities. If there is little hope of payoff, it is best to sit tight rather than to waste energy. Real estate agents who enter the business during an economic downturn may be making a mistake. Students who are failing a course would sometimes do best to drop it and try another subject. Farmers who plant their fields during a drought may go broke. If, by contrast, we come upon a short-lived opportunity, then it may be best to make a major, intense effort, despite the possible risks, in order to have a chance at a big payoff. When a million dollars in cash fell out of the back of an armored car on the streets of Detroit, a few people who made an intense, brief effort profited nicely.

A better understanding of the functions of sadness will soon be essential. We are fast gaining the capacity to adjust mood as we choose. Each new generation of psychotropic drugs has increasing power and specificity with fewer side effects. Decades ago there was a hue and cry about "soma," the fictional drug that made people tolerate tedious lives in Aldous Huxley's *Brave New World*. Now that similar substances loom as a reality, strangely little is being said. Do people not realize how fast this train is moving? We certainly should try to relieve human suffering, but is it wise to eliminate normal low mood? Many people intuitively feel it is wrong to use drugs to change mood artificially, but they will have a hard time arguing against the use of nonaddicting drugs with few side effects. The only medical reason not to use such drugs is if they interfere with some useful capacity. Soon—very soon—people will be clamoring to know when sadness is useful and when it is not. An evolutionary approach provides a foundation for addressing these questions.

We are aware that this analysis is vastly oversimplified. People are not controlled by some internal calculator that crudely motivates them to maximize their reproductive success. Instead, people form deep, lifelong emotional attachments and experience loves and hates that shape their lives. They have religious beliefs that guide their behavior, and they have idiosyncratic goals and ambitions. They have networks of friends and relatives. Human reproductive resources are not like the squirrel's cache of nuts. They are, instead, constantly changing states of intricate social systems. All these complexities do not undercut our simple arguments; they just highlight the urgency of blazing the trail of functional understanding that the adaptationist program may provide for human emotions.

While some low mood is normal, some is clearly pathological. The causes of such pathology are complex. Genetic factors are important determinants of manic-depressive disorder, a condition in which mood swings wildly from the depths of depression to aggressive euphoria. Having one parent with manic-depressive disorder increases your risk of that disorder by a factor of 5, and having two parents increases it by a factor of 10 to a likelihood of nearly 30 percent. These genes are not rare—manic-depressive illness occurs in 1 out of 100 people. Our next, by now familiar, question is, Why are these genes maintained in the gene pool? The answer is equally familiar: They probably offer some advantage, either in certain circumstances or in combination with certain other genes. A study by Nancy Andreasen, professor of psychiatry at the University of Iowa, found that 80 percent of the faculty at the renowned Iowa Writer's Workshop had experienced some kind of mood disorder. Is creativity a benefit of the genes that cause depression? The disease wreaks havoc in some individual lives, but the genes that cause it seem nonetheless to offer a fitness advantage either to some people with the disorder or to other people in whom the gene does not cause the disorder but has other, beneficial effects.

John Hartung, an evolutionary researcher at the State University of New York, has suggested that depression is common in people whose abilities threaten their superiors. If a person with lower status demonstrates his or her full abilities, this is likely to bring attack from the more powerful superior. The best protection, Hartung suggests, is to conceal your abilities and to deceive yourself about them so as to more readily conceal your ambitions. This could well explain some otherwise mysterious cases of low self-esteem in successful people. Hartung's theory reminds us of the complexity of human emotions.

Another major effort to understand mood has come from a group of researchers who are pursuing British psychiatrist John Price's theory of the role of mood in human status hierarchies. They have argued that depression often results when a person is unable to win a hierarchy battle and yet refuses to yield to the more powerful person. They suggest that depression is an involuntary signal of submissiveness that decreases the likelihood of attacks by dominants. In case studies they describe how submitting voluntarily can end depression.

UCLA researchers Michael Raleigh and Michael McGuire have found a brain mechanism that connects mood and status. In studies of vervet monkeys, they found that the highest-ranking (alpha) male in each group had levels of a neurotransmitter (serotonin) that were twice as high as those of other males. When these "alpha" males lost their position, their serotonin levels immediately fell and they huddled and rocked and refused food, looking for all the world like depressed humans. These behaviors were prevented by the administration of antidepressants, such as Prozac, that raise serotonin levels. Even more astounding, if the researchers removed the alpha male from a group and gave antidepressants to some other randomly chosen male, that individual became the new alpha male in every instance. These studies suggest that the serotonin system may function, in part, to mediate status hierarchies and that some low mood may be a normal part of status competitions. If this is so, one cannot help but wonder what will happen in large corporations as more and more depressed employees start taking antidepressants.

Still another approach to understanding depression is based on the increase of the state that occurs when the amount of daylight decreases in the fall. The large number of people affected with this seasonal affective disorder (SAD) and its strong association with cold climates have suggested to many researchers that low mood may be a variant or remnant of a hibernation response in some remote ancestor. The preponderance of women with SAD has suggested that the response may somehow regulate reproduction.

Are there novel aspects of our modern environment that make depression and suicide more likely? While every age seems to have believed that people are not as happy as they were in earlier times, some recent evidence suggests that we may actually be in an epidemic of depression. A team of distinguished investigators looked at data from 39,000 people in nine different studies carried out in five diverse areas of the world and found that young people in each country are far more likely than their elders to have experienced an episode of major depression. Furthermore, the rates were higher in societies with higher degrees of economic development. Much remains to be done to confirm this finding, but it justifies an intense study of novel aspects of modern life that might contribute to dramatic increases in depression. We will mention only two: mass communications and the disintegration of communities.

Mass communications, especially television and movies, effectively make us all one competitive group even as they destroy our more intimate social networks. Competition is no longer within a group of fifty or a hundred relatives and close associates, but among five billion people. You may be the best tennis player at your club, but you are probably not the best in your city and are almost certainly not the best in your country or planet. People turn almost every activity into a competition, whether it be running, singing, fishing, sailing, seducing, painting, or even bird watching. In the ancestral environment you would have had a good chance at being best at something. Even if you were not the best, your group would likely value your skills. Now we all compete with those who are the best in all the world.

Watching these successful people on television arouses envy. Envy probably was useful to motivate our ancestors to strive for what others could obtain. Now few of us can achieve the goals envy sets for us, and none of us can achieve the fantasy lives we see on television. The beautiful, handsome, rich, kind, loving, brave, wise, creative, powerful, brilliant heroes we see on the screen are out of this world. Our own wives and husbands, fathers and mothers, sons and daughters can seem profoundly inadequate by comparison. So we are dis-satisfied with them and even more dissatisfied with ourselves. Extensive studies by psychologist Douglas Kenrick have shown that after being exposed to photos or stories about desirable potential mates, people decrease their ratings of commitment to their current partners.

Our new technology also dissolves supportive social groups. For members of our socially oriented species, the worst punishment is solitary confinement, but many modern, anonymous groups are not much better. They often consist mostly of competitors with only an occasional comrade and no blood relatives. Extended families disintegrate as individuals scatter to pursue their economic goals. Even the nuclear family, that last remnant of social stability, seems doomed, with more than half of all marriages now ending in divorce and more and more children being born to single women.

We have a primal need for a secure place in a supportive group. Lacking family, we turn elsewhere to meet this need. More and more people have their social base in groups of friends, twelve-step programs such as Alcoholics Anonymous, support groups of all kinds, or psychotherapy. Many people turn to religion in part because of the group it provides. Some people advocate "family values" in hopes of preserving a threatened but cherished way of life. Most of us want most of all to be loved by someone who cares about us for ourselves, not for what we can do for them. For many, the search is bitter and fruitless.

LACK OF ATTACHMENT

Pre-evolutionary theories, both psychoanalytic and behavioral, explained the bond between mother and child as the result of feeding and caretaking. Primatologist Harry Harlow began to challenge these theories with studies of monkeys at the University of Wisconsin in the early 1950s. Infant monkeys were separated from their mothers and provided with two surrogate mothers, one a wire form with a baby bottle full of milk, the other a soft cloth-covered form without a bottle. Although infants got milk from the wire mother, it was the cloth surrogate they clung to, screaming if it was removed. Harlow concluded that there must be a special mechanism that evolved to facilitate the bonding of mother and infant. Inspired by Rene Spitz's studies of the social inadequacy of children raised in orphanages, Harlow next raised monkey infants in isolation. Such monkeys never became normal. They could not get along with other monkeys, had great difficulty in mating, and neglected or attacked any babies they had.

John Bowlby, an English psychiatrist, attended seminars with biologist Julian Huxley in 1951 and was inspired to read the imprinting experiments done by Nobel Prize-winning ethologist Konrad Lorenz. During a very specific critical period early in life, baby goslings imprint on their mothers or any other appropriate-sized moving object they encounter. Konrad Lorenz's boots were sufficiently similar, and many photos show him being trailed by a line of goslings. Bowlby wondered if many of his patients' difficulties were sequelae of problems with early attachment. As he looked at their first relationships, he found problems everywhere. Some had mothers who had never wanted them, others had mothers who were too depressed to respond to smiles and coos. Many had heard their mothers threaten to kill themselves and had grown up under this specter. People's early difficulties matched the problems they experienced as adults. They could not trust people, they expected to be rejected, and they felt they had to please people or they would be abandoned. Bowlby perceptively recognized that some of the clinging and withdrawal behavior of neglected babies might be adaptive attempts to engage the mother. Instead of criticizing patients for being "dependent," he recognized that they were trying to protect themselves from a feared separation.

Psychologist Mary Ainsworth and her colleagues did the controlled studies that brought Bowlby's theories to mainstream psychology. She put young children into a room and observed their behavior when the mother left and later returned. On the basis of this "strange situation" test, she classified babies into those who were securely attached and those who were anxiously attached or who avoided their mothers on reunion. Which group the child fit into strongly predicted many other characteristics from group-play patterns to personality characteristics many years later. Much remains to be done to determine what the relationship is between attachment problems and adult psychopathology and how it relates to genetic factors. Psychiatrists should not forget that mothers provide not only early experiences for their children; they also provide genes. At present we have reason to believe that many problems adults have in getting along with other people may have their origins in problems with the first attachment.

CHILD ABUSE

Child abuse seems to have become epidemic among us. How can this be? Why would we attack our own children, the vehicles of our reproductive success? Are some parents more likely to abuse than others? Canadian psychologists Martin Daly and Margo Wilson's evolutionary perspective led them to wonder if the presence or absence of a blood relationship between parents and children might predict the likelihood of child abuse. Because of the vagaries in the reporting of child abuse, they looked at an outcome that was easy to count and hard to hide—murders of children by their parents. The correlation was stronger than even they had dared to imagine. The risk of fatal child abuse for children living with one nongenetic parent is seventy times higher than it is for children living with both biological parents. This finding was not explainable by any tendency of families with stepparents to have more alcoholism, poverty, or mental illness. In several decades of research, no other risk factor has proved anywhere near as powerful in predicting child abuse. Many who have studied child abuse for decades never thought to look at the significance of kinship, but to evolutionists this was an obvious suspect.

Daly and Wilson were inspired, in part, by studies on infanticide in animals carried out by California anthropologist Sarah Hrdy and others. When Hrdy reported in 1977 that male langur monkeys routinely tried to kill the infants of females in a group they had just taken over from another male, no one wanted to believe her. She reported that the monkey mothers tried to protect their infants but often did not succeed. When they failed, nursing stopped, estrus came quickly, and the monkey mothers promptly mated with the males who had killed their infants. Hrdy noted that males who killed existing infants would increase their reproductive success because the cessation of nursing brought the females into estrus so they could become pregnant with the offspring of the new male sooner.

Subsequent field research has confirmed Hrdy's findings and extended them to many other species. Male lions kill existing cubs when they begin mating with new females. Among mice, the mere smell of a strange male often induces miscarriage—apparently an adaptation to prevent wasting investment on babies that are likely to be killed. Animals are inevitably designed to do whatever will increase the success of their genes, grotesque though the resulting behavior may seem.

The tendency for male animals to kill the offspring of other males in certain circumstances is an evolved adaptation. Is child abuse in humans in any way related? We had thought not, both because human males don't routinely take over a group of breeding females with young offspring and because many foster fathers are obviously capable of providing excellent care for children who are not their own. We had guessed that children are abused not because of an evolved adaptation but because a normal adaptation failed when one of the parents had too little early contact with the child to facilitate normal attachment. However, studies by anthropologist Mark Flinn in Trinidad have found that stepparents still treat their stepchildren more harshly than their natural children, regardless of the amount of early contact with the baby. More is involved in forming human attachments than merely spending time together. Much more research is needed to explore this murky intersection of biology and culture.

SCHIZOPHRENIA

The symptoms of schizophrenia, unlike those of anxiety and depression, are not a part of normal functioning. Hearing voices, thinking that others can read your mind, emotional numbness, bizarre beliefs, social withdrawal, and paranoia appear together as a syndrome not because they are parts of an evolved defense. It is more likely that one kind of brain damage can cause many malfunctions, just as heart damage can cause shortness of breath, chest pain, and swollen ankles. Schizophrenia disrupts the perceptual-cognitive-emotional-motivational system. This is another way of saying that we still don't know how to describe the higher levels of brain function.

Schizophrenia affects about 1 percent of the population in diverse societies worldwide. The notion that it is a disease of civilization seems to be incorrect, although there have recently been suggestions that the course of the disease is worse in modern societies. Compelling evidence suggests that susceptibility to schizophrenia depends on certain genes. Relatives of schizophrenics are several times more likely than other people to get the disease, even if they were raised by nonschizophrenic adoptive parents. If one identical twin has schizophrenia, the chance of the other getting it is about 50 percent, while the risk for a nonidentical twin is about 25 percent. There is also evidence that schizophrenia decreases reproductive success, especially in men. These observations call up our standard question: What can account for the high incidence of genes that can decrease fitness? Selection against the genes that cause schizophrenia is strong enough that they should be far less common if their presence were due simply to mutation balanced by selection. Furthermore, the relatively uniform rates of schizophrenia suggest that the responsible genes did not arise recently but have been maintained for millennia. It appears that the genes that cause schizophrenia must somehow confer an advantage that balances the severe costs.

The most likely possibility is that these genes are advantageous in combination with certain other genes, or in certain environments, much in the way a single sickle-cell gene is advantageous even though having two such genes causes sickle-cell anemia. Or it might be that the genes that predispose to schizophrenia have other effects that offer a slight advantage in most people who have them, even though a small proportion develop the disease. A number of authors have speculated on the kinds of advantages that might accrue to people who have genes that predispose to schizophrenia: perhaps they increase creativity or sharpen a person's intuitions about what others are thinking. Perhaps they protect against some disease. Some have suggested that the tendency to suspiciousness itself may compensate somewhat for the disadvantages of schizophrenia. Evidence for these ideas remains scattered, but they are worth pursuing. Support is provided by evidence of high levels of accomplishment in relatives of schizophrenics who are not affected by the disease. This whole area is just beginning to be explored.

SLEEP DISORDERS

Sleep, like so many other bodily capacities, commands our attention only when it goes awry, which it does for many people in many ways. For sleep, as for so many things, timing is often the crucial factor. Most sleep problems involve an inability to sleep at the proper time or a tendency to sleep at the wrong time. Insomnia affects more than 30 percent of the population and is the spur to a huge industry, from over-the-counter sleeping pills to specialized medical clinics. The people who suffer from daytime sleepiness are often the same ones who don't sleep well at night. Sleepiness is a bother when you are trying to read in the evening, a handicap after the alarm rings in the morning, and a positive danger if it happens while you are driving.

Then there are dreams and their disorders, nightmares and night terrors. Some people experience a kind of lack of coordination of the aspects of sleep and become conscious while still dreaming and unable to move, a frightening state indeed. People with narcolepsy slip suddenly into dreaming sleep in the midst of everyday activities, sometimes so swiftly that they fall and injure themselves. And then there are the people with sleep apnea, who intermittently stop breathing during sleep with resulting nighttime restlessness, daytime tiredness, and even brain damage. In order to understand these problems, we need to know more about the origins and functions of normal sleep.

Is sleep a trait that has been shaped by natural selection? There are several reasons to think so. First, the trait is widespread among animals and perhaps universal among vertebrates. In some animals that seem not to sleep, such as dolphins, one half of the brain in fact sleeps while the other stays awake, possibly because they must repeatedly swim to the surface to breathe. Second, all vertebrates seem to share the same sleep regulation mechanisms, with the center that controls dreaming sleep consistently located in the ancient parts of the brain. Third, the patterns of mammalian sleep, with its periods of rapid eye movement and rapid brain waves, are also shared with birds, whose evolution diverged from ours before the time of the dinosaurs. Fourth, the wide variation in the actual patterns of sleep, even in closely related mammals, suggests that whatever kind of sleeping was done by our most recent common ancestor could evolve rapidly to match the species' particular ecological niche. Finally, if deprived of sleep, all animals function poorly.

In order to better understand sleep difficulties, we would like to understand how the capacity and necessity for sleep increase fitness. One major contribution to the problem came in 1975 from British biologist Ray Meddis, who proposed that the amount and timing of our sleep are set by our potential for productive activity in different phases of the day–night cycle. As one reviewer of Meddis's book put it, our motivation to sleep at night arises from the desirability of staying off the streets. If there are special dangers in being abroad in the dark and little likelihood of positive accomplishment then, we are better off resting. This explains why humans and other animals benefit from a daily cycle of activity, but it does not explain why we sleep instead of just spending the night quietly awake, ready for any opportunities or dangers that may arise. It also does not explain why we have become so dependent on sleep that its lack makes us barely able to function.

Here is one possible perspective on the evolutionary origins of sleep. Imagine that some distant ancestor needed no sleep. If one line of its descendants had experienced greater dangers at one part of the day–night cycle (let's assume for simplicity that it was night) and greater opportunities during the day, then individuals who were inactive at night would have had a fitness advantage. As the species gradually came to confine its activity to the daylight hours, its nocturnal quiescence grew ever more prolonged and profound until it reliably spent many hours of every night inactive.

Given such a reliable daily period of inactivity, other evolutionary factors would be expected to act. It is unlikely that all needed cellular maintenance activities would proceed equally well whether an animal were awake or asleep. If some needed processes worked more efficiently when the brain was disengaged from its usual tasks, selection would act to delay them during the wakeful day and catch up during the night, thus favoring development of the state we recognize as sleep. In this way, as suggested in 1969 by Ian Oswald of Edinburgh University, some brain maintenance processes would be confined more and more to sleep and we would become more and more dependent on sleep. During this period, of course, it would be necessary for sleeping individuals to be quite safe, otherwise sleep would quickly have been selected against. Just as we became dependent on getting vitamin C from foods only because we could reliably get plenty of it, the steady availability of a period of safe rest was necessary before certain bodily maintenance mechanisms could be carried out only during sleep. One implication is that a search for metabolic processes confined to sleep, or taking place at a much greater rate during sleep, will provide insights on why we need to sleep. Indeed, brain scans have shown that protein synthesis is greatest during dreamless sleep and that mechanisms for synthesizing certain neurotransmitters can't keep up with daytime utilization and therefore must catch up at night. Furthermore, cell division is fastest in all tissues during sleep.

Once sleep was established for physiological repair, natural selection might well have relegated other functions to this period. Those most often suggested have been the memory-regulation functions. Researchers Allan Hobson and Robert McCarley have argued that dreaming sleep supports the physiology that consolidates learning. Francis Crick and Graeme Mitchison have evidence that dreaming sleep functions to purge unnecessary memories, much as we periodically discard unnecessary files from our computers. We won't consider these suggestions in detail but will only point out only that these are not necessarily mutually exclusive alternatives, nor are they at odds with Oswald's idea that sleep evolved as a period of tissue repair. None of this contradicts Meddis's observation that sleep regulates activity periods depending on the animal's ecology. Like other traits, sleep undoubtedly has many important functions. While each hypothesized function needs to be tested, support for one alternative provides evidence against another only if the functions are incompatible. Studies of sleep patterns in many different animal groups in relation to their ways of life and evolutionary relationship to one another could provide helpful evidence.

Now that we are seldom threatened by nocturnal predators such as tigers, and now that artificial light makes productive activity possible throughout the night, the need for regular sleep has become a great bother, especially when we fly across the world and our bodies insist on living according to our original time zone. Looking for the functions of sleep may well provide the knowledge we need to adapt it better to our present needs or, at the very least, to make it possible to read in the evening without falling asleep and then to sleep soundly through the night despite our worries about the crises tomorrow might bring.

DREAMING

Dreaming has interested people since the dawn of history and no doubt through much of prehistory. In recent years, many theories have been proposed about the functions of dreams, from Freud's theory of dreams fulfilling forbidden wishes to Francis Crick's theory that dreams erase and reorganize memories. But the debate has been so inconclusive that some current major authorities, like Harvard's Allan Hobson, can still argue that dreams may have no specific function but are mainly epiphenomena of brain activities. This seems unlikely to us, given the simple observation that deprivation of dreaming sleep causes severe psychopathology. For instance, cats kept on tiny islands in a pool were able to sleep, but the loss of muscle tone that accompanies dreaming sleep slipped them into the water and woke them. Such deprivation of dreaming sleep made these unfortunate cats wild and hypersexual and shortened their lives.

Even without delineating the function of dreams, an evolutionary approach can contribute to their understanding. Donald Symons, an evolutionary anthropologist at the University of California (Santa Barbara), recently proposed that there are, for evolutionary reasons, serious constraints on the stimuli we experience in dreams. While individual sleep behavior varies enormously, we tend, in dreams, to experience a wealth of our own actions and of sights but very little sound, smell, or mechanical stimulation. We can dream about doing things without actually moving because our motor nerves are paralyzed when we are in the kind of sleep that permits dreaming. We remember what people in dreams look like and what they tell us, but we do not remember as easily what their voices sounded like. We may remember enjoying a dreamworld glass of wine, but we often cannot recall its bouquet. We can dream that someone strikes us but may not remember what it felt like.

The reason for these constraints, Symons suggests, is that they were required by Stone Age realities. We could afford visual hallucinations, because closed eyes made sight useless; it was too dark for effective vision anyhow. By contrast, a cry of alarm, the smell of a tiger, or the panicky grasp of a child were important cues that required unimpaired vigilance of our senses of hearing, smell, and touch. Some species sleep with their eyes open, but we sleep with our ears open: we cannot let our dreams distract us from important sounds. Symons' theory explains some of the peculiarities of dreaming (and predicts some not yet noticed), and it will stand or fall according to how well its expectations conform to actual findings on the sensory composition of dreams. So far it seems to account for most of the available evidence.

THE FUTURE OF PSYCHIATRY

Psychiatry has recently emulated the rest of medicine by devising clear (if somewhat arbitrary) diagnostic categories, reliable methods of measuring symptoms, and standard requirements for experimental design and data analysis. Psychiatric research is now just as quantitative as that in the rest of medicine. Has all this apparent rigor brought psychiatry acceptance as just another medical specialty like neurology, cardiology, or endocrinology? Hardly. The research findings are solid, but they are not connected in any coherent theory. In its attempt to emulate other medical research by searching for the molecular mechanisms of disease, psychiatry has ironically deprived itself of precisely the concepts that provide the tacit foundation for the rest of medical research. By trying to find the flaws that cause disease without understanding normal functions of the mechanisms, psychiatry puts the cart before the horse.

Research on the anxiety disorders exemplifies the problem. Psychiatrists now divide anxiety disorders into nine subtypes, and many researchers treat each as a separate disease, investigating its epidemiology, genetics, brain chemistry, and response to treatments. The difficulty is, of course, that anxiety is not itself a disease but a defense. To appreciate the problems this creates, imagine what would happen if doctors of internal medicine studied cough the way modern psychiatrists study anxiety. First, internists would define "cough disorder" and create objective criteria for diagnosis. Perhaps the criteria would say you have cough disorder if you cough more than twice per hour over a two-day period or have a coughing bout that lasts more than two minutes. Then researchers would look for subtypes of cough disorder based on factor-analytic studies of clinical characteristics, genetics, epidemiology, and response to treatment. They might discover specific subtypes of cough disorders such as mild cough associated with runny nose and fever, cough associated with allergies and pollen exposure, cough associated with smoking, and cough that usually leads to death. Next, they would investigate the causes of these subtypes of cough disorder by studying abnormalities of neural mechanisms in people with cough disorders. The discovery that cough is associated with increased activity in the nerves that cause the chest muscles to contract would stimulate much speculation about what neurophysiological mechanisms could make these nerves overly active. The discovery of a cough-control center in the brain would give rise to another set of ideas as to how abnormalities in this center might cause cough. The knowledge that codeine stops cough would lead other scientists to investigate the possibility that cough results from deficiencies in the body's codeinelike substances.

Such a plan of research is obviously ludicrous, but we recognize its folly only because we know that cough is useful. Because we know that cough is a defense, we look for the causes of cough not in the nerves and muscles that generate a cough, or even in the brain mechanisms that regulate cough, but instead in the situations and stimuli that normally arouse the protective cough reflex. While some rare cases of cough may be caused by abnormalities of the cough-regulation mechanisms, the vast majority are adaptive responses that expel foreign matter from the respiratory tract. Only after searching for such a natural stimulus does a physician consider the possibility that the cough-regulation mechanism itself might be awry.

Many psychiatrists have studied individual differences in susceptibility to anxiety with the worthy goal of helping the many people who experience panic, tension, fear, and sleeplessness throughout their lives. Nonetheless, this approach fosters much confusion. What if research on cough were to focus on those individuals who have a lifelong tendency to cough in response to the least stimulus? Such people would be told they have a cough disorder. Soon there would be campaigns to identify people predisposed to cough disorder in order to find the genes that cause this abnormality in the cough-regulation mechanism. There undoubtedly are people with a genetic susceptibility to ready coughing, but studying them would tell us little about the cause of most coughs.

There are limits to this analogy. Anxiety is much more complicated than cough, its functions are less obvious, and it varies much more from individual to individual. More important, the cues that arouse anxiety are far less tangible than those that arouse cough. Cough is caused by foreign material in the respiratory tract, while anxiety is aroused by diverse cues processed by the mind in mysterious ways. The most obvious anxiety cues are images of dangerous objects or stimuli that have been paired with pain or some other noxious stimulus. Most clinical anxiety is aroused, however, by complex cues that require subtle interpretation. If, for example, the boss doesn't greet you, you are not invited to a meeting, and a friend avoids you on a day when layoff notices are to be distributed, you may feel serious apprehension. If it is your birthday, however, and you suspect a surprise party may be in the works, the same stimuli will arouse a very different reaction. This example only begins to tap the complexity of the mental systems that regulate anxiety. Many wishes and feelings never make it to consciousness but nonetheless cause anxiety. The woman whose panic attacks started when she began an affair insisted that the two were unrelated. Just because many of the cues that cause anxiety are hard to identify does not mean that they are not there, and it certainly does not mean that the anxiety they cause is useless or a product of abnormal brain mechanisms.

Conversely, just because much anxiety is normal, that does not mean it is all useful. Furthermore, many anxiety disorders *are* caused by genetic pre-dispositions. We don't yet know whether these are best understood as genetic defects or normal variations. Certainly, the kinds and dangerousness of various threats vary considerably from one generation to the next, and this should maintain considerable genetic variation in the anxiety-regulation mechanisms.

If psychiatry stays on its current course, it will be left treating only those disorders caused by demonstrable brain defects, while the pains and suffering of everyday life will be left to other clinicians. This would be unfortunate for patients as well as psychiatrists. The rest of medicine treats normal defensive reactions; why shouldn't psychiatry do the same? In this as well as other ways, an evolutionary view is psychiatry's route to genuine integration with the rest of medicine. An intensive effort to understand the functions of the emotions and how they are normally regulated would provide, for psychiatry, something comparable to what physiology provides for the rest of medicine. It would provide a framework in which pathopsychology could be studied like patho-physiology, so that we can understand what has gone wrong with the normal functioning of bodily systems. There is every expectation that an evolutionary approach will bring the study of mental disorders back to the fold of medicine, relying not on a crude "medical model" of emotional problems but on the same Darwinian approach that is so useful in the rest of medicine.

2 Evolutionary biology: A basic science for psychiatry?

M.T. McGuire[1], L. Marks[2], R.M. Nesse[3], A. Triosi[4]
[1]Department of Psychiatry-Biobehavioral Sciences, School of Medicine, University of California at Los Angeles, USA. [2]Institute of Psychiatry, DeCrispigny Park, London, United Kingdom. [3]Department of Psychiatry, School of Medicine, University of Michigan, Ann Arbor, Michigan, USA. [4]Clinica Psychiatrica, Università di Roma, Italy.

Evolutionary biology has much to offer psychiatry. It distinguishes between ultimate and proximate explanations of behavior and addresses the functional significance of behavior. Subtheories, frequently voiced misconceptions, specific applications, testable hypotheses and limitations of evolutionary theory are reviewed. An evolutionary perspective is likely to improve understanding of psychopathology, refocus some clinical research, influence treatment and help integrate seemingly unrelated findings and theoretical explanations.

INTRODUCTION

Recent advances in evolutionary biology have implications for psychiatric theory, research and clinical practice. Evolutionary theory introduces a broad and much needed deductive framework; it facilitates the functional analysis of behavior; it identifies important differences between ultimate causes and proximate mechanisms; it promotes a reassessment of current views about etiology and pathogenesis; and it alters treatment strategies and options. Evolutionists acknowledge that much human behavior is a product of personal and cultural experience, but argue that mind and culture themselves are products of evolution and are better understood when analyzed within the evolutionary framework.

Our assessment of the contributions that an evolutionary point of view can make to psychiatry begins with an analysis of its theoretical contributions followed by a discussion of common misconceptions. Possible applications to psychiatry are then evaluated. Finally, the limitations of the theory are reviewed.

Only selected parts of evolutionary theory are discussed. More comprehensive discussion of the theory can be found in Williams (1), Wilson (2) and Alexander (3).

OVERVIEW OF THE EVOLUTIONARY APPROACH TO PSYCHIATRY

Behavior

Consider behaviors such as acquiring a mate, sexual intercourse, having offspring, parent–offspring bonding, stranger anxiety, infant and juvenile play, sibling rivalry, competition over resources, preferential investment of resources in kin, reciprocal exchanges among nonkin, competition for social status, recognition and rejection of cheaters, deception of others and self-deception. Natural selection has shaped predispositions (strong biases) to engage in such behaviors. Predispositions range from strong (such as withdrawal from a painful stimulus) to weak, such as preference for particular styles of music).

The strengths of predispositions vary across individuals. Experience and learning, which is also an evolved capacity, modify predispositions. Environmental options and constraints interact with evolved and prioritized behavior strategies to affect the probability of immediate and long-term behavior. Psychological mechanisms (such as cognitive and psychodynamic ones) filter, modify, organize and focus information that influences behavior. Behaviors to which most persons are not predisposed (such as playing the piano) can be mastered, but usually after considerable effort. Nonetheless, the general behavior profiles and patterns of human behavior are set by the species' genome and, within limits, unfold in predictable ways.

The above and other behaviors are of special interest to psychiatry for several reasons: 1) mental disorders are associated with detectable abnormalities in the expression of such behaviors, such as reduced frequency of reciprocation (4–6); 2) an adequate understanding of some mental disorders (such as phobias, depression and somatoform disorders) requires an appreciation of the functional significance of such behaviors and of the evolved mechanisms that regulate them (7, 8); and 3) treatment strategies may change (for example greater emphasis on functional outcomes and increased attention to environmental variables) with increasing appreciation of the evolutionary perspective.

Natural selection favors brain mechanisms that result in behaviors conferring a reproductive advantage. Generally, such behaviors are neither atypical, nor pathological. With few exceptions, however, mental disorders are atypical, pathological and maladaptive. Evolutionary theory provides a framework for analyzing adaptive behavior, the mechanisms that regulate it and the circumstances interfering with its normal expression (9).

Psychopathology can be illuminated by insights into its normal adaptive precursors. Most phobias, for example, are exaggerated normal fears (10, 11); minor adaptive rituals such as perfectionism are precursors for obsessive-compulsive disorder (10;) normal mood swings can be viewed as precursors for manic-depressive illness (12); and normal sadness and social withdrawal may be precursors to clinical depression (13–15).

Subtheories

Since the early 1960s, a number of testable subtheories have been developed to explain specific behaviors. Examples include: inclusive fitness or kin selection, reciprocal altruism, parent–offspring conflict, and cognitive/feeling mechanisms.

Inclusive fitness.   Preferential investment in kin is prominent in humans, as it is in other species. The tendency is to invest more in close than in distant kin, and for parents to invest more in offspring than vice versa. Hamilton (16) postulated that certain kin-related behavior is selected because it favors individuals who share genes. A behavior costly to the self may nevertheless evolve if it increases the survival and reproduction of kin who share the genes responsible for that predisposition. Kin-selection theory explains how altruistic behavior among kin facilitates the replication of genes shared by kin. The theory predicts, for example: that parents will invest more in their offspring than vice versa; that such investment is greater with higher parental assessment of the offspring's reproductive potential; and that stepchildren are more likely to be abused than biological offspring. These predictions are well supported by evidence (17-19).

Reciprocal altruism.   Although kin selection explains investment in kin, unrelated individuals also help each other (20). Such reciprocity exchanges are not confined to humans. Vampire bats, for example, share their blood meals after returning to their roost at dawn (21). Such exchanges even occur between species (22); alarm calls by one species alert members of other species, and cleaner fish remove parasites from inside the mouths and gills of larger fish who protect cleaners from predation (23).

Reciprocal altruism theory predicts: 1) A will help B (nonkin) if, in A's view, the probability of reciprocation by B times the probable benefit of this reciprocation equals or exceeds the initial cost to A (reciprocal behavior is distinguished from mutualism, where both parties gain simultaneously); 2) failure to reciprocate evokes moralistic aggression; 3) nonreciprocation will rise at the end of a period of association (24); and 4) nonreciprocators will have fewer allies. These predictions are also supported by available evidence (25, 26).

Evolutionary theory also explains why such emotions as pride, happiness, guilt and moralistic anger and such behaviors as guilt induction, intimidation and social ostracism have evolved. They facilitate reciprocal relationships (20, 25, 27, 28). Much of development and learning deals with refining reciprocal behaviors, such as how to successfully manage reciprocity exchanges without being exploited or rejected — battles among children often focus on who owes what to whom (29). Deviations from expected patterns of early kin and nonkin social relationships may contribute to disordered reciprocity relationships later in life (30).

Parent–offspring conflict and sibling rivalry. Although cooperation between parents, offspring and siblings is promoted by the genes they share in common, conflicts can be explained by the fact that many of their genes are not shared (31). Parental fitness (the number of parental genes replicated among offspring is enhanced by the reduction of investment in maturing offspring in order to sooner reproduce again. Existing offspring try to counter this reduction and maximize their own fitness by delaying the birth of new siblings and by extracting as much from parents as they can. The tendency in many species for offspring to object to weaning supports this view. The conflict has a natural end-point when existing offspring's inclusive fitness is increased more by having a sibling with many shared genes than by continuing to try to extract more resources from parents (31).

Sibling rivalry has a parallel explanation and may arise in the same way. Siblings aid each other because they share genes, but simultaneously compete for parental resources.

Other conflicts. Similar evolutionary-based explanations account for male–female differences and aspects of marital relationships. Males, for example, are more promiscuous, take more physical risks, and engage in more antisocial behavior (2, 32, 33). Spousal relationships combine reciprocity, kin selection and the management of conflict between kin. Spouses' mutual dependence for their reproductive success leads to common interests and reduces conflict (34), while conflict results from pressures on the partner to provide more care for off-spring (31), to raise offspring in specific ways, to help nongenetic relatives or to reciprocate help more completely.

Cognitive/feeling mechanisms. Specific mental capacities appear to have evolved to serve specific functions, such as the ability to spot cheaters (35–38). Similar points apply to assessing the value of different types of reciprocation, the reproductive potential of offspring and the adaptive value of different behaviors.

The cognitive, physiological and behavioral predispositions that characterize fear offer selective advantages in dangerous situations (10).

Behavior that is phylogenetically predisposed is not necessarily inevitable, however. Indeed, it can, on occasion, be changed dramatically (10). For example, the fear of blood injury is strongly familial, develops in childhood and is characterized by a vasovagal response and syncope. Yet it can be permanently eliminated with a few hours of systematic exposure therapy. The same applies to strongly predisposed fears of snakes or other animals. (Similarly, even innate defensive responses in molluscs, mantids and birds can be eliminated by habituation analogous to exposure therapy.) The capacity for change is a built-in, selected trait that adjusts the behavioral preferences characteristic of the species.

A better understanding of such evolved mechanisms is likely to deepen our insights into psychopathology. For instance, stranger anxiety, separation anxiety and phobias of heights, animals, storms and leaving one's home range appear to be prepotent stimuli to which pre-prepared fear is readily connected (10). Over-responsiveness and/or rigidity of such mechanisms may help to explain some anxiety disorders. In other disorders, deficits in mechanisms for reciprocity negotiation seem probable. Such deficits may be a product of proximate mechanisms leading to social isolation and associated chronic depression.

An important aspect of evolved cognitive/feeling mechanisms is the distinction between symptoms and disorders. Some mental signs and symptoms, such as anxiety, sadness, irritability and withdrawal may be normal and adaptive when not severe. Like other aversive states, such as pain and nausea, they may point to circumstances liable to decrease individual fitness, but not necessarily be manifestations of disorders (7, 39). Interfering with their expression thus may be disadvantageous for the patient, just as blocking coughing or vomiting reflexes can be dangerous for patients with pulmonary or gastrointestinal infection. (Such behaviors are distinguishable from signs and symptoms that are more direct consequences of mental disorders, such as hiding from others because of persecutory delusions.)

The evolutionary arguments discussed thus far are reasonable, intuitively acceptable and supported by research findings in some respects. Several points relevant to psychiatry emerge. First, many behaviors are strongly predisposed, such as sibling rivalry, moralistic aggression and familial rejection of nonmaturing relatives. Second, some features of psychopathology reflect the prepotency and preparedness of responses. Third, features of disorders may reflect the normal operation of an adaptive response. Depression following the loss of a loved one or a decline in social status is not only expected from an evolutionary perspective (13), but also may be temporarily adaptive in evoking social support from kin and friends (40). Similarly, jealousy, anger, deception, self-deception and anxiety may be temporarily adaptive. Fourth, evolutionary interpretations are compatible with proximate mechanism explanations, such as postulated physiological changes associated with depressive disorders, inheritance of disorder vulnerability (pedigree studies) or compromised learning following aversive early experiences. Evolutionary theory offers existing psychiatric theories a context in which interrelationships between different findings and explanations emerge, and ultimate evolutionary and proximate mechanism explanations are clarified.

MISCONCEPTIONS ABOUT EVOLUTIONARY THEORY

Evolutionary Theory Applies Mainly to Other Animals

This view appears to assume that evolutionary biology consists primarily of reconstructing a species' phylogeny. Evolutionists argue instead that even if humans had no close phylogenetic relatives, evolutionary theory (or a similar theory) would be necessary to help explain human behavior. Mechanisms of adaptation operate primarily at the individual level and shape behavior accordingly (functional analysis). Viewing humans in an evolutionary context leads to predictions that fit many otherwise hard to explain facts (such as prepotency for many behaviors, step-parent abuse, sibling rivalry and parent–offspring conflict). Moreover, the theory leads to unexpected connections that are unlikely to be made without its guidance. Examples include: the possible adaptiveness of some antisocial behavior (such as cheating as an adaptive strategy) (41); abandonment of kin who are poor reproductive bets; child abuse by step-parents; male and female sexual jealousy and possessiveness (42); and agoraphobia as an extratraterritorial fear associated with past threats when venturing outside the home range (10, 43, 44).

Any species-characteristic behavior has a distribution limited in width by natural selection. Individuals vary in capacities to empathize, reciprocate, develop new goal-achievement strategies, compete and maintain psychological and/or psychological homeostasis (45). Human variations in these behaviors may have led to successful adaptation in many different environments. Seeming facets of disorders, both symptoms and personality, may thus be consequences of a range of variation rather than manifestations of psycho-pathology. In evolutionary terms a trait can be regarded as biologically normal if it enhances adaptive capacities. Severe psychopathology nearly always reduces fitness (46). Compared to normal people, those with mental disorders help kin less and are less helped by kin; they more often fail to reciprocate help from nonkin and have fewer friends; and they have reduced resource access and control (McGuire, submitted).

Evolutionary theory provides psychiatry with some explanatory tools regarding individual differences: 1) a framework that specifies the range of adaptive species-characteristic behavior patterns against which the which the behavior of individuals can be compared; 2) a general theory and subtheories to interpret the adaptive significance of behavior; and 3) a framework to explain cross-person differences in attributes (trait distribution).

Evolutionary Biology Ignores Individual Learning

The human capacity to learn is vastly greater than that of other species. The view that evolutionary biology ignores individual learning seems to arise from the incorrect assumption that if something has been learned then it has no evolutionary roots. However, the capacity to learn has been selected, like every other trait (47). Each species, including *Homo sapiens*, learns certain things more easily than others. Evolutionists do not ask, "Is it learned or innate?", but rather, "How easily can this particular response be learned?". A child's readily learning to speak, for example, reflects built-in design features based on adaptive cognitive, sensory, and behavioral algorithms. Playing the piano, however, is difficult to learn—it has not been selected for.

Culture is an Alternative to Evolutionary Explanations

It is a mistake to see biology and culture (a set of behavioral rules) as sharp opposites (48–50). Culture is not an alternative explanation to evolutionary theory. Rather, the ability to absorb culture is an evolved trait. Behavioral predispositions shape culture and are shaped through it, leading, for example, to stable patterns of sexuality, pair-bonding, child-rearing, nonkin reciprocation and social status relationships. The forms of these behaviors vary across societies, but all societies have stable patterns and values associated with strongly predisposed behavior. Amplification of biological predispositions is illustrated by avoidance of inbreeding (incest taboos), which is observed across cultures and among all studied primates (51). Similarly, deviant behavior (such as excessive risk-taking, impulsive behavior and non-reciprocation) that jeopardizes others' health and resource control evokes rejection of the deviant (25).

Evolutionary Ideas are not Relevant to Treatment

Advances in basic knowledge are more likely to lead to better formulations of treatment-relevant problems than to immediate changes in treatment procedures. Optimal treatment and prevention presupposes detailed knowledge about etiology and pathogenesis. Pediatric hospital procedures improved following Bowlby's evolutionary-based studies of attachment behavior. Appreciating the high probability of child abuse among stepchildren is likely to increase the recognition of the need for vigorous preventive measures. Therapists who understand the principles of reciprocal altruism and the possible functions of self deception and repression (52, 53) are more likely to enhance the rehabilitation of social skills. And attention to person–environment interactions is likely to optimize the selection of therapeutic recommendations: for example, teaching patients to select social environments that are responsive to their needs.

Evolutionary Hypotheses Cannot be Tested

Evolutionary hypotheses are eminently testable. For example, Daly et al. (42) provide extensive support for the prediction that, in most societies, sexual jealousy should be more extreme in males than in females. Essock-Vitale & McGuire (18) confirm that, within kin networks, resources flow from older to younger persons. Buss (54, 55) has shown that the frequency of divorce increases in infertile marriages. There is mounting evidence for the prepotency and preparedness of fear (10). Scenarios of past evolutionary events cannot be proven, but the number of possible scenarios can be limited, because given scenarios predict certain outcomes, some of which can be tested. For example, the hypothesis that domain-specific cognitive and feeling mechanisms mediate reciprocal exchange implies that basic exchange rules will be comparable across cultures, and that precursors will be present in our close phylogenetic relatives (35).

Natural Selection Should Eliminate Genes for Mental Disorders

If most mental disorders are maladaptive, then why do they persist? Evolutionists have advanced several explanations for the persistence of mental disorders. First, atypical or deviant traits tend only to reduce, not eliminate, the number of offspring. Thus, once a disorder appears in a population, it may remain for a considerable time. Reduced reproductive success is seen in obsessive-compulsive disorder, for example, but success is only marginally lower than among normals (10). Second, many disorders (such as late-onset depression, Huntington's disease and Alzheimer's disease) mostly appear after peak reproduction periods, so that inclusive fitness is less affected.

A third possibility is heterosis, in which even if it is maladaptive to have the entire set of genes that is needed to produce a given disorder, having some of them (short of the number necessary for the full disorder) may be advantageous in certain environments. Possessing all the genes for sickle cell anemia (homozygous state) leads to an early death, but carrying only some of them (heterozygous state) enhances resistance to malaria. Manic-depressive psychosis and obsessive-compulsive disorder are maladaptive, but cyclothymic and meticulous personalities may provide an adaptive advantage in certain environments. (A variation of this idea has been suggested for the persistence of senescence (44, 56): the very genes that lead to senility in old age may be those that confer some benefit in youth.)

Fourth, recessive traits may be hard for natural selection to eliminate if they only partially compromise adaptation, and many forms of mental illness are so infrequent that selection may be slow. Finally, some behaviors that are disorders in one culture might not be disorders in other cultures. Dyslexia, some forms of antisocial behavior and certain unstable personality variants are examples.

Existing Theories in Other Disciplines Explain Findings at Least as well as Evolutionary Theory

Evolutionists accept this view for certain features of current theories. Evolutionary theory does not replace other psychiatric theories. Rather, it 1) offers an additional perspective, 2) helps explain heretofore overlooked and understudied features of disorders and 3) provides an integrating framework. By adding ultimate causation to the current focus on proximate factors (such as genes, physiology, learning and psychodynamics), the theory identifies biases and constraints of behavior and physiological systems. Proximate psychiatric theories explain many of the mechanisms of disorders, such as the biochemical explanations of depression, reduced serotonin turnover among chronic abusive criminals (57) and petty criminality as the substrates on which evolution acts (58-60). Evolution can help to explain why these mechanisms exist at all.

The degree to which psychiatry is likely to incorporate an evolutionary perspective will depend on specific applications that inform our understanding and improve treatment. We now turn to the subject of applications.

APPLICATIONS

Criteria for Distinguishing Normal from Abnormal Behavior

The current criteria for defining mental disorders include: 1) association with a somatic lesion (anatomical to molecular); 2) statistical deviances from normality (such as excessive self-centeredness, learning disabilities and bipolar illness); and 3) subjective distress. Some authors have suggested "biological disadvantage" as a more appropriate criterion for identifying mental disorders (61, 62). This view accords with an evolutionary approach. A disorder must impose some form of fitness disadvantage. Statistical deviance does not directly equate with disorders—mental retardation is a disorder but genius is not. Moreover, it is difficult to know whether a condition is pathological without considering the environment in which it occurs. Depression may be adaptive in a supportive social environment, just as schizoid personality may be adaptive in isolated areas. Insofar as our present-day environment differs from past environments in which current traits are adaptive, past adaptive behaviors may become maladaptive (such as the prepotency of animal fears being more fitting for our ancestors). Subjective suffering has a high probability of association with maladaptive situations, whether caused by external circumstances or by brain disorders. Feelings of pleasure and pain probably evolved to tell us whether prevailing circumstances arc adaptive (27). Yet, even emotional suffering may be useful, just as pain, nausea and fatigue are useful, although all indicate the presence of some danger.

The preceding points imply that both the features of disorders and the disorders themselves should be evaluated in the context of evolution. Further, features of disorders may be adaptive or result as a consequence of ultimate causation. These possibilities result in alternative etiological explanations of disorders, raise questions about classification and imply different approaches to treatment.

Pathogenesis

Evolutionary theory focuses attention on distinctions between etiology (cause) from pathogenesis (mechanism). Showing that depression is associated with alterations in norepinephrine or serotonin neurotransmission (mechanism) does not reveal its cause (etiology). Biochemical alteration may be a common end product reflecting an environmental or genetic etiology, or both. Serotonin neurotransmission is altered by changes in social status, and testosterone and cortisol levels rise in response to a variety of social events (25, 63). Such changes, in turn, alter the probability of behavior (such as responsiveness to others and vigilance), how information is processed and response to drugs (64). Certain social interactions are as essential for physiological and psychological homeostasis among adults as they are among infants. Persons vulnerable to mental disorders tend to have reduced capacities to manage their social environments to produce homeostasis and a greater probability of developing a disorder. (45). Such evolutionary-oriented studies focus on behavior–physiology interactions and provide data for the empirical foundation of a more comprehensive model of mental disorders (65).

Evolved Psychological Mechanisms

As mentioned, natural selection is likely to have favored the development of cognitive/feeling mechanisms preadapted to particular situations. Examples include: respond immediately to perceived external danger; avoid or retaliate against those who inflict pain; assess others' ability to reciprocate helping; detect cheaters; and be vigilant towards actual and potential competitors. The characterization of such mechanisms is likely to be a major focus of research during the next decade. This research should lead to a description of mental disorders in terms such as underactive and overactive mechanisms (for example, over-reading or under-reading environmental dangers) as well as in the specification of such responses to behavior, physiological states and functional consequences: for example, chronic anxiety results from an overactive response to danger and/or from the failure of mechanisms that inform one that a danger has passed. Conversely, we may come to recognize new disorders characterized by defects in capacities for anxiety, normal sadness and jealousy. A clear implication is that appropriate treatment depends on both the mechanism involved and how it is awry (66).

Functional Capacities and Disorder Classification

Functional deficits are considered in Axis V in DSM-III-R, but they are accorded far less importance in the day-to-day practice than are Axes I and II. The concept of function and functional deficits is not the province of evolutionary theory. However, evolutionary theory provides a conceptual framework in which to organize and interpret functions and, in an evolutionary-derived classification, an assessment of functional capacities would be a pivotal taxonomic category. Persons with high anxiety, moderate depression, self-deception, mild bipolar illness and, in some instances, schizophrenia, often function above average. The same is true for some people who have socially unattractive traits, such as extreme self-centeredness and extreme needs to dominate and control others. For some disorders, decreased functional capacity is the primary finding, as is the case with antisocial personality and malingering.

Assessment of functioning may also help explain within-disorder variance among current classification categories. Generalized anxiety disorder with minimal functional consequences may be classified separately from generalized anxiety disorder with major functional consequences. A focus on functional capacities would also alter treatment strategies and choices. A number of drugs that effectively reduce symptom intensity also reduce functional capacities (such as decreased motivation and ability to concentrate).

Integrating Current Theories

Advocates of one school of psychiatry frequently disregard findings developed by other schools. Biological psychiatrists are seldom interested in the findings of psychoanalysts or social psychiatrists, and some behaviorists ignore physiological aspects of mental disorders. Can such parochialism be changed?

Evolutionary theory can encompass the major conceptual frameworks of psychiatry, help integrate relevant findings, appraise new ones and introduce additional possible explanations. Biological psychiatry focuses on genetic-physiological predispositions and proximate mechanisms contributing to disorders, social psychiatry on environmental contributions, behavioral psychiatry on atypical behavior and psychoanalysis on thoughts and feelings. Each of these focuses may best explain certain abnormal features, although in differing degrees within and across disorders. The addition of ultimate causation (such as predispositions to behave in certain species-characteristic ways, functional assessment, the possible adaptive function of certain features of disorders, trait distribution and the physiological consequences of person–environment interactions) enriches the database of psychiatry and allows us to address what is intuitively obvious, the concept of multiple bases for disorders.

Evolutionary theory also offers psychiatry a deductive framework and a set of testable hypotheses. For example: multiple family placements of young children during critical periods of development are predicted to lead to both suboptimal refinement or learning of basic social skills and to the expression of certain predisposed traits that otherwise might not be expressed; diminution of within-disorder adaptive traits because of drug treatment would be predicted to result in noncompliance with treatment recommendations; and relinquishment of behavior that is offensive to others will occur only if alternative behaviors are associated with desired benefits.

Limitations of evolutionary theory

A number of questions and unresolved issues remain. The limits of evolutionary explanations have not been fully explored, particularly where 2 or more tendencies conflict (such as reciprocate by helping another *vs* invest in kin). For some behaviors, evolutionary explanations may prove to be the most parsimonious: for example, excessive risk-taking, antisocial behavior and depression following loss. Nevertheless, proximate events (such as the critical physiological details of a drug overdose) associated with many disorders are best judged from existing theories.

Second, there may be limits to the degree to which evolutionary theory can be applied to individuals. The current form of the theory derives largely from population genetics and behavioral ecology, which focus on the behavior of groups, not of individuals. Potential difficulties due to this history are illustrated by considering trait distribution: on the one hand, the concept informs our understanding of trait variance; on the other, there are limits to what can be inferred from a distribution curve to an individual. Similar limitations apply to all major etiological and pathogenic theories of psychiatry.

Third, the weights assigned to and the timing of many experiences are not significantly informed by the theory. Although there is general agreement throughout psychiatry and among evolutionary biologists on the critical importance of certain developmental experiences in the shaping of individuals the importance of specific events and the time-frames in which they optimally occur remains largely an empirical issue. Extreme upbringing conditions (such as the total social deprivation of infants) have clear developmental effects, as do instances of the absence of essential neurochemicals for normal development (such as Tay-Sachs disease) or chromosomal aberrations (such as Down's syndrome). However, much of our knowledge is based on atypical situations that do not themselves directly inform our understanding of the complex process of development, its timing, and the impact of conditions generally accepted as being within the normal range.

CONCLUSION

A strong case can be made for evolutionary biology deepening our perspective by clarifying the concepts and explanatory power of ultimate to proximate explanations and by offering psychiatry an integrating paradigm. The theory puts humans back into an ecological context and raises questions about the normal operation of adaptive mechanisms, particularly those elicited by unusual circumstances. Perhaps surprisingly, its understanding and recognition of variation results in a particularly humanistic orientation to people's problems.

Acknowledgement

The authors wish to thank the late Robert J. Stoller for his helpful comments on an earlier draft.

REFERENCES

1. Williams, G.C. (1966). *Adaption and natural selection*. Princeton: Princeton University Press.
2. Wilson, M. ,& Daly, M. (1985). Competitiveness, risk taking, and violence: the young male syndrome. *Ethol Sociobiol*, *6*, 59–73.
3. Alexander, R.D. (1979). *Darwinism and human affairs*. Seattle: University of Washington Press.
4. McGuire, M.T., & Fairbanks, L.A. (Ed.) (1977). *Ethological psychiatry*. New York: Grune & Stratton.
5. McGuire, M.T., & Essock-Vitale, S.M. (1981). Psychiatric disorders in the context of evolutionary biology: a functional classification of behavior. *J Nerv Ment Dis.*, *169*, 672–686.
6. McGuire, M.T., & Essock-Vitale, S.M. (1982). Psychiatric disorders in the context of evolutionary biology. *J Nerv Ment Dis*, *170*, 9–20.
7. Nesse, R.M. (1984). An evolutionary perspective on psychiatry. *Compr Psychiatry*, *25*, 575–580.
8. Nesse, R.M., & Lloyd, A.T. (in press). The evolution of psychodynamic mechanisms. In J. Barkow, L. Cosmides, & J. Tooby (Eds.), *The adaptive mind: evolutionary psychology and the generation of culture*. Oxford: Oxford University Press.
9. Feirman, J. (Ed.) (1987). The ethology of psychiatric populations. *Ethol Sociobiol*, *8*, 1S–163S.
10. Marks, I.M. (1987). *Fears, phobias, and rituals*. Oxford: Oxford University Press.
11. Nesse, R.M. (1987). An evolutionary perspective on panic disorder and agoraphobia. *Ethol Sociobiol*, *8*, 73S–83S.
12. Gardner, R. (1982). Mechanisms in manic-depressive disorder. *Arch Gen Psychiatry*, *39*, 1436–1441.
13. Price, J.S. (1967). The dominance hierarchy and the evolution of mental illness. *Lancet*, *7502*, 243–246.
14. Price, J.S., & Sloman, L. (1987). Depression as yielding behavior: an animal model based on Schjelderup-Ebbe's pecking order. *Ethol Sociobiol*, *8*, 85S–98S.

15. Akiskal, H.S. (1985). Interaction of biologic and psychologic factors in the origin of depressive disorders. *Acta Psychiatr Scand, 319*, 131–139.
16. Hamilton, W.D. (1964). The genetical evolution of social behavior. *J Theoret Biol, 7*, 1–64.
17. Daly, M., & Wilson, M. (1985). Child abuse and other risks of not living with both parents. *Ethol Sociobiol, 6*, 197–210.
18. Essock-Vitale, S.M., & McGuire, M.T. (1985). Women's lives viewed from an evolutionary perspective. II. Patterns of helping. *Ethol Sociobiol, 6*, 155–173.
19. Essock-Vitale, S.M. (Submitted). Social relationships, reproductive success, and demographic characteristics.
20. Trivers, R.L. (1971). The evolution of reciprocal altruism. *Q Rev Biol, 46*, 35–57.
21. Wilkinson, G.S. (1988). Reciprocal altruism in bats and other mammals. *Ethol Sociobiol, 9*, 85–100.
22. Taylor, C., & McGuire, M.T. (Eds.) (1988). Reciprocal altruism: 15 years later. *Ethol Sociobiol, 9*, 67–267.
23. Trivers, R.L. (1985). *Social evolution*. Menlo Park, CA: Benjamin Cummings.
24. Axelrod, R. (1984). *The evolution of cooperation*. New York: Basic Books.
25. McGuire, M.T., & Raleigh, M.J. (1986). Behavioral and physiological correlates of ostracism. *Ethol Sociobiol, 7*, 187–200.
26. Essock-Vitale, S.M., & McGuire, M.T. (1990). Social and reproductive histories of depressed and anxious women. In C.M. Bell (Ed.), *Sociobiology and the social sciences*. Lubbock, TX: *Texas Tech University Press*, 105–118.
27. Nesse, R.M. (Submitted). *Toward an evolutionary explanation of the capacity for happiness and sadness.*
28. McGuire, M.T., & Essock-Vitale, S. (1987). Altruistic and affiliative behavior in the family and among friends: possible interpretations. *Soc Sci Info, 26*, 385–402.
29. Charlesworth, W.R., & La Freniere, P. (1983). Dominance, friendship, and resource utilization in preschool children's groups. *Ethol Sociobiol, 4*, 175–186.
30. Bowlby, J. (1973). *Attachment and loss*. Vol. 2. London: Hogarth Press.
31. Trivers, R.L. (1974). Parent–offspring conflict. *Am Zool, 14*, 249–264.
32. Deaux, K. (1976). *The behavior of women and men*. Monterey, CA: Brooks & Cole, 1976.
33. Symons, D. (1979). *The evolution of human sexuality*. New York: Oxford University Press.
34. Sloman, L., & Price, J.S. (1987). Losing behavior (yielding subroutine) and human depression: proximate and selective mechanisms. *Ethol Sociobiol, 8*, 99S–109S.
35. Tooby, J., & Cosmides, L. (1988). Evolutionary psychology and the generation of culture. I. Theoretical consideration. *Ethol Sociobiol, 9*, 29–50.
36. Cosmides, L., & Tooby, J. (1988). Evolutionary psychology and the generation of culture. II. Case study: a computational theory of social exchange. *Ethol Sociobiol, 10*, 51–97.
37. Barkow, J., Cosmides, L., & Tooby, J. (Eds.) (in press). *The adapted mind: evolutionary psychology and the generation of culture*. Oxford: Oxford University Press.
38. Buss, D.M. (1984). Evolutionary biology and personality psychology: towards a conception of human nature and individual differences. *Am Psychol, 39*, 1135–1147.
39. Alexander, R. (1987). *The biology of moral systems*. New York: Aldine de Gruyter, 110.
40. Lewis, A.J. (1934). Melancholia: a clinical survey of depressive states. *Br J Psychiatry, 24*, 277–378.
41. Harpending, H.C., & Sobus, J. (1987). Sociopathy as an adaption. *Ethol Sociobiol, 8*, 63S–72S.
42. Daly, M., Wilson, M., & Weghorst, S.J. (1982). Male sexual jealousy. *Ethol Sociobiol, 3*, 11–27.
43. Barkow, J.H. (1989). *Darwin, sex, and status*. Toronto: University of Toronto Press.
44. Nesse, R.M. (1989). Panic disorders: an evolutionary view. *Psychiatry Ann., 18*, 478–483.
45. McGuire, M.T., & Troisi, A. (1987). Physiological regulation–deregulation and psychiatric disorders. *Ethol Sociobiol, 8*, 9S–25S.

46. McGuire, M.T. (1979). Sociobiology: its potential contributions to psychiatry. *Persp Biol Med*, *23*, 50–69.
47. Livesey, P. (1986). *Learning and emotion: a biological synthesis*. Vol. 1: Evolutionary processes. Hillsdale, NJ: Lawrence Erlbaum.
48. Durham, W.H. (1976). The adaptive significance of cultural behavior. *Hum Ecol*, *4*, 89–121.
49. Boyd, R., & Richerson, P.J. (1985). *Culture and the evolutionary process*. Chicago: University of Chicago Press.
50. Richerson, P.J., & Boyd, R. (1988). The role of evolved predispositions in cultural evolution. *Ethol Sociobiol*, *10*, 195–210.
51. Bishof, N. (1972). The biological foundation of the incest taboo. *Soc Sci Info*, *11*, 7–26.
52. Lockard, J.S., & Paulhus, D.L. (Eds.) (1988). *Self-deception: an adaptive mechanism?* Englewood Cliffs, NJ: Prentice Hall.
53. Nesse, R.M. (1990). The evolutionary functions of repression and the ego defenses. *J Am Acad Psychoanal*, *18*, 260–285.
54. Buss, D.M. (1985). Human mate selection. *Am Sci*, *73*, 47–51.
55. Buss, D.M. (in press). Sex differences in human mate preferences: evolutionary hypotheses tested in 37 cultures. *Behav Brain Sci*.
56. Linnoila, M., Virkkunen, M., Scheinin, M. et al. (1983). Low cerebrospinal fluid 5-hydroxyindoleacetic acid concentration differentiates impulsive from nonimpulsive violent behavior. *Life Sci, 33*, 2609–2614.
57. Cloninger, C.R., Sigvardsson, S., Bohman, M. et al. (1982). Predisposition to petty criminality in Swedish adoptees. I. Genetic and environmental heterogeneity. *Arch Gen Psychiatry, 39*, 1233–1241.
58. Cloninger, C.R., Sigvardsson, S., Bohman, M. et al. (1982). Predisposition to petty criminality in Swedish adoptees. II. Cross-fostering analysis of gene–environment interaction. *Arch Gen Psychiatry, 39*, 1242–1247.
59. Cloninger, C.R., Sigvardsson, S., Bohman, M. et al. (1982). Predisposition to petty criminality in Swedish adoptees. III. Sex differences and validation of the male typology. *Arch Gen Psychiatry, 39*, 1248–1253.
60. Scadding, J.G. (1967). Diagnosis: the clinician and the computer. *Lancet, 7502*, 877–882.
61. Kendall, R.E. (1975). The concept of disease and its implications for psychiatry. *Br J Psychiatry, 127*, 305–315.
62. Hofer, M.A. (1984). Relationships as regulators: a psychobiologic perspective on bereavement. *Psychosom Med, 46*, 183–197.
63. McGuire, M.T., Raleigh, M.J., & Johnson, C. (1983). Social dominance in adult male vervet monkeys. II. Behavioral, biochemical relationships. *Soc Sci Info, 22*, 311–328.
64. Engle, G. (1977). The need for a new medical model: a challenge for biomedicine. *Science, 196*, 129–136.
65. Crawford, C.B. (1989). The theory of evolution: of what value to psychology? *J Compr Psychol, 103*, 4–22.

3

Evolutionary epidemiology: Darwinian theory in the service of medicine and psychiatry

Daniel R. Wilson
Departments of Psychiatry and Biological Anthropology, University of Cambridge, UK 19 Clarkson Road, Cambridge CB3 0EH, England

Received 22-II-1993

ABSTRACT

Epidemiology is a science of disease which specifies rates (illness prevalences, incidences, distributions, etc.). Evolution is a science of life which specifies changes (gene frequencies, generations, forms, function, etc.). 'Evolutionary Epidemiology' is a synthesis of these two sciences which combines the empirical power of classical methods in genetical epidemiology with the interpretive capacities of neo-darwinian evolutionary genetics. In particular, prevalence rates of genetical diseases are important data points when reformulated for the purpose of analysis in terms of their evolutionary frequencies. Traits which exceed *prevalences beyond the rates of mutation* (in Hardy–Weinberg calculations) or evidence unusual *range of phenotypic reaction* are of special interest. This is because traits which did not confer advantages in the environment of evolutionary adaptation cannot accede, through natural selection, to anything but low rates of genomic prevalence.

Evolutionary epidemiology is, in all of medicine, of particular promise in ongoing efforts to better understand psychopathology. Many complexities of phenotypic adjustment arise when new developmental demands are placed on an 'old' genome. The new and complex biosocial ecology of human mass society now evokes different phenotypes than those in the prehistorical ecology to which the genome is structurally and functionally better adapted. Some of these new phenotypes are darwinian failures. In this paper, the theoretical implications of evolutionary epidemiology are extended and some tentative points of clinical application (particularly to psychiatry) are offered.

Acta Biotheoretica **41**: 205–218, 1993. © 1993 *Kluwer Academic Publishers. Printed in the Netherlands.*

1. AN OVERVIEW OF THE EVOLUTIONARY AGENDA

Since the work of Charles Darwin we have known that traits become common, essentially, via promotion of characteristics advantageous to the struggle for existence in the environment of evolutionary adaptation. That is, genes evolve by means of natural selection.

Darwinian evolution through natural selection has, as an organizing principle, greatly influenced most of the abstract, natural and social sciences over the past century (Ruse, 1986). Its consequences have now begun to extend to the arts and letters (Paglia, 1990). Even the rarefied domains of philosophy and theology are beginning to grasp the extraordinary range and power of evolutionary thought (Wilson, 1991).

Yet surprisingly, medicine generally has so far enjoyed little benefit from the unique insights of the evolutionary point of view. Within medicine itself, psychiatry and related studies—until only very recently—have remained almost wholly unenlightened by the evolutionary perspective. This in spite of pioneering efforts by Darwin (1868) to draw human behavior into the domain of evolutionism as well as Freud's keen interest in evolutionary ideas as they relate to depth psychology (Sulloway, 1979; Ritvo, 1990).

Even as 'evolutionary psychology' acquires cachet (Pershonok, 1993), it is ironic that almost nowhere has there yet been substantial exploration of the evolved roots of human behavioral pathology. Several useful, early forays stand out (Huxley et al., 1964; Price 1972; Gardner, 1982; Chance, 1988; Gilbert, 1989; Glantz & Pearce, 1990; Badcock, 1990). Psychopathologists are, of course, intensively interested in the neural, humoral, immunological, genetical and all other manner of physiological aspects of human behavior and its abnormalities. They likewise and with care scrutinize the psychoanalytical, cognitive, interpersonal, social, cultural and other diverse determinants of disordered behavior. But however heralded has been the 'biological revolution' in psychiatry, it seems nonetheless that evolution, that most inclusive science of biology, has yet to comprehensively inform theories of or therapeutics within medicine or psychopathology (Barash, 1977).

Darwinism is now capturing the more direct attention of physicians, psychiatrists and biomedical researchers. The advent of the technologies giving rise to the Human Genome Initiative has surely made questions regarding the genetical evolution of disease of more than merely a peripheral interest to some physicians or psychopathologists. Moreover, the conceptual limitations of medicine generally and, in particular, both psychoanalysis and biological psychiatry have all become more clear during a time of marked advances in ideas about social biology and genetics. With such a darwinian renewal comes the prospect for a truly integrating model of normal human behavior and its pathology. A systematic theory of psychopathology may be emerging that is neither brainless or mindless, nor for that matter, sexless (Eisenberg, 1986).

Whatever the reasons, the incorporation of the scientific vigor of a darwinian framework is a trend to be welcomed by all interested in a complete and systematic conceptualization of medicine and psychiatry.

This is because principles to be abstracted from the taxonomic study of human behavioral forms and their distributions, both normal and abnormal, will generate a deeper comprehension of the laws of ecology from which pathological phenomena have originated and evolved (Wilson, in press). Such principles will eventually reorder theories, teaching and therapeutics within psychiatry and allied fields. It is an approach of more empirical breadth and philosophical vigor than any in the existing schools of psychopathology.

Still, an evolutionary approach to the study of normative behavior is itself rather new. Thus that the root causes of some pathological behavior are better understood as remnants of past adaptive behaviors is so entirely new an idea that little is done with it throughout the world of science: there exist no comprehensive texts or courses of study with a specific focus on the positive evolutionary roots of psychopathology. Basic or clinical research protocols are as yet of limited influence, being both new and small.

But clearly, formal psychiatric study and research, both theoretical and empirical, is warranted to incorporate and systematize the clear conceptual implications of the principles of darwinian evolution. Efforts to comprehend both normative and psychopathological behavior will benefit greatly from a thorough examination at an evolutionary vantage.

2. IMPEDIMENTS TO THE STUDY OF EVOLUTION AND HUMAN BEHAVIOR

There are several reasons that evolution has not yet substantially established itself within the purview of psychopathological studies. Most of these derive from social, political and historical concerns regarding the theory of evolution itself. Scandal still easily attaches or, more accurately, is attached to the enterprise of understanding human behavior in terms of evolution by means of darwinian natural selection. Thus, the introduction of darwinian ideas to the study of psychopathology has been inhibited in the first instance because human evolutionism remains somehow controversial. This is true not just of scientifically premature policy ambitions of some social biologists, but in some quarters of even the general principles of evolutionary biology themselves.

Long still stretch the shadows of inhumane social spencerianism, related eugenical mistakes and pseudoscientific bigotries. These and other abberant policies promulgated over the past century remain, quite justifiably, the source of enduring unease. The Scopes' monkey trial, fascist distortions and other less perverse but still misguided policies remain within living memory of many. Such ideologically dark and politically clumsy efforts to apply evolutionism to the human race ought not to be passed over lightly. Any research agenda which at all appears likely to dust off this tragic legacy arouses fear and loathing.

So, it is in such a seamy intellectual milieu as this, that psychopathologists with interests in human evolution invite further indemnification of double stigma. Evolution is, as noted, itself a residually controversial area of science. Controversy is stirred all the more when human evolutionism is joined with the central interests of psychopathology, which themselves are often the focus of considerable popular and even medical derision (abnormalities of thought, mood, sex, aggression, etc.). Novel darwinian studies of these abnormalities in persons so socially marginalized and misunderstood is work that is unlikely to appeal to the mainstream imagination.

It comes as no surprise that some critics express fear of restrictive social policies seen as inevitably consequent to studies of human evolution. For a time such concerns were voiced rather stridently by some who prejudged the agenda to be one of reactionary reductionism (Gould & Lewontin, 1979). These contretemps have subsequently been the basis for a virtual cottage industry of historiographic criticism largely pertaining to the implications of human evolutionism in its social, behavioral and political dimensions (Bowler, 1992). As such, the anxieties provoked by human social biology are, nonetheless, part and parcel of ongoing and serious discourse in the annals of philosphy and history of science for more than two centuries (Alexander, 1987). These recent arguments, especially those pertaining to human sociobiology, have generated more heat than light and are now, thankfully, on the wane. They are not germane to the topic here at hand. It is sufficient for the present purpose to say that studies pertaining to human evolution must maintain the highest of ethical standards and that derivative policy recommendations ought (if any) to be few, narrow and the subject of considerable skepticism.

Quite apart from all these ethical considerations one huge inhibition remains to thwart the nascent enterprise of evolutionary psychopathology: evolution is vast. The scales of time and complexity are astounding. It may be a phenomenon just too big and intricate to properly consider at all (Kendrew, 1978). This is a nearly insurmountable hurdle.

It is a hurdle which does not, however, defy every leap of inquiry. There is emerging a subdiscipline within evolutionary science which retains a manageable medical scope while also harnessing some of the extraordinary power of the facts of evolution (Wilson, 1992). Evolutionary epidemiology is an inherently biomedical synthesis of several basic operations borrowed from evolution and epidemiology. Its aim is to translate prevalence rates, as known to epidemiologists, into frequency rates, as known to geneticists. This synthetic method can thereby deduce which gene systems have a population prevalence so high as to be explained only with reference to a long period of advantageous natural selection in the past environment of evolution.

3. THEORETICAL EVOLUTIONARY EPIDEMIOLOGY: A MEDICAL PRIMER

Evolutionary epidemiology is simple but powerful (Wilson, 1992). It is a method based on the understanding that the concept of 'prevalence' as used by epidemiological geneticists is, in essential ways, equivalent to the concept of 'frequency' as used by evolutionary geneticists. It is necessary to review the technical meaning of these terms. Prevalence refers to the rate of existence of a disease (gene) within a population. Frequency, similarly, refers to the rate of existence of a gene (disease) within a population. These two concepts can be melded in a rigorous fashion to deduce a number of remarkable insights concerning the ultimate origins of genes now predisposing to phenotypic pathologies of body and mind. Simply stated, genes common enough to have evolved by means of natural selection can have done so only by virtue of advantages conferred to lineages which carried such genes *even if such genes now express a degree of phenotypic disease*. Darwinian evolution is, after all, a reflection of past intergenerational increases in the demographic representation of healthy reproductive lines and reductions in unhealthy ones. Darwinism offers a rare longitudinal rather than a common cross-sectional perspective.

Allison's (1954) work on sickle-cell anemia is the founding contribution to what is now emerging as a more systematic approach to diverse questions regarding the evolved basis of epidemiologically prevalent genetic illness. Though the full theoretical and practical implications of such an evolutionary epidemiology are only now gaining the attention of medical researchers, Allison's was the first proof that carriers of 'disease' genes were endowed with superior darwinian fitness in certain ecosystems. The prevalence of what had been thought of as simply 'bad' genes was inexpliably high in such ecosystems. Carriers were, it was soon learned, resistant to the ravages of malaria. The malarial organism and the human blood system had co-evolved in the environment of evolutionary adaptation. Sickle-cell anemia, however pathological it is today, *was selected into the human genome*.

But sickle-cell anemia is not a universal morbidity of the human genome. It is, rather, a special gene system which arose in special environments. It is, to some extent, thought of as an idioethnic curiosity of limited medical interest: Africans have it, Laplanders do not. Moreover, it is essentially a disease of somatic, as opposed to behavioral, pathophysiology. Still, it provides the conceptual foundation on which might be built a more considerable research program (Cavalli-Sforza & Bodmer, 1976).

Within this framework, much epidemiological data can be reconsidered from an evolutionary genetical standpoint. Such reconsideration will lead to fresh implications about the ancient origins, ongoing processes and current phenotypic modulation of 'disease' genes. There is, then, a vast amount of extant and high quality genetic epidemiological data which will yield new clinical knowledge upon consideration from an explicitly evolutionary point of view. The body of genetic epidemiology accumulated over the past century of medical studies is quite amenable to reformulation into terms appropriate for analysis by the theorems of population genetics. Of special interest in this considerable body of primary data are the many genetic polymorphisms with significant population prevalence. Studies which synthesize evolution and epidemiology will repay any careful analysis which seeks to clarify how natural selection operates on these variant alleles. Such studies may not only demonstrate some clinical syndromes to be epiphenomena of highly evolved forms, but will also, necessarily, stimulate new ideas and insights in paleoanthropology.

In any case, such a program of research will eventually expand medical understanding of the theoretical and clinical consequences of evolutionary epidemiology. Inherent is the fact that several important gene systems now expressing 'pathological' phenotypes had—in a darwinian sense—intrinsic positive qualities that account for their frequency at the high rates observed today. More immediately, several essential tasks are to:

(1) prove that certain 'disease' genes now manifesting pathology can have evolved only via advantages favored in the course of natural selection (as population polymorphisms)

(2) learn how a normative essence suffuses some genetic pathology and conferred selective advantage over the course of evolution

(3) devise therapies aimed at evoking latent healthful phenotypes or, at least, to reduce those environmental events which evoke pathological manifestations in the course of development.

4. THEORETICAL EVOLUTIONARY EPIDEMIOLOGY: A PSYCHIATRIC PRIMER

The clinical and theoretical importance of evolutionary epidemiology extends to not just the physical aspect of medicine, but also to the psychological. The body of psychiatric genetic epidemiology accumulated over the past century is large and cogent. Indeed, indirect genetic analysis has had a long and prosperous, if unpresupposing, role in psychiatric research (Goodwin & Jamieson, 1990). This body of data is quite amenable to reformulation into terms appropriate for reanalysis with the theorems of population genetics. Of special interest in this body of data are the many genetic polymorphisms with significant population prevalence. Careful examination of these variant alleles will likely prove that some have been sustained by the operations of natural selection.

Indeed, evolutionary epidemiology may require a refinement in the notion of disease itself, at least as such a label might be attached to several of the most common and genetical syndromes in medicine and especially psychiatry. Several important psychiatric conditions (manic-depression, sociopathy, obsessive-compulsivity, anxiety and even drug abuse and some disorders of personality) are so common and so strongly epigenetic that their epidemiologcal frequencies surpass even quite conservative thresholds of evolutionary selection. The deduction follows that such frequency thresholds were surpassed due to the darwinian selection of genes advantageous over the course of evolution. They most certainly served, and perhaps still serve, useful functions in human society.

This is not, necessarily, to aver that such genes now express entirely healthy phenotypes. Such would be something of a naturalistic fallacy in reverse. The current environments to which young humans are exposed and in which their phenotypes develop are, by and large, different than those in which much relevant human, primate, mammalian and reptilian ancestry achieved increasingly optimal and evolutionarily stable strategies (Wilson, in press).

This underscores the point that the same genes which conferred advantages in the environment of evolution might, upon ontogenic exposure to new biosocial ecology, form deleterious phenotypes. Developmental and social forces become important etiological factors by which the ecological cues of the modern environment *nurture nature* in emergent, not evolved, ways. The deleterious expressions of such genes are not 'genetic *qua* genetic' but truly the product of gene–environment interactions.

Thus, even a disease phenotype which is 100% penetrant, twin concordant and mendelian dominant retains a component of environmental expression. This component is a function of the differences between the ideal and the real phenotypes (Wilson, 1975). These two phenotypes arise, respectively, in the environment of evolutionary adaptation (to which the genome and ideal phenotype are, at equilibrium, adapted) and the environment of ontogenic adjustment (in which the genome is evoked to express the real phenotype).

All this is of importance both for paleoanthropology and the full appreciation of continuing advantages, if any, of these 'disease' genes. Clinically, there must be potential, if latent, benefits of the ideal phenotype residual in genes now more typically expressive of diseased real phenotypes. There are, of course further ethical, legal, social and even theological consequences to be explored with respect to these latencies and potential.

But the main objective here is to explain a method by which standard epidemiological data concerning genetical disease rates can be reanalyzed from an evolutionary point of view. Again, the point of such reanalysis is to establish whether such genetical systems have accumulated over the course of evolution due to the effects of darwinian natural selection. With the business of "how" specified, attention can be turned in earnest to questions as to who, when, where and why all this happened (Mayr, 1963).

With this comprehensive view of genetic processes by which is expressed the modern extended phenotype (Dawkins, 1976), certain major epigenetic diseases—most notably mental illnesses—can be better appreciated as atavisms of previously adaptive hominoid biopatterns. An improved grasp of the adaptive essence of mental illness may well lead to their destigmatisation while, also, giving rise to improved methods of rehabilitation.

5. APPLIED EVOLUTIONARY EPIDEMIOLOGY

Evolutionary mechanisms, generally, require eons of favorable selections for new mutations to obtain epidemiological prevalence at substantial rates. The threshold rate is not precisely known for specific genes and involves highly technical adjustments for rates of such things as mutation, back-mutation, fertility, penetrance and dominance. The calculation of threshold rates also assumes broadly stable environmental conditions, i.e., an environment of evolutionary adaptedness.

The mathematical clarification of such evolutionary dynamics is the aim of population genetics. The Hardy–Weinberg equilibrium is perhaps the fundamental theorem of population genetics, as every student of evolution may remember. The equation summates genetical fluctuations across generations in a precise way to specify the net effects of evolution via natural selection (Cavalli-Sforza & Bodmer, 1976). Genes arise by mutation and are selected for or against over time. If a new gene is helpful enough for long enough, it will accumulate. Genes at prevalences well beyond frequency of spontaneous mutation, except in decidedly unusual circumstances, were selected into the genome on the basis of positive characteristics expressed in the phenotype. They evolved.

As a rule, prevalence above the mutation rate is likely when a gene occurs in the frequency range of 1/10,000 to 1/1,000 members of a population (Wilson, 1975). Therefore, in mammalian systems rates much above 0.001% are suggestive of past positive natural selection and rates beyond 0.01% highly suggestive. Given average mutation rates and neutral fertility effects it is unlikely that a deleterious gene should attain a frequency of much more than 0.01%. Moreover, to accrete even this random level in the genome might take many generations—up to 10,000. If a simple gene system occurs to such a degree it was, though not necessarily is, abidingly adaptive.

On the other hand, deleterious mutations cannot achieve high prevalences spontaneously nor even via neutral selection (Kimura, 1955). Consequently, the majority of inherited abnormalities should be rare as a function, more or less, of mutation rate divided by fertility and penetrance. Genetic diseases should be, by definition, of very low prevalence (e.g., achondroplasia) and are often enclosed within sporadic idioethnic lines (e.g., Tay-Sachs disease). Prevalence of even a deleterious gene will equilibrate over generations at a rate balancing new mutations against the selective pressure, e.g., in achondroplasia the equilibrium frequency is one in eight thousand births for what is a classic autosomal dominant condition; Tay-Sachs is seen only rarely and in certain lineages: some Ashkenazi Jews have it, Laplanders do not (Dobzhansky, 1962). Neither of these conditions evidence past positive selection and, indeed, such positive attributes are not to be predicted in the established tests of evolutionary epidemiology. Though strongly genetic, they are too rare to have been promoted by natural selection: they are counter-exemplary evolutionary 'noise' existing, more or less, at equilibrium rates.

As noted earlier, there is a limit to the range of phenotypic reactive adjustment to ecological change or novel environs. This is true whether the genes concerned were adaptive, neutral or deleterious. Beyond these limits, environmental fluctuations extrude genes which are less flexible in expressing a reproducible phenotype. Heredity does not predict the future but rather transmits the past. While future environments are presupposed to be similar to past ones, they cannot be exactly anticipated by the genome. Some genes are, however, more supple in achieving a phenotype fit to new circumstances. These tensions played out across generations are what natural selection is all about: heredity is specific to population and environs, especially the environment of past evolution. Still, any archetype (including, specifically, evolutionarily stable strategies of behavior) was abidingly adapted to life in a past ecosystem.

Indeed, in some cases, elements of the environment were so stable as to have been phylogenetically interiorized into the genome. Given time and stability diversity converges upon the normative which converges upon the ideal. It is in this frame of thought that the example of the essential amino acids in the human diet comes to mind (Wilson, 1991). We have lost the capacity to constuct certain of these molecules even though our lives depend upon them. They have been so consistently available as foodstuffs for so long in the environment of our ancestry that our lineage has lost the capacity to anabolize them *de novo*. These features of the environment of our evolutionary adaptedness are—by means of evolutionary dialectics—now interiorized into our genome. Perhaps the best evidence of such curious interiorization lies in the fact that such deletion mutations induce little evolutionary consequence. The selection which accounts for most current gene prevalences took place in the past environment of evolution. This environment has substantially changed—in the blink of a darwinian eye—with the rise of complex culture which constrains the genome in ways not anticipated in the pleistocene environment of human evolution.

Therefore, studies of human behavior which do not vigorously consider these evolutionary parameters are comparable to Zuckerman's (1932) early and elegant but erroneous assessments of 'normal' primate behavior as derived from his observations of creatures in captivity (Wilson, 1975). One need not invoke the spirit of Rousseau to acknowledge the parallels between primates in a zoo and the enclosures of human nature brought about by contemporary society. Evolved tendencies are distorted in each. Behavior in the zoo is a property emergent from past selection in evolution. But, selection in the past environment accounts for much persistent human genomic structure and function. Yet the once predominant conditions of this past environment have changed rapidly with the rise of complex culture which increasingly encloses human nature (Weber, 1970).

In any case, if current phenotypes can be identified as the robust expressions of genes which themselves have population prevalences higher than predicted by Hardy–Weinberg calculations, then the genes evolved via the past natural selection of inherently favorable characteristics. This is true, with only technical exceptions, no matter how pathologic may be the phenotypes now unfolding from the genes nor how elusive or subtle may be the appreciation of the advantages.

Still, if and when the thresholds of epigenetic vigor and high frequency are simultaneously surpassed, then the two major conditions of the deductive premises upon which evolutionary epidemiological reasoning is based are satisfied. Consequently, the gene locus must have evolved by virtue of beneficial characteristics expressed, at least, in the course of natural selection. This approach, inchoate in Allison's work in sickle-cell anemia, has been recently formalized as a more general system (Wilson, 1992). Genetic loci of 'disease', both somatic and behavioral, can be assessed as to the likelihood of their having been evolved in the environment of their evolution on the basis of their advantageous characteristics in the struggle for existence.

6. EVOLUTIONARY EPIDEMIOLOGY: PSYCHOPATHOLOGY REASSESSED

For all the scientific and especially the popular disdain to which psychiatric theory and practice is sometimes subjected, its backbone of epidemiological research is surprisingly strong. Some of the most common, well validated and reliably diagnosed disorders of the human genome have been established within the field of psychiatry. In passing, it is useful to recall that validity and reliability are basic, if technical, terms widely used in epidemiology. The former expresses the meaningfulness of a given category of description and the latter expresses the repeatability with which such descriptions are made by different observers.

Indeed, on closer examination it appears that several of the genes most common in the entire human genome express psychopathology (e.g., manic-depression, sociopathy and obsessive-compulsive disorder). Thus they have been marked darwinian successes. Moreover, these same diagnoses are universal features of the human genome which evidence few, if any, ontogenic idiosyncracies of epidemiology due to geographic ethnic, cultural, racial or other influences on the phenotype. Therefore, their darwinian success was an enduring and universal feature of the evolutionary history of the structure and function of the genome of the entire species.

Again, the high prevalence (as population polymorphisms) of such abiding genomic traits points to intrinsic, if overlooked, positive characteristics that caused them to be so avidly retained by long-term and wide-spread natural selection. These genes and their phenotypic expressions can be said to be highly canalized (Wimsatt, 1989).

So far, only indirect, phenotypic descriptions of psychopathology have been firmly established. The era of direct, genotypic description is at hand. This era should prove interesting since some diagnostic categories thought to denote discrete diseases may ultimately prove to be mere phenotypic variants of the same etiological genes. Such genomic equivalence through phenotypic 'co-morbidity' can only mask much higher aggregate genetic prevalence rates (Hudson & Pope, 1990; Kendler et al., 1992). If so, the indices of their twin concordance, prevalence and natural selection will be all the higher.

But, much important psycopathology can already be regarded as the product of natural selection. This is true even without recourse to the greater genetic frequencies which are necessarily involved in concepts of a broader spectrum of extended phenotypes. It is likewise true even without recourse to direct gene analysis. In the era of modern science it is easy to forget that gene characteristics and behavior can be quite usefully scrutinized without direct biochemical technology as the ingenuity of both Darwin and Mendel demonstrated so remarkably. In any case, indirect methods of epidemiology will remain the most useful approach to research in psychiatric research until techniques of direct gene studies are better validated (Hyman & Nestler, 1993).

A recent, well-designed program has generated indirect population genetics data highly (if unintentionally) amenable to reanalysis in the genetic terms of evolutionary epidemiology. The National Institutes of Mental Health (USA) comprehensive, community-based Epidemiological Catchment Area Program (ECA) studies are excellent examples of highly reliable and valid multicenter data on mental disorders in America (Eaton et al., 1981). The program analyzes data derived from structured interviews utilizing highly systematic diagnostic criteria in the best descriptive tradition established by Kraepelin (1904).

Perhaps the best example of how evolutionary epidemiological analysis belies any simplistic notions of 'disease' status can be appreciated with the reconsideration of bipolar disorder, i.e., manic-depression. This syndrome of cyclical moodswings, sexuality, sociability, hypermentation and the like is quite common. Prevalence has been estimated at 0.6% to 4.0% depending upon the rigor with which the phenotype is defined. In the ECA it was noted as carrying a lifetime risk of 1.2% (Eaton et al., 1981). Twin concordance rates, adoptee studies and family risk studies have long suggested a strong genetic contribution in the phenotype (Mollica, 1988). Even a highly conservative concordance estimate is that at least 65% of the phenotype of identical twins is due to direct genetic expression; moreover, concordance may well exceed 90% (Hyman & Nestler, 1993).

More recent direct gene studies have begun to trace the chromosomal locale of operative gene(s) (Egelund et al., 1987; Hodgkinson et al., 1987). These studies are complicated by terminological problems of 'lod-scoring' but are, none-the-less, most promising. Such direct studies have identified pedigrees consistent with autosomal dominance as the prime etiology although the interpretation of these findings remain somewhat obscured by inconsistences arising from the application of gene analytic techniques to categories of psychiatric diagnosis (Hyman & Nestler, 1993).

The manic-depressive phenotype is both strongly genetic and common. Conservatively estimated, its prevalence is at least 0.5% with a degree of twin concordance of at least 65%. *Taken together, these facts lead to the highly conservative deduction that bipolar disorder is some three hundred times more common than might be calculated from Hardy–Weinberg equilibrium predictions alone:*

$$(P/E = S) = [0.325]/[0.001) = 325$$

(where 'P' is prevalence [adjusted by concordance, etc., {0.5×65%}] and where 'E' is the frequency known or estimated by Hardy–Weinberg law then 'S' is the evolutionary epidemiological index of natural selection).

Moreover, with the higher prevalence figures emerging from the ECA (1.2%) and with an extended clinical spectrum (and the higher rates of twin concordance that such a spectrum denotes, i.e., 90%), a more realistic estimate is that the manic-depressive phenotype is one thousand times more common than it would be in the absence of the sustained operations of natural selection:

$$(P/E = S) = [1.2]/[0.001] = 1200$$

In any case, these genes so greatly exceed their predicted rate prevalence as to be explained only with reference to their promotion in the operations of natural selection sustained in the environment of evolutionary adaptation (Wilson, 1992).

Evolutionary epidemiology will further revise psychopathologic theory and practice as pertains to other syndromes, as well. The deductive methods of evolutionary epidemiology suggest that natural selection promoted genetic lineages now expressing (1) sociopathy, (2) depression, (3) some anxiety-panic disorders, (4) obsessive-compulsivity, (5) certain dyslexias, (6) the biological underpinnings of some personality disorders and, (7) the biological underpinnings of some substance abuse syndromes.

7. AN OUTLINE OF THE EVOLUTIONARY ROOTS OF PSYCHOPATHOLOGY

The genetical and epigenetical processes (ranging from the molecular to the evolutionary) by which phenotypes are expressed will be greatly clarified by the Human Genome Initiative. Thus, within a generation a great many somatic and behavioral genes will be testable in terms of their definitive evolutionary epidemiological status. Candidate syndromes which satisfy the conditions of requisite prevalence (e.g., above Hardy–Weinberg estimates) and epigenetic mediation (e.g., high twin concordance or similar mendelian characters) will no doubt be found. A full understanding of their ideal function is to be achieved only with an appreciation of the conditions of their natural selection in the past environment of evolutionary adaptation.

So it is that primary data from medical epidemiology await systematic reassessment in light of evolutionary anthropology. It appears that some psychopathologic phenotypes are produced not by transient genetical errancy, but by positive selection in a darwinian sense. But having deduced that the human condition was advanced and improved by the presence of genes linked to current psychopathological phenotypes such as manic-depression, it remains an ambitious task to reconcile all of this with current theories. Practical applications are even more elusive. Still, it remains to be explained as to "how" this happened (Mayr 1961). Methods of analysis borrowed from paleo-anthropology are perhaps the best means by which to frame novel data synthesized in an evolutionary epidemiological approach. Once these crucial theoretical points are better understood, clinical uses will surely follow.

It is important to emphasize that evolutionary epidemiology methods are not merely pseudoscientific or even speculative. Gene frequencies are gene frequencies whether one is studying bacteria, fruitflies or humans. High frequencies, with only rare and technical exceptions, evolve by means of natural selection. Again, certain genes now expressing psychopathological phenotypes are of frequencies so high as to be explained only by the selection of intrinsic advantages over the course of evolution. Moreover, this cannot be refuted (unless the primary data of either epidemiological or evolutionary genetics are wrong from the outset). But, as it runs so counter to the grain of common sense it is rather hard to accept.

That may be, but it all makes rather more uncommon sense in light of what we know about the environment of human evolutionary adaptedness in prehistory. Human paleoanthropology, therefore, offers support to and is itself strengthened by an evolutionary view of psychopathology. That is to say the evolutionary origins of genes and their adaptive prehistoric phenotypes are perhaps more easily understood than are the deranged expressions evoked from identical genes in the contemporary environment.

For hominoids, including humans, a cardinal adaptation is to roles in the cohesive, foraging, kinship band replete with sexual and cross-generational tensions. Hominoid evolution long optimised its sociophysiological processes in these small kinship bands (Barchas, 1986). For how long? Some fifty million years or more. Just how small? Some fifty to 200 individuals. There were, moreover, kinship ties, life-long group membership and face-to-face interpersonal relations. Within this adaptive niche sustained perhaps since before India collided with Asia, hominoids attuned their increasingly complex assertions of affective, sexual and symbolic traits to the resonating structure and content of kin and social relations in the group (Crook, 1985).

Thus systems of communication evolved to integrate group behavior to become a feature of sociophysiological regulation of group roles and rank. By such naturalistic hominoid politics were individuals promoted, demoted, adulated, admonished or extruded by the group. This behavioral schema was a remarkable mammalian and primatological refinement of and improvement upon mere reptilian systems of intimidation and violence. Such regulation is an extension, then, of ancient modes of communication clarifying status; a descendant of reptilian behavioral adaptations now some 300 million years old. Deep at the core of human affiliative capacity and cortico-limbic sentimentality lies the reptilian brain with a sombre repertoire of conflict which can yet be mobilized under certain conditions (MacLean, 1990).

As roles in the kinship band were emerging as a main selective pressure, hominoid neural-humoral systems gradually evolved archetypic small-group processes. Consequently, regulatory norms of humans are those which attune the individual to the social group. From this viewpoint, psychopathology is essentially the study and classification of dissonance in group tuning mechanisms (Gilbert, 1989). Put another way, it is the study of the dehiscence of individuals from the cohesive, or "viscous", band (Hamilton, 1964). Such mechanisms of dehiscence arise directly from the facts of hominoid band life: face-to-face relationships for life in groups of some tens to hundreds, strong convergence between personal roles and social status, and conscious bonds of kinship. Mechanisms of kin-group selection and reciprocal altruism thus linked sex, status, social relations to displays of affective and symbolic significance among individuals in the group.

Such groups of neuropsychologically complex, socially sensitive and intensely interactive anthropoids were advantaged by genotypic characteristics which express pathologic phenotypes only when removed from their typical ecology, like Zuckerman's apes or urban humans. For example, the genes which now render individuals vulnerable may have once been more salubrious to the individual and group by means of: extended but acceptable range of affective display, libido, creativity, energy, sensitivity, spontaneity, intellect and other cardinal features of the syndrome such as charisma and leadership (Goodwin & Jamieson, 1990). Such traits would have been avidly retained in the genome. They also are characteristic of breeding groups evolving more cavalier reproductive behavior in richer and less saturated ecosystems (Wilson & Daly, 1978). Unfortunately, the fascinating subject of so-called "r and K" biopatterns, however relevant to the aims of psychiatry, is properly the subject of extensive review and well beyond the scope at hand.

8. EPILOGUE: CLINICAL COMMENTS

It is only humane for theoretical work in medicine to state clearly what may be any clinical consequences. Whatever the promise of an evolutionary view, humans must adapt to the environment of their ontogeny not that of their phylogeny. But some useful guides to treatment may derive from a more coherent idea of the phylogenetic utility of traits which are now ontogenically troublesome.

For example, restorative social, psychological and vocational efforts might be more guided to moderate the friction induced by the incompatibilities rubbing of ontogenic needs against phylogenetic trends—which can be said to be the ultimate etiological source of the patient's suffering.

Moreover, an evolutionary perspective fosters a more poignant view of those who suffer: they may have been the most well adjusted to past environments. It seems likely that some psychopathology may now be evinced from strongly canalized specialities of the phenotype such as could happen only in a highly evolved lineage of small groups, social foragers. Evolutionary science can emancipate much psychopathology from the grip of a wholly negative con-ceptualization. This in itself is quite a relief to many patients who otherwise suffer not only the ravages of a primary disease of phenotypic reativity but also a secondary stigmatization due to social ignorance regarding the naturalistic roots of mental suffering.

While more rational means of rehabilitation and treatment may emerge from a darwinian view, they ought not simply to target a nostalgia for the past. The suffering of persons whose genes might have been healthier in an extinct ecology is not ameliorated by any idealization of the evolved nature of contemporary illness. Treatment must have instead an aim to bridge the incongruities which arise between the ecology to which the genome was tailored and that which it must wear.

Still, destigmatization may begin in earnest as we all experience some degree of loss in that the modern ecosystem is no longer so fully attuned for the elaboration of optimal human phenotypes. Most can modulate, via more supple processes of epigenesis, these incongruities with only trivial neurotic and existential angst. But those suffering severe neurotic or even psychotic derangements are simply stretched beyond the flexibility of their genotypes by the contemporary phenotypic demands engendered by ontogeny. They are the true discontents of civilization.

REFERENCES

Alexander, R.C. (1987). *The Biology of Moral Systems*. Hawthorne, N.Y., Aldine.

Allison, A.C. (1954). Notes on sickle cell polymorphism. *Annals of Human Genetics, 19*, 39–57.

Badcock, C. (1990). *Oedipus in Evolution*. Oxford, Blackwell.

Barchas, P.R. (1986). Sociophysiologic orientation to small groups. In: E.J. Lawler, ed., *Advances in Group Processes, vol. 3*. Greenwich, CT, JAI Press.

Barash, D.P. (1977). *Sociobiology and Behavior*. N.Y., Elsevier.

Bowler, P.J. (1992). *The Environmental Sciences*. London, Fontana Press.

Cavalli-Sforza, L.L. and W.F. Bodmer. (1976). *Genetics, Evolution and Man*. San Francisco, Freeman.

Chance, M.R.A, ed. (1988). *Social Fabrics of the Mind*. London, LEA.

Crook, J.H. (1980). *The Evolution of Human Consciousness*. Oxford, Oxford.

Darwin, C.R. (1868). Queries about expression for anthropological inquiry. In: *Annual Report of the Board of Regents of the Smithsonian Institution for the year 1867*. Senate Misc. doc. 86: 324.

Dawkins, R. (1976). *The Selfish Gene*. Oxford, Oxford.

Dobzhansky, T. (1962). *Mankind Evolving*. New Haven, Yale.

Eaton, W.W., et al, (1981). The Epidemiologial Catchment Area Program of the National Institutes of Mental Health. *Public Health Rep* 96, 319–325.

Eisenberg, L. (1986). Mindlessness and brainlessness in psychiatry. *Br. J. Psychiatry*, 148, 497–508.

Egelund, J.A, et al, (1987). Bipolar affective disorders linked to DNA markers on chomosome 11. *Nature 325*, 789–87.

Gardner, R. J. (1982). Mechanisms in major depressive disorder: an evolutionary model. *Arch. of Gen. Psychiatry 39*, 1436–1441.

Gilbert, P. (1989). *Human Nature and Suffering*. London. LEA.

Glantz, K. and J. Pearce (1989). *Exiles from Eden*. N.Y., Norton.

Goodwin, F. and K.R. Jamieson (1990). *Manic-Depressive Illness*. Oxford, Oxford.

Gould, S.J. and R. C. Lewontin (1979). The spandrels of San Marco and the panglossian paradigm. *Proc. R.S. (Lon.) B205:* 581–98.

Hamilton, W.D. (1964). The genetical evolution of social behaviour (I. II). *J. Theor. Biol.* 7: 1–52.

Hodgkinson, S., et al, (1987). Molecular evidence for heterogeneity in manic-depression. *Nature 325:* 805–808.

Hudson, J. and H. Pope (1990). Affective spectrum disorder. *Am. J. Psychiatry*, (47) 1: 552–564.

Huxley, Sir J.S., E. Mayr, H. Osmond and A. Hoffer (1964). Schizophrenia as a genetic morphism. *Nature 204:* 220–225.

Hyman, S. and E. Nestler (1993). *The Molecular Foundations of Psychiatry*. Washington, APA Press.

Kendler, K., et al, (1992). Major depression and generalized anxiety disorder: same genes, (partly) different environments? *Arch. Gen. Psychiatry (49) 9:* 716–722.

Kendrew, Sir J. (1978). Introduction. In: R. Duncan and M. Smith, eds., *The Encyclopedia of Ignorance*. N.Y., Pocket Books.

Kimura, M. (1955). Stochastic processes and distribution of gene frequencies in natural selection. *Cold Spring Harbour Sym. on Quant. Biol., 22*: 33–53.

Kraepelin, E. (1904). *Lectures on Clinical Psychiatry.* London, Baillière.

MacLean, P.D. (1990). *The Triune Brain in Evolution.* N.Y., Plenum.

Mayr, E. (1961). Cause and effect in biology. *Science, 134*: 1501–06.

Mayr, E. (1963). *Animals, Species and Evolution.* Cambridge, Harvard.

Mollica, R.F. (1988). Mood disorders: epidemiology. In: H.I. Kaplan and B.J. Sadock, eds., *Comprehensive Textbook of Psychiatry V.* Baltimore, Williams and Wilkins.

Paglia, C. (1990). *Sexual Personae.* New Haven, Yale.

Pershonok, D. (1993). Personal Communication.

Price, J.S. (1972). Genetic and phylogenetic aspects of mood variation. *Intl. J. M.H, 1*: 124–144.

Ritvo, L.B. (1990). *Darwin's Influence on Freud.* New Haven, Yale.

Ruse, M. (1986). *Taking Darwin Seriously.* Boston, Blackwell.

Sulloway, F.J. (1979). *Freud: Biologist of the Mind.* N.Y., Basic Books.

Weber, M. (1970). *Max Weber: Essays in Sociobiology.* (H.H. Gerth and C.W. Mills, transls. and eds.), London, Routledge, Kegan, Paul.

Wilson, D.R. (1991). A healthy approach to the end of life! Proceedings of the Andover-Newton Theological Seminary Annual Colloquium, Boston.

Wilson, D.R. (1992). Evolutionary epidemiology. *Acta Biotheoretica, 40:* 87–90.

Wilson, D.R. (in press). Toward a dynamic taxonomy of behaviour.

Wilson, E.O. (1975). *Sociobiology.* Cambridge, Harvard.

Wilson, M. and Daly, M. (1978). *Sex, Evolution and Behavior.* North Scituate, MA, Duxbury Books.

Wimsatt, W. (1989). Evolutionary entrenchment. (Proceedings of the Human Behavior and Evolution Society Second Annual Meeting), *Ethology and Sociobiology,* 10 (5).

Zuckerman, S. (1932). *The Social Life of Monkeys and Apes.* London, Kegan, Paul.

4 Fear and fitness: An evolutionary analysis of anxiety disorders

Isaac M. Marks
Institute of Psychiatry, London
Randolph M. Nesse
University of Michigan Medical School, Department of Psychiatry, Ann Arbor

This article reviews the evolutionary origins and functions of the capacity for anxiety, and relevant clinical and research issues. Normal anxiety is an emotion that helps organisms defend against a wide variety of threats. There is a general capacity for normal defensive arousal, and subtypes of normal anxiety protect against particular kinds of threats. These normal subtypes of normal anxiety protect against various anxiety disorders. Anxiety disorders arise from dysregulation of normal defensive responses, raising the possibility of a hypophobic disorder (too little anxiety). If a drug were discovered that abolished all defensive anxiety, it could do harm as well good. Factors that have shaped anxiety-regulation mechanisms can explain prepotent and prepared tendencies to associate anxiety more quickly with certain cues than with others. These tendencies lead to excess fear of largely archaic dangers, like snakes, and too little fear of new threats, like cars. An understanding of the evolutionary origins, functions, and mechanisms of anxiety suggests new questions about anxiety disorders.

Received January 23, 1994; revised September 17, 1994.

Address reprint requests and correspondence to: Isaac M. Marks, M.D., Institute of Psychiatry, London, SE5 8AF, U.K., or to Randolph M. Nesse, M.D., The University of Michigan Medical School, Department of Psychiatry, C440, Med-Inn Bldg., Ann Arbor, MI 48109-0840, U.S.A. E-mail: Nesse@um.cc.umich.edu

Ethology and Sociobiology 15: 247–261 (1994)

0162-3095/94/$7.00

INTRODUCTION

Nearly everyone recognizes that anxiety is a useful trait that has been shaped by natural selection. Even good things, however, cease to be good when they become excessive. Too much anxiety can be disabling. If a drug were found that abolished all anxiety for all time it could be as harmful as a drug that induced anxiety of crippling degree. Adaptive modulation is the keynote to success. This point is best understood from an evolutionary perspective on the origins and functions of anxiety. Such a framework can illuminate current clinical and research issues.

Anxiety is one kind of emotion. Why do emotions play such a central part in our lives? Many researchers now view emotions as response patterns shaped by natural selection to offer selective advantages in certain situations (Plutchik and Kellerman 1980; Marks 1987; Lelliott et al. 1989). The bodily, behavioral, and cognitive responses that constitute emotions are a preprogrammed pattern of responses that increase ability to cope with threats or seize opportunities.

Each emotion can be thought of as a computer program designed to accomplish some specific fitness task particularly well (Nesse 1990). If the current task is courtship, romantic love is helpful. If one is being betrayed, anger is useful. If a tiger is attacking, then fearful flight and avoidance are best. If people are disapproving, then social anxiety may be appropriate. Different emotions, however, must be orchestrated, just as endocrine function must be coordinated in an endocrine orchestra. Emotional responses must fit changing adaptive challenges, with each emotion fitting a particular kind of situation.

Anxiety increases fitness in dangerous situations which threaten a loss of reproductive resources. Such resources include not only life and health, but also relationships, property, status, reputation, skill, and anything else that could increase Darwinian fitness. Given this function of anxiety, we would expect it to be aroused by any cues that indicate a risk of loss. If each subtype of anxiety evolved to deal with a particular kind of danger (as we will suggest), then the features of each anxiety subtype and the signals that arouse it should match the corresponding danger.

Prior Work on Evolution and Anxiety

The utility of fear and anxiety has long been recognized. Darwin's book on emotions emphasized the communication aspect of fear (Darwin 1872). The function of separation anxiety was pointed out by Bowlby (1973), Marks (1987), Ainsworth (Ainsworth et al. 1978), Klein (1981, p. 248), and many others. The adaptive functions of components of the stress response were laid out long ago by Cannon (1929) and later by Frankenhaeuser (Konner 1990). It has also long been known that fear is more easily linked to certain cues than to others (Marks 1969; Seligman 1970; Paley 1970 [1802]; Ruse 1988; Mineka et al. 1980).

We still lack, however, a systematic analysis of the evolutionary origins and functions of anxiety. Little research has demonstrated the advantages of anxiety, and almost no one has looked for disorders characterized by too little anxiety. There are several reasons for these gaps in our knowledge. Most writings on the functions of anxiety apologize about "speculatively" addressing such "teleological" issues, even though biologists have known for 30 years that questions about the evolutionary function of a trait are not teleological at all and that hypotheses about such functions can be tested just like any other (Marks 1974). Complex traits can be shaped by natural selection only if they serve functions that increase fitness. Hypotheses about these functions are not matters for speculation but for clear formulation and rigorous testing.

Testing of evolutionary hypotheses is now the focus of most research into animal behavior (Alcock 1989), especially by behavioral ecologists (Krebs and Davies 1991), who emphasize the functional significance of behavior, not just the descriptions dwelt on by earlier ethologists. These methods are only just beginning to be applied to the study of human behavior (Howard 1991; Barkow et al. 1992; Smith 1982). Therefore, few data-based studies of humans are available as yet. By highlighting the value of this approach and its clinical and research significance, we hope to encourage work on human anxiety that builds on the models provided by behavioral ecology. Even before then, we suggest that this perspective can provide some guidance in answering current questions about anxiety and its disorders.

Subtypes of Anxiety

A question of major concern is how to split (or lump) the various kinds of anxiety disorders, and how to justify the taxonomy. Some researchers emphasize the similarities of all anxieties and postulate the unity of all anxiety disorders. Others stress the differences between different kinds of anxiety, positing several distinct disorders, each with its own etiology, phenomenology, and treatment. An evolutionary perspective suggests a middle ground between these two extremes. General anxiety probably evolved to deal with threats whose nature could not be defined very clearly. Subtypes of anxiety probably evolved to give a selective advantage of better protection against a particular kind of danger.

To illustrate this, consider another defense, the immune response. Humans have a capacity for both a general immune response and for specialized immune responses. Antigens arouse general responses, such as lymphocyte monitoring for the presence of foreign material, inflammation, fever, pain, and malaise. They also arouse specific responses, such as immunoglobulins to bacterial infection, interferon to viral invasion, eosinophils to parasites, and natural killer cells to cancer.

Like antigens, other external threats arouse both general and more specific responses. General threats arouse general anxiety-inducing vigilance, physiological arousal, and planning for defense. Specific threats elicit specific patterns of behavioral defense (Edmunds 1974; Janzen 1981). High places evoke freezing; social threats arouse submission; predators provoke flight. An evolutionary view suggests that different types of fear should share many aspects because reactions (e.g., rise in heart rate) that are useful in one kind of danger are likely to also help other kinds. Furthermore, the presence of one threat makes it likely that others are present too. A hunter-gatherer who is excluded from the group becomes more vulnerable not only to predators but also to starvation, climatic extremes, and falling off cliffs and into holes in unknown territory.

The utility of different kinds of anxiety depends in part on the four ways in which anxiety can give protection (Marks 1987). Two of them parallel the body's ways of dealing with foreign material: (1) *Escape (flight) or avoidance (preflight)* distances an individual from certain threats in the way that vomiting, disgust, diarrhea, coughing, and sneezing put physical space between the organism and a pathogen. (2) *Aggressive defense* (anger, clawing, biting, or spraying with noxious substances) harms the source of the danger just as the immune system attacks bacteria. (3) *Freezing/immobility* may benefit by (a) aiding location and assessment of the danger, (b) concealment, and (c) inhibiting the predator's attack reflex. (4) *Submission/appeasement* is useful when the threat comes from one's own group. Inhibition of impulses probably fits best under this category.

Multiple strategies can, of course, be used together. Squid escape by jet propulsion in a cloud of concealing ink. Puffer fish look ferocious, and their spines harm the predator's mouth. Agoraphobics freeze in panic and then dash for home. Social phobics avoid or escape from authority figures if they can, and submit if they cannot. Obsessive-compulsives avoid "contamination" if possible; if they can't, they try to escape from it by washing. Any of the above four strategies can involve deception (Krebs and Dawkins 1984). An escaping rabbit runs straight ahead, but then circles furtively behind the pursuer. When a cat is threatened, its fur stands on end, making it seem larger. A possum plays dead.

In summary, the anxiety subtypes probably exist because of the benefits of having responses specialized to deal with particular dangers, but is unlikely that anxiety subtypes have differentiated into completely unrelated response patterns. To the extent that various anxiety disorders are exaggerations of various subtypes of normal anxiety, anxiety disorders can likewise be expected to be partially, not fully, differentiated.

The Relationship Between General Anxiety and Panic

Can an evolutionary perspective illuminate the relationship between general anxiety and panic? Are anxiety and panic separate, or on a continuum? Mild threat causes a general increase in anxiety that helps to locate the source and type of danger and to plan possible ways to deal with it. Extreme or sudden danger is more likely to produce panic. General anxiety commonly precedes panic. A similar relationship is observed with the two related defenses of nausea and vomiting. Nausea stops one from eating (useful if the food being ingested is toxic), and leads one to avoid foods that induced nausea (also useful). Extreme nausea culminates in vomiting, which expels the contents of the stomach. Occasionally there can be vomiting without preceding nausea, just as there can be sudden panic without preceding anxiety.

Many components of the anxiety and panic response are those which Cannon recognized as useful in situations in which "fight or flight" are the adaptive responses (Cannon, 1929). Cannon noted the functions of many of these components. Epinephrine acts on platelet beta receptors to enhance clotting and on the liver to release glucose. Cardiovascular changes speed blood circulation. Circulation patterns change so that less blood goes to the skin and gut, and more to the muscles. Hyperventilation raises oxygen import and carbon dioxide export. Sweating cools the body and makes it slippery. A sense of imminent doom galvanizes preventive action and forestalls dawdling. These components form a reliable constellation in the anxiety/panic response, which is partly mediated by adrenergic receptors (a proximate explanation). They act together to increase fitness in the face of danger (the evolutionary explanation that is needed in addition to the proximate one).

These aspects of anxiety and panic are largely similar whether cued by heights, animals, thunderstorms, darkness, public places, separation, or social scrutiny. Their similarity reflects the value of this defense against a wide array of threats.

Other Subtypes of Anxiety and Specific Threats

The features of many anxiety subtypes are well matched to the task of defending against particular types of threats. On the hypothesis that anxiety disorders represent extremes of normal forms of anxiety, we will not distinguish here between normal and pathological states.

1. Fear:
    a. Heights induce freezing instead of wild flight, thus making one less liable to fall.
    b. Blood or injury cues produce a diphasic vasovagal response ending in bradycardic syncope. Such fainting may reduce blood loss after injury and, like death feigning, inhibit further attack by a predator (Marks 1988).
    c. Public places and being far from home arouse a cluster of mild fears that guard against the many dangers encountered outside the home range of any territorial species. Agoraphobia can be seen as an intensification of such extraterritorial fear (Nesse 1987; Lelliott et al. 1989).

d. Traumas are followed by fear and avoidance of anything reminiscent of the original trauma. A natural tendency to such seeming "overreaction" is understandable given the high cost of failure to avoid any possibility of reexperiencing a mortal danger.

e. Social threats evoke responses that promote group acceptance, for example, submission to dominants and to norms of dress, mien, odor, speech, customs, beliefs. This prevents dangerous extrusion from the group. Mild shyness and embarrassment can promote acceptance. If shyness and embarrassment are excessive, however, then fitness suffers, as in several anxiety disorders: pervasive shyness in avoidant personality disorder; gaze aversion and fear of scrutiny, of shaking, and of blushing in social phobia; fear of excreting near others in sphincteric phobias (Marks 1987, pp. 362-371); terror of looking or smelling abnormal in dysmorphophobia; fear of behaving antisocially in obsessive-compulsive disorder. Impulses to behave in ways that would cause social rejection may arouse general anxiety without the subject being aware of those punishable impulses, thus helping to conceal them from others (Nesse 1990). We do not emphasise a distinction between fear of specific dangers and anxiety aroused by nonspecific dangers or unconscious impulses, because in all cases the state, whether anxiety or fear, is aroused by a cue that indicates a threat to reproductive resources.

2. Fear-like patterns:
    Some threats evoke specific discomforts not usually called anxiety.

    a. Food aversions are conditioned much less easily to anxiety and to pain than to nausea and vomiting.

    b. Threat of losing one's mate to a rival evokes jealousy that includes not only anxiety but also seeking of reassurance and aggression to try to avert loss. This pattern is intensified in morbid jealousy, which often includes obsessive ruminations and ritualistic checking on possible infidelity of the partner.

    c. The normal gag reflex stops material entering the upper respiratory tract. Hypersensitivity of this reflex may cause undue gagging with intense pharyngeal discomfort (Wilks and Marks 1983).

3. Obsessive-compulsive (OC) behaviors
    The anxiety and sense of compulsion in obsessive-compulsive disorder (OCD) may be a caricature of the motivational mechanisms that drive and prioritize normal behavioral routines. Such routines are parodied by OC rituals, which distort priorities.

    a. Many behavioral sequences are best completed to their functional end; if left unfinished, time and energy are likely to be wasted. Tension motivates persistence until closure is effected. Many obsessive-compulsives seem to lack the "fiat" we experience that marks the end of one sequence of thoughts or actions (James 1893). Such patients feel tense and must continue repeating thoughts or actions until they "feel right."

b. Many behavioral sequences are best executed one at a time, otherwise energy may be frittered away on disparate tasks, none of which are completed. The excess orderliness of OCD also wastes energy by doing tasks one by one to perfection, regardless of their importance, while leaving vital tasks undone.

c. Parasitism and infection are reduced in mammals by grooming and in birds by preening (Hart 1990). In many primate species, grooming also smoothes social interaction, as when a defeated baboon grooms the victor intensely after a fight. Many obsessive-compulsives wash and groom endlessly; if not allowed to do this, they often feel disgust or other discomfort rather than anxiety.

d. Group membership requires attention to others' needs. Disregard of these makes ostracism likely. In OCD, there is maladaptive overconcern with the risk of harming others.

e. Hoarding guards against future shortages and is protective in environments of scarcity. It is grotesquely exaggerated in some obsessive-compulsives.

It is unclear why obsessive-compulsives explain (rationalize) their fears and rituals in a more complex manner than do phobics. Perhaps different cognitive mechanisms are deranged in obsessive-compulsives as compared to phobics.

To summarize this section, the features of anxiety disorder subtypes largely correspond to various dangers humans have faced during their evolution. As noted above, subtypes of anxiety are not completely distinct because multiple threats are common, and because so many aspects of anxiety defend against many, not just one, kinds of danger. The most recent genetic evidence is consistent with this view. A study of 2,163 female twin pairs concludes: "[W]e found strong evidence of the existence both of genetic and environmental risk factors unique to each kind of phobia and for genetic and environmental risk favors that influenced all phobia subtypes. Our results were midway between the two extreme hypotheses regarding the interrelationship of the subtypes of phobias: (1) the subtypes of phobias are distinct, unrelated syndromes and (2) the subtypes of phobias represent minor variations of a single disorder." (Kendler 1992, p. 279).

It should be possible to create a taxonomy for anxiety disorders that reflects the origin and functions of normal anxiety. Just as various components of the normal immune response can respond too much (anaphylaxis), too little (hypoimmune disorders), or to the wrong cue (allergy) or wrong target (auto-immune disease), so anxiety can be excessive (as in general anxiety or panic disorders), deficient (hypophobia), or in response to a stimulus that is not dangerous (simple/specific phobias). The immune disorders are being unraveled by increasing understanding of the normal functions and mechanisms of the immune system. The anxiety disorders will also make more sense as we learn about the normal functions of the components of the anxiety system and the mechanisms that mediate them.

Defense Regulation

Defenses enhance survival only when appropriate to the degree and type of threat. If a defense is deficient, excessive, or inappropriate in form, then fitness suffers. People who lack the capacity for pain die young because their tissues get damaged (Stevens 1981); those with excessive pain are also disabled. Suppressing the cough reflex makes pneumonia likely; too much coughing can cause cerebral hemorrhage. Stopping vomiting or diarrhea may lead to death by toxin absorption (DuPont and Hornick 1973); too much vomiting or diarrhea can kill by dehydration. The systems that regulate these defenses have been fine-tuned to detect the form and amount of threat and respond appropriately.

Anxiety, too, is beneficial only if carefully regulated. Too much disables. Too little anxiety leads to behavior that makes us more likely to fall off a cliff, be attacked by a wild beast, or hurt by other humans, or to act in ways that lead to social exclusion. People with too little anxiety do not come to psychiatrists complaining of deficient fear, so their disorders, the "hypophobias," still await formal description.

The regulation of anxiety is an example of the benefit–cost tradeoffs that make every organism "a bundle of selective compromises" (Alexander 1975). While a grazing deer that lifts its head every few seconds to scan for predators has less time to eat, mate, and care for offspring, one that lifts its head too little may eat more, but is at greater risk of being eaten itself. How are such factors balanced?

The law of diminishing returns applies to anxiety, as to so much else. A little anxiety may yield marked protective gains but more fear may not be worth the costs. Selection pressure for fearfulness tapers off at the point where the incremental cost of further fear starts to rise above the incremental protection it yields. Evolved defenses often seem over-responsive (Marks 1987) because repeated false alarms may cost less than a single failure to respond when the danger is great (Nesse 1990). Anxiety at the mere hint of danger is therefore common, even though it may appear needless to a casual observer. Because the costs of erring on the side of caution are usually less than those of risk taking, it is no wonder that anxiety disorders are frequent.

Different environments select for different degrees of fear. On long-isolated islands without predators, many species lost their tendency to flee, fight, or hide. When humans arrived and brought in predators, the tame indigenous species were often killed off rapidly. The point is captured in the phrase "Dead as a dodo."

Regulation of Anxiety by Cues of Danger

It would be grossly inefficient to become anxious only after actual pain or loss. Instead, the nervous system has been shaped so that anxiety arises in response to cues that denote potential threats. Most of the dangers an individual is likely to encounter have already been survived by its forebears. Individuals who recognized and responded to a hint of such threats lived longer and had more descendants than those who had to learn from bitter experience. Selection thereby shaped a nervous system that makes us attend intently to certain cues—this is *prepotency* (Marks 1969; Ohman and Dimberg 1984) or *salience*. For instance, snake- or eye-like patterns arouse anxiety more easily than do other patterns. We are also predisposed to learn certain reactions to certain stimuli—this is *preparedness* (Seligman 1970). For instance, heights and snakes evoke fear rather than nausea, while bad food produces nausea rather than fear. *Prepotent* attention to particular patterns of stimulation is the first step on the path to *prepared* reactions to those patterns.

Fear develops quickly to minimal cues that reflect ancient dangers. As with imprinting, where experience inscribes the precise parental features that the offspring recognizes, so it is often better to convey the specifics of danger by rapid learning than by rigid genetic encoding. This avoids wasteful defense against safe stimuli. African plains' animals are less fearful of predators' presence per se than of their approach, their hunting intent, and other signs of danger (Marks 1987).

Prepared rapid learning of fear is partly mediated by the reactions of caretakers and peers. Keen observation and imitation of them is itself a prepared response. When an infant sees a visual cliff or a stranger, it looks at mother frequently to monitor her response (Marks 1987). If she smiles, this reassures; if she shows alarm, this augments her baby's fear. Rhesus monkeys are born without snake fear. Enduring fear develops after a few observations of another rhesus taking fright at a snake, but not after seeing it take the same fright at a flower (Mineka et al. 1984). Likewise, a fawn is not born with fear of a wolf, but lifelong panic is conditioned by seeing its mother flee just once from a wolf.

Prepared fears tend to manifest at the age when they become adaptive (Marks 1987). Height fear emerges in infants shortly before they start crawling at six months (Scarr and Salapatek 1970) and rises with crawling experience (Berthenthal et al. 1983). As the two-year-old child explores further afield, animal fears emerge. As young people leave home, agoraphobia arises.

Both prepotency and preparedness leading to a nonrandom distribution of fears (Marks 1987). Stimuli that come to be feared are mostly ancient threats: snakes, spiders, heights, storms, thunder, lightning, darkness, blood, strangers, social scrutiny, separation, and leaving the home range. Most phobias are exaggerations of these natural fears.

Unlike the prepared fears and phobias just noted, we rarely fear cues that have been harmless in our past, for example, wood, leaves, flowers, stones, or shallow water. Aversion therapists found it hard to induce fear of alcohol in alcoholics, or of women's clothes in tranvestites (Gelder and Marks 1970). Nor do we easily develop fear of evolutionarily recent dangers (Cook et al. 1986). Few fear motor cars, guns, cigarettes, or alcohol, despite knowing that these now kill far more people than do snakes, spiders, or sharks. Not having been present long enough to materially alter our genetic endowment, such modern perils are feared too little. It is difficult for even the great intelligence of humans to override genetic predispositions. Head and heart unite more easily when new threats relate to earlier ones. When they do, then fear of those threats may develop easily, but often in unmodulated fashion. Excessive fears of dentists and of AIDS grow out of ancient fear of injury and of infection.

Two tales show how food aversion conditions more easily when a novel food is paired with nausea than with pain. The first is of biased learning. Seligman (1970) developed nausea and vomiting some hours after a meal that included his first tasting of béarnaise sauce. Despite knowing that his affliction was probably viral, he acquired a lasting aversion to béarnaise sauce. His learning overrode his logic. The second tale is of failure to condition. Marks developed intense epigastric pain but no nausea while eating catfish for the first time. After 14 hours of agony, intestinal obstruction from an intussuscepted Meckel's diverticulum was found and corrected. No aversion to catfish followed. Such conditioning of food aversion to nausea rather than pain makes evolutionary sense; gastrointestinal toxins give rise to nausea and vomiting more than to pain.

Parents have difficulty training their offspring to fear evolutionarily recent dangers. It is hard for parents to "shift [children's] attitudes toward fear of matches, knives, bottles, dangerous sports, and the like, or toward tolerance and affection for uncles, aunts, physicians, cod liver oil, green vegetables, keeping on mittens and the like. Progress is slow" (Thorndike 1935). Thorndike here describes prepotency and preparedness for both fear and attraction. Our nervous system is neither a tabula rasa nor a clockwork machine. In addition to built-in biases, it has flexibility; its preexisting pathways can be strengthened or weakened according to certain rules that make it able to fine-tune its responses to various environments.

Benefits and Costs

There is an interesting tradeoff between biases and flexibility. Biases allow swift response to old threats with a minimum of experience, but at the cost of false alarms to cues that no longer indicate danger. The lack of other biases also has costs: We adapt slowly to some evolutionarily recent dangers. Though we fear much that now carries little risk, we accept many new perils with equanimity. We have too much fear of spiders, but too little fear of driving fast, saturated fat, and very loud music.

Our brain's flexibility does help us to (slowly) learn anxiety to totally new dangers, but this carries the cost of frequent misconnections of anxiety to cues that do not signal danger. We make inappropriate connections, thrust meaning on random sequences, and develop superstitious fears. We make false correlations between events (Mineka and Tomarken 1989) and misattribute them, particularly when anxious. People who are poor judges of probability report more experiences of illusory causality (Blackmore 1990a,b).

Cognitive Biases

Our cognitive mechanisms seem to have built-in biases shaped by natural selection. These biases usually give the right answer in daily life, but they can go wrong in circumstances that were rare in our evolutionary past. We attend to and fear rare events more than common ones: a jumbo jet crash more than daily road deaths, a rare new syndrome more than heart disease (Tversky and Kahneman 1974). We undervalue base rates in calculating risk (Kahneman et al. 1982). We attend unduly to superficial similarities to the problem at hand (Nisben and Ross 1980). We remember recent events more than those long past. We use accessible information that is unreliable rather than search for more valid data further afield. Abstract learning is more domain-specific than previously believed (Fodor 1983; Cosmida and Tooby 1981). This specificity is beneficial, because the possibilities for action are infinite. As Cosmides and Tooby (1987, p. 296) put it: "When a tiger bounds toward you, what should your response be? Should you file your toenails? Do a cartwheel? Sing a song? Is this the moment to run an uncountable number of randomly generated response possibilities through the decision rule? And again, how could you compute which possibility would result in more grandchildren? The alternative: Darwinian algorithms specialized for predator avoidance, that err on the side of false positives in predator detection, and, upon detecting a potential predator, constrain your response to flight, fight or hiding." Emotions are good examples of domain-specific mechanisms. Anxiety evolved to deal efficiently with the domain of danger and its subtypes differentiated to avert specific threats within that domain.

Implications for Research and Treatment

Current anxiety research often seeks syndrome-specific neurophysiological defects. Although such defects undoubtedly exist for some parents with some syndromes, exclusive reliance on this approach leads to difficulties. First, if anxiety is a normal defense, then some marked anxiety is likely to be, like being very tall, at the tail end of a Gaussian distribution. Different anxiety thresholds may often reflect, not specific defects, but individual polygenic variation similar to that which accounts for variation in susceptibility to cough, vomiting, or fever.

Second is the difficulty in neatly dividing anxiety disorders into mutually exclusive subtypes when each may in fact respond to a particular danger but none is completely differentiated from any other. If this is correct, then attempts to delineate mutually exclusive anxiety disorders are likely to fail.

Third is the problem in deciding which physiological aspects of anxiety reflect abnormalities and which merely reflect normal operation of the anxiety system. The sites, pathways, and neurotransmitters that regulate anxiety, like those that regulate normal vomiting, are its cause only in the superficial sense of being part of a long mediating chain. Anxiolytic drugs may correct no primary defect but rather block defensive responses well downstream from the initiating problem. Likewise, "[B]rain imaging data do not address the cause of OCD in any way whatsoever. . . . [M]ental activity as well as motor behavior, regardless of 'cause,' is mediated by the biochemical processes of the brain. Brain imaging data merely provide clues to some of the sites of abnormal cerebral activity of complex mentation and behavioral patterns of [OCD]" (Baxter 1990).

"Pharmacological dissection" seeks to delineate specific syndromes on the basis of response to particular drugs. But a single drug, even one that affects only a specific brain system, can affect many etiologically diverse conditions. Just as the analgesic effects of aspirin are not a sound basis for classifying arthritis, so antidepressants do not help us classify the many conditions in which they reduce dysphoria—anxiety, depression, schizophrenia, Alzheimer's disease, multiple sclerosis, and carcinoma. Current drugs for anxiety may be more like aspirin for pain than like insulin for juvenile-onset diabetes.

Exposure therapy is similarly nonspecific in its effects. Prolonged and repeated nontraumatic exposure to anxiety cues activates the evolved habituation mechanism that down-regulates fear. Without habituation to repeated stimulation, continual overresponding would prevent normal living. The lasting improvement from exposure therapy tells us little about how a phobia began but perhaps something about how avoidance maintains the established disorder.

The Heuristic Value of an Evolutionary Perspective

An evolutionary view can help explain otherwise puzzling features of anxiety by suggesting new and testable hypotheses about its function, and a search for relevant evidence. To take an example, stranger fear arises worldwide in infants at about six months of age. In trying to explain this, Marks when writing *Fears, Phobias, and Rituals* (1987) reasoned that a fear that is so transcultural is likely to be adaptive. At age six months, babies start to crawl away from mother and encounter strangers more often. Were strangers especially dangerous to infants in our recent evolutionary past? A search for relevant evidence found much that was emerging. Infanticide by stranger turned out to be so common that it is a strong selective force in primates as well as other species (Hrdy 1977). Abundant documentation also emerged that even today human infants are far more likely to be killed or abused by strangers than by familiars (Daly and Wilson 1989).

Without an evolutionary perspective the above hypothesis would not have been thought of and the evidence not have been sought. It was not a post hoc prediction; Marks did not know that such evidence was emerging at the time he began to look for it. Had infanticide turned out to be rare, the hypothesis would have been falsified.

Another new testable hypothesis arising out of an evolutionary view concerns agoraphobia. Mild "normal" agoraphobia seems homologous to fear of leaving the home range in territorial animals, a situation fraught with danger in the wild. Being away from home should thus be a prepotent cue for fear in normal young adults. An aversive event such as the hearing of repeated screams should evoke more anxiety (indicating prepotency) and condition more avoidance (showing preparedness) when it occurs in a public place far from, rather than near, home, even when familiarity has been controlled. Marks suggested this test to van den Hout; the results born out the prediction (van den Hout, unpublished).

An evolutionary perspective might also explain why general anxiety is not always aversive and can even be pleasurable. Millions flock to be thrilled by horror movies, the big wheel, tightrope walkers, and the like. Perhaps this is a form of play behavior, like so many other enjoyable games that help us deal better with real problems when the time comes. Young mammals spend much time in play that teaches them the game of life (Smith 1982). Hypotheses to test this view should be formulable.

The four defensive strategies noted earlier—escape, aggression, freezing and submission—are deployed to varying degrees in different subtypes of anxiety, in accordance with their utility. Examples include the greater prominence of nausea rather than anxiety in food phobias, and of syncope rather than flight in blood/injury phobias. Predictions yet to be tested include these hypotheses: (a) Submission is more marked in social than animal phobias, (b) freezing is more pronounced in fear of heights than of animals, and (c) flight is more pronounced in fear of animals than in fear of heights. Close matching of the features of anxiety subtypes to the threats they defend against demands the testing of many such predictions. This major research program is likely to reveal unsuspected facets of anxiety and its disorders.

CONCLUSION

The capacity for anxiety, like other normal defenses, has been shaped by natural selection. Anxiety disorders, like disorders of other defensive systems, are mainly disorders of regulation that entail excessive or deficient responses. As we steadily unravel the neurophysiology of the mediating mechanisms we need to remember that even if we knew every connection of every neuron, every action of every transmitter, our understanding would remain inadequate until we also knew the function for which those mechanisms were shaped. If we find drugs that offer reduction of anxiety without major side effects or dependency, then we will urgently need to know more about when anxiety is useful and when it is not. In the meantime, more knowledge about the adaptive significance of anxiety and its subtypes, and the normal mechanisms that regulate them, will help us make even more rapid progress in understanding and treating anxiety disorders.

Helena Cronin made many valuable criticisms of the manuscript, as did members of the Evolution and Psychiatry Project at the Department of Psychiatry at the University of Michigan.

REFERENCES

Ainsworth, M.D., Bichar, C., Waters, E., and Wall, S. *Patterns of Attachment: A Psychological Study of the Strange Situation*, Hillsdale, NJ: Erlbaum, 1978.

Alcock, J. *Animal Behavior: An Evolutionary Approach.* Sunderland, MA: Sinauer, 1989.

Barkow, J., Cosmides, L., and Tooby, J. (Eds.) *The Adapted Mind*, New York: Oxford Unversity Press, 1992.

Baxter, L. Neuroimaging in obsessive compulsive disorder: seeking the mediating neuroanatomy. *Obsessive Compulsive Disorder.* 167–188, 1990.

Berthenthal, B.L., Campos, J.J., and Capplovitz, K.S. Self-produced locomotion: an organizer of emotional, cognitive, and social development in infancy. In *Continuities and Discontinuities in Development*, R.M. Emde and Harmon, R. (Eds.), New York: Plenum, 1983.

Blackmore, S. Living in a nonrandom world. *The Guardian*, London, 1990a.

Blackmore, S. The lure of the paranormal. *New Scientist.* 62–69, 1990b.

Bowlby, J. *Separation: Anxiety and Anger*, New York: Basic Books, Inc, 1973.

Canon, W.B. *Bodily Changes in Pain, Hunger, Fear, and Rage: Researches into the Function of Emotional Excitement.* New York: Harper and Row, 1929.

Cook, E.W., Hodes, R.L., and Lang, P.J. Preparedness and phobia: effects of stimulus content on human visceral conditioning. *Journal of Aboral Psychology* 95(3): 195–207, 1986.

Cosmides, L., and Tooby, J. From evolution to behavior: evolutionary psychology as the missing link. In *The Latest on the Best: Essays on Evolution and Optimality.* J. Dupre (Ed.). Cambridge, MA: MIT Press, 1987.

Daly, M. and Wilson, M. *Homicide*, New York: Aldine, 1989.

Darwin, C. *The Expression of the Emotions in Man and Animals*, Chicago: University of Chicago Press, 1965 (1872).

DuPont, H.L., and Hornick, R.B. Adverse effect of Lomotil therapy in shigellosis. *Journal of the American Medical Association* 226: 1525–1528, 1973.

Edmunds, M. *Defence in Animals*, Harlow, Essex, England: Longman, 1974.

Fodor, J. *Modularity of Mind*, Cambridge, MA: MIT Press, 1983.

Gelder, M.G., and Marks, J.M. Transsexualism and faradic stimulation. In *Transsexualism and Sex Reassignment*, R. Green (Ed.). Baltimore, MD: Johns Hopkins University Press. 1970.

Hart, B.L. Behavioral adaptations to pathogens and parasites: five strategies. *Neuroscience and Biobehavioral Review* 14: 273–294, 1990.

Howard, J.C. Disease and evolution. *Nature* 352: 565–567, 1991.

Hrdy, S.B. Infanticide as a primate reproductive strategy. *American Scientist* 65: 40–49, 1997.

James, W. *The Principles of Psychology*, New York: Holt, 1893.

Janzen, D.H. Evolutionary physiology of personal defense. In *Physiological Ecology: An Evolutionary Approach to Resource Use*, C.R. Townsend and P. Calow (Eds.) Oxford: Blackwell, 1981, pp. 145–164.

Kahneman. D., Slovic, P. and Tversky, A. *Judgement Under Uncertainty: Heuristics and Biases.* Cambridge University Press, 1982.

Kendler, K.S., Neale, M.C., et al. The genetic epidemiology of phobias in women: the interrelationship of agoraphobia, social phobia, situational phobia, and simple phobia. *Archives of General Psychiatry* 49: 273–281, 1992.

Klein, D.F. *Anxiety Reconceptualized*, New York: Raven Press, 1981.

Konner, M. *Why the Reckless Survive*, London: Penguin, 1990.

Krebs, J., and Davies, N. *Behavioral Ecology: An Evolutionary Approach,* Oxford: Blackwell.

Krebs, J.R. and Dawkins, R.D. Animal signals; mind-reading and manipulation. In *Behavioral Ecology: An Evolutionary Approach.* J.R. Krebs and N.B. Davies (Eds.). Sunderland. MA: Sinauer, 1984, pp. 380–402.

Lelliott, P., Marks, I., McNamee, G., and Tobens, A. Onset of panic disorder with agoraphobia: toward an integrated model. *Archives of General Psychiatry* 46(11):1000–1004, 1989.

Marks, I.M. *Fears and Phobias*, New York: Academic Press, 1969.

Marks, I.M. *Fears, Phobias, and Rituals*, New York: Oxford University Press, 1987.

Marks, I.M. Blood-injury phobia; a review. *American Journal of Psychiatry* 145(10): 1207–1213. 1988.

Mayr, E. Teleological and teleonomic, a new analysis. *Boston Stud. Philo. Sci.* 14: 91–117, 1974.

Mineka, S. Davidson, M., Cook, M., and Keir, R. Observational conditioning of snake fear in rhesus monkeys. *Journal of Abnormal Psychology* 93: 355–372, 1984.

Mineka, S., Keir, R., and Price, V. Fear of snakes in wild and laboratory-reared rhesus monkeys (*Macaca mulatta*). *Anim. Lrn. Behav.* 8(4): 653–663, 1980.

Mineka, S., and Tomarken, A. The role of cognitive biases in the origins and maintenance of fear and anxiety disorders. In *Aversion, Avoidance, and Anxiety: Perspectives on Aversely Motivated Behavior*, L. Nilsson and T. Archer (Eds.)., Hillsdale, NJ: Erlbaum, 1989.

Nesse, R.M. An evolutionary perspective on panic disorder and agoraphobia. *Ethology and Sociobiology* 8: 73S–83S, 1987.

Nesse, R.M. Evolutionary explanation of emotions. *Human Nature* 1(3): 261–289, 1990a.

Nesse, R.M. The evolutionary functions of repression and the ego defenses. *Journal of the American Academy of Psychoanalysis* 18(2): 260–285, 1990b.

Nisbett, R., and Ross, L. *Human Inference: Strategies and Shortcomings of Social Judgment*, Englewood Cliffs, NJ: Prentice-Hall, Inc., 1980.

Öhman, A., and Dimberg, U. An evolutionary perspective on human social behavior. In *Sociopsychology*. W.M. Waid (Ed.). New York: Springer, 1984.

Paley, W. *Natural Theology*, Westmead, England: Gregg International Publications, 1970 (1802).

Plutchik, R. and Kellerman, H. *Theories of Emotion*, Orlando: Academic Press, Inc., 1980.

Ruse, M. *Philosophy of Biology Today.* Albany, NY: State Unviersity of New York, 1988.

Scarr, S., and Salapatek, P. Patterns of fear development during infancy. *Merrill-Palmer Quarterly* 16: 53–90, 1970.

Seligman, M. On the generality of the laws of learning. *Psychological Review* 77: 407–418, 1970.

Smith, P.K. Does play matter? The functional and evolutionary aspects of animal and human play. *Behavioral & Brain Sciences* 5: 139–184, 1982.

Stevens, K.M. Pain: evolutionary background and primary stimulus. *Medical Hypotheses* 7: 51–54, 1981.

Thorndike, E.I., *The Psychology of Wants, Interests, and Attitudes,* London: Appleton-Century, 1935.

Toft, C.A., Aeschlimann, A., and Bolis, L. (Eds.) *Parasite-Host Associations: Coexistence or Conflict?* New York: Oxford Univeristy Press, 1991.

Tversky, A., and Kahneman, D. Heuristics and biases. *Science* 185: 1124–1131, 1974.

vanden Hout, M. Agoraphobia: an extraterritorial fear. Unpublished manuscript.

Wilks, C.G.W., and Marks, I.M. Reducing hypersensitive gagging. *British Dental Journal* 155: 263–265, 1983.

5 An evolutionary perspective on panic disorder and agoraphobia

Randolph M. Nesse
Department of Psychiatry, University of Michigan

Panic, when viewed ethologically, is not pathological in itself; it is rather an adaptation that evolved to facilitate escape in dangerous situations. Patients with panic disorder have panic with normal form, but the attacks occur in the absence of real danger. The agoraphobia syndrome can be understood as a related adaptation that is expected after repeated panic attacks. These hypotheses account for many aspects of panic and agoraphobia that are difficult for proximate theories to explain, and they suggest new research questions and strategies.

The advances in ethology that have transformed the study of animal behavior are just now being applied to problems of psychopathology. Although most psychiatrists acknowledge the utility of animal models for understanding human behavior, few understand such fundamentals of ethology as the need for evolutionary explanations of behavioral capacities in addition to proximate explanations of the physiological and psychological mechanisms that mediate behavior. The situation is worsened by the tendency of psychiatrists to work only in one of three paradigms—analytic, behavioral, or neurophysiological—without recognizing that all three are limited to questions of proximate causation. Furthermore, recent advances in the biological treatment of mental symptoms have led many to the illogical conclusion that neurophysiological defects underlie most mental disorders. This makes it difficult to consider the possibility that some mental symptoms may, despite their distressing nature, have specific evolved adaptive functions.

The enormous conceptual and experimental progress of the field of animal behavior might long ago have stimulated a new perspective on psychopathology except for three impediments. To begin with, humans are notoriously difficult to study ethologically because their extraordinary learning capacities allow diverse adaptive strategies in a wide variety of habitats. Second, normal behavior patterns of humans have not been extensively investigated in an evolutionary framework. Finally, an additional set of complex issues arises when we try to explain pathology instead of normal behavior. These problems have so far largely precluded the kind of hypothesis testing that is now standard in the field of animal behavior. The speculations that substitute often chagrin animal scientists. We must, however, start somewhere if psychiatry is to share the firm foundation that evolutionary theory provides for the understanding of behavior. A sensible approach is to propose and test hypotheses about specific mental disorders using the large body of data that has already been gathered based on other paradigms.

It is useful to distinguish two categories of medical problems, those that result from defects and those that are normal defenses. Examples of the former include the Babinski sign, which reliably indicates a defect in an upper motor neuron, and paralysis, which indicates some defect in the neuromuscular system. Congestive heart failure also results from defects, although a variety of compensatory mechanisms are also in evidence. Some medical problems are fundamentally different, however, in that they are coordinated response patterns that have evolved to fulfil specific defensive functions. The cough reflex, for example, although usually observed only in the presence of disease or trauma, is an adaptive capacity for clearing foreign material from the pulmonary system. If it is impaired, infection and death are likely. Similar defense mechanisms include the capacities for vomiting, diarrhea, and pain. Although distressing and associated with disease or trauma, they result not from defects, but from the normal operation of adaptive systems.

This distinction is important for two reasons. First, medical interventions that counteract the effects of defects are likely to benefit patients, whereas eliminating defenses is likely to be harmful. The tragic history of thymus gland irradiation illustrates the hazards of eliminating defensive systems that are mistaken for disease. Second, defects and defenses require different kinds of explanation. An analysis of evolutionary origins and functions is required for a defense but is inappropriate for a defect. The immediate cause of a defect is an etiological agent that may disrupt many systems, whereas the immediate cause of a defensive response is a stimulus that acts upon sensors with specific connections to the response mechanism. Although both require physiological explanations, a defense is an integrated series of responses organized to serve a particular function, whereas a defect may involve deficits and compensatory responses in diverse bodily systems.

Do panic attacks result from a defect in a mechanism, or are they a defense? I shall argue that panic is an adaptive defense that facilitates escape from mortal danger; that the abnormality in people with panic disorder is not the occurrence of panic per se, but rather that the attacks occur when there is no real danger; and that agoraphobia can best be understood as a potentially adaptive consequence of repeated panic attacks. This hypothesis accounts for many aspects of panic and agoraphobia that cannot be fully explained by hypotheses from the three main proximate paradigms in psychiatry—psychoanalysis, behaviorism, and neurophysiology. I shall briefly review the facts about panic and agoraphobia and then consider the relative ability of each of the four hypotheses to account for these facts.

REVIEW OF PANIC DISORDER AND AGORAPHOBIA

Panic disorder has long been recognized as a consistent syndrome, although it has been called by many terms, including Dacosta's syndrome, soldier's heart, neurasthenia, and anxiety hysteria (Wooley 1976). The onset of symptoms is usually in the late twenties or early thirties. The 6-month prevalence of panic disorder in major U.S. cities is approximately 6 per 1000 for men and 10 per 1000 for women. For agoraphobia, the prevalence is approximately 20 per 1000 for men and 50 per 1000 for women (Weissman 1985). To provide an overview, a composite history is presented that incorporates experience with over 100 patients with panic disorder or agoraphobia as well as data from published reports (Tuma and Maser 1985; and other references).

The problem typically begins with a sudden attack of overwhelming anxiety that occurs "from out of the blue" while the person is away from home. A feeling that death is imminent and an overwhelming need to "get out of here' displace all other thoughts. Shortness of breath and pounding of the heart precede actual movement. Sweating, flushing, dizziness, chest pain, and other physical symptoms are common. The episode lasts 15–45 minutes and is followed by exhaustion for 24 hours. Days then pass without incident until a second episode suddenly occurs, often in a situation similar to that of the first attack. The person returns home immediately and seeks the company of relatives. Attacks soon become more frequent, and the person spends hours trying to discern the cause in diet, life circumstances, and other factors. Medical evaluation is sought, but findings are not specific, and the patient is told that the symptoms result from "stress" or "hyperventilation." A minor tranquilizer is often prescribed, which reduces anxiety about having attacks, but does not prevent the attacks themselves (Klein 1980). As additional attacks occur, the person avoids more and more situations, finally preferring not to leave home alone. Attacks continue to occur in the home, and the person tries to keep a relative or friend nearby at all times.

After several months the intense brief episodes of anxiety fade, but the person continues to experience intense anxiety in certain situations — being alone or in crowds, being alone in wide open space, or being in any place where exit is difficult, especially lines, movies, or airplanes (Sheehan et al. 1980; Marks 1970; Marks and Gelder 1966; Arrindell 1980). Finally the patient reads about the disorder in a newspaper article and consults a psychiatrist who specializes in treating anxiety disorders. This anxiety specialist explains that psychotherapy is not a reliable treatment (Nemiah 1980; Weiss 1964), but that antidepressant medication will stop the panic attacks (Klein 1980; Sheehan 1982; Zitren et al. 1978, 1980) and that the anticipatory anxieties can be relieved by behavioral exposure therapy (Zitren et al. 1980). After several months of treatment the person is substantially improved but continues to experience apprehension about whether symptoms will recur when the medication is stopped.

THE SYNDROME OF PANIC

First, let us consider the adequacy of the four hypotheses for explaining the consistent association of the signs, symptoms, and behaviors that comprise the syndrome of panic. Freud suggested that the signs of anxiety—especially excitement, rapid heartbeat and rapid breathing—resemble the state of sexual arousal (Strachey 1959; Fenichel 1945). This explanation fits his original sexual deprivation theory, but it does not explain the chest pain, the wish to flee, feelings of doom, and the cold knot in the abdomen. He later came to believe that the form of panic was determined by birth trauma (Strachey 1959), despite equally serious differences between the two phenomena. Freudian theory thus fails to account for many of the symptoms that characterize the panic syndrome.

Learning theorists usually have not tried to explain the panic syndrome per se. The original panic attack is viewed as an unconditioned response that spreads to new stimuli by stimulus generation (Marks et al. 1971; Jansson and Govan 1982; Chambless and Goldstein 1980). The elicitors of the original unconditioned response are however, rarely evident. Even if they were, the syndrome of panic symptoms, with its remarkable consistency across patients with widely varying histories, would remain unexplained.

Neurochemical theories seeking to delineate the brain mechanisms that control and mediate anxiety will continue to extend our understanding of the physiological mediators of panic (Uhde et al. 1985). Regardless of how adequate such proximate theories become, however, it will also be necessary to consider the evolutionary origins of the brain mechanisms that give humans the capacity for panic (Hinde 1982; Mayr 1982). Can the panic syndrome be accounted for by "sympathetic arousal," for example? The fact that behavior patterns and subjective symptoms cannot be elicited by hormone administration casts doubt on such a proposition. Moreover, even a complete description of the neuroendocrinology underlying panic would not encompass the adaptive emotional and behavioral responses that occur in many species during emergencies. The emphasis on functional significance inherent in Cannon's (1926) phrase "fight or flight" seems to have been forgotten by those who believe that a proximate explanation would alone be sufficient. Tricyclic antidepressants and monoamine oxidase inhibitors are very effective at stopping panic attacks, and this effect is unrelated to the amount of depression the patient is experiencing (Sheehan et al. 1982; Zitren et al. 1983). The known effects of these medications on amine neurotransmitters, and the involvement of the sympathetic nervous system in panic (Nesse et al. 1984; Stokes 1985) suggest that they act by influencing these systems. This conclusion may well be correct, but it does not imply that an organic defect is necessarily present. If panic is indeed a complex defense mechanism, then we should not be surprised that panic attacks can be blocked by disrupting the system at a number of different points.

Susceptibility to panic disorder is genetically transmitted (Torgersen 1983). Although this fact may seem to imply that an organic defect is involved, it is equally compatible with the view that panic is an adaptive defense. Like any other trait, the threshold for the panic response should be normally distributed in a population. Data from rhesus monkeys suggest substantial genetically determined differences in anxiety levels (Suomi et al. 1981). People with panic disorder may be at one end of such a distribution. If this is the case, then the current confident search for a specific defect could prove fruitless. My guess is, however, that some cases of panic disorder will turn out to result from defects in the mechanism that regulates the expression of panic. This is based on the fact that panic attacks often come "out of the blue" in perfectly safe surroundings. Moreover, they usually occur with substantial frequency for a period of several months and then go away (Raskin et al. 1982). This seems unlikely to represent simply an inherited threshold difference. Whether an inherited defect turns out to be important or not, the research seeking it will help us to understand the genetic, developmental, and environmental factors that regulate the threshold for and expression of panic.

Many aspects of panic disorder that are difficult for other theories to explain make sense if the syndrome is viewed as an adaptation that evolved to facilitate flight from life-threatening danger. The sudden increase in the rate and strength of cardiac contractions sends extra blood to the muscles while the gut feels empty and the skin blanches and becomes cold as blood is shunted elsewhere. Rapid and deep breathing increases blood oxygen content. Cooling sweat is secreted, muscles tighten and tremble, and the endocrine system prepares for catabolism (Nesse et al. 1984; Mason 1968). Intense mental activity is focused on planning escape. When the overwhelming urge to flee is translated into action, all effort is concentrated on escape. The direction of flight is towards home and trusted kin, a behavior pattern typical of animals that rely on homes and kin for protection. These aspects of the panic syndrome are exactly what one would expect in a behavior pattern that facilitates escape. Of the 12 symptoms that define a panic attack according to the third edition of the American Psychiatric Association Diagnostic and Statistical Manual (DSM-III) (American Psychiatric Association 1980), 8 either directly aid flight or are secondary manifestations of responses that aid flight. By excluding "life-threatening situations" from consideration, the DSM-III tacitly acknowledges that this response is expected in the face of serious danger.

Donald Klein's closely related view of panic and agoraphobia (1981) is also based on ethological considerations, but he emphasizes the similarities of panic to childhood separation anxiety and its evolutionary function of maintaining proximity of toddler and parent, as proposed by Bowlby (1973). Klein's theory views panic as a regression phenomenon, in contrast to the view presented here that emphasizes its normal adaptive function in adults. Several facts suggest that panic in adults is different from separation anxiety in children. First, the behaviors exhibited are phenomenologically different. Crying and withdrawal, or searching for the parent, predominate in separation anxiety, whereas flight and the physiological preparation for it predominate in panic. Second, panic disorder usually begins in the late twenties and is not continuous with the peak of separation anxiety in childhood. Third, panic is recorded as a normal response to danger, not to separation. Despite these differences, panic and separation anxiety may be intimately related. Normal development may transform one anxiety into the other, and developmental interference may cause a person to exhibit a combination of the two behavior patterns in circumstances that vaguely threaten separation or physical danger.

In summary, the various components of the syndrome of panic and their reliable association cannot be fully explained by analytic, behavioral, or neurophysiological theories. A combination of these theories may eventually give us an adequate proximate explanation of the mechanisms of panic. If panic is an evolved adaptation, however, then a separate evolutionary explanation is also required. The hypothesis that the capacity for panic serves the function of facilitating escape from mortal danger is consistent with the available facts about the panic syndrome and implies that panic does not necessarily involve an organic defect.

THE AGORAPHOBIA SYNDROME

Although described in the DSM-III as a separate syndrome, agoraphobia is almost always a complication of repeated panic attacks. In 95% of the agoraphobics evaluated in our anxiety clinic, agoraphobia developed after repeated "spontaneous" panic attacks. Agoraphobia is another remarkably consistent syndrome. Patients share the same fears of wide-open spaces, closed-in places, being alone, being in crowds, and being far from home (Marks 1969, 1970; Sheehan et al. 1980; Matthew et al. 1981; Arrindell 1980). How can the nature and consistency of these fears be explained?

Dynamic theory interprets the street in this syndrome as a symbol for sexual opportunities and interprets being alone as an opportunity for forbidden masturbation (Strachey 1959). Convincing support for the generality of these interpretations is not available. Even if it were, they would not explain other aspects of the agoraphobia syndrome, such as the consistent fear of lines, travel by public transportation, and being far away from home. Learning theory suggests that each panic attack conditions additional stimuli, and that fears therefore generalize until the patient is afraid to leave home (Chambless and Goldstein 1981). This appears to be true, but it leaves unexplained the fact that home-bound patients do not develop fear of the home and the consistent constellation of fears in different people. After association with panic attack, a previously neutral situation may gain the capacity to elicit anxiety. Learning theory attributes this to classical conditioning. This one-trial learning is, however, quite different from the learning of a salivation response after repeated pairings of a conditioned stimulus with food. Learning is itself a product of natural selection and is constrained by the evolutionary history of each species (Seligman and Hager 1912; Hamilton 1975). Where one-trial learning is adaptive—for instance food aversion learned after a single episode of gastrointestinal illness—it may well be preserved in the species (Bernstein 1978). If danger were encountered at a particular spot, individuals who were ready to flee upon coming again to the same spot would have a selective advantage. Agoraphobics do not develop fear of the specific object of attention at the moment of panic, but of the general area in which the attack occurred. This tendency may represent an example of "prepared learning" (Seligman 1971). Moreover, certain situations, because of their association with increased risk of danger during primate evolution, may have acquired the capacity to decrease the threshold for panic. An open landscape without trees offers no safe refuge; a closed-in space increases the risk of being trapped. Being alone and being among strangers far from home are situations that also increase risk for humans. The need for proximity to kin, repeatedly induced by panic attacks, may explain the dependency of people with agoraphobia. Attack by carnivores must have been a serious risk, but strange humans could have posed an even greater risk. These factors may help to explain the relative frequency of panic and agoraphobia in women. Women might benefit more than men from a low panic threshold and a tendency to avoid distant or isolated places because they are relatively less able to defend themselves because of the difficulty of flight with children, because they represent a potential reproductive resource for another group, and because food-gathering typically requires shorter excursions than does hunting. The efficacy of behavioral exposure therapy is also consistent with an evolutionary view of the function of agoraphobic fears. Many simple phobias are probably prepared fears, and their repeated elicitation without bad effects decreases the fear. Behavior theory leads to effective treatment but offers only a partial etiologic explanation.

In summary, people with a prepared tendency to be apprehensive in certain situations have a survival advantage, and repeated experiences of danger are an ideal cue for the avoidance of these situations. This hypothesis explains the constellation of fears that comprise the agoraphobia syndrome, the distinctive conditions that relieve these fears, and the fact that agoraphobia is a common complication of repeated panic attacks. The other theories cannot. Whether agoraphobic tendencies are latent in all of us, or are atavistic remnants possessed only by a few, is a question for further study.

IMPLICATIONS

A theory that considers the adaptive functions of panic attacks can explain many aspects of panic and agoraphobia that other theories cannot. An evolutionary explanation for panic and agoraphobia is not an alternative to proximate theories; it is rather the necessary other half of a complete explanation of any biological phenomenon. Therefore, support for the above proximate explanations does not undermine the above evolutionary explanation. Opponents of the evolutionary explanation proposed must argue either that the phenomenon has not been directly shaped by natural selection and has no adaptive function or that the proposed function is incorrect. An answer to the question, "What evolutionary forces have shaped the capacity for panic?" leaves open separate questions about learning, dynamic conflicts, the specific neurochemical mechanisms that mediate the capacity, and whether or not the mechanism is defective in people with panic disorder. Because other psychiatric conditions also likely have adaptive aspects, an evolutionary perspective on panic may provide a structure for a biopsychosocial model of panic disorder that can serve as a paradigm for improved understanding of other psychiatric disorders.

How can the proposed theories about the evolutionary functions of panic and agoraphobia be tested? Even if they are consistent with the large body of accumulated fact and can explain evidence that other theories cannot, our confidence in them must be limited until they successfully predict new findings. This task is difficult because panic is a rare phenomenon that cannot be ethically and reliably elicited in a laboratory setting. Nonetheless, a variety of predictions are possible, based on three requirements for an adequate evolutionary explanation: (1) that the capacities should be genetically influenced, (2) that the elicitors, form, and effects of the behaviors should be consistent with the proposed function, and (3) that individuals who lack the capacity should be, under natural conditions, at a fitness disadvantage directly related to the proposed function.

1. If the capacities for panic and agoraphobia are genetically based, then syndromes similar to agoraphobia and panic disorder should be observed in most humans in a variety of cultures. Although some evidence on the nature of anxiety in other cultures is available, specific studies of panic and agoraphobia are needed. Other primate species should show similar responses, modified to fit their environment. Stress reactions have been studied extensively in primates, but field researchers may not have looked for this specific pattern, as distinct from fear.

2. Specific precipitants of panic and the fears of agoraphobics should be predicted by the theory. Any situation that indicates mortal threat should reliably elicit panic attacks in normal people. Such situations might be difficult to study in the laboratory, but data on the precipitants and nature of panic in normal people would be valuable evidence.

3. Panic threshold should be normally distributed in the population. If panic patients form a second peak in the distribution, then this would support the search for an organic defect. If they are simply on the tail of the distribution, then a defect is less likely. Unfortunately, I can see no easy way to measure panic threshold. Perhaps nonpanic indicators of panic threshold could be used.

4. The proposed function of panic attacks should predict new details about the attacks. For instance, many animals freeze for a moment when danger is first sensed, presumably to decrease chances of detection by a predator. Observation of freezing behavior in a rabbit prompted me to ask panic patients if they experienced momentary freezing or paralysis at the onset of an attack. Of 15 patients, 5 said that this was a prominent symptom that no one had ever asked about before.

5. The consequences of panic should be adaptive in dangerous situations. Individuals deprived of this response should be at a fitness disadvantage. If there were a way to pharmacologically deprive wild primates of the capacity for panic without confounding side effects, the theory predicts that they would be subject to increased predation.

6. Medications that block panic attacks by blocking the mechanism of panic expression should also block normal panic. Other medications may simply reset the panic threshold closer to normal.

7. Agoraphobia should be precipitated only after repeated panic attacks. In a consecutive series of cases reported elsewhere, only 1 out of 53 patients with panic attacks and agoraphobia had the onset of agoraphobia first, with panic attacks usually occurring for several months before the onset of the agoraphobia.

Finally, an ethological perspective has benefits in the clinic. Most patients with panic attacks arrive worried that they are crazy, weak, medically ill, or all three. I have found, with several dozen patients, that a simple explanation of the adaptive function of panic in normal people is readily grasped and greatly appreciated. Patients who understand this do not ask, like others, "So, Doctor, is it physical or psychological?" This understanding of their symptoms allows them to take responsibility for cooperating with treatment without having to feel responsible for the illness itself. An ethological approach organizes the symptoms in a comprehensible way and offers a perspective that can promote a strong therapeutic alliance for the integrated biological, psychological, and social treatment of panic disorder and agoraphobia.

REFERENCES

Arrindell, W.A. (1980). Dimensional structure and psychopathology correlates of the fear survey schedule (FSIII) in a phobic population: A factorial definition of agoraphobia. *Behavior Research and Therapy 18*, 229–242.

Bernstein, I.L., (1978). Learned taste aversions in children receiving chemotherapy. *Science 200*, 1302–1303, 1978.

Bowlby, J. *Separation.* (1978). New York. Basic.

Cannon, W.B. (1926). The emergency function of the adrenal medulla in pain and the major emotions. *American Journal of Physiology, 33*, 356–372.

Chambless, D.L., and Goldstein, A.J. (1980). Clinical treatment of agoraphobia. In *Phobia: Psychological and Pharmacological Treatment*, M.R. Mavissakalian and D.H. Barlow (Eds.). New York: Guilford.

Crowe, R.R., Noyes, R. Jr., Pauls, D.L., and Slyman, D.J. (1983). A family study of panic disorder. *Archives of General Psychiatry 40*: 1065–1069.

Diagnostic and Statistical Manual of Mental Disorders, 3rd ed. (1980). Washington D.C. American Psychiatric Association Press.

Fenichel, O. (1945). *The Psychoanalytic Theory of Neurosis*. New York. Norton.

Hamilton, W.D. (1975). Innate Social Aptitudes of Man: An approach from evolutionary genetics. In *Biosocial Anthropology*, R. Fox (Ed.). New York: Wiley.

Hinde, R.A. *Ethology.* (1982). New York: Oxford University Press.

Jansson, L., and Lars-Govan, O. (1982). Behavioral treatments for agoraphobia: An evaluative review. *Clinical Psychology Review 2*: 311–336.

Klein, D.F. (1981). Anxiety reconceptualized. In *Anxiety: New Research and Changing Concepts*, D.F. Klein and J. Rabkin (Eds.). New York: Raven.

Marks, I.M. (1969). *Fears and Phobias.* New York: Academic.

Marks, I.M. (1970). Agoraphobic syndrome (phobic anxiety state). *Archives of General Psychiatry 23*: 538–553.

Marks, I.M. and Gelder, M.G. (1966). Different ages of onset in varieties of phobia. *American Journal of Psychiatry 123*: 218–221.

Marks, I.M., Boulougouris, J., and Marset, P. (1971). Flooding versus desensitization in the treatment of phobic patients. A cross over study. *British Journal of Psychiatry 119*: 353–375.

Mason, J.W. (1968). Overall hormonal balance as a key to endocrine functions. *Psychosomatic Medicine 30*: 791–808.

Matthew, A.M., Gelder, M.G., and Johnson, D.W. (1981). *Agoraphobia: Nature and Treatment.* New York: Guildford.

Mayr, E. (1982). *The Growth of Biological Thought: Diversity, Evolution and Inheritance.* Cambridge, MA: MIT Press.

Nemiah, J.C. (1980). Phobic disorder. In *Comprehensive Textbook of Psychiatry*, 3rd ed. H.I. Kaplan, A.M. Freedman, and Sadock, B.J. (Eds.). Baltimore, Williams & Wilkins.

Nesse, R.M., Curtis, G.C., Thyer, B.A., McCann, D., and Huber-Smith, M.J. (1984). Adrenergic function in panic anxiety patients. *Archives of General Psychiatry 41*: 771–776.

Nesse, Curtis, G.C., Thyer, B.A., McCann, D., and Huber-Smith, M.J. (1985). Endocrine and cardio-vascular responses during phobic anxiety. *Psychosomatic Medicine 47*: 320–332.

Raskin, M., Peeke, H.V.S., Dickman, W., and Pinkster, H. (1982). Panic and generalized anxiety disorders: Developmental antecedents and precipitants. *Archives of General Psychiatry 39*: 687–689.

Seligman, M.E.P. (1971). Phobias and preparedness. *Behavior Therapy 2*: 307–320.

Seligman, M.E.P., and Hager, J.L. (Eds.). (1972). *Biological Boundaries of Learning.* New York: Appleton–Century–Crofts.

Sheehan, D.V. (1982). Panic Attacks and phobias. *New England Journal of Medicine 307*: 156–158.

Sheehan, D.V., Ballenger, J., and Jacobsen, G. (1980). Treatment of endogenous anxiety with phobic, hysterical and hypochondriacal symptoms. *Archives of General Psychiatry 37*: 51–59.

Stokes, P.E. (1985). The neuroendocrinology of anxiety. In *Anxiety and the Anxiety Disorders.* A.H. Tuman, and J.D. Maser (Eds.). Hillsdale, NJ: Erlbaum.

Strachey, J. (1959). Editor's introduction. In S. Freud *Inhibitions, Symptoms and Anxiety.* New York, Norton, pp. 3–12.

Suomi, S.S., Kramer, G.W., Baysinger, C.M., and DeLizio, R.D. (1981). Inherited and experiential factors associated with individual differences in anxious behavior displayed by rhesus monkeys. In *Anxiety: New Research and Changing Concepts*, D.F. Klein and J. Rabkin (Eds.). New York: Raven.

Tuma, A.H., and Maser, J.D. (1985). *Anxiety and the Anxiety Disorders.* Hillsdale, NJ: Erlbaum.

Torgersen, S. (1983). Genetic factors in anxiety disorders. *Archives of General Psychiatry 40*: 1085.

Uhde, T.W., Roy-Byrne, P.P., Vittone, B.J., Boulenger, J.P., and Post,R.M. (1985). Phenomenology and Neurobiology of Panic Disorder. In A.H. Tuman and J.D. Maser (Eds.) *Anxiety and the Anxiety Disorders.* Hillsdale, NJ: Erlbaum.

Weissman, M.M. (1985). The Epidemiology of anxiety disorders: rates, risks, and familial patterns. In *Anxiety and the Anxiety Disorders.* A.H. Tuman and J.D. Maser (Eds.). Hillsdale, NJ: Erlbaum.

Wooley, C.F. (1976). Where are the diseases of yesteryear? *Circulation 53*: 745–751.

Zitren, C.M., Klein, D.F., and Woerner, M.G. (1978). Behavior Therapy, supportive psychotherapy, imipramine and phobias. *Archives of General Psychiatry 35:* 307–316.

Zitren, C.M., Klein, D.F., and Woerner, M.G. (1980). Treatment of agoraphobia with group exposure in vivo and imipramine. *Archives of General Psychiatry 37*: 63–72.

Zitren, C.M., Klein, D.F., Woerner, M.G., and Ross, D.C. (1983). Treatment of phobias. I. Comparison of imipramine hydrochloride and placebo. *Archives of General Psychiatry 40:* 125–138.

6

A cognitive developmental approach to morality: Investigating the psychopath

R.J.R. Blair[a,b]
[a]MRC Cognitive Development Unit, 4 Taviton Street, London WC1H 0BT, UK
[b]Department of Psychology, University College London, 26 Bedford Way, London WC1H 0AH, UK

Various social animal species have been noted to inhibit aggressive attacks when a conspecific displays submission cues. Blair (1993) has suggested that humans possess a functionally similar mechanism which mediates the suppression of aggression in the context of distress cues. He has suggested that this mechanism is a prerequisite for the development of the moral/conventional distinction; the consistently observed distinction in subject's judgements between moral and conventional transgressions. Psychopaths may lack this violence inhibitor. A causal model is developed showing how the lack of this mechanism would explain the core behavioural symptoms associated with the psychopathic disorder. A prediction of such a causal model would be that psychopaths should fail to make the moral/conventional distinction. This prediction was confirmed. The implication of this finding for other theories of morality is discussed.

1. INTRODUCTION

According to DSM-III-R (American Psychological Association, 1987), the essential feature of antisocial personality disorder (APD) is "a pattern of irresponsible and antisocial behaviour beginning in childhood or early adolescence and continuing into adulthood". Individuals with APD "tend to be

Reprinted from *Cognition: International Journal of Cognitive Science* Cognition 57 (1995) 1–29, A cognitive developmental approach to morality: investigation the psychopath
0010-0277/95/$09.50 © 1995 Elsevier Science B.V. All rights reserved
SSDI 0010-0277(95)00676-1
Received March 7, 1994, final version accepted July 28, 1994

irritable and aggressive and to get repeatedly into physical fights and assaults, including spouse- or child-beating" (American Psychological Association, 1987). Psychopaths[1] show "early behavioural problems and they are described as "lacking remorse or guilt" and as being "callous/lacking empathy" (items 12, 6 and 8 on Hare's (1985a) Psychopathy Checklist). They show, in summary, an early onset of extremely aggressive behaviour that is not tempered by any sense of guilt or empathy with the victim.

Given the recurrent theme of the early onset of psychopathic behaviour, it would seem reasonable to describe the disorder in developmental terms. However, many theories of psychopathy have ignored this development aspect. For example, the "frontal/limbic system" position of Gorenstein (1982; Gorenstein & Newman, 1980) makes no reference to development.[2] Nor is there reference to development in either Hare, Williamson, and Harpur's (1988) discussion of the relationship between psychopathy and language or in Gough's (1948) paper suggesting that psychopathy is due to a deficit in role taking. Mullen (1992) does describe psychopathy as a developmental disorder but the individuals he describes as psychopathic do not match the criteria of APD in DSM-III-R or the criteria of psychopathic according to Hare's (1980, 1985a) Psychopathy Checklist (PCL).

The main exceptions to these adevelopmental approaches are what might be termed the Punishment positions of Eysenck (e.g., 1964) and Traster (1978). These authors suggest a model of the development of morality and from this make claims as to the impairment in psychopaths. These authors principally claim that socialization is achieved through punishment. Remorse, for example, is viewed as a consequence of conditioning: "Conscience is a conditioned reflex" (Eysenck, 1964). The basic position of these authors is that anxiety, induced by the transgression being punished, becomes associated with the transgression. This argument is extended to the claim that psychopathy is a consequence of a deficiency in conditionability. Early work did suggest that psychopaths might be impoverished in "conditionability". Lykken (1957) observed that psychopaths were significantly inferior to normal controls and a "neurotic sociopathic" group in attaining a conditioned galvanic skin response to a buzzer that had previously been paired with an electric shock. However, the central thrust of the Punishment positions has been discredited. Developmental studies have clearly demonstrated that punishment is not associated with a reduction in antisocial behaviour; instead, the use of inductive techniques (e.g., asking the child how the victim of the act feels) is

---

[1]The diagnostic criteria for APD and psychopathic disorder are similar. Hare (1985b) found that 73% of those patients diagnosed as APD by two clinicians fulfilled Hare's criteria for psychopathy. It is plausible to suggest that the two criteria are two correlated behavioural descriptions of the same disorder.

[2]Though Damasio, Tranel, and Damasio (1991) do draw a distinction between "acquired sociopathy" following frontal damage in adulthood and clinical, DSM-III (1980) defined sociopathy following damage "during the development of his personality".

associated with a reduction in antisocial behaviour; see Hoffman (1977) for a review.

1.1. A Violence Inhibition Mechanism

Several ethologists (Eibl-Eibesfeldt, 1970; Lorenz, 1966) have proposed the existence of mechanisms which control aggression in some social animal species. These ethologists noted that the display of submission cues to a conspecific aggressor resulted in the termination of the attack. For example, dogs when attacked by a stronger opponent bare their throats. This results in the cessation of the fight. Blair (1993) proposed a model of the development of morality which implies a specific cause for psychopathy. He suggested that humans might possess a functionally analogous mechanism: a violence inhibition mechanism (VIM). He considered VIM to be a cognitive mechanism which, when activated by non-verbal communications of distress (i.e., sad facial expression, the sight and sound of tears), initiates a withdrawal response; a schema will be activated predisposing the individual to withdraw from the attack. In line with this suggestion, Camras (1977) has observed that the display of distress cues (a sad facial expression) does result in the termination of aggression in 4- to 7-year-olds. She studied the use and the effect of facial expressions in children defending possessions. When a child displayed a sad facial expression when resisting another child's attempt to take a possession, the aggressor child usually terminated his/her demands and allowed the original possessor to continue playing "for a relatively long time".

Distress cues are assumed to activate predispositions to withdraw in any observer who processes them, regardless of whether that observer is the aggressor or a bystander. However, this does not imply that the final behavioural responses of all observers who process a victim's distress cues are the same. The activation of VIM in any observer will predispose him/her to withdraw from the situation. However, VIM is not the only cognitive device controlling behaviour; for example, there are the executive functions (e.g., the Supervisory Attentional System; see Norman & Shallice, 1986). These other cognitive devices may determine the final response. Thus, in a given aggressive situation, an attacker may continue to attack and an observer initiate an intervention; in both cases, the VIM-mediated predisposition to withdraw will have been overruled by executive functioning. Finally, the strength of the withdrawal response is assumed to be a function of the degree of activation of VIM. An isolated sad facial expression may excite limited withdrawal. A screaming, sobbing individual may excite much greater withdrawal.[3]

---

[3]Again, it should be noted that the activation of VIM does not inevitably result in the withdrawal of the individual from the situation. The operation of executive functions may overrule the activation of VIM; the individual may help the distressed person. Frequent instances of helping a distressed individual may result in the development of an approach schema. In this case helping behaviour could become the prepotent response to certain distress cue situations.

1.2. Developmental Consequences of VIM

Blair (1993) suggested that VIM is a prerequisite for the development of three aspects of "morality": the moral emotions (e.g., sympathy, guilt, remorse and empathy), the inhibition of violent action and the moral/conventional distinction.

(1) *The moral emotions.* Behavioural interruptions have been claimed to induce arousal responses (e.g., Meyer, 1956; Mandler, 1984). Mandler (1984) has claimed that emotions are a consequence of the interpretation of arousal through a process of "meaning analysis". In addition, Mandler has claimed that the interpretation of arousal following a withdrawal response results in the consequent emotional state being experienced as aversive. As stated above, Blair (1993) suggested that the operation of VIM results in the interruption of ongoing behaviour; the activation of VIM results in a withdrawal response which will directly interrupt ongoing behaviour. Following Mandler, Blair suggested that the arousal induced by the activation of VIM will be interpreted as one of the moral emotions. In addition, since VIM initiates a withdrawal response, he suggested that these moral emotions would be experienced as aversive. In line with this, several studies have demonstrated that perceived distress in others generates an aversive emotional reaction that can be measured as physiological arousal in observers (e.g., Bandura & Rosenthal, 1966; Berger, 1962; Craig & Lowery, 1969; Krebs, 1975).[4]

Empathy is defined as "an affective response more appropriate to someone else's situation than to one's own" (Hoffman, 1987, p. 48). It is an emotional response to another's state. Empathy is frequently considered to be a product of role taking (Batson, Fultz, & Schoenrade, 1987). Role taking is the creation of a representation of another's internal state—a calculation of what the other might be thinking/feeling given their situation. Empathy is thus an emotional response to a representation of another's internal state. However, for the purposes of the present paper this definition will be narrowed further; empathy will be considered to be an emotional reaction to a representation of the distressed internal state of another. The intention here is to provide an account of arousal to the thought of another being distressed as opposed to the sight or sound of their distress. It is empathy, defined in this way, that is most relevant to the description of the psychopath.

During normal development, individuals will witness other individuals displaying distress cues resulting in the activation of VIM. On many occasions the observers may role take with the distressed victims; they will calculate

---

[4]Mandler (1984) has claimed that the interpretation of arousal following an approach response results in the valancy of the consequent emotional state being positive. Batson (see, for a review, Batson, Fultz, & Schoenrade, 1987) has found that subjects report the emotional experience associated with approach (helping) tendencies to distress cues as being positive. Adjectives subjects use to describe the experience are: tender, warm and soft-hearted.

representations of the victim's internal state (e.g., "she's suffering"; "what a poor little boy"; "he must be cold and hungry"). There will thus be pairings of distress cues activating VIM with representations formed through role taking. It is suggested here that the representations formed through role taking will become, through classical conditioning, trigger stimuli for VIM. Distress cues can be seen as unconditioned stimuli (US) for the unconditioned response (UR): the activation of VIM. Representations formed through role taking, paired with the US of the distress cues of the target of the role taking, will result in these representations becoming conditioned stimuli for the conditioned response of VIM activation. Thus, an individual may generate empathic arousal to just the thought of someone's distress (e.g., "what a poor little boy") without distress cues being actually processed. In line with this, film sequences, where victims talk about their conditions (potentially initiating role taking in observers) but where they do not actually show distress cues, have been found to induce physiological arousal changes in observers (Eisenberg, Fabes, Bustamante, Mathy, Miller, & Lindholm, 1988; Eisenberg et al., 1992; Fabes, Eisenberg, & Eisenbud, 1993).

(2) *The inhibition of violent action.* As stated above, the postulated operation of VIM initiates a withdrawal response resulting in the on-line interruption of violent action. However, and in addition, it is suggested that *developmentally* VIM results in the inhibition of violent action. The normally developing child will be negatively reinforced by the distress cues every time he engages in any aggressive activity. Through classical conditioning this should result in even the thought of aggression being aversively reinforced; the thought of the aggression will come to trigger VIM. Hence, over time, the child will be less likely, *ceteris paribus*, to engage in violent actions.[5]

(3) *The moral/conventional distinction.* The moral/conventional distinction is the distinction between moral and conventional transgressions found in the judgements of children and adults. Within the literature on this distinction (e.g., Arsenio & Ford, 1985; Nucci & Turiel, 1978; Siegal & Storey, 1985; Smetana, 1981, 1985; Smetana & Braeges, 1990; Tisak & Turiel, 1988; see, for a review, Turiel, Killen, & Helwig, 1987), moral transgressions have been defined by their consequences for the rights and welfare of others, and social conventional transgressions have been defined as violations of the behavioural uniformities that structure social interactions within social systems.

---

[5]Of course, if the child is rewarded for his attacks, particularly during the attack, either by material gain or by peer/parental praise, the child is likely to overrule VIM and continue the attack. Such a child, by continuing to fight, will obviously not experience a withdrawal response. Consequently, such a child will not experience the aggression as aversive (assuming they do not have to withdraw from the fight because they lost the conflict). Indeed, they may even enjoy the violence (if the aggressor continues to approach the victim child). Such a child will not be less likely to engage in future violent action. Indeed, they may be more likely to aggress.

The judgements, "criterion judgements" as Turiel (1983) termed them, that children have been asked to make about moral and conventional transgressions can be divided into two broad categories: seriousness and modifiability. Usually, children and adults judge moral transgressions as more serious than conventional transgressions. For example, while all of the transgression situations, whether moral or conventional, are generally judged not *permissible*, conventional transgressions are more likely to be judged *permissible* than moral transgressions (Smetana, 1985, 1986; Smetana & Braeges, 1990; Tisak & Turiel, 1988; Weston & Turiel, 1980). In addition, subjects generally state that moral transgressions are more *serious* than conventional transgressions or rank them as more *serious* than conventional transgressions (Nucci, 1981; Smetana, 1981, 1985; Smetana & Braeges, 1990; Smetana, Bridgeman, & Turiel, 1983; Stoddart & Turiel, 1985). As regards the modifiability category of criterion judgements, the research indicates that moral transgressions are judged *differently* from conventional transgressions. For example, moral transgressions are judged less *rule contingent* than conventional transgressions (Arsenio & Ford, 1985; Smetana, 1981, 1985; Smetana et al., 1983; Smetana, Kelly, & Twentyman, 1984; Nucci, 1981; Nucci & Nucci, 1982; Nucci & Turiel, 1978; Weston & Turiel, 1980); individuals state that moral transgressions are not permissible even in the absence of prohibiting rules while conventional transgressions are judged permissible if there is no rule prohibiting them. In addition, moral transgressions are less under *authority jurisdiction* (the act would not be permissible even if the teacher says that you can do the act) than conventional transgressions (Laupa & Turiel, 1986; Tisak & Turiel, 1984, 1988; Turiel, 1983). The moral/conventional distinction has been found in the judgements of children from the age of 39 months (Smetana, 1981) and across cultures (e.g., Hollos, Leis, & Turiel; 1986; Nucci, Turiel, & Encarnacion-Gawrych, 1983; Song, Smetana, & Kim, 1987).

1.3. Theories of the Moral/Conventional Distinction

The existing framework of models of the moral/conventional distinction (e.g., Smetana, 1983; Turiel, 1977, 1983; Turiel et al., 1987; Turiel & Smetana, 1984) involves the suggestion that the distinction is a result of the formation of two independent conceptual domains (see Turiel & Davidson, 1986). These authors have proposed that the child constructs these domains from the qualitatively different social interactional consequences of moral and conventional transgressions. This *construction* process has not been well specified by most authors. However, Turiel (1983) has described two forms of manipulation of gathered data which result in the *construction* of what he terms "judgements of moral necessity". These two forms are: manipulations of past experiences and counter-factual reasoning. Turiel (1983) states that "the child will connect his or her experience of pain (an undesirable experience) to the observed experience of the victim" (p. 43). According to Turiel, by forming this connection the child will generate a proscription against the event which resulted in the victim. In addition, Turiel (1983) states that the child will arrive at "judgements of moral necessity" through comparison of the performance of the act itself with its opposite. If the constructed consequences of its non-occurrence (there is no victim) are judged to be more "desirable" than the consequences of its occurrence (the victim is harmed), then inferences will be made regarding how people should act in these circumstances. As stated above, the child will judge the presence of a victim as undesirable if he has connected his own experience of pain with that of the victim.

According to Turiel, these same manipulations, when applied to conventional transgressions, will not result in automatic proscriptions. First, Turiel does not consider that there are any past experiences that might result in the generation of proscriptions. Second, Turiel argues that comparison of a conventional act with its opposite will not result in one situation being judged as obviously superior to the other. Taking, for example, the conventional transgression of talking in class, Turiel considers that there is no intrinsic basis for a requirement that children do not talk in class. According to Turiel (1983), it is social organizational factors, such as consensus, rules and authority, that provide meaning to conventional proscriptions.

In summary, therefore, the origin of the moral/conventional distinction, according to Turiel, is the child's *construed* connection between his personal experience of pain and the observed experience of the victim. It is a consequence of this connection that the child judges any act that results in a victim as wrong whatever the context. It is the child's experience of his own pain that makes the observed experience of the victim aversive. It would thus be predicted from this that an individual who has never experienced pain would not make the moral/conventional distinction.

Blair (1993), in contrast, suggested that VIM is a prerequisite for the development of the moral/conventional distinction. He claimed that the activation of VIM mediates the performance on the moral/conventional distinction task but that this only occurs after representations of moral transgressions have become stimuli for the activation of VIM. He suggested that repeated pairing of representations of the transgression with the distress cues that are being caused by the act results in these representations of the transgression becoming, through classical conditioning, conditioned stimuli for the activation of VIM. Since conventional transgressions, by definition, do not result in victims, they are therefore never paired with distress cues and will not therefore become stimuli for the activation of VIM. Blair (1993) claimed that it was the on-line operation of VIM which determines the moral/conventional distinction. He suggested that the withdrawal response following the activation of VIM is experienced, through meaning analysis, as aversive (following Mandler's, 1984, position on value). He suggested that it was this sense of aversion to the moral transgression that resulted in the act being judged as bad. Manipulations of the transgression's context (i.e., stating that there is no rule against the transgression) would not alter the activation of VIM by the details of the transgression. Thus, according to this position, the transgression would still be judged bad. Conventional transgressions would not generate this sense of aversion. They are defined as transgressions only by the presence of rules. Removal of the rule, by modifying the transgression context, and the transgression should no longer be judged as bad to do.[6]

1.4. A Developmental Account of Morality

In Fig. 1, the developmental consequences of VIM are represented as a causal model. Causal models are divided into three levels: physiological, cognitive and behavioural (see Morton & Frith, 1993). The relationship of connected elements within a causal model is one of causality. Normally, causal models are applied to abnormal development where the absence of a particular neural structure has cognitive and behavioural consequences; e.g., in autism. In this case, "cause" has a straightforward meaning. In the case of normal development, it has the implication of critical necessity. Thus, the model in Fig. 1 represents the claim that VIM causes the development of the moral emotions; i.e., VIM is critically necessary if the moral emotions are to develop normally. Fig. 1 also represents two alternative accounts of the development of VIM: either as the maturation of a physiological structure or as the result of the experience of certain early socialization events. It is possible that VIM is an innately specified physiological structure. Alternatively, VIM may be a consequence of the very early experience of socialization to withdraw from certain distress cue contexts; e.g., when another's distress cues have been caused by the self. Fig. 1 represents the claim that the autonomic nervous system (ANS) is necessary for the development of all emotions; the ANS provides the arousal which is interpreted as an emotion through meaning

---

[6]It should be noted that a distinction between morality and convention is also made for positive acts. For example, Smetana et al. (1983) found that moral positive actions (e.g., comforting a young child) were ranked by subjects as better to do than conventional positive actions (e.g., wearing the school's uniform). The VIM position makes no direct predictions about the moral/conventional distinction in positive actions nor does it make specific claims as to why we should approve of moral positive actions. It could be argued that moral positive actions are evaluated as good if they result in the termination of a situation evaluated as bad because of the activation of VIM (i.e., a distressed other). In this case, VIM would be conceptualized as a prerequisite for the development of the moral/ conventional distinction in positive acts. Alternatively, it could be argued that VIM has no role in the development of approval for moral positive acts, that VIM is only involved in the development of disapproval for moral transgressions. In this case, VIM would have no role in the development of the moral/conventional distinction for positive acts. At present, these two positions have not been empirically resolved.

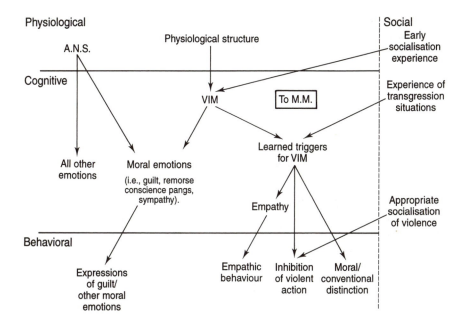

FIG. 1. A causal model of the developmental consequences of VIM.

analysis (Mandler, 1984). VIM, specifically, allows the development of the moral emotions. VIM, when activated, generates arousal which will be interpreted as one of the moral emotions (see above). In addition, pairing of the activation of VIM with representations of the transgression situation or representations formed through role taking of the victim's experience will, through classical conditioning, result in the expansion of the VIM trigger database.[7] This expansion allows the experience of empathy,[8] the development of additional inhibitions on violence and the expression of the moral/ conventional distinction (see above).

---

[7]For this expansion of the trigger database to occur, VIM must actually control behaviour: the individual must withdraw from the transgression situation. If the individual continues to approach the victim (perhaps because of peer pressure to inflict greater damage), the individual will associate any representations of the victim's plight or the transgression situation with the approach response. Such an individual is most likely to be aggressive in future.

[8]Empathy, defined as above, is an emotional reaction to a representation of the distressed internal state of another; i.e., an emotional reaction to a representation of the form "she's suffering"; "what a poor little boy"; "he must be cold and hungry".

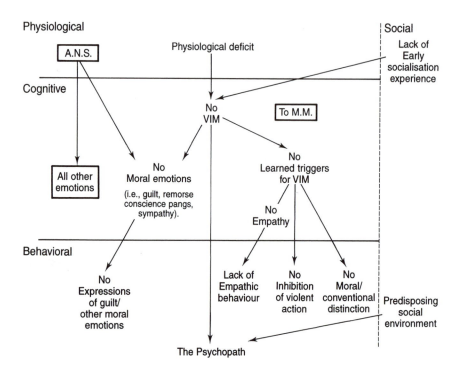

FIG. 2. A causal model of the developmental consequences of an absence of VIM.

1.5 A Developmental Account of Psychopathic Disorder

Fig. 2 represents the hypothesized consequences of an absence of VIM as a causal model. Elements within a causal model that are unaffected by the absence of another element are shown "protected" within boxes. Thus, in Fig. 2, the Theory of Mind Mechanism (Leslie, 1987, 1988) and "All other emotions" are shown as independent of the development of VIM. In line with this, Blair et al. (in press) found that psychopaths, relative to nonpsychopaths, are not impoverished on "Theory of Mind" tasks while Patrick, Bradley, and Lang (1993) observed that psychopaths showed arousal to fear stimuli.

In Fig. 2, the absence of VIM is conceptualized as either a consequence of a physiological deficit or the absence of early socialization experiences. The lack of VIM will result in the absence of the moral emotions. An absence of the moral emotions is reported in the clinical description of psychopathy (Karpman, 1941; Hare, 1985a). The lack of VIM will obviously prevent the addition of learned triggers for the activation of VIM: Normally, representations held during the display of distress cues will come to activate VIM through classical conditioning. For example, representations of the victim's internal state, formed through role taking, will come to activate VIM. Obviously, without VIM, this will not occur; there will be no pairings of representations of the victim's internal state with the activation of VIM because there will be no activation of VIM. Psychopathy is associated with the inability to feel empathy with the victim (Hare, 1985a). As stated above, not only does VIM interrupt violent action on line (in the context of distress cues) but it also developmentally inhibits violent action. The child with VIM will be, *ceteris paribus*, negatively reinforced following any action that results in the display of distress cues by a victim. The child without VIM would not be negatively reinforced; he would, therefore, be much more likely to show violent tendencies from a very early age. Psychopaths are associated with considerable violent tendencies from a very early age (American Psychological Association, 1987; Hare, 1985a). Thus, the core features of the behavioural description of the psychopath—the early onset of extremely aggressive behaviour that is not tempered by any sense of guilt or empathy with the victim—are all direct causal predictions of a lack of VIM.

Now it is the case that, in general, a cognitive deficit is not determinate at the behavioural level. Thus, a lack of VIM need not result in the individual becoming a psychopath. Psychopaths are defined, for clinical purposes, by the frequency of their criminal and other antisocial acts. A lack of VIM does not of itself motivate an individual to commit aggressive acts. A lack of VIM just means that one source of the interruption of violent action is lost. Thus, in Fig. 2, the development of the psychopath is represented as a consequence of the lack of VIM together with either unspecified cognitive or environmental factors. It is perhaps possible that the development of the psychopath may require deficits within executive functioning as well as within VIM; that both sources of behavioural inhibition must be impaired in order for the child to develop as a psychopath. Certainly, there have been reports of impairments in executive functioning in psychopaths in the literature (e.g., Gorenstein, 1982). It can therefore be predicted that there may exist a population who show the same callous behaviour and lack of moral emotions as the psychopath. These individuals, because of either the lack of the cognitive factors or the social environment predisposing them to crime, would not be known to the legal and psychiatric services. However, at the cognitive level, these individuals would show at least one of the same structural deficits as the psychopath: the lack of VIM.

Finally, Fig. 2 represents two unique predictions of the VIM position: individuals lacking VIM should fail the moral/conventional distinction and fail to internally generate moral justifications. Blair (1993) has suggested that the operation of VIM mediates the moral/conventional distinction (see above). If psychopaths lack VIM they should fail to demonstrate this distinction. VIM may also be a prerequisite for the internal generation of moral meta-knowledge; i.e., the individual's consciously accessible theories about why moral transgressions are bad to do. Children have been consistently found to justify their opinions about moral transgressions by references to the *victim's welfare and by appeals to fairness* (e.g., Arsenio & Ford, 1985; Nucci, 1981; Smetana, 1985; Song et al., 1987). Blair (1993) suggested that when the individual is asked why a moral transgression is bad, he should be able to do some sort of causal analysis which will determine that the distress to the other is the object which activated the withdrawal response; i.e., it is the object that is bad. Blair suggested that without VIM the individual will judge acts as bad only because he has been told that they are bad (by parents/peers). Without VIM, if the subject is asked about why the act is bad, he will make reference to what he has been told.

Previous investigations of the moral reasoning of the psychopath have been exclusively conducted within the paradigmatic framework of Kohlberg (1969; Colby & Kohlberg, 1987). While it appears clear that the moral reasoning of delinquents is at a lower level than that of normal controls[9] (see Blasi, 1980; Trevathan & Walker, 1989) it is more debatable whether the moral reasoning of psychopaths is at a lower level than that of criminal controls. Fodor (1973) found that the moral reasoning of psychopathic youths was at a lower level than the moral reasoning of other delinquents. Campagna and Harter (1975) found the moral reasoning of sociopaths to be lower than that of non-incarcerated normals, even when controlling for mental age. Jurkovic and Prentice (1977) found that psychopaths give evidence of less mature moral reasoning than other groups of delinquent and normal youths. However, Lee, and Prentice (1988) only found that delinquents responded at a lower level than non-delinquents; the psychopaths did not reason at a lower level than the other delinquent groups.

Also, the above studies used scales of psychopathy (e.g., Quay's Behaviour Problem Checklist) that are of doubtful validity (see Hare & Cox, 1978). This methodological deficit was remedied by Trevathan and Walker (1989), who utilized Hare's Psychopathy Checklist. Trevathan and Walker (1989) observed a tendency for the psychopaths to reason at a lower level than non-psychopathic controls but this was not significant. However, both groups of delinquents scored at a significantly lower level than non-incarcerated controls. Thus, while it is clear that criminal groups may reason at a lower level than non-criminal controls, it is uncertain whether the moral reasoning of psychopaths is lower than that of other criminal groups.

No previous work has investigated whether the psychopath makes a distinction between moral and conventional rules. No previous work has looked at moral meta-knowledge. This is despite the fact that both of these are fundamental aspects of the normal development of morality. The VIM position

---

[9]Though the reasons for this are not (see Blasi, 1980).

would predict that the psychopath should fail to make a distinction in his judgements between moral and conventional transgressions and that he will not make victim-based justifications of why moral transgressions are bad to do. In summary, it was predicted that:

(1) that psychopaths will not make a distinction between moral and conventional rules;
(2) that psychopaths will treat moral rules as if they were conventional; that is, under permission conditions, the psychopaths will say that moral as well as conventional transgressions are OK to do;
(3) that psychopaths will be less likely to make references to the pain or discomfort of victims than the non-psychopath controls.

2. METHOD

2.1. Design

The experiment involved a 2 × 2 repeated measures factorial design. The independent variables were the two different subject groups (psychopaths and non-psychopathic controls) and the two different domains of story (moral and conventional). The dependent variable was the responses of the subjects to the questions about the transgression situation.

2.2. Subjects

Ten psychopaths and 10 non-psychopath controls took part in this study. All were obtained through contacts in Broadmoor and Ashworth Special Hospitals and had been admitted to the hospitals under the legal category of Psychopathic Disorder. The files of all the subjects were examined to obtain a Psychopathy Checklist (PCL) score in accordance with the guidelines of Hare (1985a). Wong (1988) has shown that PCL scores derived entirely from file data can be valid and reliable. Four items on the PCL were not scored: items 1 ("Glibness/ superficial charm"), 2 ("Grandiose sense of self worth"), 4 ("Pathological lying") and 13 ("Lack of realistic, long term goals"). These items were neglected because of the difficulty of obtaining such information from the files. However, Hare states that "as many as 5 items can be omitted without any appreciable reduction in reliability" (Hare, 1985a, p. 10). The subjects were then divided into two groups according to their score on the PCL: one high for psychopathy (the psychopaths), one low for psychopathy (the nonpsychopaths). All of the subjects were male and white. All of the subjects had committed crimes of violence. Indeed, all of the subjects apart from one of the high PCL scorers (i.e., one of the psychopaths) had killed. Full subject characteristics are shown in Table 1.

Two-way ANOVAs (comparing the two subject groups) were undertaken for each of the subject criteria. These revealed no significant differences in age

TABLE 1
Means for each of the subject criteria (standard deviations in parentheses)

Group	N	Age	IQ (WAIS)	Raven's matrices score	Hare's psychopathy score[a]
Psychopaths	10	33.3 (7.7)	91.6 (17.2)	6.4 (2.1)	31.6 (2.1)
Non-psychopaths	10	37.5 (9.43)	92.7 (16.0)	6.3 (3.3)	16.1 (4.6)

[a]To gain a score out of 40 when only 16 items were being measured the score from the 16 items (out of 32) was multiplied by 40/32.

between the two groups ($F(1, 18) = 1.10$; n.s.). The two tests of intelligence revealed no significant differences between the groups either when using the WAIS[10] ($F(1, 12) = 0.08$; n.s.) or Raven's Advanced matrices ($F(1, 18) = 0.01$; n.s.).

2.3. Materials

The stories used to measure the moral/conventional distinction were all taken from the literature. The four moral stories involved a child hitting another child, a child pulling the hair of another child and the victim cries, a child smashing a piano and a child breaking the swing in the playground. The four conventional stories involved a boy child wearing a skirt, two children talking in class, a child walking out of the classroom without permission and a child who stops paying attention to the lesson and turns his back on the teacher. Subject's responses to questions were recorded on standard scoring sheets.

2.4. Procedure

Subjects were tested in one of the interview rooms attached to the ward on which the subject was housed. Before the study commenced the subjects were introduced to the experimenter and informed about what they were to do. Subject consent forms were taken.

Before any of the transgressions scenes were read out to the subjects, they were informed that all of the scenes would occur within a school environment. It was decided to place the transgressions scenes within a school environment, as opposed to a ward or other adult environment, because piloting had shown

[10]WAIS scores were obtained from the patients' files and not by the present experimenter. WAIS scores were not available for three of the psychopaths and three of the non-psychopaths. Because of the incompleteness of these data, all of the subjects were submitted Raven's Advanced matrices.

that teachers were regarded by the subjects as legitimate authority figures for children. Some subjects did not regard nurses as legitimate authority figures for other adults.

Each of the transgression scenes was read out to the subject one at a time. The order of presentation of the transgression scenes was randomized across subjects. After the transgression scene had been presented, the subject was asked four questions:

(1) "Was it OK for X to do Y?" (Examining the subject's judgement of the *permissibility* of the act.)
(2) "Was it bad for X to do [the transgression?]" and then "On a scale of one to ten, how bad was it for X to do [the transgression]?" (Examining the subject's judgement of the *seriousness* of the act.)
(3) "Why was it bad for X to do [the transgression]?" (Examining the subject's *justification categories* for the act.)

The subject was then told:

"Now what if the teacher said before the lesson, before X did [the transgression], that "At this school anybody can Y if they want to. Anybody can Y."

The subject was then asked a final question:

(4) "Would it be OK for X to Y if the teacher says X can?" (Examining the rule's *authority jurisdiction*.)

All responses were recorded by hand on a standard scoring sheet.

2.5. Scoring Procedure

The scoring procedure followed that commonly used in the literature (e.g., Smetana, 1981; Smetana & Braeges, 1990). The answers to all questions, except three, were scored categorically. *Yes* responses were assigned a score of 0, and *no* (*not* OK) responses a score of 1. Subjects could thus achieve a cumulative score of between 0 and 4 for each of the domains for each of the questions. Question 3 was scored according to the value (between 1 and 10) the subject had given that transgression. The justifications of the subjects were scored according to categories similar to those used in previous research (e.g., Smetana, 1985). The justification categories are shown in Table 2. Two coders scored all justifications, and inter-rater reliability was high (91%).

3. RESULTS

3. 1. Criterion Judgements

Table 3 presents the means and standard deviations of moral and conventional judgements for each of the criterion judgements for both subject groups. Three 2 (Domain) × 2 (Group) ANOVAs were performed on the subject's responses

TABLE 2
A description of the justification categories

	Description
Other's welfare	Any reference to the welfare of the victim (e.g., "it will hurt him")
Normative references	Any reference, even implicit (e.g., "It's not acceptable to do that"), to rules
Disorder statements	Any reference to the disruption caused by the transgression (e.g., "It will distract the class").
Lack of change	Any reference to the long-term implications of the transgression (e.g., "If he gets away with it now he'll always do it")
Rudeness	Any reference to the rudeness of the transgression (e.g., "It's bad manners")
Other	Any other response

for each of the three criterion judgements. These three ANOVAs revealed main effects of domain for all three judgements: *permissibility*, $F(1, 38) = 9.51$, $p = .05$; *seriousness*, $F(1, 38) = 8.83$, $p < .01$, and; *authority jurisdiction* (modifiability), $F(1, 38) = 30.07$, $p < .001$). Moral transgressions were judged significantly less *permissible*, more *serious* and less *authority dependent* than conventional transgressions.

Significant group differences were only shown in the results of the ANOVA on the *authority jurisdiction* (modifiability) criterion judgement. This ANOVA showed a main effect of group $F(1, 38) = 5.53$, $p < .05$ and a significant Domain × Group interaction $F(1, 38) = 9.97$, $p < .01$. However, a simple effects analysis using two-way ANOVAs to examine the moral/conventional distinction of the two groups independently revealed different patterns of responding for the two groups. The non-psychopaths made a significant moral/conventional distinction on all three criterion judgements (*permissibility*, $F(1, 18) = 11.76$, $p < .05$;

TABLE 3
The means and standard deviations of moral (M) and conventional (C)
judgements for each of the criterion judgements for each of the subject groups

	Criterion judgements					
	Permissibility		Seriousness		Modifiability	
	M	C	M	C	M	C
Psychopaths	0.98	0.93	8.28	6.42	0.95	0.80
	(0.08)	(0.17)	(1.66)	(3.04)	(0.16)	(0.33)
Non-psychopaths	1.00	0.75	8.04	4.72	1.00	0.38
	(0.00)	(0.26)	(2.11)	(3.29)	(0.00)	(0.34)

seriousness, $F(1, 18) = 6.49$, $p < 05$; *authority jurisdiction*, $F(1, 18) = 53.47$, $p < .001$). However, the psychopaths did not make a significant moral/conventional distinction on any of the criterion judgements (*permissibility*, $F(1, 18) = 0.56$, n.s.; *seriousness*, $F(1, 18) = 2.58$, n.s.; *authority jurisdiction*, $F(1, 18) = 2.08$, n.s.).

It seems therefore that while the responding of the psychopaths and non-psychopaths was only significantly different for the *authority jurisdiction* (modifiability) criterion judgement, the two groups can be differentiated (see Fig. 3). As predicted (prediction 1; see the simple effects analysis), the psychopaths did not show a moral/conventional distinction on any of the criterion judgements. However, in contrast to prediction 2, the psychopaths did not judge moral transgressions as conventional on the *authority jurisdiction* criterion judgement; i.e., *authority dependent*. Indeed, psychopaths did the opposite, judging conventional transgressions as moral on this criterion judgement; i.e., not *authority independent*.

Analysis of individual subject data reveals the difference in the pattern of responding of the two subject groups even more clearly. Table 4 reveals the differences between individuals in the two groups in their pattern of responding on the *authority jurisdiction* question. Table 4 reveals how many of the subjects in each of the two groups judged how many of the conventional transgressions to be *authority independent*. All of the subjects (other than one psychopath) judged that all of the moral transgressions were *authority independent*.

Table 4 clearly shows the difference between the two groups. Six psychopath (as opposed to 1 non-psychopath) subjects did not distinguish between moral and conventional transgressions on the *authority jurisdiction* question at all; all of these subjects thought that the transgression was not OK even if the teacher said that it was. In addition, a two (group)-way ANOVA, performed on the "quality of the moral/conventional distinction" score, revealed that the

TABLE 4
The number of psychopaths and non-psychopaths in each of the "quality of the moral/ conventional distinction" categories

Group	*Quality of the moral/conventional distinction*		
	No distinction	*Mild distinction*	*Clear distinction*
Psychopaths	2	2	8
Non-psychopaths	1	8	1

No distinction = no transgressions were judged *authority independent*; mild distinction = 1 transgression was judged *authority independent*; clear distinction = 2 or more transgressions were judged *authority dependent*.

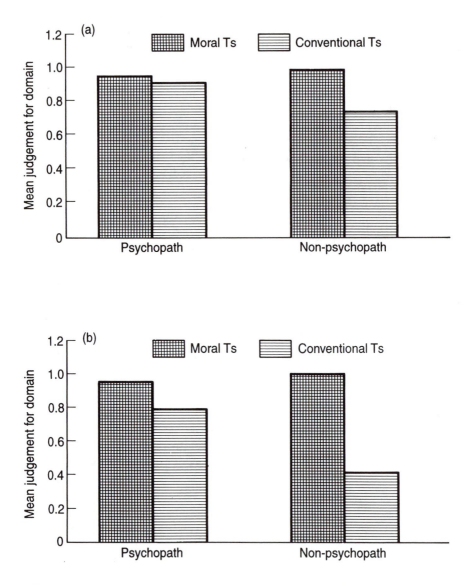

FIG. 3. Results of the psychopath and non-psychopath subjects on the *permissibility* (a) and *modifiability* (b) questions.

psychopaths were judging significantly more of the conventional transgres–
sions as moral ($F(1, 18) = 8.10$; $p < :05$).

Only 2 psychopaths as opposed to 8 controls made a clear moral/
conventional distinction (i.e., considered that more than two of the

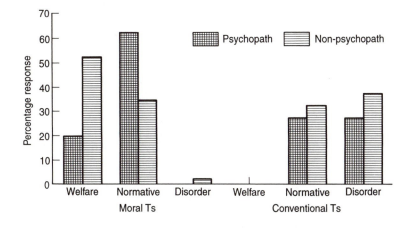

FIG. 4. Proportionate use of justification categories by psychopath and non-psychopaths for moral and conventional transgressions.

conventional transgressions were OK to do under the permission conditions). Even then, 1 of these 2 psychopaths actually viewed all transgressions, apart from the 2 physical violence transgressions, as permissible under permission conditions; this subject, unlike all the other 19 studied, considered that property damage, under permission conditions, was permissible.

3.2. Justification Categories

Table 5 and Fig. 4 depict subjects' proportionate use of justifications for (combined) moral and conventional items. It seems that, regardless of group,

TABLE 5
The proportionate use by the psychopath and non-psychopath subjects of the justification categories

	Group			
	Psychopath		Non-psychopath	
	M	C	M	C
Other's welfare	17.5	0.00	52.50	0.00
Normative references	52.50	42.50	35.00	25.00
Disorder statements	0.05	22.50	2.50	32.50
Lack of change	12.50	7.50	2.50	12.50
Rudeness	0.00	17.50	2.50	17.50
Other	12.5	10.00	5.00	12.5

M, moral; C, conventional.

victim's welfare reasoning was more commonly used to justify moral items while *disorder* statements and *rudeness* were more commonly used to justify conventional items. Indeed, a 2 (Group) × 2 (Domain) ANOVA, performed on the *victim's welfare* justification category, revealed a main effect for domain. This ANOVA also revealed a main effect of group ($F(1, 38) = 6.76; p < .05$). As predicted (prediction 3), psychopaths are significantly less likely to justify items by references to the *victim's welfare*. There was also a significant Group × Domain interaction ($F(1, 36) = 6.76; p < .05$). This was a product of the fact that this difference between the groups was only present for the moral items; no conventional items were justified through references to *victim's welfare*.

Examination of *victim's welfare* justification by the individual subject revealed that 5 of the psychopaths and 9 of the non-psychopaths used this form of justification at least once. Of the 5 psychopaths who used this justification, 2 were the 2 subjects who showed a clear moral/conventional distinction (see Table 4) and 1 was 1 of the subjects who made a mild moral/conventional distinction. The 1 non-psychopath who did not use *other's welfare* justifications did, however, make a clear moral/conventional distinction.

3.3. Individual Item PCL Scores and the Moral/Conventional Distinction

It was decided to investigate the relationship between the subject's score on each of the items of the PCL and his tendencies to judge conventional transgressions as moral and to make references to *victim's welfare* in his justifications. Table 6 shows those PCL items which significantly correlated with the tendency to judge conventional transgressions as moral and the tendency to make *victim's welfare* justifications. Table 7 shows the inter-correlations between total PCL score, tendency to judge conventional

TABLE 6

Individual items on the PCL which significantly correlated with tendency to judge conventional transgressions as moral and tendency to make *victim's welfare* justifications

PCL item	Tendency to judge conventional transgressions as moral	Tendency to make *victim's welfare* justifications
Lack of remorse or guilt	0.74**	−0.48
Callous/lack of empathy	0.41	−0.55
Early behavioural problems	n.s.	−0.60*
Juvenile delinquency	n.s.	−0.57
Criminal versatility	0.60	−0.49

$* = p < .01; \quad ** = p < .001.$

TABLE 7

Intercorrelations of total PCL score, tendency to judge conventional transgressions as moral and tendency to make *victim's welfare* justifications

	Tendency to judge conventional transgressions as moral	Tendency to make victim's welfare justifications
Total PCL score	0.45[a]	−0.47
Tendency to make *victim's welfare* justifications	−0.54	

[a]This correlation is not significant.

transgressions as moral and tendency to make *victim's welfare* justifications. These two tables show three significant correlations of individual PCL items with tendency to judge conventional transgressions as moral ("lack of remorse or guilt", "callous/lack of empathy" and "criminal versatility"). Total PCL score also correlated significantly with this tendency. Five individual test items and the total PCL score correlated significantly with the tendency to make *victim's welfare* justifications. In addition, tendency to make *victim's welfare* justifications correlates significantly with tendency to judge conventional transgressions as moral.

4. DISCUSSION

The present study examined the form of the moral/conventional distinction made by psychopaths and non-psychopaths and the categories used by these subjects when they justify their judgements. This study revealed: first, and in line with predictions, that while the non-psychopaths made the moral/conventional distinction, the psychopaths did not; secondly, and in contrast with predictions, that psychopaths treated conventional transgressions like moral transgressions rather than treating moral transgressions like conventional transgressions; and thirdly, and in line with predictions, that psychopaths were much less likely to justify their items with reference to *victim's welfare*.

It should be noted that while these results were broadly in line with predictions, they would not be expected from an analysis of the literature. As reported above, the observation in individuals of a moral/conventional distinction is a particularly robust phenomenon; it is found across ages (e.g Nucci, 1981) and across cultures (e.g., Song et al., 1987). Indeed, Blair (submitted) found that children with autism made the distinction. In fact, all other populations examined have been found to make this distinction.

It should also be noted that these findings cannot be explained as a result of poor parenting strategies (this includes neglect or child abuse). While clinicians have reported that many psychopaths have been abused as children, not all have, nor have the non-psychopath population used here been free of this abuse. More importantly, Smetana et al. (1984), examining the moral/ conventional distinction in abused children, found that these children did make the distinction.

Indeed, these findings cannot easily be accommodated within the existing framework of accounts of the moral/conventional distinction (e.g., Smetana, 1983; Turiel, 1977, 1983; Turiel et al., 1987; Turiel & Smetana, 1984). These authors have suggested that the moral/conventional distinction is a result of the formation of two, independent conceptual domains (see Turiel & Davidson, 1986). These authors have proposed that the child *constructs* these domains from the qualitatively different social interactional consequences of moral and conventional transgressions. Such a framework would have to account for the present findings as indicating that the psychopath has not *constructed* the moral domain either because of a failure in the construction process or because of a lack of experience of the social interactional consequences of moral and conventional transgressions. Taking the second possibility first: given the activities of the psychopaths it is highly unlikely that they have not been exposed to the social interactional consequences of moral and conventional transgressions. It would therefore probably be easier to explain the present findings in terms of a deficit within the *construction* process in psychopaths. The only detailed description of the *construction* process is that provided by Turiel (1983). He states that two forms of the manipulation of gathered data result in the *construction* of "judgements of moral necessity": manipulations of past experience and counter-factual reasoning. In summary, both of these manipulations result in judgements of moral necessity if the child has *constructed* a connection between his own personal experience of pain and the observed experience of the victim. It would thus be predicted that an individual who has never experienced pain would not make the moral/conventional distinction. However, there is no reason to believe the psychopaths do not experience pain. Nor is there any empirical reason to believe that psychopaths are any less likely to form *connections* between concepts than the normal population.

Two potential alternative ways of generating "judgements of moral necessity" might be by either role taking or empathizing with the victim. Representations of another's plight, formed through role taking, have previously been suggested to motivate the observer to alleviate that plight (Gough, 1948). In addition, emphatic responses are assumed to motivate prosocial behaviour (Hoffman, 1987) and inhibit violent action (Feshbach, 1983; Gibbs, 1987; Perry & Perry, 1974; Samenov, 1984). As stated above, role taking is defined as the "imaginative transposing of oneself into the thinking and acting of another" (Feshbach, 1978). As Batson states: "Perspective taking is the psychological variable most often assumed to be the antecedent of specifically empathic reactions to another's distress" (Batson et al., 1987, p.172). Thus, empathizing involves role taking. To role take an individual must be able to "mentalize" (see Leslie, 1987, 1988) where "mentalizing" involves the representation of mental states of others. If, when the individual is role taking, he is forming a representation of the mental state of the other he is, by definition, "mentalizing". Children with autism have been demonstrated to be incapable of "mentalizing" (e.g., Baron-Cohen, Leslie & Frith, 1985; Leslie & Frith, 1988). Therefore, according to the above definitions, these children cannot either role take or empathize. However, children with autism do make the moral/conventional distinction (Blair, submitted). Therefore, neither role taking nor empathy can be prerequisites for successful performance on the moral/conventional distinction task.

Turning to the position detailed in the Introduction, there is no reason to believe that children with autism lack VIM and, therefore, their demonstration of the moral/conventional distinction is not surprising. While children with autism may not be able to represent a mental state of another's distress, this distress, as a visual or aural cue, will activate their VIM. Developmentally, representations of transgressions which commonly cause distress in victims (moral transgressions) will become triggers for VIM due to their pairing with VIM activation as a consequence of the observation of distress cues (see above). Thus, in children with autism, as in normally developing children, representations of moral transgressions will activate VIM.

As regards the three predictions made in the Introduction for psychopaths, it can be seen that two out of the three were confirmed. If psychopaths lack VIM they should fail to distinguish in their judgements between moral and conventional transgressions. Most of the psychopaths in the present study did not distinguish between these two transgression situations in their judgements. If psychopaths lack VIM they should show impoverished victim-based moral meta-knowledge. The psychopaths in the present study demonstrated significantly less reference to victim-based moral meta-knowledge than the non-psychopaths. In addition, as regards the VIM position, the findings displayed in Tables 6 and 7 should be considered. Total PCL score correlated with both tendency to judge conventional transgressions as moral and tendency to make *victim's welfare* justifications. There is an association between degree of psychopathy and both failure to make the moral/conventional distinction and failure to make *victim's welfare justifications*. More important, however, are the significant correlations between individual PCL items and both moral/conventional scores. All the individual PCL items which correlate significantly with either of the measures of failure on the moral/conventional distinction task would be predicted primary consequences of a lack of VIM. In particular, in this respect, is the very significant correlation between lack of remorse or guilt and tendency to judge conventional items as moral. The causal model presented in Fig. 2 specifically predicts the absence of moral emotions in the psychopath.

The third prediction, that the psychopaths should treat moral transgressions as conventional, was disconfirmed. The psychopaths treated conventional transgressions as if they were moral. In the Introduction, it was suggested that when an individual learns of a moral transgression, VIM is activated by the presence of a victim. It was suggested that VIM activation results in a withdrawal response resulting in arousal. This arousal, associated with the withdrawal response, is experienced as aversive. The act which elicited this arousal is associated with the aversiveness; it is considered undesirable. Even if the transgression situation is changed, i.e., there is no rule prohibiting the moral transgression, VIM will still be activated by the presence of the victim, and so the act will still be considered not OK to do. In contrast, when an individual processes a conventional transgression VIM will not be activated and there will be no aversive arousal. The individual will therefore consider that any conventional transgression that is not prohibited by a rule is OK to do.

This account implies: first, that the psychopath should judge moral and conventional transgressions similarly; and, secondly, that the psychopath should process all transgressions as conventional (*authority dependent*) because, given the lack of VIM, no aversive arousal should be generated. As stated above, the first prediction was confirmed; psychopaths did judge moral and conventional transgressions similarly. However, psychopaths judged all transgressions as moral, not conventional. However, this second finding is not incompatible with the VIM position. Indeed, perhaps this finding is not surprising. These subjects were all incarcerated and presumably motivated to be released. All wished to demonstrate that the treatments they were receiving were effective. They therefore would be motivated to show how they had learned the rules of society (notice the predominance of normative statement justifications from both groups; 45% of the psychopaths' and 34% of the non-psychopaths' justifications were of this form). The psychopaths manifest this desire on the *authority jurisdiction* criterion judgement, by suggesting that all transgressions are *authority independent*. I suggest that this is because the psychopaths lack VIM and thus are unable to identify the distinguishing features differentiating moral and conventional transgressions. This inability, coupled with a desire to demonstrate adherence to societal rules, results in their judgement of all the transgressions as authority independent. The non-psychopaths, in contrast, though presumably equally motivated to be released, are incapable of ignoring the distinguishing features of moral and conventional transgressions because of the operation of VIM, and thus answer the *authority jurisdiction* question appropriately.

Examining the justifications produced by subjects when they were explaining why they thought the transgressions were not OK to do (see Table 5 and Fig. 3), it can be seen that psychopaths and non-psychopaths used similar justifications if the transgression was conventional but not if the transgression was moral. If the transgression was moral, nonpsychopaths used predominantly *other's welfare* justifications ("it hurts") while psychopaths used predominantly *normative* justifications (i.e., "it's wrong" or "it's not socially acceptable"). This result was as predicted. Without VIM the individual may not associate the pain of the other with the transgression and thus will not justify the act's wrongness by referring to the welfare of others.

It could be suggested, from Table 5 and Fig. 4, that the psychopaths, though they failed to make a moral/conventional distinction in their criterion judgements, are making a moral/conventional distinction in their justifications. They certainly do show a tendency to give different justifications for moral and conventional transgressions. However, this cannot be taken as evidence against the position proposed here. In the Introduction, the moral/conventional transgressions distinction was defined as the distinction in an individual's *judgements* between moral and conventional transgressions. It was suggested that the activation of VIM by representations of moral, but not conventional, transgressions was responsible for this distinction. It was also suggested that VIM was a prerequisite for the internal generation of justifications centred on the plight of the victim. However, it was not suggested that VIM had a role in the generation of any other form of justification category. Indeed, there is no reason to believe that it should have. What justification category an individual gives for a specific transgression will be a function of the salient aspects of that transgression. There is no reason to believe that the salient features of a moral transgression should be identical to those of a conventional transgression (outside of the fact that moral transgressions necessarily result in victims). Indeed, there is reason to believe that they should not be. Moral transgressions (e.g., one individual hitting another) need not result in classroom disorder. The conventional transgressions used in the present study (e.g., talking in class) necessitate classroom disorder. Thus, the fact that the psychopaths give different non-victim-based justifications for moral and conventional transgression cannot be used against the position being advocated here.

In conclusion, this study confirmed two predictions of the causal model presented as Fig. 1. Psychopaths are significantly more likely to fail to make the moral/conventional distinction and they are significantly less likely to make reference to the welfare of others. While this study has not proven that psychopaths lack VIM, it has provided evidence that is in line with the position.

ACKNOWLEDGEMENTS

This research was conducted in partial fulfilment of the requirements for the degree of PhD at University College London. James Blair was supported by a Science and Engineering Research Council studentship and a Wellcome Mental Health Training Fellowship (ref. 37132/Z/92/2/1.4Q). The author would like to thank the staff at

Broadmoor and Ashworth Hospitals, particularly Ms. C. Sellars, Dr. I. Strickland, Ms. F. Clark and Dr. A.O. Williams. He is also grateful to Professor J. Morton, Professor R. Blackburn, Dr. Tidmarsh and Dr. Lisa Cipolotti for their comments on earlier drafts of this paper.

Portions of this article were presented at the Experimental Psychology Society meeting, London, January 1994.

REFERENCES

American Psychological Association (1987). *Diagnostic and Statistical Manual of Mental Disorders, 3rd revised edition (DSM-III-R)*. Washington, DC: American Psychological Association.

Arsenio, W.F., & Ford, M.E. (1985). The role of affective information in social-cognitive development: children's differentiation of moral and conventional events. *Merrill-Palmer Quarterly, 31*, 1–17.

Bandura, A., & Rosenthal, T.L. (1966). Vicarious classical conditioning as a function of arousal level. *Journal of Personality and Social Psychology, 3*, 54–62.

Baron-Cohen, S., Leslie, A.M. & Frith, U. (1985). Does the autistic have a "Theory of Mind"? *Cognition, 21*, 37–46.

Batson C.D., Fultz J., & Schoenrade, P.A. (1987). Adults' emotional reactions to the distress of others. In N. Eisenberg & J. Strayer (Eds.), *Empathy and its development* (pp. 163–185). Cambridge, UK: Cambridge University Press.

Berger, S.M. (1962). Conditioning through vicarious instigation. *Psychological Review, 69*, 450–466.

Blair, R.J.R. (submitted). Morality in the autistic child.

Blair, R.J.R., Sellars, C., Strickland, I., Clark, F., Williams, A.O., Smith, M., & Jones, J. (in press). Theory of mind in the psychopath. *Journal of Forensic Psychology*.

Blair, R.J.R., Sellars, C., Strickland, I., Clark, F., Williams, A.O., Smith, M., & Jones, J. (submitted). Role taking in the psychopath.

Biasi, A. (1980). Bridging moral cognition and moral action: a critical review of the literature. *Psychological Bulletin, 88*, 1–45.

Campagna, A.F., & Harter, S. (1975). Moral judgements in sociopathic and normal children. *Journal of Personality and Social Psychology, 31*, 199–205.

Camras, L.A. (1977). Facial expressions used by children in a conflict situation. *Child Development, 48*, 1431–1435.

Colby, A., & Kohlberg, L. (1987). *The measurement of moral judgement*. New York: Cambridge University Press.

Craig, K.D., & Lowrey, J.H. (1969). Heart rate components of conditioned vicarious autonomic responses. *Journal of Personality and Social Psychology 11*, 381–387.

Damasio, A.R., Tranel, D., & Damasio, H.C. (1991). Somatic markers and the guidance of behavior: theory and preliminary testing. In H.S. Levin, H.M. Eisenberg & A.L. Benton (Eds.), *Frontal lobe function and dysfunction*, (pp. 217–229). New York: Oxford University Press.

Eibl-Eibesfeldt, I. (1970). *Ethology: The biology of behaviour*. New York: Holt, Rinehart & Winston.

Eisenberg, N., Fabes, R.A., Bustamante, D., Mathy, R.M., Miller, P.A., & Lindholm, E. (1988). Differentiation of vicariously induced emotional reactions in children. *Developmental Psychology, 24*, 237–246.

Eisenberg, N., Fabes, R.A., Carlo, G., Troyer, D., Speer, A.L., Karbon, M., & Switzer, G. (1992). The relations of maternal practices and characteristics to children's vicarious emotional responsiveness. *Child Development, 63*, 583–602.

Eysenck H.J. (1964). *Crime and personality*. London: Routledge & Kegan Paul.

Fabes, R.A., Eisenberg, N., & Eisenbud, L. (1993). Behavioral and physiological correlates of children's reactions to others in distress. *Developmental Psychology, 29,* 655–663.

Feshbach, N.D. (1978). Studies of empathic behaviour in children. In H.A. Maher (Ed.), *Progress in experimental personality research.* New York: Academic Press.

Feshbach, N.D. (1983). Learning to care: a positive approach to child training and discipline. *Journal of Clinical Child Psychology, 12,* 266–271.

Fodor, E.M. (1973). Moral development and parent behaviour antecedents in adolescent psychopaths. *Journal of Genetic Psychology, 122,* 37–43.

Gibbs, J.C. (1987). Social processes in delinquency: the need to facilitate empathy as well as sociomoral reasoning. In W.M. Kurtines & J.L. Gewirtz (Eds.), *Moral development through social interaction* (pp. 301–321). New York: Wiley.

Gorenstein, E.E. (1982). Frontal lobe functions in psychopaths. *Journal of Abnormal Psychology, 91,* 368–379.

Gorenstein, E.E., & Newman. J.P. (1980). Disinhibitory psychopathology: a new perspective and a model for research. *Psychological Review, 37,* 301–315.

Gough, H.G. (1948). A sociological theory of psychopathy. *American Journal of Sociology, 53,* 359–366.

Hare, R.D. (1980). A research scale for the assessment of psychopathy in criminal populations. *Personality and Individual Differences, 1,* 111–119.

Hare, R.D. (1985a). *Scoring manual for the psychopathy checklist.* Unpublished manuscript. University of British Columbia, Vancouver, Canada.

Hare, R.D. (1985b). A comparison of procedures for the assessment of psychopathy. *Journal of Consulting and Clinical Psychology, 53,* 7-16.

Hare, R.D., & Cox, D.N. (1978). Clinical and empirical conceptions of psychopathy, and the selection of subjects for research. In R.D. Hare & D. Schalling (Eds.), *Psychopathic behaviour: Approaches to research.* Chichester: Wiley.

Hare, R.D., Williamson, S.E., & Harpur, T.J. (1988). Psychopathy and language. In T.E. Moffitt & A.M. Sarnoff (Eds.), *Biological contributions to crime causation. NATO Advanced Science Series D: Behaviour and Social Sciences* (pp. 68–92). Dordrecht: Martinus Nijhoff.

Hoffman, M.L. (1977). Empathy, its development and prosocial implications. In C.B. Keasey (Ed.), *Nebraska symposium on motivation* (Vol. 25, pp. 169–218). Lincoln: University of Nebraska Press.

Hoffman, M.L. (1987). The contribution of empathy to justice and moral judgment. In N. Eisenberg & J. Strayer (Eds.), *Empathy and its development* (pp. 47-80). Cambridge, UK: Cambridge University Press.

Hollos, M., Leis, P., & Turiel, E. (1986). Social reasoning in children and adolescents. *Journal of Cross Cultural Psychology, 17,* 352–374.

Jurkovic, G.J., & Prentice, N.M. (1977). Relation of moral and cognitive development to dimensions of juvenile delinquency. *Journal of Abnormal Psychology, 86,* 414–420.

Karpman, B. (1941). On the need for separating psychopathy into two distinct types: the symptomatic and the idiopathic. *Journal of Criminal Psychopathy, 3,* 112–137.

Kohlberg, L. (1969). Stage and sequence: the cognitive-developmental approach to socialization. In D.A. Goslin (Ed.), *Handbook of socialisation theory and research.* Chicago: Rand McNally.

Krebs, D.L. (1975). Empathy and altruism. *Journal of Personality and Social Psychology, 32,* 1134–1146.

Laupa, M., & Turiel E. (1986). Children's conceptions of adult and peer authority. *Child Development, 57,* 405–412.

Lee, M. & Prentice, N.M. (1988). Interrelations of empathy, cognition and moral reasoning with dimensions of juvenile delinquency. *Journal of Abnormal Child Psychology, 16,* 127–139.

Leslie A.M. (1987). Pretence and representation: the origins of "Theory of Mind". *Psychological Review, 94,* 412–426.

Leslie, A.M. (1988). Some implications of pretence for mechanisms underlying the child's theory of mind. In P.L. Astington, P.L. Harris, & D.R. Olson (Eds.), *Developing theories of the mind.* Cambridge: Cambridge University Press.

Leslie, A.M. & Frith, U. (1988). Autistic children's understanding of seeing, knowing and believing. *British Journal of Developmental Psychology, 6,* 315–324.

Lorenz, K. (1966). *On aggression.* New York: Harcourt Brace Jovanovich.

Lykken, D.T. (1957). A study of anxiety in the sociopathic personality. *Journal of Abnormal and Social Psychology, 55,* 6–10.

Mandler, G. (1984). *Mind and body.* New York: Norton.

Mayer, L.B. (1956). *Emotion and meaning in music.* Chicago: University of Chicago Press.

Morton, J., & Frith U. (1993). Causal modelling: a structural approach to developmental psychopathology. In D. Cicchetti & D.H. Cohen (Eds.), *Manual of developmental psychopathology.* New York: Wiley.

Mullen, P.E. (1992). Psychopathy: a developmental disorder of ethical action. *Criminal Behaviour and Mental Health, 2,* 234–244.

Norman, D., & Shallice, T. (1986). Attention to action: willed and automatic control of behaviour. In R.J. Davidson, G.E. Schwartz. & D. Shapiro (Eds.), *Consciousness and self-regulation.* New York: Plenum Press.

Nucci, L. (1981). Conceptions of personal issues: a domain distinct from moral or societal concepts. *Child Development, 52;* 114–121.

Nucci, L., & Nucci, M. (1982). Children's responses to moral and conventional transgressions in free-play settings. *Child Development, 52,* 1337–1342.

Nucci. L., & Turiel, E. (1978) Social interactions and the development of social concepts in preschool children. *Child Development, 49,* 400–407.

Nucci, L., Turiel, E., & Encarnacion-Gawrych, G.E. (1983). Social interactions and social concepts: analysis of morality and convention in the Virgin Islands. *Journal of Cross Cultural Psychology, 14,* 469–487.

Patrick, C.J., Bradley, M.M., & Lang, P.J. (1993). Emotion in the criminal psychopath: startle reflex modulation. *Journal of Abnormal Psychology, 102,* 82–92.

Perry, D.G., & Perry, L.C. (1974). Denial of suffering in the victim as a stimulus to violence in aggressive boys. *Child Development, 45,* 55–62.

Samenov, S.E. (1984). *Inside the criminal mind.* New York: Random House.

Siegal, M., & Storey, R.M. (1985). Day care and children's conceptions of moral and social rules. *Child Development, 56,* 1001–1008.

Smetana, I. (1981). Preschool children's conceptions of moral and social rules. *Child Development, 52,* 1333–1336.

Smetana, J. (1983). Social-cognitive development: domain distinctions and coordinations. *Developmental Review, 3,* 131–147.

Smetana, J. (1985). Preschool children's conceptions of transgressions: effects of varying moral and conventional domain-related attributes. *Developmental Psychology, 21,* 18–29.

Smetana, J. (1986). Preschool children's conceptions of sex-role transgressions. *Child Development, 57,* 862–871.

Smetana, J., & Braeges, J.L. (1990). The development of toddlers' moral and conventional judgements. *Merrill-Palmer Quarterly, 36,* 329–346.

Smetana, J., Bridgeman, D.L., & Turiel, E.. (1983). Differentiation of domains and prosocial behaviour. In D.L. Bridgeman (Ed.), *The nature of prosocial development: Interdisciplinary theories and strategies.* New York: Academic Press.

Smetana, J., Kelly, M., & Twentyman, C.T. (1984). Abused, neglected and nonmaltreated children's conceptions of moral and social-conventional transgressions. *Child Development, 55,* 277–287.

Song, M., Smetana, J.G., & Kim, S.Y. (1987). Korean children's conceptions of moral and conventional transgressions. *Developmental Psychology, 23,* 577–582.

Stoddart, T., & Turiel, E. (1985). Children's concepts of cross-gender activities. *Child Development, 56*, 1241–1252.

Tisak, M.S., & Turiel, E. (1984). Children's conception of moral and prudential rules. *Child Development 55*, 1030–1039.

Tisak, M.S., & Turiel, E. (1988). Variation in seriousness of transgressions and children's moral and conventional concepts. *Developmental Psychology, 24*, 352–357.

Trasler, G. (1978). Relations between psychopathy and persistent criminality: methodological and theoretical issues. In R.D. Hare & D. Schalling (Eds.), *Psychopathic behaviour: Approaches to research.* Chichester: Wiley.

Trevathan, S., & Walker, L.J. (1989). Hypothetical versus real-life moral reasoning among psychopathic and delinquent youth. *Development and Psychopathology, 1*, 91–103.

Turiel, E. (1977). Distinct conceptual and developmental domains: social convention and morality. In H.E. Howe & C.B. Keasey (Eds.), *Nebraska symposium on motivation.* Lincoln: University of Nebraska Press.

Turiel, E. (1983). The development of social knowledge: *Morality and convention.* Cambridge, UK: Cambridge University Press.

Turiel, E., & Davidson, P. (1986). Heterogeneity, inconsistency, and asynchrony in the development of cognitive structures. In I. Levin (Ed.), *Stage and structure: Reopening the debate*. Norwood, NJ: Ablex Press.

Turiel, E., Killen M., & Helwig, C.C. (1987). Morality: its structure, functions, and vagaries. In J. Kagan & S. Lamb (Eds.) *The emergence of morality in young children* (pp. 155–245). Chicago: University of Chicago Press.

Turiel, E., & Smetana, J. (1984). Social knowledge and action: the coordination of domains. In W.M. Kunines & J.L. Gewirtz (Eds.) *Morality, moral behaviour and moral development: Basic issues in theories and research.* New York: Wiley.

Weston, D., & Turiel, E. (1980). Act–Rule relations: children's concepts of social rules. *Development Psychology, 236*, 417–424.

Wong, S, (1988). Is Hare's Psychopathy Checklist reliable with the interview? *Psychological Reports, 62*, 931–934.

7

Evolutionary social psychology and family homicide

Martin Daly and Margo Wilson
McMaster University

Homicide is an extreme manifestation of interpersonal conflict with minimal reporting bias and can thus be used as a conflict "assay." Evolutionary models of social motives predict that genetic relationship will be associated with mitigation of conflict, and various analyses of homicide data support this prediction. Most "family" homicides are spousal homicides, fueled by male sexual proprietariness. In the case of parent–offspring conflict, an evolutionary model predicts variations in the risk of violence as a function of the ages, sexes, and other characteristics of protagonists, and these predictions are upheld in tests with data on infanticides, parricides, and filicides.

Homicide within the family is a theme of great psychological significance. In many mythologies, the primordial murder was a fratricide or patricide. Freud's "Oedipal theory" made the urge to kill one's father a normal element of the male psyche;[1] Bloch[2] maintains that the "central preoccupation of childhood" is the fear of parental filicide. Moreover, the murderous impulses are apparently manifest not just in imagination, but in action. Two prominent experts on domestic violence in the United States have written.[3]

> With the exception of the police and the military, the family is perhaps the most violent social group, and the home the most violent social setting, in our society. A person is more likely to be hit or killed in his or her home by another family member than anywhere else or by anyone else.

M. Daly is a professor and M. Wilson is a research associate in the Department of Psychology, McMaster University, Hamilton, Ontario, Canada L8S 4K1.

These allegations present a puzzle from the perspective of contemporary evolutionary theories of social motives and behavior.[4-7] The species-typical appetites, aversions, motives, emotions, and cognitive structures of all creatures, including *Homo sapiens*, have been shaped by selection to produce social action that is effectively "nepotistic": action that promotes the proliferation of the actor's genetic elements in future generations, by contributing to the survival and reproductive success of the actor's genetic relatives. Apprehensions of self-interest—such as the absence of pain and hunger, or the positive satisfactions derived from social and sexual successes and from the well-being of one's children—evolve as tokens of expected genetic posterity ("expected" in the statistical sense of that which would be anticipated from past evidence). It follows that individual self-interests conflict because of rivalry for representation in future gene pools.[8] Genetic relatedness is a predictor of reduced conflict and enhanced cooperation because the genetic posterities of blood relatives co-vary (are promoted by common exigencies) in direct proportion to their degree of relatedness. The heuristic value and essential soundness of this theoretical framework have been abundantly confirmed by recent research on nonhuman animals,[6, 7, 9] and there is a growing body of empirical studies indicating its applicability to human sociality, too.[9-13]

What, then, of family violence? We propose (i) that genetic relationship is associated with the mitigation of conflict and violence in people, as in other creatures; and (ii) that evolutionary models predict and explain patterns of differential risk of family violence.

We shall focus on an extreme form of interpersonal violence: homicide. One may protest that homicides are too infrequent and extreme to illuminate conflict generally, but there is advantage in focusing on acts so dire. The issues over which people are prepared to kill are surely those about which they care most profoundly. Moreover, because homicide is viewed so seriously, there is less reporting bias in homicide archives than in the records of any lesser manifestation of conflict. Homicides thus provide an exceptionally valid "assay" of interpersonal conflict.

GENETIC RELATIONSHIP AND MITIGATION OF HOMICIDE RISK WITHIN FAMILIES

Criminological studies of homicide in the United States[14] have generally used a limited categorization of victim–killer relationships. In a classic study of homicides in Philadelphia,[15] for example, "relatives" constituted almost one-fourth of all victims, and most of these were spouses; blood relatives and in-laws were not distinguished, together constituting just 6.5% of solved cases. These results are apparently typical: "Relatives" have never been found to exceed one-third of any substantial sample of U.S. homicides, and, wherever spouses have been distinguished, they outnumber all other relatives combined. In two studies, genealogical and marital relatives were distinguished: 19% of Detroit homicide victims in 1972 were related to their killers by marriage compared to 6% by blood[16]; 10% of Miami victims in 1980 were marital relatives of their killers compared to 1.8% blood relatives.[17]

These data suggest that blood kin may be relatively immune from lethal violence in the United States,[18] given the high frequency and intensity of interactions among relatives. However, in order to decide whether this is really so, one needs some sort of denominator representing "opportunity": the number and availability of potential victims in different categories of relationship to potential killers. One approach to this problem is to confine attention to cases involving members of the same household, so that the universe of accessible potential victims can be specified. Given the prevailing household compositions in Detroit in 1972, for example, coresidents unrelated to the killer by blood, whether spouses or not, were more than 11 times more likely to be slain than coresiding genetic relatives.[11, 16] Comparable analyses have not been conducted in other U.S. cities (nor can they be with information in typical data sets, since coresidence has not ordinarily been recorded); however, the fact that the distribution of victim–killer relationships in Detroit was unexceptional suggests that similar results would obtain.

Another approach to the issue of whether kinship mitigates conflict when opportunity is controlled entails comparing the distribution of relationships between killers and their victims with the distribution of relationships between collaborators in homicide. The logic is this: If conflict and cooperation were to arise merely in proportion to the frequency and intensity of interactions, relatively intimate types of relationships would provide more opportunities for both. Those intimate links that are prevalent among victim–killer relationships should thus prove to be similarly prevalent among co-offenders. But such is not the case. Among co-accused pairs of killers in Miami, for example, 29.6% were blood relatives—as compared to just 1.8% of victims and killers.[17] In fact, the average degree of relatedness between collaborative killers is far higher than the corresponding value for victim and killer in every society for which a relevant sample of cases is available, including tribal horticulturalists, medieval Englishmen, Mayan villagers, and urban Americans.[11]

STEP-RELATIONSHIPS

A particularly apt comparison for assessing effects of (perceived) relationship on conflict is that between the parent–offspring relationship and surrogates thereof. Parental solicitude has evolved to expend animals' resources (and even their lives) in enhancing the reproductive prospects of their descendants.[19, 20] It is therefore not surprising that parental solicitude evolves to be discriminative with respect to predictors of the offspring's probable contribution to the parent's genetic posterity.[21] One implication is that substitute parents will often care less profoundly for "their" children than will genetic parents.

"Cruel stepparent" stories are cross-culturally ubiquitous[22] and reflect a recurring dilemma. Mothers and fathers have been widowed or abandoned with dependent children throughout human history, whereupon the fate of the children became problematic. A worldwide solution to the problem of single parents unable or unwilling to raise their children is fosterage to close relatives such as maternal grandparents.[23] In some societies, widows are customarily married to their dead husbands' brothers (the levirate); in others, widows with dependent children may spurn remarriage and reside with siblings or other close relatives. In the absence of such arrangements, children come under the care of stepparents who may have no benevolent interest in their welfare. In a study of the foraging Ache Indians of Paraguay, for example, Hill and Kaplan[24] traced the careers of 67 children raised by mother and stepfather after the natural father's death: 43% had died, of various causes, before their 15th birthdays, as compared to just 19% of those raised by two surviving parents.

Children in stepparent families are disproportionately often injured in industrial nations, too. The specific kinds of injuries involved suggest that such children are not at risk merely by virtue of decreased parental vigilance and supervision, but are also more often assaulted.[25, 26] When injuries are attributed to "child abuse," the difference between stepparent and generic parent homes is large and is independent of risk attributable to low socioeconomic status, maternal youth, family size, or personality characteristics of the abusers.[27, 29] Abusive stepparents are discriminative, sparing their own children within the same household.[28, 30] Presently available data do not reveal whether stepmother or stepfather households entail greater risks.[31]

Overrepresentation of stepfamilies in child abuse samples might be dismissed as a product of reporting biases but for the fact that stepparents are even more strongly overrepresented in cases of child homicide, where biases of detection and reporting are presumably minimal. An English sample of "fatal battered baby cases" included 15 killed by stepfathers and 14 by genetic fathers,[32] although fewer than 1% of same-age English babies dwelt with stepfathers.[25] Similarly, an Australian sample of fatally battered babies included 18 slain by substitute fathers compared to 11 by genetic fathers.[33] A child living with one or more substitute parents in the United States in 1976 was approximately 100 times more likely to be fatally abused than a same-age child living with genetic parents.[11] Age-specific rates of being killed by step- or genetic parents in Canada are shown in Fig. 1.

In view of the costs of prolonged "parental" investment in nonrelatives, it may seem remarkable that step-relationships are ever peaceful; let alone genuinely affectionate. However, violent hostility is rarer than friendly

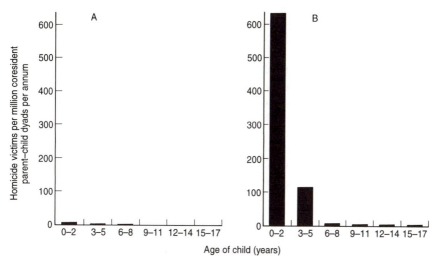

FIG. 1. Age-specific rates of homicide victimization by (A) genetic parents ($n = 341$ victims) or (B) stepparents ($n = 67$), Canada, 1974 to 1983. [Adapted from (11) with permission © 1988, Aldine de Gruyter]

relations even among nonrelatives; people thrive by the maintenance of networks of social reciprocity and by establishing reputations for fairness and generosity that will make them attractive exchange partners.[34] The kindly deportment of most stepparents may prove to be explicable mainly in the context of reciprocity with the genetic parent; moreover, insofar as indulgence toward unrelated children is a general attribute of men (or other male animals), it may be attributable to sexual selection as a result of female mate choice.[35] The fact remains, however, that step-relationships lack the deep commonality of interest of the natural parent–offspring relationship, and feelings of affection and commitment are correspondingly shallower.[29, 36] Differential rates of violence are one result.

SPOUSAL CONFLICTS

The customary extension of the category "relative" to encompass spouses and in-laws is metaphorical, but not arbitrary. By cooperative rearing of joint offspring, mates in a species with biparental care forge a powerful commonality of interest analogous to that existing between blood relatives.[37] Indeed, the generic interests of an exclusively monogamous pair coincide even more closely than those of blood relatives.[34] However, two considerations act against the evolution of perfect harmony in mated pairs: (i) the possibility of extra-pair reproduction and (ii) the partners' nepotistic interest in the welfare of distinct sets of collateral kin.

Mutual progeny contribute to spousal harmony, whereas children of former unions contribute to spousal conflict.[38] U.S. divorce statistics reflect these effects of children: For a given duration of marriage, children of former unions elevate divorce rates, whereas children of the present union reduce them.[39] We predict parallel influences of children on spousal homicide rates. There is some evidence that the presence of stepchildren is associated with spousal homicide,[11, 40, 41] but available data do nor permit quantitative assessment of the risks in households of various compositions.

In many animals (including people in their environments of evolutionary adaptation), female reproduction is resource-limited whereas the reproductive capacities of females are themselves the limiting "resource" for males. Male reproductive output in such species has a higher ceiling and greater variance than that of females, with the result that reproductive competition is more intense and dangerous among males (5, 19, 42). One tactic in such competition is sequestering and guarding mates, which increases in utility (relative to alternative tactics like maximizing copulatory contacts) in species with biparental care, since parentally investing males can be fooled about paternity.

Human marriage is a cross-culturally general institutionalization of reproductive alliance, entailing mutual obligations between the spouses during child-rearing, rights of sexual access (often but not necessarily exclusive and usually controlled by the husband), and legitimization of the status of progeny. Men take a proprietary view of women and their reproductive capacity, as witness the widespread practices of bridewealth[43] and claustration and infibulation of reproductively valuable women,[44] and the near universality of sexually asymmetrical adultery laws that treat poaching by rival males as a property violation.[45, 46]

Male sexual proprietariness is the dominant issue in marital violence. In studies of "motives" of spousal homicide, the leading identified substantive issue is invariably "jealousy".[11] Interview studies of North American spouse killers indicate that the husband's proprietary concern with his wife's infidelity or her intention to quit the marriage led him to initiate the violence in an overwhelming majority of cases, regardless of whether it was the husband or wife who ended up dead.[11, 41] Similarly, in other cultures, wherever motives in a sample of spousal homicides have been characterized in detail, male sexual proprietariness has proven relevant to more than half of those homicides.[11] Sexual proprietariness evidently lies behind most nonlethal wife beating, too,[46, 47] suggesting that spousal homicides are not primarily cold-blooded "disposals," but are the tip of the iceberg of coercive violence. Men strive to control women by various means and with variable success, while women strive to resist coercion and maintain their choices. There is brinkmanship in any such context, and homicides by spouses of either sex may be considered the slips in this dangerous game.[48]

This view of spousal violence as the coercive tactic of proprietary men suggests that women will be extremely at risk when perceived as likely to end the relationship. Indeed, there is a remarkable prevalence of recently estranged wives among homicide victims. In an Australian study,[33] 98 of 217 women slain by their husbands (45%) were separated or in the process thereof, compared to just 3 of 79 men slain by their wives (4%). Estrangement has also been implicated in spousal homicides in Canada.[11] A correct apprehension of the lethal risk in deserting a proprietary husband is surely one factor in the reluctance of many abused wives to leave.

The above considerations suggest, moreover, that young wives may be especially at risk, for two reasons: Youth per se makes the woman more attractive to rival men,[49] and the short duration of the marriage means that deep commonalities of interest have yet to be forged, making the marriage potentially unstable.[50] In Canada, young wives are indeed likeliest to be spousal homicide victims (Fig. 2). One might attribute this differential risk to the fact that young women are married to young men, the most homicidal demographic category, but the woman's age is apparently more relevant to spousal homicide risk than the man's;[11] the wife's declining risk as a function of age is apparent within each age class of husbands (although risk rises again for wives much older than their husbands). To date, no analysis has fully unconfounded the variables of the two parties' ages and marital and reproductive histories in order to assess their separate relevances to spousal homicide risk.[51]

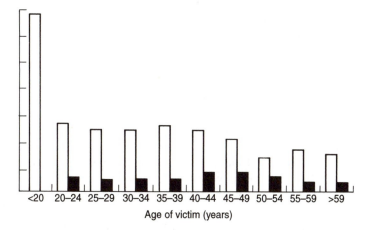

Age of victim (years)

FIG. 2. Age-specific rates of homicide victimization within legal marriages for (open bar) women killed by their husbands ($n = 528$) and (solid bar) men killed by their wives ($n = 124$), Canada, 1974 to 1983.[11] Age-related variations in spousal homicide victimization are significant for wives ($\chi^2(9) = 44.2, P < 0.001$), but not for husbands ($\chi^2(9) = 10.6, P > 0.3$). [Adapted from (11) with permission © 1988. Aldine de Gruyter]

PARENT–OFFSPRING CONFLICT AND VIOLENCE

Parents and children engage in frequent battles of wills, major and minor. Traditional social scientific views of these conflicts attribute them to imperfect adaptation in one or the other party, for example, "immature" egoism in the child or poor parenting skills.

Trivers[52] proposed a radically different perspective on parenting and socialization: Even though offspring are the parents' means to genetic posterity, parent–offspring conflict is an endemic feature of sexually reproducing organisms, because the allocation of resources and efforts that would maximize a parent's genetic posterity seldom matches that which would maximize a particular offspring's. Selection favors inclinations in both parties to achieve one's own optimum against the wishes and efforts of the other. This theory accounts for the seemingly maladaptive phenomenon of weaning conflict, as well as for disparate parental and offspring attitudes to collateral kin, "regression" to earlier stages of development on the birth of a sibling, and adolescent identity crises.[7, 21, 52, 53] In some circumstances, an offspring's reproductive prospects (according to cues that were predictive in the species' environment of evolutionary adaptation) may be insufficient to offset that offspring's detrimental effect on the parent's capacity to pursue other adaptive action, in which case parental solicitude may be expected to fail.[54]

People everywhere recognize that parents may sometimes be disinclined to raise a child, and anthropologists have collected much information about the circumstances in which infanticide is alleged to be common, acceptable, or even obligatory. If parental inclinations have been shaped by selection, there are at least three classes of circumstances in which we might anticipate some reluctance to invest in a newborn: (i) doubt that the offspring is the putative parent's own, (ii) indications of poor offspring quality, and (iii) all those extrinsic circumstances, such as food scarcity, lack of social support, and overburdening from the demands of older offspring, that would have made a child unlikely to survive during human evolutionary history.[55] The great majority of ethnographic accounts of infanticide in nonindustrial societies reflect one or other of these three categories of strategic allocation of lifetime parental effort.[56, 57]

Moreover, we may expect maternal psychology to exhibit sensitivity to the mother's own residual reproductive value: A newborn's compromising effects on the mother's future diminish with maternal age, and hence maternal willingness to jettison an infant may also be expected to decrease. This prediction is upheld (Fig. 3).[58] This maternal age effect is not an artefact of marital status; it is observed in both married and unmarried women.[11]

Evolutionary considerations suggest several predictions about filicide in relation to the child's age, too. In ancestral environments, the child's probability of attaining adulthood and contributing to its own and its parents' genetic posterity increased with age, especially during infancy, as the child

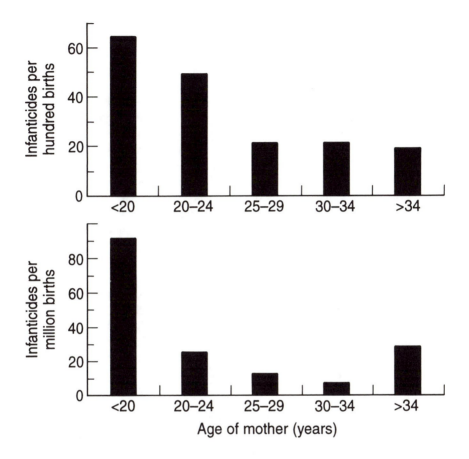

FIG. 3. Rates of infanticides by mothers as a function of maternal age, among (A) Ayoreo Indians of South America[58] ($n = 54$ victims), and (B) in Canada, 1974 to 1983[11] ($n = 87$). [(A) is reprinted from (58) with permission © 1984, Aldine de Gruyter; (B) is adapted from (11) with permission © 1988, Aldine de Gruyter]

passed through a stage of high mortality risk. The predicted consequence is that parental psychology should have evolved to cherish the child increasingly over a prolonged period, as the child's reproductive value increased. Hence:

1. Parents are expected to be more willing to incur costs on behalf of offspring nearer to maturity[59] and to be more inhibited in the use of dangerous tactics when in conflict with such offspring. Filicide rates are thus predicted to decline with the child's age, whereas no such effect is predicted in the case of child homicides by nonrelatives, whose valuation of the child is not expected to parallel that of the parents.

2. This decline is predicted to be negatively accelerated and concentrated in the first year postpartum, because (i) in the environments of human evolutionary adaptation, the lion's share of the prepubertal increase in reproductive value occurred within the first year, and (ii) insofar as parental disinclination reflects a "strategic" assessment of the reproductive episode, an evolved assessment mechanism should be such as to terminate hopeless ventures as early as possible.

3. Filicides perpetrated by the mother are predicted to be a more steeply declining function of the child's age than those perpetrated by the father, because (i) women's reproductive life spans end before those of men, so the utility of alternative reproductive efforts declines more steeply for women than for men; (ii) the extent to which children impose greater opportunity costs on mothers than on fathers is probably maximal in infancy; and (iii) phenotypic and other evidence of paternity may surface after infancy and is expected to be relevant to paternal but not to maternal solicitude.[45, 60]

All these predictions gain support from the Canadian data in Fig. 4.

Offspring kill parents, too. Because violence toward parents, like violence toward children, is associated with economic and other stressors,[61] and because parricides often follow a history of parental mistreatment of the eventual killer,[62] one might expect factors related to the risk of filicide to affect the risk of parricide in a directionally similar fashion. An evolutionary theoretical perspective, however, suggests one likely exception to this generalization. Just as a parent's valuation of an offspring is predictably related to the ages (reproductive values) of both parties, so too is the offspring's valuation of the parent. An offspring of a given age may be expected to disvalue an elderly parent more than a younger one. These considerations suggest that parental age at the child's birth will have opposite effects on the rates of violence perpetrated by parent and offspring against each other, and the data in Fig. 5 are supportive.

An alternative to Trivers's[7, 52] evolutionary analysis of parent–offspring conflict is Freud's "Oedipal theory": It is allegedly a normal phase of infant male psychosocial development to lust after mother and wish father dead.[1] [Freud[63] later developed a less detailed theory of an analogous girlish love of father and antipathy toward mother.] An evolutionary perspective suggests that Freud apprehended two distinct parent–offspring conflicts and conflated them. There is indeed a conflict between father and infant son over the wife-mother, but it is not sexual rivalry. The optimal birth interval from the child's perspective exceeds that from the father's and it is not implausible that toddlers have evolved specific adaptive strategies to delay the conception of a sibling,[64] including tactics to diminish mother's sexual interest and thwart father's access to her. In many societies, there is a later conflict between father and son over the timing of the son's accession to reproductive status, often subsidized by the

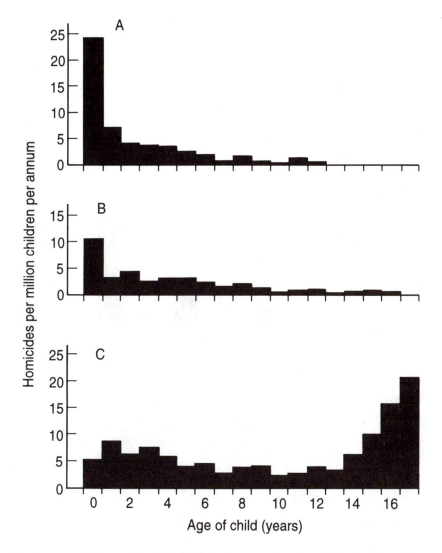

FIG. 4. Age-specific rates of homicide victimization among Canadian children, 1974 to 1983. (A) Slain by mothers (*n* = 198 victims), (B) by fathers (*n* = 154), and (C) by persons other than genealogical relatives (*n* = 493).

father at a cost to his own continuing reproductive ambitions; this later conflict is "sexual," but it is not over the mother.

If Trivers's[7, 52] evolutionary model is correct, then conflict between parents and young children exists irrespective of the child's sex. According to Freud, children are in conflict primarily with the parent of the same sex, at least in the

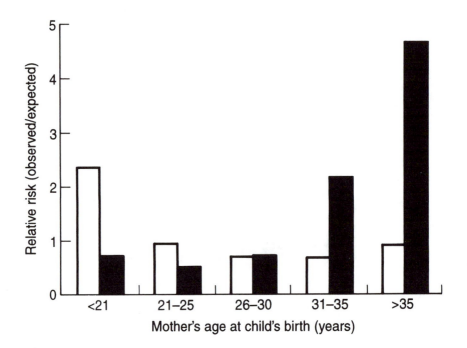

FIG. 5. Parent–child homicides perpetrated (open bar) by the mother (filicide, $n = 190$ victims) or (solid bar) upon her (matricide, $n = 61$), as a function of her age at the child's birth, Canada, 1974 to 1983. Relative risk is the ratio of the observed number of cases over the number expected if cases were distributed in proportion to the numbers of births to Canadian women in each age category in the calendar year of each filicide victim or matricide perpetrator's birth. Both distributions depart from number expected (filicides, $\chi^2(4) = 66.5$, $P < 0.001$; matricides, $\chi^2(4) = 56.9$, $P < 0.001$). No comparable analysis of parental filicides and patricides is possible because of lack of information on age-specific fertility of men in the population-at-large.

"Oedipal phase" (ages 2 to 5 years)[65] if not from birth; such a same-sex contingency in parent–offspring antagonisms is allegedly endemic to the human condition. Trivers's account predicts no such infantile same-sex contingency although elements of sexual rivalry could arise later. Canadian data on parent–offspring homicide cases support Trivers's view (Table 1), as do British and U.S. data.[66]

CONCLUDING REMARKS

Analyses of "family violence" have hitherto ignored crucial distinctions among relationships. Elucidation of the nature of relationship-specific confluences and conflicts of interest requires a conception of the fundamental nature of self-

TABLE 1

Parent–offspring homicides in Canada, 1974 to 1983, cross-tabulated by sex of killer and victim and by offspring age. Table entries are numbers of victims; 13 cases in which both parents were charged are excluded. All cases in which the child was 10 years old or less are filicides; "circumpubertal" cases include 31 filicides and 24 parricides; "adult" offspring cases include 26 filicides and 148 parricides. Only after puberty is there a same-sex contingency in parent–offspring violence; ns, not significant.

Offspring stage (age, in years)	Victim's sex	Killer's sex		Test of contingency
		Male	Female	
Infantile (0–1)	Male	24	53	
	Female	17	50	$\chi^2(1) = 0.6$
	Percentage male	58.5	51.5	ns
"Oedipal" (2–5)	Male	21	21	
	Female	27	27	$\chi^2(1) = 0.0$
	Percentage male	43.8	43.8	ns
"Latency" (6–10)	Male	21	19	
	Female	10	5	$\chi^2(1) = 0.9$
	Percentage male	67.7	79.2	ns
Circumpubertal (11-16)	Male	28	9	$\chi^2(1) = 0.0$
	Female	14	4	ns
	Percentage male	66.7	79.2	
Adult (≥ 17)	Male	104	8	
	Female	47	15	$\chi^2(1) = 10.1$
	Percentage male	68.9	34.5	$P < 0.01$

interest. Evolutionary theory provides such a conception by considering perceived self-interests to be evolved tokens of expected genetic posterity. From this perspective, the spousal relationship is unique in its potential for generating shared interests and betrayals thereof, and the commonalities and conflicts of interest even among blood relatives are relationship-specific.

The application of such an evolutionary model to the study of violence (or other social behavior) is neither simple nor direct. In particular, an evolutionary model need not imply that the behavior in question effectively promotes the reproductive success of the actors or their relatives. Homicide is a rare, extreme product of motivational mechanisms whose outputs are only expected to be adaptive on average, and in environments not crucially different from those in which we evolved. Murder-suicides forcefully illustrate why adaptation is most usefully sought at a psychological level of abstraction rather than in each category of overt behavior. Men are far more likely than women to commit suicide after killing a spouse[11, 33] and are especially likely to do so when the couple are estranged. A frequently expressed rationale is "If I can't have her, no one can." In such a case, the killer has apparently fallen into futile spite, but the counterproductiveness of sexual proprietariness in these extreme cases hardly gainsays its candidate status as a masculine psychological adaptation. The more typical consequences of fierce proprietariness have surely been effective deterrence of rivals and coercive control of wives. Similarly, the proposition that discriminative parental affection has been favored by selection is not undermined by the consideration that fatal child abuse may land a stepfather in jail. Although specific acts may be maladaptive (especially in evolutionarily novel environments), selection has shaped the social motives, emotions, and cognitive processes underlying them. Evolutionary psychological constructs like "discriminative parental solicitude" or "male sexual proprietariness" are domain-specific, but they influence a range of actions both conflictual and cooperative. The evolutionary psychological hypotheses that we have tested against homicide data should be further assessed with less extreme behavioral measures of conflict and with positive measures of harmony and solicitude.

Evolutionary models have enabled us to predict and discover patterned variations in the risk of lethal violence, as a function of the parties' ages, circumstances, and specific relationships to one another. As predicted, genetic relationship is associated with a softening of conflict, and people's evident valuations of themselves and of others are systematically related to the parties' reproductive values. Evolutionary theory can provide a valuable conceptual framework for the analysis of social psychologies.[7, 11, 34, 49, 67]

REFERENCES AND NOTES

1. Freud, S. (1900). *The Interpretation of Dreams*. New York: Basic Books. (1913). *Totem and Taboo*. New York: Norton.
2. Bloch, D. (1978). *So the Witch Won't Eat Me: Fantasy and the Child's Fear of Infanticide*. New York: Grove.
3. Gelles, R.J. & Straus, M.A. (1985). In A.J. Lincoln and M.A. Straus (Eds.), *Crime and the Family* (pp. 88–110). Springfield, IL: Thomas.
4. Hamilton, W.D. (1964). *J. Theor. Biol.*, 7, 1.
5. Williams, G.C. (1966). *Adaptation and Natural Selection*. Princeton, NJ: Princeton University Press.
6. Wilson, E.O. (1975). *Sociobiology*. Cambridge, MA: Belknap. Wittenberger, J.F. (1981). *Animal Social Behavior*. Boston: Duxbury. Daly, M. & Wilson, M. (1983). *Evolution and Behaviour*. Belmont, CA: Wadsworth. Krebs, J.R. & Davies, N.B. (Eds.) (1984). *Behavioural Ecology*. Oxford: Blackwell, ed. 2. Rubenstein, D.I. & Wrangham, R.W. (Eds.) (1986). *Ecological Aspects of Social Evolution*. Princeton, NJ: Princeton University Press.
7. Trivers, R.L. (1985). *Social Evolution*. Menlo Park, CA: Benjamin/Cummings.
8. Notwithstanding the focus on individuals and their genetic nonidentity, theoretical work on social evolution and the research inspired thereby have been little concerned with genetically based phenotypic variation. Instead, researchers have been primarily concerned to identify adaptive, species-typical (or sex-typical), faculative social strategies.
9. Alexander, R.D. & Thinkle, D.W. (Eds.) (1981). *Natural Selection and Social Behavior*. New York: Chiron.

10. Chagnon, N. & Irons, W. (Eds.) (1979). *Evolutionary Biology and Human Social Behavior.* North Scituate, MA: Duxbury.
11. Daly, M. & Wilson, M. (1988). *Homicide.* Hawthorne, NY: Aldine de Gruyter.
12. Betzig, L.L., Borgerhoff Mulder, M. & Turke, P.W. (Eds.) (1988). *Human Reproductive Behaviour.* Cambridge: Cambridge University Press.
13. Crawford, C., Smith, M. & Krebs, D. (Eds.) (1987). *Sociobiology and Psychology.* Hillsdale, NJ: Erlbaum.
14. For example, see Loftin, C. & Parker, R.N. (1985). *Criminology, 23,* 269. Messner, S.F. & Tardiff, K., *ibid*, p. 241; Williams, K.R. & Flewelling, R.L., *ibid.*, *25* , 543.
15. Wolfgang, M.E. (1958). *Patterns in Criminal Homicide.* Philadelphia: University of Pennsylvania Press.
16. Daly, M. & Wilson, M. (1982). *Am. Anthropol.*, *84,* 372.
17. Wilbanks, W. (1984). *Murder in Miami.* Lanham, MD: University Press of America.
18. Elsewhere, blood relatives often constitute a larger proportion of homicide victims than in the United States. Fratricides constitute a significant component of the homicide rate, for example, in certain agricultural societies in which the family farm is not practicably partionable, so that one's brother is one's principal rival.[11] In general, rates of family homicides seem to be less variable between countries than rates of other killings,[11] so that family homicides are proportionately significant wherever the overall homicide rate is low. Further assessment of the influence of (perceived) relatedness on rates of violence will require the development of new models incorporating the effects of social access, competition, and other social structural variables.
19. Trivers, R.L. (1972). In B. Campbell (Ed.), *Sexual Selection and the Descent of Man 1871–1971* (pp. 136–179). Chicago: Aldine.
20. In most dyadic relationships, reciprocity is carefully monitored and imbalances are resented as exploitative [L. Betzig, in (12), pp. 49–64; pp. 49–64; N.A. Berté, in (12), pp. 83–96; S.M. Essock-Vitale and M.T. McGuire, *Ethol. Sociobiol*, *6*, 155 (1985); H. Kaplan and K. Hill, *Curr. Anthropol*, *26*, 223 (1985)]. Parental altruism is different in that the flow of benefits is prolongedly, cumulatively, and ungrudgingly unbalanced.
21. Daly, M. & Wilson, M. (1988). *Nebr. Symp. Motiv.*, *35,* 91.
22. Cox, M.R. (1892). *Cinderella: 345 Variants.* London: The Folk-lore Society. Thompson, S. (1955). *Motif-Index of Folk Literature.* Bloomington: Indiana University Press.
23. Silk, J.B. (1980). *Am. Anthropol.*, *82,* 799.
24. Hill, K. & Kaplan, in (12), pp. 291–305.
25. Wadsworth, J., Burnell, I., Taylor, B. & Butler, N. (1983). *J. Epidemiol. Community Health*, *37,* 100.
26. Fergusson, D.M., Fleming, J. & O'Neill, D.P. (1972). *Child Abuse in New Zealand.* Wellington: Government of New Zealand Printer.
27. Wilson, M., Daly, M. & Weghorst, S. (1980). *J. Biosoc. Sci.*, *12,* 333.
28. M. Daly and M. Wilson (1985). *Ethol Sociobiol.*, *6,* 197.
29. Wilson M. & Daly, M. (Eds.) (1987). In R.J. Gelles and J.B. Lancaster (Eds.), *Child Abuse and Neglect* (pp. 215–232). Hawthorne, NY: Aldine de Gruyter.
30. Lightcap, J.L., Kurland, J.A. & Burgess, R.L. (1982). *Ethol. Sociobiol.*, *3,* 61.
31. Neither do presently available data permit the assessment of risks to adoptees. We predict that such risks will be less than to stepchildren for several reasons: (i) adoption "by stranger" is primarily the recourse of childless couples, strongly motivated to simulate a natural family experience, whereas step-relationships arise incidentally to the establishment of a desired mateship; (ii) adoptive parents are equally unrelated to their wards and thus avoid the conflict of one party's "parental" efforts benefiting the other's children; (iii) couples wishing to adopt are screened for suitability and may return children who do not work out; and (iv) adoptive couples are much more affluent on average than either stepparent or genetic parent families.
32. Scott, P.D. (1973). *Med. Sci. Law*, *13,* 197.

33. Wallace, A. (1986). *Homicide: The Social Reality*. Sydney: New South Wales Bureau of Crime Statistics and Research.
34. Alexander, R.D. (1987). *The Biology of Moral Systems*. Hawthorne, NY: Aldine de Gruyter.
35. Connor, R.C. (1562). *Anim Behav.*, *34*, 1562. Smuts, B.B. (1986). *Sex and Friendship in Baboons*. Hawthorne, NY: Aldine de Gruyter. Yanagisawa, Y. & Ochi, H. (1986). *Anim. Behav.*, *34*, 1769.
36. Duberman, L. (1975). *The Reconstituted Family*. Chicago: Nelson-Hall. Flinn, M.V. (1988). *Ethol. Sociobiol.*, *9*, 335.
37. Marital extension of the concept of "family" opens the door to a variety of manipulative metaphorical usages of kinship terminology [N.A. Chagnon, in (12), pp. 23–48; N.W. Thornhill, thesis, University of New Mexico, Albuquerque (1987); G.R. Johnson, S.H. Ratwik, J.T. Sawyer, in *The Sociobiology of Ethnocentrism*, V. Reynolds, V. Falger, I. Vine, Eds. (Croom Helm, London, 1987), pp. 157–174].
38. Messinger, L. (1976). *J. Marriage Fam. Counseling*, *2*, 193. Ambert, A.M. (1986). *J. Marriage Fam.*, *48*, 795.
39. Becker, G.S., Landes, E.M. & Michael, R.T. (1977). *J. Polit. Econ.*, *85*, 1141. White, L.K. & Booth, A. (1985). *Am. Sociol. Rev.*, *50*, 689.
40. Binda, J.J.M. (1980). In R. Brana-Shute and G. Brana-Shute (Eds.), *Crime and Punishment in the Caribbean*. Gainesville, FL: Centre for Latin American Studies. Kalmuss, D. & Seltzer, J.A. (1986). *J. Marriage Fam.*, *48*, 113. Lundsgaarde, H.P. (1977). *Murder in Space City*. New York: Oxford University Press.
41. Chimbos, P.D. (1978). *Marital Violence*. San Francisco: R & E Research Associates.
42. Bateman, A.J. (1948). *Heredity*, *2*, 349. Thornhill, R. & Thornhill, N.W. (1983). *Ethol. Sociobiol.*, *4*, 137. Wilson, M. & Daly, M. (1985). *Ibid.*, *6*, 59. Although the focus of this article is family homicides, the majority of lethal violence occurs between unrelated men and involves competition for material, social, and sexual resources that were directly related to reproductive success in the environments of human evolution [(11); Chagnon, N.A. (1988). *Science*, *239*, 985].
43. Comaroff, J.L. (Ed.) (1980). *The Meaning of Marriage Payments*. London: Academic Press. Borgheroff Mulder, M. in (12), pp. 65–82.
44. Dickemann, M., in (9), pp. 417–438. Hosken, F.P. (1979). *The Hosken Report: The Genital and Sexual Mutilation of Females*. Lexington, MA: Women's International Network News.
45. Wilson, M. (1987). *Unit. Toronto Fac. Law Rev.*, *45*, 216.
46. Daly, M., Wilson, M. & Weghorst, S.J. (1982). *Ethol. Sociobiol.*, *3*, 11.
47. Anglo-American tort actions illustrate the proprietary rights of men over women's sexual and reproductive capacities [Backhouse, C. (1986). *Dalhousie Law J.*, *10*, 45; Sinclair, M.B.W. (1987). *Law Inequality*, *5*, 33; Brett, P. (1955). *Aust. Law J.*, *29*, 321].
48. Legal traditions all over the world acknowledge that violent rages on the part of cuckolds are to be expected and excuse them to varying degrees (11, 45). The recognition that cuckolds are inclined to violence does not in itself explain why such violence should be deemed justified; the acknowledged temptations to theft, by contrast, are usually considered an argument for stiffer (deterrent) penalties. Legitimation of the cuckold's use of violence is analogous to the legitimation of self-defense and protection of property and reflects a social contract among those men who "own" women.
49. Symons, D. (1979). *The Evolution of Human Sexuality*. Oxford: Oxford University Press.
50. Age-specific divorce rates are maximal at shortest marital duration [Norton, A.J. & Moorman, J.E. (1987). *J. Marriage Fam.*, *49*, 3].
51. Homicide rates are 9 times higher in common-law unions than in legal marriages in Canada (11) and 13 times higher in Australia (33). The large number of common-law couples in U.S. spousal homicide samples [Bourdouris, J. (1971). *J. Marriage Fam.*, *33*, 667; (11, 15, 17)] suggests that a similar situation prevails in the United States, but the U.S. census does not distinguish common-law marriages. Common-law unions may be especially risky for several

reasons, including short duration, lack of commitment, children of other unions, and relative poverty. Research into their exceptional risk is needed.

52. Trivers, R.L. (1974). *Am. Zool.*, *14*, 249.
53. Slavin, M.O. (1985). *Psychoanal. Contemp. Thought*, *8*, 407.
54. Evolutionary considerations suggest that human maternal attachment is likely to entail three distinct processes with different time courses: an assessment in the immediate postpartum of the prospects for a successful rearing, followed by a discriminative attachment to the child, and a gradual deepening of love and commitment proceeding over several years [M. Daly and M. Wilson, in (13), pp. 293–309].
55. Alexander, R.D. (1979). *Darwinism and Human Affairs*. Seattle: University of Washington Press.
56. Dickeman, M. (1975). *Annu. Rev. Ecol. Syst.*, *6*, 107; Minturn, L. & Stashak, J. (1982). *Behav. Sci Res.*, *17*, 70.
57. Daly, M. & Wilson, M. (1984). In G. Hausfater and S.B. Hrdy (Eds.), *Infanticide* (pp. 487–502). Hawthorne, NY: Aldine de Gruyter.
58. Bugos, P. & McCarthy, L. *ibid.*, pp. 503–520.
59. Andersson, M., Wiklund, C.G. & H. Rundgren. (1980). *Anim. Behav.*, *28*, 536; Patterson, T.L., Petrinovich, L. & James, D.K. (1980). *Behav. Ecol. Sociobiol*, *7*, 227; Pressley, P.H. (1981). *Evolution*, *35*, 282.
60. Daly, M. & Wilson, M. (1982). *Ethol. Sociobiol.*, *3*, 69.
61. Pillemer, K.A. & Wolf. R.S. (Eds.) (1986). *Elder Abuse*. Dover, MA: Auburn House.
62. Corder, B.F., Ball, B.C., Haizlip, T.M., Rollins, R. & Beaumont, R. (1976). *Am. J. Psychiatry*, *133*, 957; Russell, D.H. (1984). *Int. J. Offender Ther. Comp. Criminol.*, *28*, 177.
63. Freud, S. (1931). *Int. Z. Psychoanal.*, *17*, 317.
64. Blurton Jones, N.G. & da Costa, E. (1987). *Ethol. Sociobiol.*, *8*, 135.
65. Freud, S. (1922). In J. Strachey, Transl. and Ed., *The Standard Edition of the Complete Psychological Works of Sigmund Freud*, vol. 18. London: Hogarth.
66. Daly, M. & Wilson, M. (in press). *J. Pers.*
67. Symons, D. in (13), pp. 121–146; Barkow, J.H. (1984). *J. Anthropol. Res.*, *40*, 367; Cosmides, L. (1985). Thesis, Harvard University, Cambridge, MA; Tooby, J. & DeVore, I. (1987). In W.G. Kinzey (Ed.), *The Evolution of Human Behavior: Primate Models* (pp. 183–237). Albany: State University of New York Press.
68. Supported by grants from the Harry Frank Guggenheim Foundation, Health and Welfare Canada, the Natural Sciences and Engineering Research Council of Canada, and the Social Sciences & Humanities Research Council of Canada. We thank M.W. Swanson, J. Bannon, and R. Hislop for access to Detroit homicide data, and J. Lacroix and C. McKie for access to Canadian homicide data. We also thank N. Chagnon, L. Cosmides, C. LaFramboise, P. Strahlendorf, D. Symons, N. Thornhill, R. Thornhill, and J. Tooby for critical comments on the manuscript.

8 The sociobiology of sociopathy: An integrated evolutionary model

Linda Mealey
*Department of Psychology, College of St. Benedict, St. Joseph,
MN 56374.*[1]
Electronic mail: lmealey@psy.ug.edu.au

Abstract: Sociopaths are "outstanding" members of society in two senses: politically, they draw our attention because of the inordinate amount of crime they commit, and psychologically, they hold our fascination because most of us cannot fathom the cold, detached way they repeatedly harm and manipulate others. Proximate explanations from behavior genetics, child development, personality theory, learning theory and social psychology describe a complex interaction of genetic and physiological risk factors with demographic and micro environmental variables that predispose a portion of the population to chronic antisocial behavior. More recent, evolutionary and game theoretic models have tried to present an ultimate explanation of sociopathy as thc expression of a frequency-dependent life strategy which is selected in dynamic equilibrium, in response to certain varying environmental circumstances. This paper tries to integrate the proximate, developmental models with the ultimate, evolutionary ones, suggesting that two developmentally different etiologies of sociopathy emerge from two different evolutionary mechanisms. Social strategies for minimizing the incidence of sociopathic behavior in modern society should consider the two different etiologies and the factors that contribute to them.

Sociopaths, who comprise only 3%–4% of the male population and less than 1% of the female population (Davison & Neale 1994; Robins et al. 1991; Strauss & Lahey 1984), are thought to account for approximately 20% of the United States prison population (Hare 1993) and between 33% and 80% of the population of chronic criminal offenders (Hare 1980; Harpending & Sobus 1987; Mednick et al. 1977). Furthermore, whereas the "typical" U.S. burglar is estimated to have committed a median five crimes per year before being

133

apprehended, chronic offenders—those most likely to be sociopaths—report committing upward of 50 crimes per year and sometimes as many as two or three hundred (Blumstein & Cohen 1987). Collectively these individuals are thought to account for over 50% of all crimes in the U.S. (Hare 1993; Loeber 1982; Mednick et al. 1987).

Whether criminal or not, sociopaths typically exhibit what is generally considered to be irresponsible and unreliable behavior; their attributes include egocentrism, an inability to form lasting personal commitments and a marked degree of impulsivity. Underlying a superficial veneer of sociability and charm, sociopaths are characterized by a deficit of the social emotions (love, shame, guilt, empathy, and remorse). On the other hand, they are not intellectually handicapped, and are often able to deceive and manipulate others through elaborate scams and ruses, or by committing crimes that rely on the trust and cooperation of others, such as fraud, bigamy, and embezzlement. The sociopath is "aware of the discrepancy between his behavior and societal expectations, but he seems to be neither guided by the possibility of such a discrepancy nor disturbed by its occurrence" (Widom 1976a, p. 614). This cold-hearted and selfish approach to human interaction at one time garnered for sociopathy the moniker "moral insanity" (Davison & Neale 1994; McCord 1983).

Sociopaths are also sometimes known as psychopaths or antisocial personalities. Unfortunately, the literature reflects varied uses of these three terms (Eysenck 1987; Feldman 1977; Hare 1970; McCord 1983; Wolf 1987). Some authors use one term or another as a categorical label, as in psychiatric diagnosis or in defining distinct personality "types"; an example is the "antisocial personality" disorder described in the Diagnostic and Statistical Manual of the American Psychiatric Association (1987). Other authors use the terms to refer to individuals who exhibit, to a large degree, a set of behaviors or personality attributes that are found in a continuous, normal distribution among the population at large; an example of such usage is "sociopathy" as defined by high scores on all three scales of the Eysenck Personality Questionnaire: extraversion, neuroticism, and psychoticism (Eysenck 1977; 1987).

Other authors make a distinction between "simple" and "hostile" (Allen et al. 1971), or "primary" and "secondary" psychopaths or sociopaths (Fagan & Lira 1980). These authors reserve the term "simple" or "primary" for those individuals characterized by a complete lack of the social emotions; individuals who exhibit antisocial behavior in the absence of this emotional deficit are called "hostile" or "secondary" psychopaths or sociopaths, or even "pseudo-psychopaths" (McCord 1983). Other authors also make a typological distinction, using the term "psychopath" to refer to antisocial individuals who are of relatively high intelligence and middle to upper socioeconomic status and who express their aberrant behavior in impressive and sometimes socially skilled behavior which may or may not be criminal, such as insider trading on the stock market (Bartol 1984). These authors reserve the term "sociopath" for those antisocial persons who have relatively low intelligence and social skills or who come from the lower socioeconomic stratum and express their antisocial nature in the repeated commission of violent crimes or crimes of property.

I will begin by using the single term "sociopath" inclusively. However, by the end of the paper I hope to convince the reader that the distinction between primary and secondary sociopaths is an important one because there are two different etiological paths to sociopathy, with differing implications for prevention and treatment.

My basic premise is that sociopaths are designed for the successful execution of social deception and that they are the product of evolutionary pressures which, through a complex interaction of environmental and genetic factors, lead some individuals to pursue a life strategy of manipulative and predatory social interactions. On the basis of game theoretic models this strategy is to be expected in the population at relatively low frequencies in a demographic pattern consistent with what we see in contemporary societies. This strategy is also expected to appear preferentially under certain social, environmental, and developmental circumstances which I hope to delineate.

In an effort to present an integrated model, I will use a variety of arguments and data from the literature in sociobiology, game theory, behavior genetics, child psychology, personality theory, learning theory, and social psychology. I will argue that: (1) there is a genetic predisposition underlying sociopathy, which is normally distributed in the population; (2) as the result of selection to fill a small, frequency-dependent, evolutionary niche, a small fixed percentage of individuals—those at the extreme of this continuum—will be deemed "morally insane" in any culture; (3) a variable percentage of individuals who are less extreme on the continuum will sometimes, in response to environmental conditions during their early development, pursue a life strategy that is similar to that of their "morally insane" colleagues; and (4) a subclinical manifestation of this underlying genetic continuum is evident in many of us, becoming apparent only at those times when immediate environmental circumstances make an antisocial strategy more profitable than a prosocial one.

1. THE MODEL

1.1. The Evolutionary Role of Emotion

As the presenting, almost defining characteristic of sociopaths is their apparent lack of sincere social emotions in the absence of any other deficit such as mental retardation or autism (Hare 1980), it seems appropriate to begin with an examination of some current models of emotion.

Plutchik (1980) put forth an evolutionary model of emotion in which he posits eight basic or "primary" emotions (such as fear, anger, and disgust) which predate human evolution and are clearly related to survival.[2] According to the model, everyone (including sociopaths) experiences these primary emotions, which are cross-cultural and instinctively programmed. "Secondary" and "tertiary" emotions, on the other hand, are more complex, specifically human, cognitive interpretations of varying combinations and intensities of the primary emotions.[3] Because they are partly dependent upon learning and socialization, secondary emotions, unlike primary emotions, can vary across individuals and cultures. Thus, the social emotions (such as shame, guilt, sympathy, and love), which are secondary emotions, can be expected to exhibit greater variability.

Griffiths (1990) points out that most of the important features of emotion argue for an evolutionary design: emotions are generally involuntary, and are often "intrusive" (p. 176); they cause rapid, coordinated changes in the skeletal/muscular system, facial expression, vocalization, and the autonomic nervous system; they are to a large extent innate, or at least "prepared" (see Seligman 1970); and they do not seem as responsive to new information about the environment as do beliefs. Griffiths argues that emotional responses to stimuli (he calls them "affect-programs" after Ekman 1971) are information-ally encapsulated, complex, organized reflexes, which are "adaptive responses to events that have a particular ecological significance for the organism" (p. 183). That is, they are likely to be highly specialized reflexive responses elicited spontaneously by the presence of certain critical stimuli, regardless of the presence of possible mediating contextual cues or cognitive assessments.

Nesse (1990) likewise posits an evolutionary model in which emotions are "specialized modes of operation, shaped by natural selection, to adjust the physiological, psychological, and behavioral parameters of the organism in ways that increase its capacity and tendency to respond to the threats and opportunities characteristic of specific kinds of situations" (p. 268). He attributes a particular role to the social emotions, a role he couches in the language of reciprocity and game theory. Presenting a classic Prisoner's Dilemma matrix, he notes which emotions would be likely to be associated with the outcomes of each of the four cells: when both players cooperate, they experience friendship, love, obligation, or pride; when both cheat or defect, they feel rejection and hatred; when one player cooperates and the other defects, the cooperator feels anger and the defector feels anxiety and guilt.

Given that these emotions are experienced *after* a behavioral choice is made, how could they possibly be adaptive? Nesse's explanation is based on the models of Frank (1988) and Hirshleifer (1987), which posit that ex post facto feelings lead to behavioral expressions that are read by others and can be used to judge a person's likely future behavior. To the extent that the phenomenological experience of emotion serves to direct a person's future behavior (positive emotions reinforce the preceding behavior whereas negative emotions punish and, therefore, discourage repetition of the behavior), the outward expression of emotion will serve as a reliable indicator to others of how a person is likely to behave in the future. Indeed, that there exist reliable, uncontrollable outward expressions of these inner experiences at all suggests that the expressions must be serving a communicative function (Dimberg 1988).

If, however, as in the case of the Prisoner's Dilemma, the most rational strategy is to be selfish and defect, why should the positive (reinforcing) emotions follow mutual cooperation rather than the seemingly more adaptive behavior of defection? Here lies the role of reputation. If a player is known, through direct experience or social reputation, always to play the "rational" move and defect, then in a group where repeated interactions occur and individuals are free to form their own associations, no player will choose to play with the known defector, who will thus no longer be provided the opportunity for any kind of gain—cooperative or exploitative. To avoid this social "shunning" based on reputation[4] and hence, to be able to profit at all from long-term social interaction, players must be able to build a reputation for cooperation. To do so, most of them must in fact, reliably cooperate, despite the fact that cooperation is not the "rational" choice for the short term. Frank (1988) and Hirshleifer (1987) suggest that the social emotions have thus evolved as "commitment devices" (Frank) or "guarantors of threats and promises" (Hirshleifer): they cause positive or negative feelings that act as reinforcers or punishers, molding our behavior in a way that is not economically rational for the short term but profitable and adaptive in situations where encounters are frequent and reputation is important.

Frank (1988) presents data from a variety of studies suggesting that people do often behave irrationally (emotionally) in many dyadic and triadic inter-actions—sometimes even when it is clear that there will be no future opportunity to interact again with the same partner. These studies support the suggestion that in social situations, one's emotional response will often prevail over logic, the reason being that such behavior is, in the long run, adaptive under conditions when one's reputation can follow or precede one. (See also Alexander 1987; Anawalt 1986; Axelrod 1986; Caldwell 1986; Dugatkin 1992; Farrington 1982; Frank et al. 1993; and Irons 1991 for more on the role of reputation.)

According to these models, emotion serves both as a motivator of adaptive behavior and as a type of communication: the phenomenological and physio-logical experience of emotion rewards, punishes, and motivates the individual toward or away from certain types of stimuli and social interactions, whereas the outward manifestations of emotion communicate probable intentions to others.

Once such reliable communicative mechanisms have evolved, however, when communication of intent precedes interaction, or when one's reputation precedes one, the conditions of interaction become vulnerable to deception through false signaling or advance deployment of enhanced reputation (e.g., Caldwell 1986). Those who use a deceptive strategy and defect after signaling cooperation are usually referred to as "cheaters," and, as many authors have pointed out (e.g., Alexander 1987; Dennett 1988; Quiatt 1988; Trivers 1971), the presence of cheaters can lead to a coevolutionary "arms race" in which potential cooperators evolve fine-tuned sensitivities to likely evidence or cues of deception, while potential cheaters evolve equally fine-tuned abilities to hide those cues.[5]

As long as evolutionary pressures for emotions as reliable communication and commitment devices leading to long-term, cooperative strategies coexist with counter-pressures for cheating, deception, and "rational" short-term selfishness, a mixture of phenotypes will result, such that some sort of statistical equilibrium will be approached. Cheating should thus be expected to be maintained as a low-level, frequency-dependent strategy, in dynamic equilibrium with changes in the environment which exist as counter-pressures against its success. This type of dynamic process has been modeled extensively by evolutionary biologists who use game theory: the topic I turn to next.

1.2. Game Theory and Evolutionarily Stable Strategies

Game theory was first introduced into the literature of evolutionary biology by Richard Lewontin (1961), who applied it to the analysis of speciation and extinction events. It was later taken up in earnest by John Maynard Smith and colleagues (e.g. Maynard Smith 1978; 1974; Maynard Smith & Price 1973 [See also Maynard Smith: "Game Theory and the Evolution of Behaviour" *BBS* 7(1) 1984.]) who used it to model contests between individuals. Maynard Smith showed that the "evolutionarily stable strategies" (ESSs) that could emerge in such contests included individuals' use of mixed, as well as fixed, strategies. Alexander (1986) writes: "It would be the worst of all strategies to enter the competition and cooperativeness of social life, in which others are prepared to alter their responses, with only preprogrammed behaviors" (p. 171).

The maintenance of mixed ESSs in a population can theoretically be accomplished in at least four ways (after Buss 1991): (1) through genetically based, individual differences in the use of single strategies (such that each individual, in direct relation to genotype, consistently uses the same strategy in every situation); (2) through statistical use by all individuals of a species-wide, genetically fixed, optimum mix of strategies (whereby every individual uses the same statistical mix of strategies, but does so randomly and unpredictably in relation to the situation); (3) through species-wide use by all individuals of a mix of environmentally contingent strategies (such that every individual uses every strategy, but predictably uses each according to circumstances); (4)

through the developmentally contingent use of single strategies by individuals (such that each individual has an initial potential to use every type of strategy but, after exposure to certain environmental stimuli in the course of development, is phenotypically canalized from that point on to use only a fraction of the possible strategies). To Buss's fourth mechanism can be added a differential effect of genotype on developmental response to the environment, thus adding another mechanism: (5) genetically based individual differences in response to the environment, resulting in differential use by individuals of environmentally-contingent strategies (such that individuals of differing genotypes respond differently to environmental stimuli in the course of development and are thus canalized to produce a different set of limited strategies given the same later conditions).

Following the leads of Cohen & Machalek (1988); Harpending & Sobus (1987); Kenrick et al. (1983); Kofoed & MacMillan (1986); and MacMillan & Kofoed (1984), I would like to suggest an evolutionary model in which sociopaths are a type of cheater-defector in our society of mixed-strategy interactionists. I will be arguing that sociopathy appears in two forms, according to mechanisms 1 and 5 (above): one version that is the outcome of frequency-dependent, genetically based individual differences in use of a single (antisocial) strategy (which I will refer to a "primary sociopathy") and another that is the outcome of individual differences in developmental response to the environment, resulting in the differential use of cooperative or deceptive social strategies (which I will refer to as "secondary sociopathy"). To support this model, I will provide evidence that there are predictable differences in the use of cheating strategies across individuals, across environments, and within individuals across environments; this evidence will integrate findings from the fields of behavior genetics, child psychology, personality theory, learning theory, and social psychology.

2. THE EVIDENCE

2.1. Behavior Genetics

For decades, evidence has been accumulating that both criminality and sociopathy have a substantial heritable component, and that this heritable component is to a large extent overlapping; that is, the heritable attributes that contribute to criminal behavior seem to be the same as those which contribute to sociopathy. Although there is no one-to-one correspondence between those individuals identified as criminals and those identified as sociopaths (indeed, the definitions of both vary from study to study), it is clear that these two sets of individuals share a variety of characteristics and that a subset of individuals share both labels (Ellis 1990b; Gottesman & Goldsmith 1993; Moffitt 1987; Robins et al. 1991).

2.1.1. Studies of criminal behavior

The behavior-genetic literature on criminal behavior suggests a substantial effect of heredity across several cultures.[6] Christiansen (1977a; 1977b), Cloninger & Gottesman (1987), Eysenck & Gudjonsson (1989), Raine (1993) and Wilson & Herrnstein (1985) review studies of twins which, taken as a whole, suggest a heritability of approximately 0.60 for repeated commission of crimes of property. (Heritability is a measure of the proportion of variance of a trait, within a population, that can be explained by genetic variability within that population; it thus ranges theoretically from 0.00 to 1.00, with the remaining population variance explained by variance in individuals' environment.) Adoption studies (reviewed in Cloninger & Gottesman 1987; Eysenck & Gudjonsson 1989; Hutchings & Mednick 1977; Mednick & Finello 1983; Mednick et al. 1987; Raine 1993; and Wilson & Herrnstein 1985) arrive at a similar conclusion.[7]

Several adoption studies were also able to demonstrate significant interactive effects not discriminable using the twin methodology. Cadoret et al. (1983); Crowe (1972; 1974); Mednick & Finello (1983); and Mednick et al. (1984) report significant gene–environment interactions such that adoptive children with both a genetic risk (criminal biological parent) and an environmental risk (criminality, psychiatric illness, or other severe behavioral disturbance in an adoptive parent) have a far greater risk of expressing criminal behavior than do adoptees with no such risk or only one risk factor, and that increased risk is more than simply an additive effect of both risk factors. In addition, Baker et al. (1989) report an interaction based on sex, in which females are more likely to transmit a genetic risk to their offspring than are males.

2.1.2. Studies of sociopathy

The literature on sociopathy suggests a pattern similar to that on criminality: Cadoret (1978); Cadoret & Cain (1980); Cadoret & Stewart (1991); Cadoret et al. (1987); Crowe (1974); and Schulsinger (1972) demonstrate a substantial heritability to sociopathy; Cadoret et al. (1990) found a gene–environment interaction similar to the one found for criminal behavior; and Cadoret & Cain (1980; 1981) found an interaction involving sex, such that male adoptees were more sensitive to the influence of environmental risk factors than were female adoptees.

The similarity of the patterns described in these two domains is to some extent due to the fact that the diagnosis of sociopathy is often based in part upon the existence of criminal activity in a subject's life history. On the other hand consider the following facts: (1) criminal behavior and other aspects of sociopathy are correlated (Cadoret et al. 1983; Cloninger & Gottesman 1987; Eysenck 1977; Morrison & Stewart 1971; Patterson et al. 1989; Wolf 1987); (2)

criminal activity is found with increased frequency among the adopted-away children of sociopaths (Moffitt 1987); (3) sociopathy is found with increased frequency among the adopted-away children of criminals (Cadoret & Stewart 1991; Cadoret et al. 1990). This all suggests that criminality and sociopathy may share some common heritable factors. For this reason, early researchers and clinicians (e.g. Cadoret 1978; Schulsinger 1972) suggested using the term "antisocial spectrum" to incorporate a variety of phenotypes considered likely to be manifestations of closely related genotypes.[8] The existence of this spectrum suggests a multifactorial, probably polygenic, basis for sociopathy and its related phenotypes. Using an analogy to "g," [See Jensen: "The Nature of the Black–White Difference on Various Psychometric Tests" *BBS* 8(2) 1985.] which is often used to refer to the common factor underlying the positive correlations between various aptitude measures, Rowe (1986) and Rowe & Rodgers (1989) use "d" to refer to the common factor underlying the various expressions of social deviance.

2.1.3. Sex differences and the "two-threshold" model

Cloninger put forth a "two-threshold" polygenic model) to account for both the sex difference in sociopathy and its spectral nature (Cloninger et al. 1975; 1978). According to the model, sociopaths are individuals on the extreme end of a normal distribution whose genetic component is (1) polygenic and (2) to a large degree, sex-limited. (Sex-limited genes, not to be confused with sex-linked genes, are those which are located on the autosomes of both sexes but are triggered into expression only within the chemical/hormonal microenvironment of one sex or the other. Common examples include beard and mustache growth in men, and breast and hip development in women.) If a large number of the many genes underlying sociopathy are triggered by testosterone or some other androgen, many more men than women will pass the threshold of the required number of *active* genes necessary for its outward expression.

According to the two-threshold model, those females who *do* express the trait must have a greater overall "dose" or "genetic load" (i.e., they are further out in the extreme of the normal distribution of genotypes) than most of the males who express the trait. This proposition has been supported by data showing that, in addition to the greater overall risk for males as opposed to females, there is also a greater risk for the offspring (and other relatives) of female sociopaths as compared to the offspring (and other relatives) of male sociopaths. This phenomenon cannot be accounted for either by sex linkage or by the differential experiences of the sexes.

Besides providing a proximate explanation for the greater incidence of male sociopathy and crime, the two-threshold model also explains on a proximate level the finding that males are more susceptible to environmental influences than females. Somewhat paradoxically, although a male will express sociopathy at a lower "genetic dose" than is required for expression in a female, the *heritability* of the trait is greater for females, meaning that the environmental component of the variance is greater for males.[9]

The two-threshold model thus explains in a proximate sense what sociobiologists would predict from a more ultimate perspective. The fact that males are more susceptible than females to the environmental conditions of their early years fits well with sociobiological theory in that the greater variance in male reproductive capacity makes their "choice" of life strategy somewhat more risky and therefore more subject to selective pressures (Buss 1988; Mealey & Segal 1993; Symons 1979). Sociobiological reasoning thus leads to the postulate that males should be more sensitive to environmental changes that (1) trigger environmentally contingent or developmentally canalized life history strategies or (2) are stimuli for which genetically based individual differences in response thresholds have evolved. (Recall mechanisms 3, 4, and 5 for the maintenance of mixed strategy ESSs in a population.)

If the evolutionary models apply, then when, specifically, would sociopathy be the best available strategy? What would be the environmental cues that, especially for boys, would trigger its development? To answer these questions, I turn to the child psychology literature, with a special focus on studies of life history strategies, delinquency, and moral development.

2.2. Child Psychology

2.2.1. Life history strategies

Beginning with Draper and Harpending's now-classic 1982 paper on the relationship between father absence and reproductive strategy in adolescents, there has been an increasing effort to view development as the unfolding of a particular life strategy in response to evolutionarily relevant environmental cues (Belsky et al. 1991; Crawford & Anderson 1989; Draper & Belsky 1990; Draper & Harpending 1982; Gangestad & Simpson 1990; MacDonald 1988; Mealey 1990; Mealey & Segal 1993; Moffitt et al. 1992; Surbey 1987). These models are based either implicitly or explicitly on the assumption that there are multiple evolutionarily adaptive strategies and that the optimal strategy for particular individuals will depend both upon their genotype and their local environment. To date, most developmental life history models address variance in reproductive strategies (for example: age at menarche or first sexual activity, number of mating partners, and amount of parental investment), but this type of modeling can also be applied to the adoption of social strategies such as cheating versus cooperation.

Perhaps the most oft-mentioned factor suggested as being relevant to the development of a cheating strategy, especially in males, is being competitively disadvantaged with respect to the ability to obtain resources and mating opportunities. Theoretically, those individuals who are the least likely to outcompete other males in a status hierarchy, or to acquire mates through female choice, are the ones most likely to adopt a cheating strategy (see, e.g., Daly & Wilson 1983; Gould & Gould 1989; Thornhill & Alcock 1983, regarding nonhuman animals, and Cohen & Machalek 1988; Kenrick et al. 1983; Kofoed & MacMillan 1986; MacMillan & Kofoed 1984; Symons 1979; Thornhill & Thornhill 1992; Tooke & Camire 1991, regarding humans). In humans, competitive disadvantage could be related to a variety of factors, including age, health, physical attractiveness, intelligence, socioeconomic status, and social skills.

Criminal behavior, one kind of cheating strategy, is clearly related to these factors. Of the seven cross-cultural correlates of crime reported by Ellis (1988), three seem directly related to resource competition—large number of siblings, low socioeconomic status, and urban residency. The four others—youth, maleness, being of black racial heritage, and coming from a single-parent (or otherwise disrupted) family background—can be plausibly argued to be related to competition as well (see, e.g., Cohen & Machalek 1988; Ellis 1988: Kenrick et al. 1983; Wilson & Herrnstein 1985). Empirical data suggest that deficits in competitive ability due to psychosis (Hodgins 1992), intellectual handicap (Hodgins 1992; Moffitt & Silva 1988; Quay 1990a; Stattin & Magnusson 1991), or poor social skills (Dishion et al. 1991; Garmezy 1991; Hogan & Jones 1983; Simonian et al. 1991) are also associated with criminal behavior. Likewise, the competitive advantages conferred by high intelligence (Hirschi & Hindenlang 1977; Kandel et al. 1988; Silverton 1988; White et al. 1989; Wilson & Herrnstein 1985) or consistent external support (Garmezy 1991) can mitigate the development of criminal or delinquent behavior in those who are otherwise at high risk.

Rape and spouse abuse, other forms of cheating strategy, appear to be related to the same life-history factors as crime (Ellis 1989; 1991a; Malamuth et al. 1991; Thornhill & Thornhill 1992). In fact, Huesmann et al. (1984), Rowe and Rodgers (1989), and Rowe et al. (1989) present evidence that there is a common genetic component to the expression of sexual and nonsexual antisocial behavior. Given the overlaps between rape, battering, and criminality in terms of life history circumstances, genetics, and apparent inability to empathize with one's victim, it would be parsimonious to postulate that they might be expressions of a single sociopathy spectrum. As such, these antisocial behaviors could be considered to be genetically influenced, developmentally and environmentally contingent cheating strategies, utilized when a male finds himself at a competitive disadvantage (see also Figueredo & McCloskey, unpublished manuscript).

Along these lines, MacMillan and Kofoed (1984) presented a model of male sociopathy based on the premise that sexual opportunism and manipulation are the key features driving both the individual sociopath and the evolution of sociopathy. Harpending and Sobus (1987) posited a similar basis for the evolution and behavioral manifestations of Briquet's hysteria in women, suggesting that this syndrome of promiscuity, fatalistic dependency, and attention-getting, is the female analogue, and homologue, of male sociopathy.

2.2.2. Delinquency

Childhood delinquency is a common precursor of adolescent delinquency and adult criminal and sociopathic behavior (Loeber 1982; Loeber & Dishion 1983; Loeber & Stouthamer-Loeber 1987; Patterson et al. 1989; Robins & Wish 1977); in fact, childhood conduct disorder is *a* prerequisite finding in order to diagnose adult antisocial personality (American Psychiatric Association 1987). As in the literature on adults, an important distinction is frequently made between two subtypes of conduct disorder in children: Lytton (1990), for example, distinguishes between "solitary aggressive type" and "group type"; Loeber (1990) distinguishes between "versatiles" and "property offenders"; and Strauss & Lahey (1984) distinguish between "unsocialized" and "socialized." I will argue that these subtypes are precursors of two types of adulthood antisociality (with "solitary aggressive," "versatile," or "un-socialized" types leading to primary sociopathy and "group," "property offender," or "socialized" types presaging secondary sociopathy). I will also argue that the differing life-history patterns of these two types of delinquents are reflections of two different evolutionary mechanisms for maintaining ESSs in a population: mechanism 1 and mechanism 5, respectively (see sect. 1.2).

Although more than half of juvenile delinquents outgrow their behaviour (Gottesman & Guildsmith 1993; Lytton 1993; Robins et al. 1991), the frequency of juvenile antisocial behaviors is still the best predictor of adult antisocial behavior and the earlier such behavior appears, the more likely it is to be persistent (Farrington 1986; Loeber & Stouthamer-Loeber 1987; Lytton 1990; Robins et al. 1991; Stattin & Magnusson 1991; White et al. 1990). The mean age at which adult sociopaths exhibited their first significant symptom is between 8 and 9 years; 80% of all sociopaths exhibited their first symptom by age 11 (Robins et al. 1991). Over two-thirds of eventual chronic offenders are already distinguishable from other children by kindergarten (Loeber & Stouthamer-Loeber 1987). Thus, by evaluating the environments of juvenile delinquents, we can fairly reliably reconstruct the childhood environments of adult sociopaths.

Studies of this sort consistently implicate several relevant environmental factors correlated with boyhood antisocial behavior: inconsistent discipline, parental use of punishment as opposed to rewards, disrupted family life (especially father absence, family violence, alcoholic parent, or mentally ill parent), and low socioeconomic status (Cadoret 1982; Farrington 1986; 1989; Loeber & Dishion 1983; Lytton 1990; McCord 1986; Offord et al. 1991; Patterson et al. 1989; Silverton 1988; van Dusen et al. 1983; Wilson &

Herrnstein 1985). Aside from the fact that all of these variables are more likely to exist when one or the other parent is sociopathetic, and the child, hence, genetically predisposed to sociopathy, behaviorist and social learning models of the dynamics of early parent–child interactions (to be described in sect. 2.4.2) have been fairly convincing in explaining how antisocial behaviors can be reinforced under such living conditions.

In line with the postulate that cheating strategies would most likely be used by individuals who are at a competitive disadvantage, Hartup (1989), Hogan & Jones (1983), Kandel et al. (1988), Loeber & Dishion (1983), Magid & McKelvie (1987), McGarvey et al. (1981), and Patterson et al. (1989) suggest that the common way in which high risk familial and environmental factors contribute to delinquency is by handicapping children with respect to their peers in terms of social skills, academic ability, and self-esteem. This noncompetitiveness then leads disadvantaged youths to seek alternative peer groups and social environments in which they can effectively compete (Dishion et al. 1991). If they are successful in the estimation of their new peer group, adopting this strategy may lead to "local prestige" (Rowe, personal communication) sufficient to commandeer resources, deter rivals, or gain sexual opportunities within the new referent group (see also Moffitt 1993). In other words, competitively disadvantaged youth may be trying to "make the best of a bad job" (Cohen & Machalek 1988, p. 495; Dawkins 1980, p. 344), by seeking a social environment in which they may be less handicapped or even superior.

The correlates of delinquency in girls are essentially the same as those for boys, although delinquency is less common in girls (Lytton 1990: Robins 1986; White et al. 1990). Caspi et al. (1993) found that delinquency in girls, as in boys, is arrived at via two different developmental trajectories. One pattern includes a history of antisocial behavior throughout childhood and a tendency to seek out delinquent peers; based on previous research (White et al. 1990), this life history trajectory is thought to lead to persistent antisocial behavior in adulthood. The second pattern is exhibited by girls who have few behavior problems in childhood, but who, upon reaching menarche, exhibit more and more frequent antisocial behaviors. The antisocial behavior of girls who show this latter pattern is thought to be more a product of environmental influence than that of girls who follow the first trajectory, as this pattern is selectively exhibited by girls who (a) have an early age of menarche and (b) are in coeducational school settings. These girls, upon reaching early sexual maturity, start associating with older male peers and exhibiting some of the antisocial behaviors that are more often displayed by older boys than by their younger female peers (see Maccoby 1986); girls who follow this trajectory are expected to "outgrow" their antisocial activities. Although the two subsets of delinquent girls would be difficult to differentiate using a cross-sectional methodology, in accordance with the model presented here, Caspi et al. (1993) consider their differing developmental histories to be of theoretical importance for longitudinal studies and of practical importance for early intervention (see Moffitt 1993 for a similar scenario regarding boys).

2.2.3. Moral development

Like the tendency to engage in antisocial behavior, an individual's tendency to engage in prosocial behavior seems to be fairly stable from an early age (Rushton 1982). Yet the development of individual differences in behavior has not been as well studied as the presumably universal stages of cognition that underlie changes in moral reasoning. Kohlberg's (1964) stage model of moral development, for example, ties advances in moral thinking to advances in reasoning ability and attributes individual differences largely to differences in cognitive ability. Although it is clear that both moral reasoning and moral behavior covary with age (Rushton 1982) and may do so in a manner consistent with some evolutionists' thinking (e.g., Alexander 1987), cognitive models alone cannot explain the absence of moral behavior in sociopaths, who are not intellectually handicapped with respect to the normal population.

Other developmental models posit the emergence of empathy and the other social emotions as prerequisites for moral behavior (see Zahn-Waxler & Kochanska 1988 for a review). Even very young children, it seems, are in a sense biologically prepared to learn moral behavior, in that they are selectively attentive to emotions—especially distress—in others (Hoffman 1978; Radke-Yarrow & Zahn-Waxler 1986; Zahn-Waxler & Radke-Yarrow 1982). Hoffman (1975; 1977; 1982), for example, suggests that the observation of distress in others triggers an innate "empathic distress" response in the child, even before the child has the cognitive capacity to differentiate "other" from "self". Accordingly, any instrumental behavior that serves to reduce the distress of the other also serves to relieve the vicarious distress of the child. Thus, very young children might learn to exhibit prosocial behavior long before they are able to conceptualize its effect on others.

In Hoffman's model, the motivation behind early prosocial behavior is the (egocentric) need to reduce one's own aversive feelings of arousal and distress. As the child ages, the range of cues and stimuli that can trigger the vicarious distress increase through both classical and operant conditioning. Eventually, when the child develops the cognitive ability to "role play," or take on another's perspective, empathic distress turns to "sympathetic distress," which motivates the prosocial behavior that is more likely to be interpreted as intentional, altruistic, and moral. Hoffman's model of prosocial behavior dovetails nicely with Hirshleifer's (1987) "Guarantor" and Frank's (1988) "Commitment" model of emotion (see sect. 1.1); the reduction in anxiety that follows cooperative or prosocial behavior reinforces such behavior, whereas the increase in anxiety which, through stimulus generalization, follows acts or thoughts of antisocial behavior will punish and therefore reduce those acts and thoughts.

Dienstbier (1984) reported an interesting series of studies testing the role of anxiety and emotional arousal on cheating. As expected, high arousal levels were associated with low cheating levels (and vice versa), but the subjects' *attribution* of the cause of high arousal was also important.When subjects were able to attribute their arousal to a cause *other than* the temptation to cheat, they found it much easier to cheat than when they had no other explanation for their arousal level. Subjects were also less willing to work to avoid punishment when they were able to attribute their arousal to an external cause rather than to an internal source of anxiety associated with the threat of punishment. Dienstbier concluded that when a situation is perceived to be "detection-free," one's temptation to cheat is either resisted or not, depending on the levels of anxiety *perceived to be associated with the temptation.*

The ability to act *intentionally* in either a prosocial or antisocial manner (or in the terms of game theory, cooperatively or deceptively), depends upon having reached a certain level of cognitive development at which it is possible to distinguish emotions of the self from emotions of others; that is, the child must pass from empathic responses to sympathetic responses (Dunn 1987; Hoffman 1975; 1977; 1984; Mitchell 1986; Vasek 1986). This transition begins to occur some time during the second year (Dunn 1987; 1988; Dunn et al. 1991; Hoffman 1975; 1982; Leslie 1987) when the child is beginning to develop what has come to be called a "theory of mind" (Premack & Woodruff 1978). [See also Gopnik: "How We Know Our Minds" *BBS* 16(1) 1993 and Tomasello et al.: "Cultural Learning" *BBS* 16(3) 1993.]

Having a theory of mind allows one to impute mental states (thoughts, perceptions, and feelings) not only to oneself, but also to other individuals. Humphrey (1976; 1983) suggests that this kind of awareness evolved in humans because it was a successful tool for predicting the behavior of others. Humphrey claims that the best strategists in the human social game would be those who could use a theory of mind to empathize accurately with others and thereby be able to predict the most adaptive strategy in a social interaction (Byrne & Whiten 1988 call this aptitude "Machiavellian intelligence.") [See also Whiten & Byrne: "factical Deception in Primates" *BBS* 11(2) 1988.] Humphrey's model is something of a cognitive equivalent of the evolutionary models of emotion discussed in section 1.1: they can probably be considered complementary and mutually reinforcing. With regard to sociopathy, the question is whether a strategist can be successful using only the *cognitive* tool of a theory of mind, without access to *emotional*, empathic information which, presumably, sociopaths lack (Mealey 1992). In the next section I will argue that this is exactly what a sociopath does.

2.3. Personality Theory

The models of normative moral development presented above are helpful but clearly insufficient to explain sociopathy. Although some adoption studies and most longitudinal studies report significant effects of social and environmental risk factors on delinquency and criminality, the magnitude of that risk *as a simple main effect* is rather small. Despite repeated exposure to inconsistent and confusing reinforcement and punishment, most children who grow up with these risk factors *do not* turn out to be sociopathic, whereas some children who do not experience such risk factors do. Studies have repeatedly shown that the effect of the environment is much more powerful for children at biological risk than for others. What is it that makes high risk environmental features particularly salient for those individuals who have a certain predisposing genotype?

2.3.1. The role of gene–environment interactions

Stimulated by the work of Howe and Plomin (Dunn & Plomin 1990; Plomin & Daniels 1987; Rowe 1983a; 1983b; 1990a; 1990b; Howe & Plomin 1981), evidence is accumulating that unlike what has been traditionally assumed, the most important environmental features and events that influence personal development are not those that are shared by siblings within a family (such as parenting style, socioeconomic status, and schooling), but rather are idiosyncratic events and relationships which are difficult to study systematically with traditional methods. Despite a shared home, individual children will encounter different microenvironments: their individual relationships with their parents will differ, and their experiences on a day to day, minute by minute basis will not overlap significantly. In addition, there will be some environmental differences which are *due* to genetic differences; children with different personalities, aptitudes, and body types will not only seek out different experiences (Caspi et al. 1987; Rowe 1990a; Scarr & McCartney 1983), but will also attribute different phenomenological interpretations to the same experiences (Dunn 1992; Rowe 1983a; 1990b). For these reasons, any two children will experience an (objectively) identical environment in different ways; there is, in some sense, no real validity to some of the operational measures we currently use to describe a child's environment (Plomin & Daniels 1987; Rowe & Plomin 1981; Wachs 1992).

Although this may sound discouraging for those who seek to apply psychological research to the prevention of crime and delinquency—and most such efforts have, in fact, been fairly unsuccessful (Borowiak 1989; Feldman 1977; Gottschalk et al. 1987; Patterson et al. 1989)—there are reasons for optimism. Palmer (1983) suggests that the "nothing works" conclusion is valid only in the sense that no single intervention technique will be successful across the board, and that targeting different strategies to different individuals should prove more successful. More and more studies are suggesting that there are at least two developmental pathways to delinquency and sociopathy and that we need to address them separately (Caspi et al. 1993; Dishion & Poe 1993; Lytton 1990; McCord 1993; Moffitt 1993; Patterson 1993; Quay 1990b; Simons 1993; White et al. 1990). The evolutionary model presented here makes specific predictions about the likely differential success of various intervention and prevention strategies for individuals arriving at their antisocial behavior via different paths: although individuals of dissimilar genotypes may end up with similar phenotypes, different environmental elements and experiences may be particularly salient for them. (This is a corollary of mechanism 5 for the maintenance of ESSs presented in sect. 1.2.).

As I will argue below, primary and secondary sociopathy seem to provide an excellent illustration of the development of similar phenotypes from different genotype–environment interactions. To the extent that we understand it now, primary sociopaths come from one extreme of a polygenic genetic distribution and seem to have a genotype that disposes them "to acquire and be reinforced for displaying antisociality" (Rowe 1990a, p. 122). That genotype results in a certain inborn temperament or personality coupled with a particular pattern of autonomic arousal which, together, seem to design the individual (1) to be selectively unresponsive to those environmental cues necessary for normal socialization and moral development and (2) to actively seek the more deviant and arousing stimuli within the environment. Secondary sociopaths, on the other hand, are not as genetically predisposed to their behavior; rather they are more responsive to environmental cues and risk factors, becoming sociopathic "phenocopies" (after Moffitt 1993) when the carrying capacity of the "cheater" niche grows. What are the predisposing *constitutional factors* that place some individuals at high risk?

2.3.2. The role of temperament

In a twin study, Rushton et al. (1986) found evidence of substantial heritability of self-reported measures of altruism, nurturance, aggressiveness, and empathy. Across twin pairs, altruism, nurturance, and empathy increased with age, whereas aggressiveness decreased; sex differences (in the expected direction) were found for nurturance, empathy, and aggression; for all measures, the environmental contributions were determined to be individual rather than familial. Methodological considerations do not allow full confidence in the numerical heritability estimates of this study, but Eisenberg et al. (1990) conclude that it reports true individual differences that are likely to be a result of genetic differences in temperament, specifically sociability and emotionality.

More recently, two additional twin studies have confirmed the findings of Rushton et al. Emde et al. (1992) reported significant heritabilities for empathy, behavioral inhibition, and expressions of negative affect, while Ghodsian-Carpey & Baker (1987) found significant heritabilities on four measures of aggressiveness in children. Like the Rushton et al. study, both of these studies also reported sex differences, and both confirmed the relative importance of nonshared, as opposed to shared, environmental influences.

A fourth twin study (Rowe 1986) used a different set of personality indices but went a step further in establishing the link between temperament and antisocial behavior. Howe's analysis suggests that, especially for males, the inherited factors correlated with one's genetic risk of delinquency are the same as those that lead to the temperamental attributes of anger, impulsivity, and deceitfulness ("self-serving dishonesty with people with whom a person ordinarily has affectional bonds," p. 528). It is interesting to note that although Rowe found that common genetic factors related temperament and delinquency, environmental factors related academic nonachievement with delinquency.

These findings provide evidence for the two-pathway model presented in section 1.2, in that such a gene–environment interaction (1) would create at least two possible routes to sociopathy or criminality, one primarily heritable and one less so; and (2) in terms of the latter, less heritable pathway, would set the stage for developmentally and environmentally contingent individual differences in antisocial behavior. In addition, in line with previously mentioned studies and the proposed model, the environmental factors Rowe found to be statistically significant varied within families and were more significant for males than for females.

Most of the research into the relationship between temperament, personality and sociopathy has been based on the extensive work of Hans Eysenck (summarized in Eysenck 1977 and 1983, Eysenck & Gudjonsson 1989, and Zuckerman 1989). Eysenck first postulated and then convincingly documented that sociopathy in particular and antisocial behavior in general are correlated with high scores on all three of the major personality dimensions of the Eysenck Personality Questionnaire: "extraversion" (versus introversion), "neuroticism" (versus emotional stability), and "psychoticism" (versus fluid and efficient superego functioning—not synonymous with psychotic mental illness; Zuckerman (1989) suggests that this scale would be better called "psychopathy"). All three of these dimensions exhibit substantial heritability, and since psychoticism is typically much higher in males than females, it is a likely candidate for one of the relevant sex-limited traits that fits Cloninger's two-threshold risk model explaining the sex difference in expression of sociopathy.

In trying to explain the proximate connections between temperament, delinquency, sociopathy, and criminal behavior, Eysenck and his colleagues devised the "General Arousal Theory of Criminality" (summarized in Eysenck & Gudjonsson 1989), according to which the common biological condition underlying all of these behavioral predispositions is the inheritance of a nervous system that is relatively insensitive to low levels of stimulation. Individuals with such a physiotype, it is argued, will be extraverted, impulsive, and sensation seeking, because under conditions of relatively low stimulation they find themselves at a suboptimal level of arousal; to increase their arousal, many will participate in high-risk activities such as crime (see also Farley 1986 and Gove & Wilmoth 1990). In general support of this model, Ellis (1987) performed a meta-analysis which found that both criminality and sociopathy were associated with a variety of indicators of suboptimal arousal, including childhood hyperactivity, recreational drug use, risk taking, failure to persist on tasks, and preference for wide-ranging sexual activity.

Additional confirmation of the arousal model comes from Zuckerman, who found a similar pattern of behaviors associated with his measure of sensation seeking. (The following summary is derived from Daitzman & Zuckerman 1980; Zuckerman 1979; 1983; 1984; 1985; 1990; 1991; and Zuckerman et al. 1980). In addition to seeking thrill and novelty, sensation seekers describe "a hedonistic pursuit of pleasure through extraverted activities including social drinking, parties, sex, and gambling," "an aversion to routine activities or work and to dull and boring people," and "a restlessness in an unchanging environment" (Zuckerman et al. 1980, p. 189). In college students, sensation seeking is correlated with the Pd (Psychopathic Deviate) scale of the Minnesota Multiphasic Personality Inventory; among prisoners it can be used to distinguish primary psychopaths from secondary psychopaths and non-psychopathic criminals (see also Fagan & Lira 1980). Zuckerman also shows that sensation seeking as a temperament appears at an early age (3–4 years), exhibits a high degree of heritability, correlates negatively with age in adults, and exhibits sex differences, with higher scores more often in males. Because it shows a relationship with both sex and age, sensation seeking (and its presumed underlying hypoarousal) may also be a good candidate for a trait that can explain the distribution and expression of sociopathy (see also Baldwin 1990).

Gray (1982; 1987), and Cloninger (Cloninger 1987a; Cloninger et al. 1993) have proposed updated versions of the Eysenck model in which the three personality factors are rotated and renamed to more clearly correspond to known neural circuitry. Gray names the three systems: the approach or behavioral activation system, the behavioral inhibition system, and the fight/flight system, Cloninger names them "novelty-seeking," "harm-avoidance," and "reward-dependence". The three factors explain the same variance in personality as Eysenck's original factors and have been shown to be independent and highly heritable (Cloninger 1987a). In addition to mapping more closely to known neural systems, these three factors are also proposed to correspond to differential activity of three neurochemicals: dopamine for behavioral activation (or novelty seeking), serotonin for behavioral inhibition (or harm avoidance), and norepinephrine for fight/flight (or reward dependence); see Charney et al. 1990; Cloninger 1987a; Depue & Spoont 1986; Eysenck 1990; and Raine 1993 for partial reviews.

2.3.3. The role of physiology

Using Cloninger's terminology sociopaths are individuals who are high on novelty seeking, low on harm avoidance, and low on reward dependence. Thus, we should expect them to be high on measures of dopamine activity, low on measures of serotonin activity, and low on measures of norepinephrine activity; data suggest that they are.

Zuckerman (1989) reports that sensation seeking is negatively correlated with levels of dopamine-beta-hydroxylase (DBH), the enzyme that breaks down dopamine, and that extremely low levels of DBH are associated with undersocialized conduct disorder and psychopathy. With respect to the two-pathway model, boys with socialized conduct disorder (those with fewer, later-appearing symptoms and who are posited to be at risk for secondary, as opposed to primary, sociopathy) had high levels of DBH.

In addition, extraverts and delinquents are reported to have lower than average levels of adrenaline (epinephrine) and norepinephrine under baseline circumstances; Magnusson (1985, as cited by Zuckerman 1989) reports that urinary epinephrine measures of boys at age 13 significantly predicted criminality at ages 18–25. High sensation seekers, criminals, and other individuals scoring high on measures of impulsivity and aggression also have significantly lower levels than others of the serotonin metabolite, 5-HIAA (Brown et al. 1982; Brown et al. 1979; Depue & Spoont 1986; Kruesi et al. 1992; Muhlbauer 1985; Haine 1993; Zuckerman 1989; 1990). These are not small effects: Raine (1993) reports an average effect size (the difference between groups divided by the standard deviation) for serotonin of 0.75; and for norepinephrine of 0.41; Brown et al. (1979) reported that 80% of the variance in aggression scores of their sample was explained by levels of 5-HIAA *alone*; Kruesi et al. reported that knowing 5-HIAA levels increased the explained variance of aggression *at a two year follow up* from 65% (using clinical measures only) to 91% (clinical measures plus 5-HIAA measures).

Levels of monoamine oxidase (MAO)—an enzyme that breaks down the neurotransmitters serotonin, dopamine, epinephrine, and norepinephrine—are also low in antisocial and sensation-seeking individuals (Ellis 1991b; Zuckerman 1989). Individual differences in platelet MAO appear shortly after birth and are stable (Raine 1993; Zuckerman 1989; 1990); Zuckerman reports an estimated heritability of 0.86. Recently, a mutant version of the gene coding for MAO-A, the version of MAO specific to serotonin, has been identified in an extended family in which the males show a history of repeated, unexplained outbursts of aggressive behavior (Brunner et al. 1993; Morell 1993); urinalysis indicated that the MAO-A is not functioning normally in the affected men.

Results of psychophysiological studies also report significant differences between sociopaths and others. Reviews of this literature can be found in Eysenck & Gudjonsson (1989), Mednick et al. (1987), Haine (1989), Haine (1993), Raine & Dunkin (1990), Trasler (1987), and Zuckerman (1990).

Among the findings are: high sensation seekers and sociopaths are more likely than lows and normals to show orienting responses to novel stimuli of moderate intensity, whereas lows and normals are more likely to show defensive or startle responses; criminals and delinquents tend to exhibit a slower alpha (resting) frequency in their electroencephalogram (EEG) than age-matched controls; high sensation seekers and delinquents differ from lows and nondelinquents in the amplitude and shape of cortical evoked potentials; extraverts and sociopaths show less physiological arousal than introverts and normals in response to threats of pain or punishment and more tolerance of actual pain or punishment; and delinquents (though not necessarily adult criminals) tend to have a lower baseline heart rate than nondelinquents.

The importance of the role of these psychophysiological factors as significant causes, not just correlates, of sociopathy is strengthened by evidence that (a) these measures of autonomic reactivity are just as heritable as the temperament with which they are associated (Gabbay 1992; Zuckerman 1989), and that (b) the same physiological variables that differentiate identified sociopaths, delinquents, and criminals from others can also significantly predict later levels of antisocial behavior in unselected individuals (Loeb & Mednick 1977 using skin conductance; Raine et al. 1990a using EEG, heart rate, and skin conductance; Raine et al. 1990b using evoked potentials; Satterfeld 1987 using EEG; and Volavka et al. 1984 using EEG). As for the reports on neurochemistry, these effects are not small; Raine (1993) reports that for heart rate, the average effect size across ten studies was 0.84.

Another important physiological variable in the distribution of sociopathic behavior is testosterone. Testosterone (or one of its derivatives) is a likely trigger for the sex-limited activation of genes required by the two-threshold model presented earlier. The mechanism of action of steroid hormones is to enter the nucleus of the cell and interact with the chromosomes, regulating gene expression. This differential activity of the genes leads to some of the individual, age, and sex differences we see in temperament, specifically, psychoticism, aggression, impulsivity, sensation-seeking, nurturance, and empathy (Ellis 1991b; Zuckerman 1984; 1985; 1991; Zuckerman et al. 1980). Variation in testosterone levels also parallels the age variation in the expression of sociopathic behavior and is correlated with such behavior in adolescent and adult males (Archer 1991; Dabbs & Morris 1990; Daitzman & Zuckerman 1980; Ellis & Coontz 1990; Gladue 1991; Olweus 1986; 1987; Rubin 1987; Schalling 1981; Susman et al. 1987; Udry 1990; Zuckerman 1985). Testosterone is thus likely to play a dual role in the development of sociopathy, just as it does in the development of other sex differences: one as an organizer (affecting traits) and one as an activator (affecting states).

Udry (Drigotas & Udry 1993; Halpern et al. 1993), unable to replicate his own 1990 study suggesting an activating effect of testosterone, has suggested that the correlation between testosterone and aggression might be due to a physiosocial feedback loop; he posits that boys with high early levels of testosterone mature faster and, being bigger, are more likely to get into fights. Since levels of testosterone, adrenaline, and serotonin have been shown to fluctuate in *response to* social conditions (Archer 1991; Kalat 1992; McGuire et al. 1983; Olweus 1987; Raleigh et al. 1991; Raleigh et al. 1984; Schalling 1987), this sociophysiological interaction creates a positive feedback loop: those who start out with high levels of testosterone and sensation seeking (and low levels of adrenaline, serotonin, and MAO) are (1) more likely than others to initiate aggressive behavior and (2) more likely to experience success in dominance interactions, leading to (3) a greater probability of experiencing further increases in testosterone, which (4) further increases the likelihood of continued aggressive behavior.

Another example of a sociophysiological feedback loop comes from Dabbs and Morris (1990), who found significant correlations between testosterone levels and antisocial behavior in lower class men but not in upper class men. They explained this by positing that upper class men are more likely, because of differential socialization, to avoid individual confrontations. If this is true, it would mean that upper class men are, because of their socialization, specifically *avoiding* the types of social encounter that might raise their testosterone (and, in turn, their antisocial behavior). This interpretation is supported by the finding (in the same study) that significantly fewer upper class than lower class men had high testosterone levels. Thus, it is possible that upper class socialization may mitigate the influence of testosterone. An alternative explanation—that the aggressive behavior associated with higher testosterone levels leads to downward social mobility—also suggests a recursive sociophysiological interaction.

Raine (1988) has argued that since upper class children are less likely than lower class children to suffer the *environmental* risks predisposing one toward sociopathic behavior, when such behavior is seen in upper class individuals, it is likely to be the result of a particularly strong genetic predisposition. Evidence supporting this has been reported by three independent studies. Wadsworth (1976) found physiological indicators of hypoarousal among upper-class, but not lower-class, boys who subsequently became delinquent. Raine (Raine 1988; Raine & Dunkin 1990; Raine & Venables 1981; 1984) found indicators of hypoarousal in his upper-class antisocial subjects, but the reverse in his lower-class subjects. Satterfeld (1987) found that of his lower-class subjects, those in a biologial high-risk group were seven times more likely to have been arrested than those in his control group, whereas among his middle- and upper-class subjects, the rate was 25 and 28 times, respectively. This outcome was a result of lower rates of criminal activity in the control groups of the middle- and upper-class subjects as compared to the lower-class controls; that is, almost all of those who had been arrested from the middle and upper class were biologically at high risk, but this was not true for the lower class subjects. The implications of these findings are of tremendous import, as they suggest that (1) the effect of the social environment might be considerably larger than suggested by adoption studies and (2) there might be different etiological pathways to sociopathy and therefore different optimal strategies for its prevention or remediation, depending upon what kind of social and environmental background the individual has experienced.

2.4. Learning Theory

Adoption studies show that the environment clearly plays an important role in the etiology of sociopathy, but that its effects are different for individuals of different genotypes. As mentioned in section 2.3.1, some of this difference is likely to be a result of gene–environment correlations, in that different environments are *sought* by individuals of different genotypes; some will be a result of differences in the *interpretation* of the same environment by individuals of different genotypes; and some will be a result of differences in environment *impinging* upon people *because* of differences in their genotype (e.g. discriminating parental treatment of two children differing in temperament). In nonadoptive families, gene–environment correlations will be even stronger because parents with certain personality types will provide certain environments for their children. These differential effects of environment on individuals of varying genetic risk for sociopathy become readily apparent when we examine the effect of the interaction between physiotype and conditioning on the process of socialization.

2.4.1. Conditioning

There is evidence that individuals with a hypoaroused nervous system are less sensitive than most people to the emotional expression of other individuals and to social influences in general (Eliasz & Reykowski 1986, Eysenck 1967 as cited in Patterson and Newman 1993). They are also less responsive to levels and types of stimuli that are normally used for reinforcement and punishment (Eliasz 1987); as a result, they are handicapped in learning through autonomic conditioning although they exhibit no general intellectual deficit (e.g., Eysenck 1977; Gorenstein & Newman 1980; Hare & Quinn 1971; Lytton 1990; Mednick 1977; Newman et al. 1985; Raine 1988; Ziskind et al. 1978; Zuckerman 1991). One of the posited consequences of this learning deficit is a reduced ability to be socialized by the standard techniques of reward and punishment that are used (especially in the lower classes and by uneducated parents) on young children. In particular, hypoaroused individuals have difficulty inhibiting their behavior when both reward and punishment are possible outcomes (Newman 1987; Newman & Kosson 1986; Newman et al. 1985; Patterson & Newman 1993; Zuckerman 1991); in situations when most people would experience an approach–avoidance conflict, sociopaths and extraverts are more likely to approach (see also Dienstbier 1984). Because of their high levels of sensation seeking, children with a hypoaroused nervous system will be more likely than other children to get into trouble and when they do, they will be less likely to be affected by, and learn from the consequences, whether those consequences are a direct result of their behavior or an indirect result such as parental punishment.

Despite continuing problems with operational definitions, recent research suggests that there might be distinguishable differences in learning between primary and secondary sociopaths, or children with unsocialized versus socialized conduct disorder (Gray 1987; Newman et al. 1992; Newman et al. 1993; Quay 1990b). Primary sociopaths, with their inability to experience the social emotions, exhibit deficits on tasks which typically induce anxiety in others, specifically, passive avoidance tasks, approach–avoidance tasks, and tasks involving punishment, but they can learn well under other conditions (Newman et al. 1992; Patterson & Newman 1993; Raine 1993; Raine et al. 1990b). Secondary sociopaths and extraverts, on the other hand, have normal levels of anxiety and responses to punishment, but they may be especially driven by high reward conditions (Doddy et al. 1986; Derryberry 1987; Newman et al. 1990).

Primary sociopaths, with diminished ability to experience anxiety and to form conditioned associations between antisocial behavior and the consequent punishment, will be unable to progress through the normal stages of moral development. Unlike most children who are biologically prepared to learn empathy, they are *contraprepared* to do so, and will remain egoistic—unable to acquire the social emotions empathy, shame, guilt, and love. They present at an early age with "unsocialized" conduct disorder. Secondary sociopaths, with normal emotional capacities, will present, generally at a later age, with "socialized" conduct disorder (Loeber 1993; Patterson 1993; Simons 1993). What socialization processes contribute to their development?

2.4.2. Social learning

In sect. 2.2.1, it was noted that a cheating strategy is predicted to develop when a male (especially) is competitively disadvantaged, and that criminal behavior (especially in males) is clearly related to factors associated with disadvantage. These factors are: large numbers of siblings, low socioeconomic status, urban residency, low intelligence, and poor social skills. How, in a proximate sense, do these variables contribute to the development of secondary sociopathy? Path models suggest a two-stage process involving a variety of cumulative risk factors (Dishion et al. 1991; Lueber 1993; McGarvey et al. 1981; Moffitt 1993; Patterson et al. 1991; Simons 1993; Snyder et al. 1986; Snyder & Patterson 1990).[10]

In the first stage, disrupted family life, associated with parental neglect, abuse, inconsistent discipline, and the use of punishment as opposed to rewards, is critical (Conger 1993; Feldman 1977; Luntz & Widom 1993; McCord 1986; Patterson et al. 1989; Simons 1993; Snyder et al. 1986; Wilson & Herrnstein 1985). Poor parenting provides the child with inconsistent feedback and poor models of prosocial behavior, handicapping the child in the development of appropriate social, emotional, and problem-solving skills. This pattern is found most frequently in parents who are themselves criminal, mentally disturbed, undereducated, of low intelligence, or socioeconomically deprived (Farrington 1986; McCord 1986; McGarvey et al. 1981), leading to a cross-generational cycle of increasing family dysfunction (e.g., Jaie et al. 1992; Luntz & Widom 1993).

In the second stage, children with poor social skills find themselves at a disadvantage in interactions with age mates; rejected by the popular children, they consort with one another (Dishion et al. 1991; Hartup 1989; Kandel et al. 1988; Loeber & Dishion 1983; Patterson et al. 1989; Snyder et al. 1986). In these socially unskilled peer groups, which will also include primary sociopathic or unsocialized conduct disorder children, delinquent, antisocial behavior is reinforced and new (antisocial) skills are learned (Maccoby 1986; Mofftt 1993). Antisocial behavior may then escalate in response to, or as prerequisite for, social rewards provided by the group, or as an attempt to obtain the perceived social (and tangible) rewards which often accompany such behavior (Moffitt 1993). As the focus of the socialization process moves outside the home, parental monitoring becomes more important (Conger 1993; Dishion et al. 1991; Forgatch 1991; Simons 1993; Snyder et al. 1986; Snyder & Patterson 1990), as does the availability of prosocial alternatives for the socially unskilled adolescent (Apter 1992; Farrington 1986; Moffitt 1993).

The development of secondary sociopathy appears to depend much more on environmental contributions than does primary sociopathy. Since it is secondary sociopathy which, presumably, has increased so rapidly and so recently in our culture, what can social psychologists contribute to our understanding of the sociocultural factors involved in its development?

2.5. Social Psychology

2.5.1. Machiavellianism

First, the use of antisocial strategies is not restricted to sociopaths. The majority of people who are arrested are not sociopathic and many people exhibit antisocial behavior that is infrequent enough or inoffensive enough to preclude arrest. Some antisocial behavior is even considered acceptable if it is expressed in socially approved circumstances. Person (1986), for example, relates entrepreneurism to psychopathy whereas Christie (1970) notes that people who seek to control and manipulate others often become lawyers, psychiatrists, or behavioral scientists; Jenner (1980) also claims that "subtle, cynical selfishness with a veneer of social skills is common among scientists" (p. 128).

Christie (see Christie & Geis 1970) developed a scale for measuring this subclinical variation in antisocial personality; he called it the "Machiavellianism" or "Mach" scale. One's Mach score is calculated by compiling answers to Likert-format queries of agreement or disagreement with statements like "humility not only is of no service but is actually harmful," "nature has so created men that they desire everything but are unable to attain it," and "the most important thing in life is winning." Adults who score high on the Mach scale express "a relative lack of affect in interpersonal relationships," "a lack of concern with conventional morality," "a lack of gross psychopathology," and "low ideological commitment" (Christie & Geis 1970, pp. 3–4); children who score high on Machiavellianism have lower levels of empathy than their age mates (Barnett & Thompson1984).

High Machs have an "instrumental cognitive attitude toward others" (Christie & Geis 1970, p. 277) and, because they are goal oriented as opposed to person oriented, they are more successful in face-to-face bargaining situations than low Machs. High Machs "are especially able communicators, regardless of the veracity of their message" (Kraut & Price 1976). In a related vein, high Machs, like sociopaths, are more resistant to confession after cheating than are low Machs, and they are rated as being more plausible liars (Dradley & Klohn 1987; Christic & Geis 1970); like sociopaths, high Machs are often referred to as "cool." According to Christie, "If Machiavellianism has any behavioral definition. . . self-initiated manipulation of others should be at its core" (p. 76). One can thus easily think of Machiavellianism as a low-level manifestation of sociopathy. It even shows a sex difference consistent with the two-threshold model (Christie & Geis 1970), an age pattern consistent with age variation in testosterone levels (Christie & Geis 1970), significant positive correlations with Eysenck's criticism and neuroticism scales (Allsopp et al. 1991), and correlation with serotonin levels (Madsen 1985).

In one study, Geis & Levy (1970) found that high Machs (who were thought to use an "impersonal, cognitive: rational, cool" approach with others), were much more accurate than low Machs (who were thought to use a "more personal, empathizing" approach) at assessing how other "target" individuals answered a Machiavellian attitudes questionnaire. Even more interesting is the result (from the same study) that the high Machs achieved their accuracy by using a nomothetic or actuarial strategy: they guessed that everyone was at about the average level without discriminating between individuals based on differences they had had an opportunity to observe during a previous experimental session. In addition, their errors tended to be random, which would fit with reports by Eliasz & Reykowski (1986) and Damasio et al.

(1990), who found that hypoaroused and antisocial individuals are less attentive to social and emotional cues than others. Low Machs, on the other hand, used an idiographic approach, and although they successfully differentiated between high scorers and low scorers, they grossly underestimated the scores of both, guessing at a level that was more reflective of their own scores than those of the population at large.

This study suggests two things: (1) Basing one's playing strategies on an "impersonal, cognitive, rational, cool" approach to others might be more accurate in the long run than using a "personal, empathizing" approach (*at least in those situations where cooperating long-term partnerships are not possible*) and (2) the errors made by those who use the personal, empathizing approach are of the kind more likely to result in playing the cooperation strategy when the cheating strategy would be more appropriate (rather than vice versa). Thus, the personal, empathizing approach is likely to make one susceptible to being exploited by others who use the impersonal cognitive approach; indeed, high Machs outcompete low Machs in most experimental competitive situations (Christie & Geis 1970; Terhune 1970).

As I have argued elsewhere (Mealey 1992), the common assumption that an empathy-based approach to predicting the behavior of others is better than a statistical approach is not necessarily correct; this belief may itself be an emotion-based cognitive bias. To have such a bias may be beneficial, however, for the same reason that emotional commitment biases are beneficial: in situations where *voluntary, long-term coalitions can be formed*, the personal, empathizing (and idealistic) low Machs might outperform the more impersonal, cognitive (and realistic) high Machs, since *low Machs would be more successful than high Machs in selecting a cooperator as a partner.*

Although two studies (Hare & Craigen 1974 and Widom 1976a) report on the strategy of sociopaths in Prisoner's Dilemma-type settings, in both studies the sociopaths were paired with one another; thus, we do not have a measure of the strategy sociopaths use against partners of their own choosing or in situations with random, rotating partners.[11] I would predict that in such settings, sociopaths, like Geis & Levy's high Mach subjects, would be less proficient than others in distinguishing between high and low Mach partners, and would thus be at a disadvantage in iterated games with a chosen partner; on the other hand (again like high Mach subjects), they should perform at better than average levels when playing with randomly assigned, rotating partners. Widom (1976b) found that when asked to guess how "people in general" would feel about different social situations sociopaths guessed that others would feel essentially the same way that they do, whereas control subjects guessed that others would feel differently. As in the Geis & Levy study, both groups were wrong, but in different ways: the sociopaths underestimated their differences from others, whereas the control subjects substantially overestimated their differences from others, suggesting that sociopaths (like high Machs) were using a nomothetic approach to prediction, where as controls (like low Machs) were using an idiographic approach.

Machiavellianism and the related propensity to use others in social encounters has generally been looked upon as a trait. An alternative perspective, however, acknowledges both the underlying variation in personality *and* the situational factors that are relevant to an individual's behavior at any given moment (e.g., Barber 1992). In line with mechanism 5 for maintaining ESSs (presented in sect. 1.2), Terhune (1970) says "actors bring to the situation propensities to act in a certain general way, and within the situation their propensities interact with situational characteristics to determine their specific behavior" (p. 229).[12] This brings us to the last question: beyond the constitutional and environmental variables that contribute to the development of individual differences in personality and antisocial behavior, what can social psychology tell us about the *within-individual* situational factors that encourage or discourage cheating strategies, and how can these be explained?

2.5.2. The role of mood

Although mood and emotion are not identical concepts, they are clearly related.[13] Mood might be thought of as a relative of emotion which clearly varies within individuals but is perhaps less an immediate response to concrete events and stimuli and more a generalized, short- to mid-term response to the environment. As such, the role of mood must be addressed by any model that relies so heavily on the concepts of emotion, emotionality and emotionlessness as determinants of behavior.

Positive mood and feelings of success have been demonstrated to enhance cooperative behavior (Cialdini et al. 1982; Farrington 1982; Mussen & Eisenberg-Berg 1977). If, as Nesse (1991) has argued, positive mood is a reflection not only of past success, but also of *anticipation of future success*, the facilitation of cooperation by positive mood could be seen as part of a long-term strategy by individuals who feel they can afford to pass up possible short-term gains for the sake of establishing a cooperative reputation.

Sad affect and feelings of failure can also affect strategy in social interactions. To the extent that sadness and feelings of failure follow losses of various sorts, individuals in these circumstances should be expected to be egoistic and selfish. In children, this is typically what is found (Baumann et al. 1981; Mussen & Eisenberg-Berg 1977). In some children, and more consistently in adults, on the other hand, sadness and feelings of future can facilitate prosocial behavior. Mussen & Eisenberg-Berg (1977) suggest that this is a result of a deliberate effort to enhance one's (diminished) reputation among others; Baumann et al. (1981) and Cialdini et al. (1982) suggest that it is a result of a deliberate effort to relieve negative affect based on prior experience that prosocial behavior often has a positive, self-gratifying effect.

If sadness is profound, that is, if one is depressed and experiencing the cognitive biases and selective attention associated with depression (Mineka & Sutton 1992; Nesse 1991; Sloman 1992), one would be expected to desist from all social interaction, being neither antisocial nor prosocial, but asocial (Nesse 1991; Sloman 1992). In this view, the lethargy and anhedonia associated with depression could be considered to be facultative lapses in the emotions or moods which typically motivate a person toward social interaction.

Hostility can also lead to cognitive biases and selective attention to relevant social stimuli. Dodge and Newman (1981) show that aggressiveness in boys is associated with the over-attribution of hostile intent to others. The authors conclude that such attributions lead to increased "retaliatory" aggression by the hostile individuals, fueling a cycle of true hostility and retaliation by all parties. It is also abundantly clear that anger and hostility, once expressed, do not lead to catharsis, but to amplified feelings and outward expressions of that anger (Tavris 1982).

Guilt, which often follows selfish behavior, typically results in an increase in subsequent prosocial behavior (Cialdini et al. 1982; Hoffman 1982); Hoffman calls this "reparative altruism." Guilt can easily be seen as one of Hirshleifer's (1987) or Frank's (1988) emotional commitment devices, compelling one to perform prosocial behavior as a means of reestablishing one's tarnished reputation.

Cialdini et al. (1982) also report that prosocial behavior increases after observing another's transgression. They explain this phenomenon within the context of what they call the "negative relief" model: prosocial behavior is performed as a means of alleviating negative feelings in general (including direct or vicarious guilt, sympathy, distress, anxiety or depression). Like Hoffman's, this model postulates that the reinforcing power of (relief provided by) prosocial behavior is learned during childhood.

Since guilt, anxiety, and sympathy are social emotions that primary sociopaths rarely, if ever, experience, there is no reason to expect that they might moderate their behavior so as to avoid them. On the other hand, there is no reason to expect that sociopaths do not experience fluctuations in mood (such as depression, optimism, or anger) in response to their changing evaluation of their prospects of success and failure. To the extent that we can manipulate the sociopath's mood, therefore, we might be able to influence his behavior.

2.5.3. Cultural variables

Competition, in addition to being one of the most important variables in determining long-term life strategy choices, is also one of the more important situational variables influencing the choice of immediate strategy. Competition increases the use of antisocial and Machiavellian strategies (Christie & Geis 1970) and can counteract the increase in prosocial behavior that generally results from feelings of success (Mussen & Eisenberg-Berg 1977). Some cultures encourage competitiveness more than others (Mussen & Eisenberg-Berg 1977; Shweder et al. 1987) and these differences in social values vary both temporally and crossculturally. Across both dimensions, high levels of competitiveness are associated with high crime rates (Farley 1986; Wilson & Herrnstein 1985) and Machiavellianism (Christie & Geis 1970).

High population density, an indirect form of competition, is also associated with reduced prosocial behavior (Farrington 1982) and increased antisocial behavior (Ellis 1988; Robbins et al. 1991; U.S. Department of Justice 1993; Wilson & Herrnstein 1985)—especially in males (Wachs 1992; see sect. 3.2.1 and references therein for ultimate, game theoretic explanations why this might occur; see Draper 1978; Foster 1991; Gold 1987; Siegel 1986; and Wilson & Daly 1993 for a variety of proximate explanations). Fry (1988) reports large differences in the frequency of prosocial and antisocial behaviors in two Zapotec settlements equated for a variety of socioecological variables; the one major difference—thought perhaps to be causal—was in land holdings per capita, with the higher levels of aggression found in the community with the smaller per capita land holdings.

Last, but not least, is the relatedness or similarity of the interactors to their partners in an interaction. Based on models of kin selection and inclusive fitness, individuals should be more cooperative and less deceptive when interacting with relatives who share their genes, or relatives who share investment in common descendants. Segal (1991) reported that identical twins cooperated more than fraternal twins in playing the Prisoner's Dilemma. Barber (1992) reported that responses on an altruism questionnaire were more altruistic when the questions were phrased so as to refer to relatives (as opposed to "people" in general), and that Machiavellian responses were thereby reduced. Rushton (1989; Rushton et al. 1984) presents evidence that people also cooperate more with others who are similar to them even though not genetically related. There are a variety of plausible evolutionary explanations for this behavior (see Mealey 1984; Pulliam 1982; and BBS commentary on Rushton 1989).

3. INTEGRATION, IMPLICATIONS, AND CONCLUSIONS

3.1. Integration: Sociopathy as an ESS leads to two types of sociopaths

3.1.1. Primary sociopathy

I have thus far argued that some individuals seem to have a genotype that disposes them "to acquire and be reinforced for displaying anti-sociality" (Rowe 1990a, p. 122). The genotype results in a certain inborn temperament or personality, coupled with a particular pattern of autonomic hypoarousal that, together, design the child to be selectively unresponsive to the cues necessary for normal socialization and moral development. This scenario is descriptive of mechanisms (sect. 1.2) of maintaining ESSs in the population; it describes the existence of frequency-dependent, genetically based individual differences in employment of life strategies. I accordingly suggest that there will always be *a small, cross-culturally similar, and unchanging baseline frequency of sociopaths:* a certain percentage of sociopaths—those individuals to whom I have referred as primary sociopaths—will always appear in every culture no matter what the sociocultural conditions. Those individuals will display *chronic, pathologically emotionless antisocial behavior throughout most of their lifespan and across a variety of situations,* a phenotype that is recognized (according to Robins et al. 1991, p. 259) "by every society, no matter what its economic system, and in any eras".[14] Since it is a genetically determined strategy, primary sociopaths should be *equally likely to come from all kinds of socioeconomic backgrounds*; on the other hand, since they constitute that small group of individuals whose physiotype makes them essentially impervious to the social environment *almost all sociopaths from the upper classes will be primary sociopaths.*[15]

Of course, because they are not intellectually handicapped, these individuals will progress normally in terms of cognitive development and will acquire a theory of mind. Theirs, however, will be formulated purely in instrumental terms, without access to the empathic understanding that most of us rely on so much of the time. They may become excellent predictors of others' behavior, unhandicapped by the vagaries and "intrusiveness" of emotion, acting, as do professional gamblers, solely on nomothetic laws and actuarial data rather than on hunches and feelings. In determining how to "play" in the social encounters of everyday life, they will use a pure cost–benefit approach based on immediate personal outcome with no "accounting" for the emotional reactions of others with whom they are dealing. Without love to "commit" them to cooperation, anxiety to prevent "deflection," or guilt to inspire repentance, they will remain fated to continually play for the short-term benefit in Prisoner's Dilemma.

3.1.2. Secondary sociopathy

At the same time, because changes in gene frequencies in the population would not be able to keep pace with the fast-changing parameters of social interactions, an additional, *fluctuating proportion* of sociopathy should be a result of mechanism 5 maintaining ESSs, which allows for more flexibility in the ability of the population to track the frequently dependent nature of the success of the cheating strategy. Mechanism 5 (genetically based individual difference in response to the environment, resulting in *differential use by individuals of environmentally contingent strategies*) would explain the development and distribution of what I have referred to as secondary sociopathy. Secondary sociopathy is expressed by individuals who are not extreme on the genetic sociopathy spectrum, but who, because of their exposure to environmental risk factors, pursue a strategy that involves *frequent, but not necessarily emotionless cheating.* Unlike primary sociopaths, secondary sociopaths will not necessarily exhibit chronic antisocial behavior, because their strategy choices will be *more closely tied to age, fluctuation in hormone levels, their competitive status within their referent group, and changing environmental contingencies.* Since secondary sociopathy is more closely tied to environmental factors than to genetic factors, secondary sociopaths will almost always come from lower class backgrounds and their numbers could vary substantially across cultures and time, tracking environmental conditions that favor or disfavor the use of cheating strategies.

The existence of this second etiological pathway to sociopathy explains the fact that cultural differences are correlated with differences in the overall incidence of antisocial behavior (Ellis 1988; Farley 1986; Gold 1987; Robins et al. 1991; Wilson & Herrnstein 1985). It also explains why, as the overall incidence of sociopathy increases, the discrepancy in the ratio of male to female sociopaths decreases (Robins et al. 1991): since secondary sociopathy is less heritable than primary sociopathy (according to this model), the effect of sex-limited genes (like that of all the genes contributing to the spectrum) should be less important for the development of secondary sociopathy, resulting in less of a sex difference. Based on this model, I would predict that, unlike what we find for primary sociopathy (see sect. 2.1.3), we should find *no differential heritability* between the sexes for secondary sociopathy (even though there will still be a sex difference in prevalence).

3.2. Implications of the Two-pathway Model

Terhune (1970) suggests that choice of strategy in experimental game situations (and, presumably, real-life settings as well) depends upon two things: (1) cognitive expectations regarding others (i.e., a theory of mind) and (2) motivational/emotional elements such as hopes and fears. Since primary sociopaths have a deficit in the realm of emotional motivation, they presumably act primarily upon their cognitive expectations of others; to the extent that they do act upon emotions, it is most likely to be upon mood and the primary emotions (like anger and fear) rather than upon the social and secondary emotions (like love and anxiety). Thus, the extent to which a society will be able to diminish the antisocial behavior of *primary* sociopaths will depend upon two things: (1) its influence on the sociopath's cognitive evaluation of *its own reputation* as a player in the Prisoner's Dilemma, and (2) the *primary emotion- or mood-inducing capacity* of the stimuli it utilizes in establishing the costs and benefits of prosocial versus antisocial behavior.

Manipulations of these two variables will also influence the numbers of secondary sociopaths by changing the size of the adaptive niche associated with antisocial behavior. In addition, since the development of secondary sociopathy is more influenced by the social environment than is the development of primary sociopathy, and since secondary sociopaths are not devoid of social emotions, changing patterns in the nurturing and socialization of children and in the socialization and rehabilitation of delinquents and adult criminals is an additional, viable possibility for reducing the overall prevalence of antisocial behavior.

3.2.1. Minimizing the impact of primary sociopaths: Society as a player in the Prisoner's Dilemma

Sociopaths' immediate decisions are based in part on their ability to form a theory of mind; and to use those expectations of others' behavior in a cost–benefit analysis to assess what actions are likely to be in their own self-interest. (This is true for both primary and secondary sociopaths.) The outcome of such analyses is therefore partially dependent on the sociopath's expectations of the behavior of other players in the game. I would argue that an entire society can be seen as a player and that the past behavior of that society will be used by the sociopath in forming the equivalent of a theory of mind to predict the future behavior of that society.

Like an individual player, a society will have a certain probability of detecting deception, a more-or-less accurate memory of who has cheated in the past, and a certain proclivity to retaliate or not, based upon a cheater's past reputation and current behavior. Since the sociopath is using a rational and actuarial approach to assess the costs and benefits of different behaviors, it is the actual past behavior of the society which will go into his calculations, rather than risk assessments inflated from the exaggerated fears or anxieties that most people feel in anticipation of being caught or punished. *Thus, to reduce antisocial behavior, a society must establish and enforce a reputation for high rates of detection of deception and identification of cheaters, and a willingness to retaliate.* In other words, it must establish a successful strategy of deterrence.

Game theory models by Axelrod and others have shown that the emergence, frequency, and stability of social cooperation is subject to an abundance of potential deterrent factors (Axelrod 1984; Axelrod & Dion 1988; Axelrod & Hamilton 1981; Boyd 1988; Boyd & Richerson 1992; Dugatkin & Wilson 1991; Feldman & Thomas 1987; Heckathorn 1988; Hirshleifer & Coll 1988; Nowak & Sigmund 1993; Vila & Cohen 1993). Among these are: *group size* (as it decreases, cooperation increases); *non-random association of individuals within the population* (as it increases, cooperation increases); *the probability of error in memory or recognition of an individual* (as it decreases, cooperation increases); *the effect of a loss on a cooperator* (as it decreases, cooperation increases); *the effect of a gain on a defector* (as it decreases, cooperation increases); *the frequency of punishment against defectors* (as it increases, cooperation increases); *the cost of punishment for the punished* (as it increases, cooperation increases); *and the cost of punishment for the punishers* (as it decreases, cooperation increases).[16]

Recent game-theoretic models are coming closer and closer to the complexity of real-world human social interactions on a large scale by examining the role of culture and technology in expanding society's collective memory of individual players' past behavior, broadcasting the costs and benefits of cooperation and defection, and the development and application of new socialization, deception-detection, and punishment techniques (see especially Dugatkin 1992; Hirshleifer & Rasmusen 1989; Machalek & Cohen 1991). These models begin to provide useful strategies for the real-world prediction and reduction of cheating strategies and antisocial behavior. (See also Axelrod 1986; Bartol 1984; Ellis 1990a; Eysenck & Gudjonsson 1989; Farrington 1979; Feldman 1977; Machalek & Cohen 1991; and Wilson & Herrnstein 1985 for some nonquantitative models and tests that incorporate some of these variables in their explanation of the socialization, punishment, and deterrence of crime.)

Since neither secondary nor primary sociopaths have a deficit in the ability to perform accurate cost–benefit analyses, increasing the *probabilities* of criminal detection, identification, and punishment can also reduce crime; a society must therefore establish a *reputation* for willingness to retaliate. (The National Research Council [1993] reports that a 50% increase in the *probability* of incarceration for any single crime reduces subsequent crime twice as much as does doubling incarceration *duration* [p. 294]). Harsher penalties can also be deterring, but only if they are *reliably* meted out.

Another key is in making the costs of cheating *salient*. Generally speaking, antisocial and uncooperative behaviors increase as the costs become more diffuse or removed in time, and prosocial and cooperative behaviors decrease as the benefts become more diffuse or remove in time (Bartol 1984; Low 1993; Ostrom 1990). For primary sociopaths, this is even more so, since their sensation-seeking physiotype makes them particularly unable to make decisions based on nonimmediate consequences. Although able to focus attention on interesting tasks for short periods, the sociopath cannot perform well under conditions of delayed gratification (Pulkkinen 1986) and is more motivated to avoid immediate costs than by threats or avoidance of future punishments (Christie & Geis 1970; Forth & Hare 1989; McCord 1983; Raine 1988; 1989). Costs associated with social retaliation must therefore not only be predictable, but swift, and the swiftness itself must also be predictable.

Another factor the sociopath will use to "compute" the potential value of an antisocial action is the cost–benefit ratio of the alternatives (Piliavin et al. 1986). For the sociopath, money and other immediate tangible rewards are more motivating than social reinforcers (such as praise) or promises of future payoff, and visual stimuli are more salient than auditory stimuli (Chesno & Kilmann 1975; Forth & Hare 1989; Raine 1989; Raine & Venables 1987; Raine et al. 1990b; Zuckerman 1990). Thus, alternatives to crime must be stimulating enough and rewarding enough to preferentially engage the chronically hypoaroused sensation seeker. This will be a difficult task to achieve, but it will be more successful if we can effectively distinguish primary from secondary sociopaths. Primary sociopaths, with their emotional, but not intellectual deficit, will be competent on some tasks on which secondary sociopaths, with deficits in social skills, emotion regulation and problem solving, will not. Possibilities might include: novelist, screenplay writer, stunt man, talk show host, disk jockey, explorer, treasure hunter, race car driver, or skydiving exhibitionist. Given that primary sociopaths will always be with us in low numbers, it would be a wise social investment to create—even on an individual basis, if necessary—a number of exciting, high-payoff alternatives for them, in order to minimize the number who may otherwise cause pain and destruction. Distinguishing between primary and secondary sociopaths is also critical for decisions about confinement and rehabilitation. Quinsey & Walker (1992) cite examples where recidivism rates went up for psychopaths, but down for nonpsychopaths, after they were exposed to the same kind of "treatment". Recidivism is much greater in primary sociopaths than in secondary sociopaths (Hare et al. 1992), and sometimes the only response is prolonged incapacitation (until they literally "grow out of it"). A recent international meeting of experts concluded that "treatment" programs dealing with primary sociopaths should be "less concerned with attempts to develop empathy or conscience than with intensive efforts to convince them that their current attitudes and behaviour (simply) are not in their own self-interest" (Hare 1993, p. 204).

3.2.2. Minimizing the prevalence of secondary sociopathy: Society as a socializing agent and mood setter

Given that secondary sociopaths have a different life history and are more responsive to environmental influences than primary sociopaths, social changes can be designed to minimize not only their impact, but their incidence. Loeber (1990) argues that each generation in our society is being raised with an increasing number of environmental risk factors, leading to increasing generation-wide deficits in impulse control. He makes specific suggestions to screen for high-risk children and institute early intervention, noting that different interventions are likely to be more or less effective given different risk factors in the child's or adolescent's life history (see also U.S. Department of Justice 1993).

One possible intervention is parent training (see Magid & McKelvie 1987 and Dumas et al. 1992 for review and programmatic suggestions). Laboratory experiments show that antisocial behaviors can be reduced and prosocial behaviors reinforced by appropriate use of modeling, induction, and behavioral modification technique (Feldman 1977; Gelfand & Hartmann 1982; Grusec 1982; Kochanska 1991; 1993; Mussen & Eisenberg-Berg 1977; Radke-Yarrow

& Zahn-Waxler 1986; Rushton 1982). Recent longitudinal studies in natural settings suggest that positive effects of good parenting, especially parental warmth and predictability, may be long lasting (Kochanska 1991; 1993; Kochanska & Murray 1992; McCord 1986).

The cause and effect relationship between parent behavior and child behavior, however, is not likely to be one-way. Children of different gender, temperament, and even social classes, respond differentially to different socialization techniques (Dienstbier 1984; Kochanska 1991; 1993; Kochanska & Murray 1992; Lytton & McCord 1993; Radke-Yarrow & Zahn-Waxler 1986), and, to some extent, difficult children *elicit* poor parents (Bell & Chapman 1986; Buss 1981; Eron et al. 1991; Lee & Bates 1985; Lytton 1990; Snyder & Patterson 1990). It is easy for parents of difficult children to lose heart, and in so doing, become even less effective (Patterson 1992). For example, studies cited in Landy & Peters (1992) found that mothers of aggressive children, like other mothers with a low sense of personal power, tend to give weak, ineffectual commands to their children.

This lack of "goodness of fit" between parental style and the needs of the child is probably an important factor in the exacerbation of conduct disorder (Landy & Peters 1992; Lee & Bates 1985; Moffitt 1993; Wachs 1992). Parents need help in identifying high-risk children. Then they need instruction in how to take a practical, assertive approach with them (see Garmezy 1991; Magid & McKelvie 1987), while using a more inductive, empathic approach with their other children (see Kochanska 1991, 1993; Kochanska & Murray 1992).

Social workers, health care providers, and employees of the criminal justice system also need to to be able to distinguish between children with different risk factors and life histories and to respond accordingly. Palmer (1983) argues that agents should be individually matched with each client/offender based on style and personality characteristics to prevent high Mach and sociopathic offenders from taking advantage of low Mach employees.

At a broader level, many sociocultural aspects of modern society seem to contribute to antisocial behaviors and attitudes (Moffitt 1993; National Research Council 1993). As a society gets larger and more competitive, both theoretical models (sect. 3.2.1) and empirical research (sect. 2.4.2) show that individuals become more anonymous and more Machiavellian, leading to reductions in altruism and increases in crime. Social stratification and segregation can also lead to feelings of inferiority, pessimism, and depression among the less privileged, which can in turn promote the use of alternative competitive strategies, including antisocial behavior (Magid & McKelvey 1987; Sanchez 1986; Wilson & Daly 1993).

Crime may be one response to the acquisition of an external locus of control (Haine et al. 1982) or learned helplessness. Learned helplessness and other forms of depression have been associated with reduced levels of serotonin (Traskman et al. 1981); since reduced levels of serotonin have also been shown to be related to increased aggression, it is likely that physiological changes mediate these psychological and behavioral changes. The neurochemical pathway involved in learned helplessness (identified by Petty & Sherman 1982) appears to be the same one identified by Gray (1982; 1987) and Cloninger (1987a) with mediation of behavioral inhibition/harm avoidance, and by Charney et al. (1990) with anxiety-mediated inhibition.

Crime may also function to obtain desirable resources, increase an individual's status in a local referent group, or provide the stimulation that the more privileged find in more socially acceptable physical and intellectual challenges (e.g., Apter 1992; Farley 1986; Farrington 1986; Lyng 1990; Moffitt 1993). According to Apter, "the vandal is a failed creative artist," a bored and frustrated sensation seeker who "does not have the intellectual or other skills and capacities to amuse or occupy himself" (1992, p. 198). Thus, in addition to making the costs of antisocial behavior greater, strong arguments can be made for providing early social support for those at risk, and for developing alternative, nonexploitative, sensation-seeking ventures that can meet the psychological needs of disadvantaged and low-skilled individuals.

3.3. Conclusions

A review of the literature in several areas supports the concept of two pathways to sociopathy:

1a. "Primary sociopaths" are individuals of a certain genotype, physiotype, and personality who are incapable of experiencing the secondary "social" emotions that normally contribute to behavioral motivation and inhibition; they fill the ecological niche described by game theorists as the "cheater strategy," and, as the result of frequency-dependent selection, will be found in low frequency in every society.

1b. To minimize the damage caused by primary sociopaths, the appropriate social response is to modify the criminal justice system in ways that obviously reduce the benefits and increase the costs of antisocial behavior, while simultaneously creating alternatives to crime that could satisfy the psychophysiological arousal needs of the sociopath.

2a. "Secondary sociopaths" are individuals who use an environmentally contingent, facultative cheating strategy not as clearly tied to genotype; this strategy develops in response to social and environmental conditions related to disadvantage in social competition and will thus covary (across cultures, generations, and even within an individual lifetime) with variation in immediate social circumstances.

2b. To reduce the frequency of secondary sociopathy, the appropriate social response is to implement programs that reduce social stratification, anonymity, and competition, intervene in high-risk settings with specialized parent education and support, and increase the availability of rewarding, prosocial opportunities for at-risk youth.

Since the genetics and life histories of primary and secondary sociopaths are so different, successful intervention will require differential treatment of different cases; we thus need to encourage the widespread adoption of common terminology and diagnostic criteria.

ACKNOWLEDGEMENTS

I would like to thank Mr. Rainer Link, who helped me get started on this project, and who collaborated with me on the first version and first public presentation of the model (Link & Mealey 1992). I would also like to extend thanks to the many individuals who provided useful comments during the revision process: J.D. Baldwin, David Buss, Patricia Draper, Lee Dugatkin, Lee Ellis, Hans Eysenck, David Farrington, Hill Goldsmith, Henry Harpending, James Kalat, John Loehlin, Michael McGuire, Randy Nesse, Jaak Panskepp, David Rowe, Sandra Scarr, Nancy Segal, Chuck Watson, David S. Wilson, and four anonymous *BBS* reviewers.

NOTES

1. As of January 1, 1996 Linda Mealey will be at the Dept. of Psychology, University of Queensland, Brisbane, Australia 4702. Email: lmealey@psych.uq.edu

2. Plutchik's eight primary emotions are: anger, fear, sadness, disgust, surprise, joy, acceptance, and anticipation. Others posit a few more (Izard 1977; 1991) or fewer (Ekman 1971; Panskepp 1982) but what is basically agreed is that primary emotions are those which can be found in other mammals, are hard-wired in the brain, are reflexively produced in response to certain stimuli, are associated with certain, sometimes species-specific, physiological responses (e.g., piloerection, changes in heart rate, facial expressions), and, in humans, are found cross-culturally and at an early age (see Ortony & Turner 1990 for a dissenting opinion).

    Note that the "social emotions," including love, guilt, shame, and remorse, do not meet the above criteria, and are not considered to be primary emotions by most authors (see Izard 1991 for another perspective). Although distinctly human, the social emotions seem to involve a critical element of learning, and, central to the argument I will be making, are not panhuman.

3. According to Plutchik, cognitive processes themselves evolved "in the service of emotions," "in order to make the evaluations of stimulus events more correct and the predictions more precise so that the emotional behavior that finally resulted would be adaptively related to the stimulus event" (1980, p. 303). This model of the relationship between emotion and cognition is somewhat similar to Bigelow's (1972), which postulates that intelligence evolved as a result of the need to *control* the emotions (especially the aggressive emotions) in the service of sociality, and Humphrey's (1976; 1983), which claims that self-awareness evolved because it was a successful tool for predicting the behavior of others.

4. See Draper (1978) and the 1986 special issue of *Ethology and Sociobiology* on ostracism for further discussion of the role of shunning with specific reference to human societies; see Hirshleifer & Rasmusen (1989) for a game theoretic model of shunning; and see Nathanson (1992) for the importance of the social emotion shame.

5. The wealth of literature on strategies that people use to detect deception in interpersonal interactions, as well as the technologies that have been developed in order to further enhance that ability in less personal social interactions, are indicators of the importance we bestow on such ability (see Zuckerman et al. 1981, Mitchell & Thompson 1986, and especially Ekman 1992).

6. Although the data are overwhelming, the particular articles cited in this section should not be considered to be independent reports, since most of the reviews cited overlap substantially in

their coverage and many authors or teams report their findings more than once in a series of updates. Interested readers should direct themselves to the most recent publications; however, older publications do contain some information not presented in the updates and are thus included for thoroughness and ease of reference.

7.   Twin study methods yield estimates of what is termed "broad heritability," which includes both "additive" genetic factors (i.e., the summed effect of individual genes on the phenotype) and "non-additive" genetic factors (i.e., the phenotypic effects of dominance interactions between homologous alleles on paired chromosomes, and the epistatic interactions between nonhomologous genes throughout the genome). Adoption study methods, on the other hand, yield estimates of what is termed "narrow heritability," which is only the additive genetic component. The additive component is that which can be selected for (or against) as it is transmitted from generation to generation, whereas the nonadditive effect is unique to each individual genotype and is broken and reshuffled with every episode of sexual recombination. Because of this difference, twin studies typically yield higher heritability estimates than adoption studies. [See also Plomin & Daniels: "Why Are Children in the Same Family So Different from One Another/" *BBS* 10(1) 1987; Plomin & Bergeman: "The Nature of Nurture" *BBS* 14(3) 1991; and Wahlsten: "Insensitivity of the Analysis of Variance to Heredity-Environment Interaction" *BBS* 13(1) 1990.]

Another difference between the twin methodology and the adoption methodology is that twin studies generally provide heritability coefficients which estimate the proportion of the *total explained variance* accounted for by genetic factors, whereas adoption studies provide heritability coefficients which estimate the proportion of the *total variance* (including measurement error) that is accounted for by additive genetic factors. Since measurement error is so large when assessing criminality, adoption studies tend to yield both smaller and more varied heritability estimates than do twin studies. The first is that heritability can change across generations—even in the absence of genetic change—due to changes in the environment; this effect cannot be assessed in either twin or adoption studies, but is only a limitation of generalizability for the former, whereas it is conflated in the latter. The second is that heritability can also be different *at different ages*. Huesmann et al. (1994), for example, report that the correlation between children's aggression level and their parents' aggression level *when measured at the same age* is greater than the correlation between the child's own aggression level at one age and at a later age. This phenomenon also results simply in limited generalizability of heritability estimates derived from twin studies, but yields conflated estimates from adoption studies.

The heritability of 0.6 reported herein is an estimate of broad heritability as derived directly from twin studies; similar estimates can also be calculated indirectly from adoption study data after accounting for measurement error, but cohort effect cannot be separated out. See Leohlin (1992) for a general discussion of twin and adoption methodologies and Emde et al. (1992) and Raine (1993) for further discussions of the relevance of methodological considerations as they pertain to interpretation of the specific studies summarized herein.

8.   There is also evidence that at least one form of alcoholism belongs to the sociopathy spectrum: Type II alcoholism, which is also much more prevalent in men than women and seems to be transmitted in the same way (Bohman et al., 1981; Cadoret 1980; Cloninger et al., 1978, 1981; McGue et al. 1992; Stabenau 1985; Zucker & Gomberg 1986). Type II alcoholism is characterized by early onset, frequent violent outbursts, EEG abnormalities, and several of the personality attributes that are often seen in sociopathy; impulsivity, extraversion, sensation seeking, aggressiveness, and lack of concern for others (Cloninger 1987b; Tarter 1988).

9.   The interesting phenomenon of differential heritability of traits across the sexes can occur, as in this case, as a result of differential (sex-limited) expression of the same genes or, as it does with Type I alcoholism (a milder, nonviolent form), as result of differential environmental experiences of the sexes (Cloninger et al., 1978). Since heritability is measured as a proportion, the value of a heritability estimate will change whenever the numerator (variance in a trait due

to genetic variance) or the denominator (total variance in the trait) changes. Since the denominator (total variance) is composed of both genetic and environmental variance, changes in either will change the heritability. This method of defining heritability also explains some other apparent paradoxes, such as how two populations (e.g., racial groups or two successive generations of a single group) could have exactly the same genotypic variation with respect to trait, but because of differences in the environments, exhibit differential phenotypes and differential heritability of the trait.

10. Like the behavior-genetic studies cited in section 2.1.1., these studies provide overwhelming data, but should not be considered as independent reports, because many overlap or update earlier work. Methodologically, although path models and the longitudinal studies from which they are derived have excellent ecological validity, they are correlational; although they improve upon cross-sectional designs by noting which factors precede others development- ally, they cannot completely sort out cause and effect—especially in the earliest stages of parent–child interactions.

11. The strategy of sociopaths against one another, although not a test of the current model, is still interesting in its own right. In the Hare and Craigen (1974) modified Prisoner's Dilemma, the majority of sociopaths, in their turn, chose from among five "plays" the choice that minimized their own pain (an electric shock) for that trial, but that maximized their partner's. Since partners took turns in selecting from the same five "plays" this strategy actually maximized pain over the long run. The alternative, pain-minimizing strategy, involved giving both oneself and one's partner a small shock—a choice that most subjects declined to use. This result seems to confirm the sociopath's inability to consider anything other than the immediate consequences of an act, as well as the ineffectiveness of delayed punishment or threat of punishment as a deterrent. In the Widom (1976a) study, sociopaths did not, in general, "defect" more often than the controls, but in the condition when subjects were informed of their partner's move on the previous trial, sociopaths were much more likely than controls to "defect" after a mutual cooperation. On this measure, at least, the sociopaths seemed to demonstrate an inability to "commit" to an ongoing cooperative relationship. [See also Caporael et al.: "Selfishness Examined" *BBS* 12(4) 1989.]

12. Terhune (1980) reports that personality is the most important factor for strategy choice *within the setting of single-trial Prisoner's Dilemma interactions*. In multiple-trial interactions, however, when players have the opportunity to learn one another's dispositions, situational factors are more important for determining play (see Frank et al., 1993). This is consistent with the idea that the establishment of reputation is a key goal, even for players who on a single trial would choose not to cooperate. For more on the idea that establishing a certain reputation within one's referent group is a conscious goal and how that might play a role in the development of antisocial behavior, see Hogan and Jones (1983) and Irons (1991).

13. For some of the debate on this issue see the series of comments and replies following Nesse (1991) in the electronic journal—*Psycoloquy*. The comments specifically addressing the relationship between mood and emotion are: Morris (1992), Nesse (1992a), Plutchik (1992), and Nesse (1992b).

14. While searching for data to test this prediction, I came across only the Robins et al. (1991) reference in support of it, and one reference in an introductory psychology text (Wade & Tavris 1993) against it. The latter stated that antisocial personality disorder "is rare or unknown in small, tightly knit, cooperative communities, such as the Inuit, religious Hutterites, and Israelis raised on the communal plan of the kibbutz" (p. 584). Contact with Dr. Tavris allowed me to follow up on the sources from which the latter statement was derived (Altrocchi 1980; Eaton & Weil 1953; and Montagu 1978). My conclusion (which is shared by Dr. Tavris in personal communication) is that the absence or rarity of sociopathy in these small, tightly knit societies is not a result of the creation of a social system in which sociopaths never develop; rather, it is that *secondary* sociopaths do not develop (keeping total numbers at the low baseline) and that primary sociopaths *emigrate*.

Small, closely knit societies have all the properties that game theoretic models indicate will reduce (*but not eliminate*) the incidence of the cheater strategy (see sect. 3.2.1). One of the most important of these features is size *per se*; the cheater strategy cannot be used repeatedly against the same interactors and remain successful (see sect. 1.2). Thus, in small societies, sociopaths are likely to do their damage, acquire a reputation, and leave—to avoid punishment and move on to greener pastures. This "roving strategist" model (Dugatkin 1992; Dugatkin & Wilson 1991; Harpending & Sobus 1987) allows for both the evolution and the maintenance of a low baseline of successful sociopaths even in small groups (like those in which we presumably evolved).

15. Despite being a genetically based strategy, because primary sociopathy is the end product of the additive *and interactive* effects of many genes, we will not be able to predict or identify individual sociopaths by knowledge of their genotype. We will, however, be able to predict which children will be at risk, given their genetic background, the same way we predict which children will be at risk given their familial and socio-cultural background. We will also be alerted to the need to differentiate between diagnoses of primary sociopathy and secondary sociopathy (and our consequent approaches to them) based upon knowledge of an already identified sociopath's genetic and environmental background.

16. Axelrod (1986) and Boyd and Richerson (1992) also consider the extension of punishment not only to cheaters, but to those cooperators who do not, themselves, punish cheaters. The presence of this strategy can lead to an ESS of practically any behavior, regardless of whether there is any group benefit derived from such cooperation. Clearly this extension of the model has some analogues with totalitarian regimes and in-groups of a variety of sorts.

REFERENCES

Alexander, R.D. (1986). Biology and law. *Ethology and Sociobiology, 7*(3/4), 329–337.

Alexander, R.D. (1987). *The biology of moral systems*. Aldine de Gruyter Pub.

Allen, H., Lindner, L., Goldman, H. & Dinitz, S. (1971). Hostile and simple sociopaths: An empirical typology. *Criminology, 9*, 27–47.

Allsopp, J., Eysenck, H.J. & Eysenck, S.B.G. (1991). Machiavellianism as a component in psychoticism and extraversion. *Personality and Individual Differences, 12*(1), 29–41.

Altrocchi, J. (1980). *Abnormal Behavior*. Harcourt Brace Jovanovich Pub.

American Psychiatric Association. (1987). *Diagnostic and statistical manual*, 3rd ed. (rev.) American Psychiatric Association.

Anawalt, H.C. (1986). Ostracism and the law of defamation. *Ethology and Sociobiology, 7*(3/4), 329–337.

Apter, M.J. (1992). *The dangerous edge: The psychology of excitement*. Free Press.

Archer, J. (1991). The influence of testosterone on human aggression. *British Journal of Psychiatry, 82*, 1–28.

Axelrod, R. (1984). *The evolution of cooperation*. Basic Books.

Axelrod, R. (1986). An evolutionary approach to norms. *American Political Science Review, 80*(4), 1095–1111.

Axelrod, R. & Dion, D. (1988). More on the evolution of cooperation. *Science, 242*, 1385–1390.

Axelrod, R. & Hamilton, W.D. (1981). The evolution of cooperation. *Science, 211*, 1290–1396.

Baker, L.A. Mack, W. Moffitt, T.E. & Mednick, S. (1987). Sex differences in property crime in a Danish adoption cohort. *Behavior Genetics, 19*(3), 355–370.

Baldwin, J.D. (1990). The role of sensory stimulation in criminal behavior, with special attention to the age peak in crime. In L. Ellis & H. Hoffman (Eds.), *Crime in biological, social, and moral contexts*. Praeger Pub.

Barber, N. (1992). *Are interpersonal attitudes, such as Machiavellianism and altruism, modified by relatedness of their targets?* Presented at the Fourth Annual Meeting of the Human Behavior and Evolution Society, Albuquerque, N.M.

Bartol, C.R. (1984). *Psychology and American law*. Wadsworth Pub.

Bell, R.Q. & Chapman, M. (1986). Child effects in studies using experimental or brief longitudinal approaches to socialization. *Developmental Psychology, 22*, 595–603.

Belsky, J., Steinberg, L. & Draper, P. (1991). Childhood experience, interpersonal development and reproductive strategy: An evolutionary theory of socialization. *Child Development, 62*(4), 647–670.

Bigelow, R. (1972). The evolution of cooperation, aggression, and self-control. In J.K. Cole & D.D. Jensen (Eds.), *Nebraska symposium on motivation*, vol. 20. University of Nebraska Press.

Blumstein, A. & Cohen, J. (1987). Characterizing criminal careers. *Science, 237*, 985–991.

Boddy, J., Carver, A. & Rowley, K. (1986). Effects of positive and negative verbal reinforcement on performance as a function of extraversion–introversion: Some tests of Gray's theory. *Personality and Individual Differences, 7*(1), 81–88.

Bohman, M., Sigvardsson, S. & Cloninger, C.R. (1981). Maternal inheritance of alcohol abuse. *Archives of General Psychiatry, 38*, 965–969.

Borowiak, M. (1989). *The effectiveness of individual therapy, group therapy, family therapy, and outdoor therapy on adjudicated juvenile delinquents: A meta-analysis*. Unpublished senior thesis, St. John's University, Collegeville, MN.

Boyd, R. (1988). Is the repeated Prisoner's Dilemma game a good model of reciprocal altruism? *Ethology and Sociobiology, 9*, 211–221.

Boyd, R. & Richerson, P.J. (1992). Punishment allows the evolution of cooperation (or anything else) in sizable groups. *Ethology and Sociobiology, 213*(3), 171–195.

Bradley, M.T. & Klohn, K.I. (1987). Machiavellianism, the control question test and the detection of deception. *Perceptual and Motor Skills, 64*, 747–757.

Brown, G.L., Goodwin, F.K., Ballenger, J.C., Goyer, P.F. & Major, L.F. (1979). Aggression in Humans correlates with cerebrospinal fluid amine metabolites. *Psychiatry Research, 1*, 131–139.

Brunner, H.G., Nelen, M., Breakefield, X.O., Ropers, H.H. & van Oost, B.A. (1993). Abnormal behavior associated with a point mutation in the structural gene for monoamine oxidase A. *Science, 262*, 578–580.

Buss, D.M. (1981). Predicting parent–child interactions from children's activity level. *Developmental Psychology, 17*, 59–65.

Buss, D.M. (1988). The evolution of human intrasexual competition: Tactics of mate attraction. *Journal of Personality and Social Psychology, 54*(4), 616–628.

Buss, D.M. (1991). Evolutionary personality psychology. *Annual Review of Psychology. 42*, 459–491.

Byrne, R.W. & Whiten, A. (1988). *Machiavellian intelligence: Social expertise and the evolution of intellect in monkeys, apes, and humans*. Oxford Science Pub.

Cadoret, R.J. (1978). Psychopathology of adopted-away offspring of biologic parents with antisocial personality. *Archives of General Psychiatry, 35*, 176–184.

Cadoret, R.J. (1982). Genotype–environment interaction in antisocial behavior. *Psychosomatic Medicine, 12*, 235–239.

Cadoret, R. (1986). Epidemiology of antisocial personality. In W.H. Reid, D. Dorr, J.I Walker & J.W. Bonner, III (Eds.), *Unmasking the psychopath: Antisocial personality and related syndromes*. W.W. Norton Pub.

Cadoret, R.J & Cain, C. (1980). Sex differences in predictors of antisocial behavior in adoptees. *Archives of General Psychiatry, 37*, 1171–1175.

Cadoret, R.J. & Cain, C. (1981). Environmental and genetic factors in predicting adolescent antisocial behavior. *The Psychiatric Journal of the University of Ottawa, 6*(4), 220–225.

Cadoret, R.J., Cain, C.A. & Crowe, R.R. (1983). Evidence for gene–environment interaction in the development of adolescent antisocial behavior. *Behavior Genetics, 13*(3), 301–310.

Cadoret, R.J. & Stewart, M.A. (1991). An adoption study of attention deficit/hyperactivity/aggression and their relationship to adult antisocial personality. *Comprehensive Psychiatry, 32*(1), 73–82.

Cadoret, R.J., Troughton, E., Bagford, J. & Woodworth, G. (1990). Genetic and environmental factors in adoptee antisocial personality. *European Archives of Psychiatry and Neurological Sciences, 239*, 231–240.

Cadoret, R.J., Troughton, E. & O'Gorman, T.W. (1987). Genetic and environmental factors in alcohol abuse and antisocial personality. *Journal of Studies on Alcohol, 48*(1), 1–8.

Caldwell, R.L. (1986). The deceptive use of reputation by stomatopods. In R.W. Mitchell & N.S. Thompson (Eds.), *Deception: Perspectives on human and nonhuman deceit*. SUNY Press.

Caspi, A., Elder, G.H. & Bem, D.J. (1987). Moving against the world: Life-course patterns of explosive children. *Developmental Psychology, 23*, 308–313.

Charney, D.S., Woods, S.W., Krystal, J.H. & Heninger, G.R. (1990). Serotonin function and human anxiety disorders. *Annals of the New York Academy of Sciences, 600*, 558–573.

Chesno, F.A. & Kilman, P.R. (1975). Effects of stimulation intensity in sociopathic avoidance learning. *Journal of Abnormal Psychology, 84*, 144–150.

Christiansen, K.O. (1977a). A review of studies of criminality among twins. In S.A. Mednick & K.O. Christiansen (Eds.), *Biosocial bases of criminal behavior*. Gardner Press.

Christiansen, K.O. (1977b). A preliminary study of criminality among twins. In S.A. Mednick & K.O. Christiansen (Eds.), *Biosocial bases of criminal behavior*. Gardner Press.

Christie, R. (1970). The Machiavellis among us. *Psychology Today, 4*(6), 82–86.

Christie, R. & Geis, F.L. (1970). *Studies in Machiavellianism*. Academic Press.

Cialdini, R.B., Kenrick, D.T. & Baumann, D.J. (1982). Effects of mood on prosocial behavior in children and adults. In N. Eisenberg (Ed.), *The Development of prosocial behavior*. Academic Press.

Cloninger, C.R. (1987a). A systematic method for clinical description and classification of personality variants. *Archives of General Psychiatry, 44*, 573–588.

Cloninger, C.R. (1987b). Neurogenetic adaptive mechanisms in alcoholism. *Science, 236*, 410–416.

Cloninger, C.R., Bohman, M. & Sigvardsson, S. (1981). Inheritance of alcohol abuse. *Archives of General Psychiatry, 38*, 861–868.

Cloninger, C.R., Christiansen, K.O., Reich, T. & Gottesman, I.I. (1978). Implications of sex differences in the prevalences of antisocial personality, alcoholism, and criminality for familial transmission. *Archives of General Psychiatry, 35*, 941–951.

Cloninger, C.R. & Gottesman, I.I. (1987). Genetic and environmental factors in anti-social behavior disorders. In S.A. Mednick, Terrie E. Moffitt, & S.A. Stack (Eds.), *The causes of crime: New biological approaches*. Cambridge University Press.

Cloninger, C.R., Reich, T., & Guze, S.B. (1975). The multifactorial model of disease transmission: Sex differences in the familial transmission of sociopathy (antisocial personality). *British Journal of Psychiatry, 127*, 11–22.

Cloninger, C.R., Svrakic, D.M. & Przybeck, T.R. (1993). A psychobiological model of temperament. *Archives of General Psychiatry, 50*, 975–990.

Cohen, L.E. & Machalek, R. (1988). A general theory of expropriative crime: An evolutionary ecological approach. *American Journal of Sociology, 94*(3), 465–501.

Conger, R. (1993). *Linking family processes to adolescent deviance*. Presented at the 45th annual meeting of the American Society of Criminology, Phoenix, AZ.

Crawford, C.B. & Anderson, J.L. (1989). Sociobiology: An environmentalist discipline? *American Psychologist, 44*(12), 1449–1459.

Crowe, R.R. (1972). The adopted offspring of women criminal offenders: A study of their arrest records. *Archives of General Psychiatry, 27*, 600–603.

Crowe, R.R. (1974). An adoption study of anti-social personality. *Archives of General Psychiatry, 31*, 785–791.

Dabbs, J.M. & Morris, R. (1990). Testosterone, social class and antisocial behavior. *Psychological Science, 1*, 209–211.

Daitzman, R. & Zuckerman, M. (1980). Disinhibitory sensation seeking personality and gonadal hormones. *Personality and Individual Differences, 1*, 103–110.

Daly, M. & Wilson, M. (1983). *Sex, evolution, and behavior*, 2nd ed. Willard Grant Press.

Damasio, A.R., Tranel, D. & Damasio, H. (1990). Individuals with sociopathic behavior caused by frontal damage fail to respond autonomically to social stimuli. *Behavioural Brain Research, 41*, 8194.

Davison G.C., & Neale J.M. (1994). *Abnormal psychology* (6th edition). John Wiley & Sons Pub.

Dawkins, R. (1980). Good strategy or evolutionary stable strategy? In G.W. Barlow & J.. Silverberg (Eds.), *Sociobiology: Beyond nature/nurture?*. Westview Press.

Dennett, D. (1988). Why creative intelligence is hard to find. *Behavioral and Brain Sciences, 11*(2), 253.

Depue, R.A., & Spoont, M.R. (1986). Conceptualizing a serotonin trait. *Annals of the New York Academy of Sciences, 487*, 47–62.

Derryberry, D. (1987). Incentive and feedback effects on target detection: A chronometric analysis of Gray's model of temperament. *Personality and Individual Differences, 8*(6), 855–865.

Dienstbier, R.A. (1984). The role of emotion in moral socialization. In C.E. Izard, J. Kagan & R.B. Zajonc (Eds.), *Emotions, cognition and behavior*. Cambridge University Press.

Dimberg, U. (1988). Facial expressions and emotional reactions: A psychobiological analysis of human social behaviour. In H.L. Wagner (Ed.), *Social psychophysiology and emotion: Theory and clinical applications*. John Wiley & Sons Pub.

Dishion, T.J., Patterson, G.R., Stoolmiller, M. & Skinner, M.L. (1991). Family, school, and behavioral antecedents to early adolescent involvement with antisocial peers. *Developmental Psychology, 27*(1), 172–180.

Dishion, T.J. & Poe, Joyanna (1993). *Parental antisocial behavior as an antecedent to deviancy training among adolescent boys and their peers*. Presented at the 45th annual meeting of the American Society of Criminology, Phoenix, AZ.

Dodge, K.A. & Newman, J.P. (1981). Biased decision-making processes in aggressive boys. *Journal of Abnormal Psychology, 90*(4), 375–379.

Draper, P. (1978). The learning environment for aggression and antisocial behavior among the !Kung (Kalahari Desert, Botswana, Africa). In A. Montagu (Ed.), *Learning non-aggression: The experience of non-literate societies*. Oxford University Press.

Draper, P. & Belsky, J. (1990). Personality development in evolutionary perspective. *Journal of Personality, 58*(1), 141–161.

Draper, P. & Harpending, H. (1982). Father absence and reproductive strategy: An evolutionary perspective. *Journal of Anthropological Research, 38*(3), 255–273.

Dugatkin, L.A. (1992). The evolution of the "con artist". *Ethology and Sociobiology, 13*(1), 3–18.

Dugatkin, L.A. & Wilson, D.S. (1991). ROVER: A strategy for exploiting cooperators in a patchy environment. *The American Naturalist, 138*(3), 687–702.

Dumas, J.E., Blechman, E.A. & Prinz, R.J. (1992). Helping families with aggressive children and adolescents change. In R.DeV Peters, R.J. McMahon & V.L. Quinsey (Eds.), *Aggression and violence throughout the lifespan*. Sage Pub.

Dunn, J. (1987). The beginnings of moral understanding: Development in the second year. In J. Kagan & S. Lamb (Eds.), *The emergence of morality in young children*. Chicago University Press.

Dunn, J. (1988). *The beginnings of social understanding*. Harvard University Press.

Dunn, J. (1992). Siblings and development. *Current Directions in Psychological Science, 1*, 6–9.

Dunn, J., Brown, J., Slomkowski, C., Tesla, C. & Youngblade, L. (1991). Young children's understanding of other people's feelings and beliefs: Individual differences and their antecedents. *Child Development, 62*, 1352–1366.

Dunn, J. & Plomin, R. (1990). *Separate lives: Why siblings are so different*. Basic Books.

van Dusen, K.T, Mednick, S.A., Gabrielli, W.F. Jr., & Hutchings, B. (1983). Social class and crime in an adoption cohort. *The Journal of Criminal Law and Criminology, 74*(1), 249–269.

Eaton, J.W. & Weil, R.J. (1953). The mental health of the Hutterites. *Scientific American, 189*(6), 32–37.

Eisenberg, N., Fabes, R.A. & Miller, P.A. (1990). The evolutionary and neurological roots of prosocial behavior. In L. Ellis & H. Hoffman (Eds.), *Crime in biological, social, and moral contexts*. Praeger Pub.

Ekman, P. (1971). Universals and cultural differences in facial expressions of emotion. In J. Cole (Ed.), *Nebraska symposium on motivation*, vol. 9. University of Nebraska Press.

Ekman, P. (1992). *Telling lies: Clues to deceit in the market place, politics and marriage*, 2nd ed. Norton Pub.

Eliasz, A. (1987). Temperament-contingent cognitive orientation toward various aspects of reality. In J. Strelau & H.J. Eysenck (Eds.), *Personality dimensions and arousal*. Plenum Press.

Eliasz, H. & Reykowski, J. (1986). Reactivity and empathic control of aggression. In J. Strelau, F.H. Farley & A. Gale (Eds.), *The biological bases of personality and behavior, vol.2: Psychophysiology, performance, and application*. Hemisphere Pub.

Ellis, L. (1987). Relationships of criminality and psychopathy with eight other apparent behavioral manifestations of sub-optimal arousal. *Personality and Individual Differences, 8*, 905–925.

Ellis, L. (1988). Criminal behavior and r/K selection: An extension of gene-based evolutionary theory. *Personality and Individual Differences, 9*(4), 697–708.

Ellis, L. (1989). *Theories of rape: Inquiries into the causes of sexual aggression*. Hemisphere Pub.

Ellis, L. (1990a). The evolution of collective counterstrategies to crime: From the primate control rule to the criminal justice system. In L. Ellis & H. Hoffman (Eds.), *Crime in biological, social, and moral contexts*. Praeger Pub.

Ellis, L. (1990b). Conceptualizing criminal and related behavior from a biosocial perspective. In L. Ellis & H. Hoffman (Eds.), *Crime in biological, social, and moral contexts*. Hoffman. Praeger Pub.

Ellis, L. (1991a). A synthesized (biosocial) theory of rape. *Journal of Consulting and Clinical Psychology, 59*(5), 631–642.

Ellis, L. (1991b). Monoamine oxidase and criminality: Identifying an apparent biological marker for antisocial behavior. *Journal of Research in Crime and Delinquency, 28*(2), 227–251.

Ellis, L. & Coontz, P.D. (1990). Androgens, brain functioning, and criminality: The neurohormonal foundations of antisociality. In L. Ellis & H. Hoffman (Eds.), *Crime in biological, social, and moral contexts*. Praeger Pub.

Emde, R.N., Plomin, R., Robinson, J., Corley, R., DeFries, J., Fulker, D.W., Reznick, J.S., Campos, J., Kagan, J. & Zahn-Waxler, C. (1992). Temperament, emotion, and cognition at fourteen months: The MacArthur longitudinal twin study. *Child Development, 63*, 1437–1455.

Eron, L.D., Huesmann, L.R. & Zelli, A. (1991). The role of parental variables in the learning of aggression. In D.J. Pepler & K.H. Rubin (Eds.), *The development and treatment of aggression*. Lawrence Erlbaum Pub.

Eysenck, H.J. (1977). *Crime and personality*, 3rd ed. Routledge & Kegan Paul Pub.

Eysenck, H.J. (1983). Personality, conditioning, and antisocial behavior. In W.S. Laufer & J. M. Day (Eds.), *Personality theory, moral development, and criminal behavior*. Lexington Books.

Eysenck, H.J. (1987). The definition of personality disorders and the criteria appropriate for their description. *Journal of Personality Disorders, 1*(3), 211–219.

Eysenck, H.J. (1990). Biological dimensions of personality. In L.A. Pervin (Ed.), *Handbook of personality theory and research*. Guilford Pub.

Eysenck, H.J. & Gudjonsson, G.H. (1989). *The causes and cures of criminality*. Plenum Press.

Fagan, T.J. & Lira, F.T. (????). The primary and secondary sociopathic personality: Differences in frequency and severity of antisocial behaviors. *Journal of Abnormal Psychology, 89*(3), 493–496.

Farley, F. (1986). The big T in personality. *Psychology Today, 20*(5), 44–52.

Farrington, D.P. (1979). Experiments on deviance with special reference to dishonesty. *Advances in Experimental Social Psychology, 12*, 207–252.

Farrington, D.P. (1982). Naturalistic experiments on helping behavior. In A.M. Colman (Ed.), *Cooperation and competition in humans and animals*. Van Nostrand Reinhold Pub.

Farrington, D.P. (1986). Stepping stones to adult criminal careers. In D. Olweus, J. Block & M. Radke-Yarrow (Eds), *Development of antisocial and prosocial behavior: Research, theories, and issues.* Academic Press.

Farrington, D.P. (1989). Early predictors of adolescent aggression and adult violence. *Violence and Victims, 4*(2), 79–100.

Feldman, M.P. (1977). *Criminal behavior: A psychological analysis.* John Wiley & Sons Pub.

Feldman, M.W. & Thomas, E.A.C. (1987). Behavior-dependent contexts for repeated plays of the Prisoner's Dilemma II: Dynamical aspects of the evolution of cooperation. *Journal of Theoretical Biology, 128,* 297–315.

Figueredo, A.J. & McCloskey, L. A. (nd). *Sex, money, and paternity: The evolutionary psychology of domestic violence.* Unpublished manuscript.

Forgatch, M.S. (1991). The clinical science vortex: a developing theory of antisocial behavior. In D.J. Pepler & K.H. Rubin (Eds.), *The development and treatment of aggression.* Lawrence Erlbaum Pub.

Forgatch, M.S., Stoolmiller, M. & Patterson, G.R. (1993). Parental affect and adolescent delinquency: A mediational model. Presented at the 45th annual meeting of the American Society of Criminology, Phoenix, AZ.

Forth, A.E. & Hare, R.D. (1989). The contingent negative variation in psychopaths. *Psychophysiology, 26,* 676–682.

Foster, D. (1991). Social influence III: Crowds and collective violence. In D. Foster & J. Louw-Potgieter (Eds.), *Social psychology in South Africa.* Lexicon Pub. (Johannesburg).

Frank, R.H. (1988). *Passions within reason: The strategic role of the emotions.* W.W. Norton Pub.

Frank, R.H., Gilovich, T. & Regan, D.T. (1993). The evolution of oneshot cooperation: An experiment. *Ethology and Sociobiology, 14,* 247–256.

Fry, D.P. (1988). Intercommunity differences in aggression among Zapotec children. *Child Development, 59,* 1008–1019.

Gabbay, F.H. (1992). Behavior-genetic strategies in the study of emotion. *Psychological Science, 3*(1), 50–55.

Gangestad, S.W. & Simpson, J.A. (1990). Toward an evolutionary history of female sociosexual variation. *Journal of Personality, 58*(1), 69–95.

Garmezy, N. (1991). Resiliency and vulnerability to adverse developmental outcomes associated with poverty. *American Behavioral Scientist, 34*(4), 416–430.

Geis, F. & Levy, M. (1970). The eye of the beholder. In R. Christie & F.L. Geis (Eds.), *Studies in Machiavellianism.* Academic Press.

Gelfand, D.M. & Hartmann, D.P. (1982). Response consequences and attributions: Two contributors to prosocial behavior. In N. Eisenberg (Ed.), *The development of prosocial behavior.* Academic Press.

Ghodsian-Carpey, J. & Baker, L.A. (1987). Genetic and environmental influences on aggression in 4- to 7-year old twins. *Aggressive Behavior, 13,* 173–186.

Gladue, B.A. (1991). Aggressive behavioral characteristics, hormones, and sexual orientation in men and women. *Aggressive Behavior, 17,* 313–326.

Gold, M. (1987). Social ecology. In H.C. Quay (Ed.), *Handbook of juvenile delinquency.* Wiley-Interscience Pub.

Gordon, D.A. & Arbuthnot, J. (1987). Individual, group, and family interventions. In H.C. Quay (Ed.), *Handbook of juvenile delinquency.* Wiley-Interscience Pub.

Gorenstein, E.E. & Newman J.P. (1980). Disinhibitory psychopathology: A new perspective and a model for research. *Psychological Review, 87*(3), 301–315.

Gottesman, I.I. & Goldsmith, H.H. (1993). Developmental psychopathology of anti-social behavior: Inserting genes into its ontogenesis and epigenesis. In C.A. Nelson (Ed.), *Threats to optimal development: Integrating biological, psychological and social risk factors.* Lawrence Erlbaum Pub.

Gottschalk, R., Davidson, W.S., II, Gensheimer, L.K. & Mayer, J.P. (1987). Community based interventions. In H.C. Quay (Ed.), *Handbook of juvenile delinquency*. Wiley-Interscience Pub.

Gould, J.L. & Gould, C.G. (1989). *Sexual selection. Scientific American Library*. W.H. Freeman Pub.

Gove, W.R. & Wilmoth, C. (1990). Risk, crime, and neurophysiologic highs: A consideration of brain processes that may reinforce delinquent and criminal behavior. In L. Ellis & H. Hoffman (Eds.), *Crime in biological, social, and moral contexts*. Praeger Pub.

Gray, J.A. (1982). *The neuropsychology of anxiety: An enquiry into the functions of the septohippocampal system*. Oxford University Press.

Gray, J.A. (1987). Perspectives on anxiety and impulsivity: A commentary. *Journal of Research in Personality, 21*, 493–509.

Griffiths, P.E. (1990). Modularity, and the psychoevolutionary theory of emotion. *Biology and Philosophy, 5*, 175–196.

Grusec, J.E. (1982). The socialization of altruism. In N. Eisenberg (Ed.), *The development of prosocial behavior*. Academic Press.

Halpern, C.T., Udry, J.R., Campbell, B. & Suchindran, C. (1993). Relationship between aggression and pubertal increase in testosterone: A panel analysis of adolescent males. *Social Biology, 40*(1–2), 8–24.

Hare, R.D. (1970). *Psychopathy: Theory and research*. John Wiley & Sons Pub.

Hare, R.D. (1980). A research scale for the assessment of psychopathy in criminal populations. *Personality and Individual Differences, 1*: 111–119.

Hare, R.D. (1993). *Without conscience: The disturbing world of the psychopaths among us*. Pocket Books.

Hare, R.D. & Craigen, D. (1974). Psychopathy and physiological activity in a mixed-motive game situation. *Psychophysiology, 11*, 197–206.

Hare, R.D., Forth, A.E. & Strachan, K.E. (1992). Psychopathy and crime across the life span. In R.DeV. Peters, R.J. McMahon & V.L. Quinsey (Eds), *Aggression and violence throughout the lifespan*. Sage Pub.

Hare, R.D. & Quinn, M.J. (1971). Psychopathy and autonomic conditioning. *Journal of Abnormal Psychology, 77*, 223–235.

Harpending, H. & Sobus, J. (1987). Sociopathy as an adaptation. *Ethology and Sociobiology, 8*(3s), 63s–72s.

Hartup, W.W. (1989). Social relationships and their developmental significance. *American Psychologist, 44*(2), 120–126.

Heckathorn, D.D. (1988). Collective sanctions and the creation of Prisoner's Dilemma norms. *American Journal of Sociology, 94*(3), 535–562.

Hirschi, T. & Hindelang, M.J. (1977). Intelligence and delinquency: A revisionist review. *American Sociological Review, 42*, 571–587.

Hirshleifer, D. & Rasmusen, E. (1989). Cooperation in a repeated prisoner's dilemma with ostracism. *Journal of Economic Behavior and Organization, 12*, 87–106.

Hirshleifer, J. (1987). On the emotions as guarantors of threats and promises. In J. Dupre (Ed.), *The latest on the best: Essays on evolution and optimality*. Bradford Books.

Hirshleifer, J. & Coll, J.C. (1988). What strategies can support the evolutionary emergence of cooperation? *Journal of Conflict Resolution, 32*(2), 367–398.

Hodgins, S. (1992). Mental disorder, intellectual deficiency, and crime: Evidence from a birth cohort. *Archives of General Psychiatry, 49*, 476–483.

Hoffman, M.L. (1975). Developmental synthesis of affect and cognition and its implications for altruistic motivation. *Developmental Psychology, 11*(5), 607–622.

Hoffman, M.L. (1977). Empathy, its development and prosocial implications. In C.B. Keasy (Ed.), *Nebraska symposium on motivation*, vol. 25. University of Nebraska Press.

Hoffman, M.L. (1978). Psychological and biological perspectives on altruism. *International Journal of Behavioral Development, 1*, 323–339.

Hoffman, M.L. (1982). Development of prosocial motivation: Empathy and guilt. In N. Eisenberg (Ed.), *The development of prosocial behavior*. Academic Press.

Hoffman, M.L. (1984). Interaction of affect and cognition in empathy. In C.E. Izard, J. Kagan & R.B. Zajonc (Eds.), *Emotions, cognition and behavior*. Cambridge University Press.

Hogan, R. & Jones, W.H. (1983). A role-theoretical model of criminal behavior. In W.S. Laufer & J.M. Day (Eds.), *Personality theory, moral development, and criminal behavior*. Lexington Books.

Huesmann, L.R., Eron, L.D., Lefkowitz, M.M. & Walder, L.O. (1984). Stability of aggression over time and generations. *Developmental Psychology, 20*(6), 1120–1134.

Humphrey, N.K. (1976). The social function of intellect. In P.P.G. Bateson & R.A. Hinde (Eds.), *Growing points in ethology*. Cambridge University Press.

Humphrey, N.K. (1983). *Consciousness regained*. Oxford University Press.

Hutchings, B. & Mednick, S.A. (1977). Criminality in adoptees and their adoptive and biological parents: A pilot study. In S.A. Mednick & K.O. Christiansen (Eds.), *Biosocial bases of criminal behavior*. Gardner Press.

Irons, W. (1991). How did morality evolve? *Zygon, 26*(1), 49–89.

Izard, C.E. (1977). *Human emotions*. Plenum Press.

Izard, C.E. (1991). *The psychology of emotions*. Plenum Press.

Jaffe, P.G., Suderman, M. & Reotzel, D. (1992). Working with children and adolescents to end the cycle of violence: A social learning approach to intervention. In R.DeV. Peters, R.J. McMahon & V.L. Quinsey (Eds.), *Aggression and violence throughout the lifespan*. Sage Pub.

Jenner, F.A. (1980). Psychiatry, biology and morals. In G.S. Stent (Ed.), *Morality as a biological phenomenon: The presuppositions of sociobiological research*. University of California Press.

Kalat, J.W. (1992). *Biological psychology*, 4th edition. Wadsworth Pub.

Kandel, E., Mednick, S.A., Kirkegaard-Sorensen, L., Hutchings, B., Knop, J., Rosenberg, R. & Schulsinger, F. (1988). IQ as a protective factor for subjects at high risk for antisocial behavior. *Journal of Consulting and Clinical Psychology, 56*(2), 224–226.

Kenrick, D.T., Dantchik, A., & MacFarlane, S. (1983). Personality environment, and criminal behavior: An evolutionary perspective. In W.S. Laufer & J.M. Day (Eds.), *Personality theory, moral development, and criminal behavior*. Lexington Books.

Kochanska, G. (1991). Socialization and temperament in the development of guilt and conscience. *Child Development, 62*, 1379–1392.

Kochanska, G. (1993). Toward a synthesis of parental socialization and child temperament in early development of conscience. *Child Development, 64*, 325–347.

Kochanska, G. & Murray, K. (1992). *Temperament and conscience development*. Presented at the Ninth Occasional Temperament Conference, Bloomington, Indiana, October 29–31, 1992.

Kofoed, L. & MacMillan, J. (1986). Alcoholism and antisocial personality: The sociobiology of an addiction. *The Journal of Nervous and Mental Disease, 174*(6), 332–335.

Kohlberg, L. (1964). Development of moral character and moral ideology. In M. Hoffman & L.W. Hoffman (Eds.), *Review of child development research*. Russell Sage Foundation.

Kraut, R.E. & Price, J.D. (1976). Machiavellianism in parents and their children. *Journal of Personality and Social Psychology, 33*(6), 782–786.

Kruesi, M.J., Hibbs, E.D., Zahn, T.P., Keysor, C.S., Hamburger, S.D., Bartko, J.J. & Rapoport, J. L. (1992). A 2-year prospective follow-up study of children and adolescents with disruptive behavior disorders: Prediction by cerebrospinal fluid 5-hydroxyindoleacetic acid, homovanillic acid, and autonomic measures? *Archives of General Psychiatry, 49*, 429–435.

Landy, S. & Peters, R. DeV. (1992). Toward an understanding of a developmental paradigm for aggressive conduct problems during the pre-school years. In R.DeV. Peters, R.J. McMahon & V.L. Quinsey (Eds.), *Aggression and violence throughout the lifespan*. Sage Pub.

Lazarus, R.S. (1991). *Emotion and adaptation*. Oxford University Press.

Lee, C.L. & Bates, J.E. (1985). Mother–child interactions at age two years and perceived difficult temperament. *Child Development, 56*, 1314–1325.

Leslie, A.M. (1987). Pretense and representation: The origins of 'Theory of Mind'. *Psychological Review, 94*(4), 412–426.

Lewontin, R.C. (1961). Evolution and the theory of games. *Journal of Theoretical Biology, 1*, 382–403.

Link, R. & Mealey, L. (1992). *"The sociobiology of sociopathy: An integrated evolutionary model".* Presented at the Conference on the Biology of Morality, Bethel College, St. Paul, MN.

Littlepage, G. & Pineault, T. (1978). Verbal, facial, and paralinguistic cues to the detection of truth and lying. *Personality and Social Psychology Bulletin, 4*(3), 461–464.

Loeb, J. & Mednick, S.A. (1977). A prospective study of predictors of criminality, III: electrodermal response patterns. In S.A. Mednick, Terrie E. Moffitt, & S.A. Stack (Eds.), *The causes of crime: New biological approaches.* Cambridge University Press.

Loeber, R. (1982). The stability of antisocial and delinquent child behavior: A review. *Child Development, 53*, 1431–1446.

Loeber, R. (1990). Development and risk factors of juvenile antisocial behavior and delinquency. *Clinical Psychology Review, 10*, 1–41.

Loeber, R. (1993). *Predictors of delinquency and violence: Longitudinal findings from the Pittsburgh youth study.* Presented at the 45th annual meeting of the American Society of Criminology Phoenix, AZ.

Loeber, R. & Dishion, T. (1983). Early predictors of male delinquency: A review. *Psychological Bulletin, 94*(1), 68–99.

Loeber, R. & Stouthamer-Loeber, M. (1987). Prediction. In H.C. Quay (Ed.), *Handbook of juvenile delinquency.* Wiley-Interscience Pub.

Loehlin, J.C. (1992). *Genes and environment in personality development.* Sage Pub.

Low, B. (1993). *Linking our evolutionary past and our ecological future: A behavioral ecological approach.* Presented at the Fifth Annual Meeting of the Human Behavior and Evolution Society, August 4–8, 1993, Binghamton, NY.

Luntz, B.K. & Widom, C.S. (1993). *A comparison of antisocial personality diagnoses and psychopathy checklist scores in a sample of non-institutionalized young adults.* Presented at the 45th annual meeting of the American Society of Criminology, Phoenix, AZ.

Lyng, S. (1990). Edgework: A social psychological analysis of voluntary risk taking. *American Journal of Sociology, 95*(4), 851–856.

Lytton, H. (1990). Child and parent effects in boys' conduct disorder: A reinterpretation. *Developmental Psychology, 26*(5), 683–697.

Maccoby, E.E. (1986). Social groupings in childhood: Their relationship to prosocial and antisocial behavior in boys and girls. In D. Olweus, J. Block & M. Radke-Yarrow (Eds.), *Development of antisocial and prosocial behavior: Research, theories, and issues.* Academic Press.

MacDonald, K.B. (Ed.) (1988). *Sociobiological perspectives on human development.* Springer-Verlag Pub.

Machalek, R. & Cohen, L.E. (1991). The nature of crime: Is cheating necessary for cooperation? *Human Nature, 2*(3), 215–233.

MacMillan, J. & Kofoed, L. (1984). Sociobiology and antisocial personality: An alternative perspective. *The Journal of Nervous and Mental Disease, 172*(12), 701–706.

Madsen, D. (1985). A biochemical property relating to power seeking in humans. *American Political Science Review, 79*, 448–457.

Magid, K. & McKelvey, C.A. (1987). *High risk: Children without a conscience.* Bantam Books.

Malamuth, N.M., Sockloskie, R.J., Koss, M.P. & Tanaka, J.S. (1991). Characteristics of aggressors against women: Testing a model using national sample of college students. *Journal of Counseling and Clinical Psychology, 59*(5), 670–681.

Maynard Smith, J. (1978). The evolution of behavior. *Scientific American, 239*, 176–192.

Maynard Smith, J. (1974). The theory of games and the evolution of animal conflict. *Journal of Theoretical Biology, 47*, 209–221.

Maynard Smith, J. & Price, G.R. (1973). The logic of animal conflict. *Nature, 246*, 15–18.

McCord, J. (1983). Personality, moral development, and criminal behavior. In W.S. Laufer & J.M. Day (Eds.), *Personality theory, moral development, and criminal behavior*. Lexington Books.

McCord, J. (1986). Instigation and insulation: How families affect antisocial aggression. In D. Olweus, J. Block & M. Radke-Yarrow (Eds.), *Development of antisocial and prosocial behavior: Research, theories, and issues*. Academic Press.

McCord, J. (1993). *From family to peer group*. Discussant at the 45th annual meeting of the American Society of Criminology, Phoenix, AZ.

McGarvey, B., Gabrielli, W.F., Jr., Bentler, P.M. & Mednick, S.A. (1981). Rearing, social class, education, and criminality: A multiple indicator model. *Journal of Abnormal Psychology, 90*(4), 354–364.

McGue, M., Pickens, R.W. & Svikis, D.S. (1992). Sex and age effects on the inheritance of alcohol problems: A twin study. *Journal of Abnormal Psychology, 101*(1), 3–17.

McGuire, M., Raleigh, M. & Johnson, C. (1983). Social dominance in adult male vervet monkeys II: Behavior–biochemical relationships. *Social Science Information, 22*, 311–328.

Mealey, L. (1984). Comment on genetic similarity theory. *Behavior Genetics, 15*(6), 571–574.

Mealey, L. (1990). Differential use of reproductive strategies by human groups? *Psychological Science, 1*(6), 385–387.

Mealey, L. (1992). Are monkeys nomothetic or idiographic? *Behavioral and Brain Sciences, 15*(1), 161–162.

Mealey, L. & Segal, N.L. (1993). Heritable and environmental variables affect reproduction-related behaviors, but not ultimate reproductive success. *Personality and Individual Differences, 14*(6), 783–794.

Mednick, S.A. (1977). A biosocial theory of learning of law-abiding behavior. In S.A. Mednick & K.O. Christiansen (Eds.), *Biosocial bases of criminal behavior*. Gardner Press.

Mednick, S.A. & Finello, K.M. (1983). Biological factors and crime: Implications for forensic psychiatry. *International Journal of Law and Psychiatry, 6*, 1–15.

Mednick, S.A., Gabrielli, W.F., Jr. & Hutchings, B. (1984). Genetic influences in criminal convictions: Evidence from an adoption cohort. *Science, 224*, 891–894.

Mednick, S.A., Gabrielli, W.F., Jr. & Hutchings, B. (1987). Genetic factors in the etiology of criminal behavior. In S.A. Mednick, Terrie E. Moffitt, & S.A. Stack (Eds.), *The causes of crime: New biological approaches*. Cambridge University Press.

Mednick, S.A., Kirkegaard-Sorense, L., Hutchings, B., Knop, J., Rosenberg, R. & Schulsinger, F. (1977). An example of biosocial interaction research: The interplay of socioenvironmental and individual factors in the etiology of criminal behavior. In S.A. Mednick & K.O. Christiansen (Eds.), *Biosocial bases of criminal behavior*. Gardner Press.

Mednick, S.A., Moffitt, T.E. & Stack, S.A. (1987). *The causes of crime: New biological approaches*. Cambridge University Press.

Mineka, S. & Sutton, S.K. (1992). Cognitive biases and emotional disorders. *Psychological Science, 3*(1), 65–69.

Mitchell, R.W. (1986). A framework for discussing deception. In R.W. Mitchell & N.S. Thompson (Eds.), *Deception: Perspectives on human and nonhuman deceit*. SUNY Press.

Mitchell, R.W. & Thompson, N.S. (1986). *Deception: Perspectives on human and nonhuman deceit*. SUNY Press.

Moffitt, T.E. (1987). Parental mental disorder and offspring criminal behavior: An adoption study. *Psychiatry, 50*, 346–360.

Moffitt, T.E. (1993). Adolescent-limited and life-course-persistent antisocial behavior: A developmental taxonomy. *Psychological Reports, 100*(4), 674–701.

Moffitt, T., Caspi, A., Belsky, J. & Silva, P.A. (1992). Childhood experience and the onset of menarche: A test of a sociobiological model. *Child Development, 63*, 47–58.

Moffitt, T.E. & Silva, P.A. (1988). IQ and delinquency: A direct test of the differential detection hypothesis. *Journal of Abnormal Psychology, 97*(3), 330–333.

Montagu, A. (1978). *Learning non-aggression: The experience of nonliterate societies*. Oxford University Press.

Morell, V. (1993). Evidence found for a possible 'Aggression Gene'. *Science, 260*, 1722–1723.

Morris, W.W. (1992). More on the mood–emotion distinction. *Psycoloquy* (an electronic journal) 3.2.1.1.

Morrison, J.R. & Stewart, M.A. (1971). A family study of the hyperactive child syndrome. *Biological Psychiatry, 3*, 189–195.

Muhlbauer, H.D. (1985). Human aggression and the role of central serotonin. *Pharmacopsychiatry, 18*, 218–221.

Mussen, P. & Eisenberg-Berg, N. (1977). *Roots of caring, sharing, and helping*. W.H. Freeman Pub.

Nathanson, D.L. (1992). *Shame and pride: Affect, sex, and the birth of the self*. Norton Pub.

National Research Council (1993). *Understanding and preventing violence*. National Academy Press.

Nesse, R.M. (1990). Evolutionary explanations of emotions. *Human Nature, 1*(3), 261–289.

Nesse, R. (1991). What is mood for? *Psycoloquy* (an electronic journal) 2.9.2.1.

Nesse, R. (1992a). Overevaluation of the mood–emotion distinction. *Psycoloquy* (an electronic journal) 3.2.1.2.

Nesse, R. (1992b). Ethology to the rescue (Reply to Plutchik) *Psycoloquy* (an electronic journal) 3.2.1.6.

Newman, J.P. (1987). Reaction to punishment in extraverts and psychopaths: Implications for the impulsive behavior of disinhibited individuals. *Journal of Research in Personality, 21*, 464–480.

Newman, J.P. & Kosson, D.S. (1986). Passive avoidance learning in psychopathic and nonpsychopathic offenders. *Journal of Abnormal Psychology, 95*(3), 252–256.

Newman, J.P, Patterson, C.M., Howland, E.W. & Nichols, S.L. (1990). *Personality and Individual Differences, 11*(11), 1101–1114.

Newman, J.P., Widom, C.S. & Nathan, S. (1985). Passive avoidance in syndromes of disinhibition: Psychopathy and extraversion. *Journal of Personality and Social Psychology, 48*(5), 1316–1327.

Nowak, M. & Sigmund, K. (1993). A strategy of win-stay, lose-shift that outperforms tit-for-tat in the Prisoner's Dilemma game. *Nature, 364*, 56–58.

Offord, D.R., Boyle, M.H. & Racine, Y.A. (1991). The epidemiology of antisocial behavior in childhood and adolescence. In D.J. Pepler & K.H. Rubin (Eds.), *The development and treatment of aggression*. Lawrence Erlbaum Pub.

Olson, S.L. (1989). Assessment of impulsivity in preschoolers: Cross-measure convergences, longitudinal stability, and relevance to social competence. *Journal of Clinical Child Psychology, 18*(2), 176–183.

Olweus, D. (1986). Aggression and hormones: Behavioral relationship with testosterone and adrenaline. In D. Olweus, J. Block & M. Radke-Yarrow (Eds.), *Development of antisocial and prosocial behavior: Research, theories, and issues*. Academic Press.

Olweus, D. (1987). Testosterone and adrenaline: Aggressive antisocial behavior in normal adolescent males. In S.A. Mednick, Terrie E. Moffitt, & S.A. Stack (Eds.), *The causes of crime: New biological approaches*. Cambridge University Press.

Ortony, A. & Turner, T.J. (1990). What's basic about basic emotions? *Psychological Review, 97*(3), 315–331.

Ostrom, E. (1990). *Governing the commons*. Cambridge University Press.

Palmer, T. (1983). The "effectiveness" issue today: An overview. *Federal Probation, 26*, 3–10.

Panskepp, J. (1982). Toward a general psychobiological theory of emotions. *Behavioral and Brain Sciences, 5*, 407–422.

Patterson, C.M. & Newman, J.P. (1993). Reflectivity and learning from aversive events. *Psychological Review, 100*(4), 716–736.

Patterson, G.R. (1992). Developmental changes in antisocial behavior. In R.DeV. Peters, R.J. McMahon & V.L. Quinsey (Eds.), *Aggression and violence throughout the lifespan*. Sage Pub.

Patterson, G.R. (1993). *Determinants and outcomes for early and late onset of police arrest.* Presented at the 45th annual meeting of the American Society of Criminology, Phoenix, AZ.

Patterson, G.R., Capaldi, D. & Bank, L. (1991). An early starter model for predicting delinquency. In D.J. Pepler & K.H. Rubin (Eds.), *The development and treatment of aggression*. Lawrence Erlbaum Pub.

Patterson, G.R., DeBaryshe, B.D. & Ramsey, E. (1989). A developmental perspective on antisocial behavior. *American Psychologist, 44*(2), 329–335.

Person, E. S. (1986). Manipulativeness in entrepreneurs and psychopaths. In W.H. Reid, D. Dorr, J.I. Walker & J.W. Bonner, III (Eds.), *Unmasking the psychopath: Antisocial personality and related syndromes*. W.W. Norton Pub.

Petty, F. & Sherman, A.D. (1982). Serotonergic mediation of the learned helplessness animal model of depression. In B.T. Ho, J.C. Schoolar & E. Usdin (Eds.), *Serotonin in biological psychiatry*. Raven Press.

Piliavin, I., Thornton, C, Gartner, R. & Matsueda, R. (1986). Crime, deterrence, and rational choice. *American Sociological Review, 51*, 101–119.

Plomin, R. & Daniels, D. (1987). Why are children in the same family so different from each other? *Behavioral and Brain Sciences, 10*, 1–16.

Plutchik, R. (1980). *Emotion: A psychoevolutionary synthesis*. Harper & Row Pub.

Plutchik, R. (1992). What is mood for? A critique. *Psycoloquy* (an electronic journal) 3.2.1.5.

Premack, D. & Woodruff, G. Does a chimpanzee have a theory of mind? *Behavioral and Brain Sciences, 4*, 515–526.

Pulkkinen, L. (1986). The role of impulse control in the development of antisocial and prosocial behavior. In D. Olweus, J. Block & M. Radke-Yarrow (Eds.), *Development of antisocial and prosocial behavior: Research, theories, and issues*. Academic Press.

Pulliam, H.R. (1982). A social learning model of conflict and cooperation in human societies. *Human Ecology, 10*(3), 353–363.

Quay, H.C. (1990a). Intelligence. In H. C. Quay (Ed.), *Handbook of juvenile delinquency*. Wiley-Interscience Pub.

Quay, H.C. (1990b). Patterns of delinquent behavior. In H. C. Quay (Ed.), *Handbook of juvenile delinquency*. Wiley-Interscience Pub.

Quiatt, D. (1988). Which are more easily deceived, friends or strangers? *Behavioral and Brain Sciences, 11*(2), 260–261.

Quinsey, V.L. & Walker, W.D. (1992). Dealing with dangerousness: Community risk management strategies with violent offenders. In R.DeV. Peters, R.J. McMahon & V.L. Quinsey (Eds.), *Aggression and violence throughout the lifespan*. Sage Pub.

Radke-Yarrow, M. & Zahn-Waxler, C. (1986). The role of familial factors in the development of prosocial behavior: Research findings and questions. In D. Olweus, J. Block & M. Radke-Yarrow (Eds.), *Development of antisocial and prosocial behavior: Research, theories, and issues*. Academic Press.

Raine, A. (1988). Antisocial behavior and social psychophysiology. In H. L. Wagner (Ed.), *Social psychophysiology and emotion: Theory and clinical application*. John Wiley and Sons, Pub.

Raine, A. (1989). Evoked potentials and psychopathy. *International Journal of Psychophysiology, 8*, 1–16.

Raine, A. (1993). *The psychopathology of crime: Criminal behavior as a clinical disorder*. Academic Press.

Raine, A. & Dunkin, J. (1990). The genetic and psychophysiological basis of antisocial behavior: Implications for counseling and therapy. *Journal of Counseling and Development, 68*, 637–644.

Raine, A., Rogers, D.B. & Venables, P.H. (1982). Locus of control and socialization. *Journal of Research in Personality, 16*, 147–156.

Raine, A. & Venables, P.H. (1981). Classical conditioning and socialization—a biosocial interaction. *Personality and Individual Differences, 2*, 273–283.

Raine, A. & Venables, P.H. (1984). Tonic heart rate level, social class, and antisocial behavior in adolescents. *Biological Psychology, 18*, 123–132.

Raine, A. & Venables, P.H. (1987). Contingent negative variation, P3 evoked potentials, and antisocial behavior. *Psychophysiology, 24*(2), 191–199.

Raine, A., Venables, P.H. & Williams, M. (1990a). Relationships between central and autonomic measures of arousal at age 15 years and criminality at age 24 years. *Archives of General Psychiatry, 47*, 1003–1007.

Raine, A., Venables, P.H. & Williams, M. (1990b). Relationships between N1, P300, and contingent negative variation recorded at age 15 and criminal behavior at age 24. *Psychophysiology, 27*(5), 567–574.

Raleigh, M., McGuire, M., Brammer, G., Pollack, D.B. & Yuwiler, A. (1991). Serotonergic mechanisms promote dominance acquisition in adult male vervet monkeys. *Brain Research, 559*, 181–190.

Raleigh, M., McGuire, M., Brammer, G. & Yuwiler, A. (1984). Social status and whole blood serotonin in vervets. *Archives of General Psychiatry, 41*(4), 405–410.

Robins, L.N. (1986). The consequences of conduct disorder in girls. In D. Olweus, J. Block & M. Radke-Yarrow (Eds.), *Development of antisocial and prosocial behavior: Research, theories, and issues.* Academic Press.

Robins, L.N., Tipp, J. & Przybeck, T. (1991). Antisocial personality. In L.N. Robins & D.A. Reiger (Eds.), *Psychiatric disorders in America.* Free Press.

Robins, L.N. & Wish, E. Childhood deviance as a developmental process: A study of 223 urban black men from birth to 18. *Social Forces, 56*(2), 449–473.

Rowe, D.C. (1983a). A biometrical analysis of perceptions of family evironment: A study of twin and singleton sibling kinships. *Child Development, 54*, 416–423.

Rowe, D.C. (1983b). Biometrical genetic models of self-reported delinquent behavior: A twin study. *Behavior Genetics, 13*(5), 473–489.

Rowe, D.C. (1986). Genetic and environmental components of antisocial behavior: A study of 265 twin pairs. *Criminology, 24*(3), 513–532.

Rowe, D.C. (1990a). Inherited dispositions toward learning delinquent and criminal behavior: New evidence. In L. Ellis & H. Hoffman (Eds.), *Crime in biological, social, and moral contexts.* Praeger Pub.

Rowe, D.C. (1990b). As the twig is bent? The myth of child-rearing influences on personality development. *Journal of Counseling and Development, 68*, 606–611.

Rowe, D.C. & Plomin, R. (1981). The importance of nonshared environmental influences on behavioral development. *Developmental Psychology, 17*, 517–531.

Rowe, D.C. & Rodgers, J.L. (1989). Behavioral genetics, adolescent deviance, and "d": Contributions and issues. In G.R. Adams, R. Montemayor & T.P. Gullotta (Eds.), *Biology of adolescent behavior and development.* Sage Pub.

Rowe, D.C., Rodgers, J.L., Meseck-Bushey, S. & St. John, C. (1989). Sexual behavior and nonsexual deviance: A sibling study of their relationship. *Developmental Psychology, 25*, 61–69.

Rubin, R.T. (1987). The neuroendocrinology and neurochemistry of antisocial behavior. In S.A. Mednick, Terrie E. Moffitt & S.A. Stack (Eds.), *The causes of crime: New biological approaches.* Cambridge University Press.

Rushton, J.P. (1982). Social learning theory and the development of prosocial behavior. In N. Eisenberg (Ed.), *The development of prosocial behavior.* Academic Press.

Rushton, J.P. (1989). Genetic similarity, human altruism, and group selection. *Behavioral and Brain Sciences, 12*(3), 503–518.

Rushton, J.P., Fulker, D.W., Neale, M.C., Nias, D.K.B. & Eysenck, H.J. (1986). Altruism and aggression: The heritability of individual differences. *Journal of Personality and Social Psychology, 50*(6), 1192–1198.

Rushton, J.P., Russell, R.J.H. & Wells, P.A. (1984). Genetic similarity theory: An extension to sociobiology. *Behavior Genetics, 14*, 179–193.

Sanchez, J. (1986). Social crises and psychopathy: Toward a sociology of the psychopath. In W.H. Reid, D. Dorr, J.I. Walker & J.W. Bonner, III (Eds.), *Unmasking the psychopath: Antisocial personality and related syndromes.* W.W. Norton Pub.

Satterfeld, J.H. (1987). Childhood diagnostic and neurophysiological predictors of teenage arrest rates: an eight-year prospective study. In S.A. Mednick, Terrie E. Moffitt & S.A. Stack (Eds.), *The causes of crime: New biological approaches.* Cambridge University Press.

Scarr, S. & McCartney, K. (????). How people make their own environments: A theory of genotype–environment effects. *Child Development, 54*, 424–435.

Schalling, D. (1987). Personality correlates of plasma testosterone levels in young delinquents: An example of person–situation interaction? In S.A. Mednick, Terrie E. Moffitt & S.A. Stack (Eds.), *The causes of crime: New biological approaches.* Cambridge University Press.

Schulsinger, F. (1972). Psychopathy: Heredity and environment. *International Journal of Mental Health, 1*, 190–206. (Reprinted in 1977 in S.A. Mednick & K.O. Christiansen (Eds.), *Biosocial bases of criminal behavior.* Gardner Press.)

Segal, N. L. (1991). *Cooperation and competition in adolescent MZ and DZ twins during a Prisoner's Dilemma game.* Presented at the Society for Research on Child Development, Seattle, WA.

Seligman, M.E.P. (1970). On the generality of the laws of learning. *Psychological Review, 77*, 407–418.

Shweder, R.A., Mahapatra, M. & Miller, J.G. (1987). Culture and moral development. In J. Kagan & S. Lamb (Eds.), *The emergence of morality in young children.* Chicago University Press.

Siegel, L.J. (1986). *Criminology.* (2nd edition). West Pub.

Silverton, L. (1988). Crime and the schizophrenia spectrum: A diathesis–stress model. *Acta Psychiatrica Scandinavica, 78*: 72–81.

Simonian, S.J., Tarnowski, K.J. & Gibbs, J.C. (1991). Social skills and antisocial conduct of delinquents. *Child Psychiatry and Human Development, 22*(1), 17–27.

Simons, R.L. (1993). *Family context and developmental timing of delinquent behaviors.* Presented at the 45th annual meeting of the American Society of Criminology, Phoenix, AZ.

Sloman, L. (1992). How mood variation regulates aggression. *Psycoloquy* (an electronic journal) 3.1.1.3.

Snyder, J., Dishion, T.J. & Patterson, G.R. (1986). Determinants and consequences of associating with deviant peers during preadolescence and adolescence. *Journal of Early Adolescence, 6*(1), 29–43.

Snyder, J. & Patterson, G. (1990). Family interaction and delinquent behavior. In H.C. Quay (Ed.), *Handbook of juvenile delinquency.* Wiley-Interscience Pub.

Stabenau, J.R. (1985). Basic research on heredity and alcohol: Implications for clinical application. *Social Biology, 32*(3–4), 297–321.

Stattin, H. & Magnusson, D. (1991). Stability and change in criminal behavior up to age 30. *The British Journal of Criminology, 31*(4), 327–346.

Strauss, C.C. & Lahey, B.B. (1984). Behavior disorders of children. In H.E. Adams & P.B. Sutker (Eds.), *Comprehensive handbook of psychopathology.* Plenum Press.

Surbey, M.K. (1987). Anorexia nervosa, amenorrhea, and adaptation. *Ethology and Sociobiology, 8*, 47S–61S.

Susman, E.J., Inoff-Germain, G., Nottelmann, E.D., Loriaux, D.L., Cutler, G.B., Jr. & Chrousos, G.P. (1987). Hormones, emotional dispositions, and aggressive attributes in young adolescents. *Child Development, 58*, 1114–1134.

Symons, D. (1979). *The evolution of human sexuality.* Oxford University Press.

Tarter, R.E. (1988). Are there inherited behavioral traits that predispose to substance abuse? *Journal of Consulting and Clinical Psychology, 56*(2), 189–196.

Tavris, C.A. (1982). *Anger: The misunderstood emotion.* Simon & Schuster Pub.

Terhune, K.W. (1970). The effects of personality in cooperation and conflict. In P. Swingle (Ed.), *The structure of conflict*. Academic Press.

Thornhill, R. & Alcock, J. (1983). *The evolution of insect mating systems*. Harvard University Press.

Thornhill, R. & Thornhill, N.W. (1992). The evolutionary psychology of men's coercive sexuality. *Behavioral and Brain Sciences*, *15*(2), 363–375.

Tooke, W. & Camire, L. (1991). Patterns of deception in intersexual and intrasexual mating strategies. *Ethology and Sociobiology*, *12*, 345–364.

Traskman, L., Asberg, M., Bertilsson, L. & Sjastrand, L. (1981). Monoamine metabolites in CSF and suicidal behavior. *Archives of General Psychiatry*, *38*, 631–636.

Trasler, G. (1987). Biogenetic factors. In H.C. Quay (Ed.), *Handbook of juvenile delinquency*. Wiley-Interscience Pub.

Tremblay, R.E. (1993). *Cognitive deficits, school achievement, disruptive behavior, and juvenile delinquency: A longitudinal look at their developmental sequence*. Presented at the 45th annual meeting of the American Society of Criminology, Phoenix, AZ.

Trivers, R.L. (1971). The evolution of reciprocal altruism. *Quarterly Review of Biology*, *46*, 35–57.

U.S. Department of Justice. (1992). Criminal victimization in the United States, 1991: A national crime victim survey report (NCJ139563).

U.S. Department of Justice. (1993). A comprehensive strategy for serious, violent, and chronic juvenile offenders: Program summary (NCJ-143453).

Udry, J.R. (1990). Biosocial models of adolescent problem behaviors. *Social Biology*, *37*, 1–10.

Vasek, M.E. (1986). Lying as a skill: The development of deception in children. In R.W. Mitchell & N.S. Thompson (Eds.), *Deception: Perspectives on human and nonhuman deceit*. SUNY Press.

Vila, B.J. & Cohen, L.E. (1993). Crime as strategy: Testing an evolutionary ecological theory of expropriative crime. *American Journal of Sociology*, *98*(4), 873–912.

Volavka, J., Mednick, S.A., Gabrielli, W.F., Matousek, M. & Pollock, V.E. (1984). EEG and crime: Evidence from longitudinal prospective studies. *Advances in Biological Psychiatry*, *15*, 97–101.

Wachs, T.D. (1992). *The nature of nurture*. Sage Pub.

Wade, C. & Tavris, C. (1993). *Psychology* (3rd edition). Harper/Collins Pub.

White, J.L., Moffitt, T.E., Earls, F., Robins, I. & Silva, P.A. (1990). How early can we tell?: Predictors of childhood conduct disorder and adolescent delinquency. *Criminology*, *28*(4), 507–533.

White, J.L., Moffitt, T.E. & Silva, P.A. (1989). A prospective replication of the protective effects of IQ in subjects at high risk for juvenile delinquency. *Journal of Consulting and Clinical Psychology*, *57*(6), 719–724.

Widom, C.S. (1976a). Interpersonal and personal construct systems in psychopaths. *Journal of Consulting and Clinical Psychology*, *44*(4), 614–623.

Widom, C.S. (1976b). Interpersonal conflict and cooperation in psychopaths. *Journal of Abnormal Psychology*, *85*(3), 330–334.

Wilson, M. & Daly, M. (1993). *Homicide as a window on modulated risk-proneness in competitive interpersonal confrontations*. Presented at the 45th annual meeting of the American Society of Criminology, Phoenix, AZ.

Wilson, J.Q. & Herrnstein, R.J. (1985). *Crime and human nature*. Simon & Schuster Pub.

Wolf, P. (1987). Definitions of antisocial behavior in biosocial research. In S.A. Mednick, T.E. Moffitt & S.A. Stack (Eds.), *The causes of crime: New biological approaches*. Cambridge University Press.

Zahn-Waxler, C. & Kochanska, G. (1988). The origins of guilt. In R.A. Thompson (Ed.), *Nebraska symposium on motivation*, vol. 36. University of Nebraska Press.

Zahn-Waxler, C. & Radke-Yarrow, M. (1982). The development of altruism: Alternative research strategies. In N. Eisenberg (Ed.), *The development of prosocial behavior*. Academic Press.

Ziskind, E., Syndulko, K. & Maltzman, I. (1978). Aversive conditioning in the sociopath. *Pavlovian Journal of Biological Science*, *13*(4), 199–205.

Zucker, R.A. & Gomberg, E.S.L. (1986). Etiology of alcoholism reconsidered. *American Psychologist, 41*(7), 783–793.

Zuckerman, M. (1979). *Sensation seeking*. Lawrence Erlbaum Pub.

Zuckerman, M. (1983). *Biological bases of sensation-seeking, impulsivity and anxiety*. Lawrence Erlbaum Pub.

Zuckerman, M. (1984). Sensation seeking: A comparative approach to a human trait. *Behavioral and Brain Sciences, 7*, 413–471.

Zuckerman, M. (1985). Biological foundations of the sensation-seeking temperament. In J. Strelau, F.H. Farley & A. Gale (Eds.), *The biological bases of personality and behavior, vol.1: Theories, measurement techniques, and development*. Hemisphere Pub.

Zuckerman, M. (1989). Personality in the third dimension: A psychobiological approach. *Personality and Individual Differences, 10*(4), 391–418.

Zuckerman, M. (1990). The psychophysiology of sensation seeking. *Journal of Personality, 58*, 313–345.

Zuckerman, M. (1991). *The psychobiology of personality*. Cambridge University Press.

Zuckerman, M., Buchsbaum, M.S. & Murphy, D.L. (1980). Sensation seeking and its biological correlates. *Psychological Bulletin, 88*, 187–214.

Zuckerman, M., DePaulo, B., & Rosenthal, R. (1981). Verbal and nonverbal communication of deception. In L. Berkowitz (Ed.), *Advances in experimental social psychology*. Academic Press.

9 The evolution of the "con Artist"

Lee Alan Dugatkin*
Department of Biological Sciences, State University of New York at Binghamton, Binghamton, New York

A series of game-theoretical models for the evolution of, what in the folk literature has become known as, the "Confidence Artist" is presented. Con artists are assumed to be noncooperators who move between groups and "prey" on naive cooperators. Cooperators learn about con artists by either direct experience or via cultural transmission about the identity (or behavior) of such individuals. Three types of transmission rules about con artists are modeled: 1) transmission rate that is independent of the frequency of con artists in the metapopulation; 2) transmission such that cooperators, with some probability, can learn about *particular* con artists who have entered their group; and 3) a type of frequency dependent transmission such that cooperators can identify con artists in proportion to their frequency in the metapopulation.

In general, cultural transmission works against con artists by 1) decreasing the critical between-patch travel time to invade a metapopulation of cooperators or 2) decreasing the equilibrial frequency of con artists (compared to the case of no cultural transmission). Depending on the mode of cultural transmission, con artists may exist at relatively high or low frequencies.

*Current address: Department of Biology, Mount Allison University, Sackville, New Brunswick, Canada.

Received January 14, 1991; revised July 15, 1991.

Address reprint requests to: Lee Alan Dugatkin, Ph.D., Department of Biology, Mount Allison University, Sackville, New Brunswick, Canada, E0A 3C0.

Ethology and Sociobiology 13: 3–18 (1992)

0162-3095/92$5.00

INTRODUCTION

Few actions in human societies appear as ubiquitous as cooperative behavior. Nonetheless, from evolutionary perspective, cooperation remains something of a mystery. We can all recall scenarios in which cheating (i.e., noncooperative behavior) yields a higher payoff than cooperating. This paradox is formalized in game theory, a branch of economics imported into evolutionary biology by Maynard Smith and Price (1973). Game theory models situations in which the payoff to an individual is dependent on his own behavior plus the behavior of others.

Perhaps the most famous game examining the evolution of cooperation is the so-called Prisoner's Dilemma (Fig. 1). The payoff structure of this game is such that if played once, the most profitable move is to defect (as $T > R$ and $P > S$). However, if both individuals defect they each receive less than had they both cooperated ($R > P$); hence the dilemma. In game theory terms cooperation is the Pareto solution while defection provides the Nash solution to the game.

Cooperation can be salvaged from the Prisoner's Dilemma in two ways. First, cooperators may preferentially interact with other cooperators (Grafen 1979; Hines and Maynard Smith 1979; Fagen 1980; Mirmirani and Oster 1978; Eshel and Cavalli-Sforza 1982; Aoki 1984). Second, a "supergame," with iterated plays between the same opponents, can be envisioned. Often, there will be no foreknowledge of how others will behave when encountered and this information must be obtained by a history of past interactions.

Usually the concept of repeated interactions is represented by a single term, w, the probability that a given interaction will be followed by another

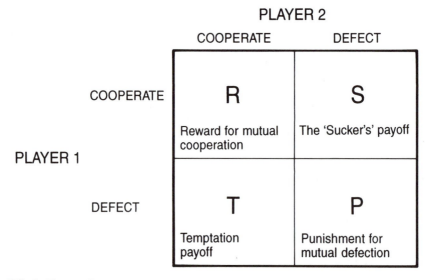

FIG. 1. The payoff matrix qualifies as a Prisoner's Dilemma if: $T > R > P > S$ and $2R > T + S$.

interaction with the same individual. If w is sufficiently high, then a strategy called tit-for-tat (TFT), which begins with a move of cooperation (C) and thereafter imitates the previous behavior of its partner, is exceptionally robust (see Axelrod and Hamilton 1981; Brown et al. 1982; Axelrod 1984; Michod and Sanderson 1985 for general treatments of TFT; and Peck and Feldman 1986; Feldman and Thomas 1987; Boyd and Lorberbaum 1987; Farrell and Ware 1989; Dugatkin 1990 for situations in which TFT can be invaded by other strategies). This rule (begin with C and copy your partner's behavior), endows TFT with three characteristics: 1) It is a "nice" strategy—it cooperates with its partner at the start of a game. 2) It is a "retaliatory" strategy—it defects when its partner defects. 3) It is a "forgiving" strategy—it "forgives" prior moves of defection by a partner if they are followed by a move of cooperation. Nice behavior allows strings of mutual cooperation to begin, retaliation prevents strings of sucker's payoffs from occurring, and forgiving allows reestablishment of strings of mutual cooperation with individuals that defect occasionally or are perceived incorrectly as having defected (Boyd 1989).

Despite the popularity of the iterated Prisoner's Dilemma model in evolutionary game theory, it presents a rarely discussed paradox: How can the assumption of random interactions between individuals in a large population be reconciled with the assumption of repeated interactions required for cooperation to evolve? One possibility is for individuals to form associations at random that persist for an unbroken string of interactions (determined by w) before terminating. Once this association is dissolved, however, the probability of it reforming is near zero, since the original association was formed at random from a large population (Axelrod and Hamilton 1981). In this scenario individuals employing TFT need only remember the previous interaction that they engaged in. It is likely that this does not demand elaborate cognitive abilities.

A second way to reconcile random interactions with repeated interactions is to assume a global population that is divided into a large number of patches within which interactions occur at random. If the patches are relatively small, then individuals within a patch will encounter each other many times. When patches are random samples of the global population, then the expected probability of encountering TFT within a patch will be identical to the proportion of TFT in the global population. Thus, the assumptions of random interactions and repeated interactions can be satisfied simultaneously (Brown et al. 1982; Getty 1987; Dugatkin and Wilson 1991).

I have previously used this second technique to examine the evolution of cooperation when defectors move between groups (Dugatkin and Wilson 1991). Consider a global population of TFT individuals that is subdivided into a large number of patches of size M + 1 individuals, such that each individual interacts with M neighbors. Assume that pairs form randomly within each patch such that an individual interacts, on average, I times (i.e., I represents an expected rather than a fixed value). Figure 2 shows the fitness of an ALL-D mutant as a function of M and I. All of the curves begin with a slope of T and end with a slope of P (see Fig. 1) as the proportion of first interactions with TFT declines from 1 to 0. The rate at which the transition occurs depends on the size of the patch. The fitness of TFT throughout the global population is simply R*I, as shown by the straight line in Fig. 2. Thus, ALL-D cannot invade a global population of TFT as long as I is sufficiently large relative to M. This example translates the term w into biologically interpretable parameters of patch size and duration. Now, however, TFT requires a memory of previous interactions with all M individuals in the patch, which may surpass the cognitive abilities of some species. However, a number of species besides humans appear able to recognize and respond appropriately towards large numbers of conspecifics (Packer 1977; Russell 1983; Wilkinson 1984; Seyfarth and Cheney 1984).

At the same time that patchy environments provide a solution to reconciling random interactions with repeated interactions, this population structure may be subject to invasion by a strategy I have called "roving defector" (ROVER: Dugatkin and Wilson 1991; also see Harpending and Sobus 1987). As Fig. 2 indicates, if the between patch travel time is not prohibitive, defectors should move (rove) from patch to patch, exploiting "naive individuals." At equilibrium, however, TFT individuals should not opt to move as the expected frequency of TFT is the same in all patches, while the expected encounter rate with unknown defectors is highest in new, unexplored patches.

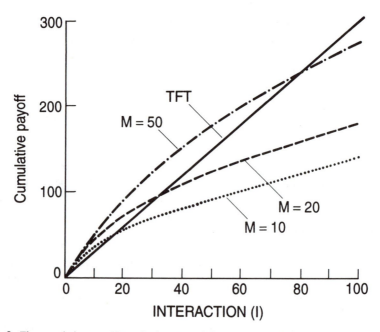

FIG. 2. The cumulative payoff to a single mutant defector and an individual using the TFT strategy in a patch saturated with TFT individuals; T = 5, R = 3, P = 1.

Here, I wish to argue that Roving defectors are analogous to what in the popular literature has been referred to as a "con artist" (Melville 1857; Kuhlman 1972; Nash 1976; Linberg 1982). Con artists move from place to place and leave only once "their cover is blown"; i.e., they are known by too many cooperators. It is in this light that I wish to analyze the evolution of the con artist in human populations.

Surprisingly, the type of cheating practiced by the confidence man has been glamorized in folk tales and thus provides one of the few examples of cheating behavior that seems to be "mythologized" in popular literature. Clearly the behavior of humans, be they con artists or cooperators, is more complex than that examined in Dugatkin and Wilson (1991). An examination of con artists requires explicitly incorporating some type of cultural transmission (Cavalli-Sforza and Feldman 1981; Boyd and Richerson 1985). That is, we must consider the case that an individual can obtain information about a particular con artist, or with con artists in general, without himself being conned. On first glance it would appear that such a modification to the model must favor cooperators. I show here that the dynamics of the game are more complex than this simple prediction leads one to believe.

THE MODEL

Before examining the effect of cultural transmission on the fate of the con artist, it may be helpful to review the original model of Dugatkin and Wilson (1991). Subsequent to this, I explicitly incorporate cultural transmission into the model.

The Metapopulation

Let the metapopulation consist of a large number of patches of size $M + 1$. TFT and ALL-D individuals, in frequencies ϕ and $(1 - \phi)$ are then randomly distributed into these patches. Encounters between individuals in a patch occur at random. The cost of moving from one patch to another is labeled τ and I assume that patches are never revisited within the memory span of the individuals involved.

Gain Curves Within a Patch and Optimal Residence Time

Within an average patch, the expectation of interacting with TFT and ALL-D remains constant at ϕ and $(1 - \phi)$, respectively. For ALL-D, the probability that a TFT individual encountered is naive (i.e., has not met that ALL-D individual before) declines from 1 to 0 as residency in the patch increases.

Fitness of ALL-D. In order to construct ALL-D's expected payoff as a function of 1 (the number of interactions in a patch) the expected number of different TFT individuals ALL-D will meet at least once is calculated. This problem is analogous to a "dice throwing" question in probability theory. Consider an M-sided dice with k-faces red, rolled I times. The expected number of red faces seen at least once during I rolls, e(I), is:

$$e(I) = k(1 - ((M - 1)/M)^I \qquad (1)$$

(see appendix for a derivation of e(I)).

Where I = the number of interactions in a patch, M = patch size, k = the number of TFT in a group (ϕM), and e(I) is the expected number of TFT individuals seen at least once during I interactions. Thus Eq. (1) becomes:

$$e(I) = \phi M(1 - ((M - 1)/M)^I \qquad (2)$$

Since each of ALL-D's interactions, aside from first encounters with TFT individuals, yield a payoff of P, we can calculate the expected value of ALL-D's cumulative payoff as a function of I:

$$G(I)ALL - D = e(I)T + (I - e(I))P \qquad (3)$$

When G(I)All-D is plotted against I (see Fig. 2), the shape is similar to those found in optimal foraging problems on patch residence time (Charnov 1976; Stevens and Krebs 1986), suggesting that there is an optimal number of encounters, I* (which could be scaled to residence time), that ALL-D should stay in a patch. As is common in marginal value problems, I assume that ALL-D can correctly assess the optimum. We referred to the optimizing ALL-D as ROVER (Dugatkin and Wilson 1991). Here, since I will consider the case of cultural transmission about cheaters, I call such a strategy "Con Artist" (hereafter referred to as CA).

Assume that the cost of traveling between patches (τ) is the lost opportunity to interact, such that τ can be expressed as a number of interactions with zero payoff. I assume that the fitness of CON-ARTIST is proportional to the average payoff per unit interaction, including both the number of interactions within the patch (I) and the number of "interactions" spent traveling between patches (τ). Thus the payoff to CA, labeled W_{CA} can be calculated as follows:

$$W_{CA} = \frac{G(I*)CA}{\tau + I*} = \frac{e(I*) + (I* - (e(I*))P}{\tau + I*} \qquad (4)$$

where I* = the optimal number of encounters CA should remain in a patch.

Since I* cannot be obtained analytically (Charnov 1976), a computer simulation that incremented I by a value of one until the maximum pay-off was achieved (e.g., the point at which the average rate of gain in the environment equals the instantaneous rate of gain in a patch) was used.

For some parameter values the optimal decision for CA is to "settle down" in a patch for its entire lifetime rather than move between patches. In all simulations an arbitrary lifetime of $L = 1000$ interactions was used to calculate the fitness of a sedentary CA. This fitness was also used whenever it exceeded the fitness calculated from Eq. (4). For symmetry, when CA settles down, I also assume a lifetime of $L = 1000$ interactions for TFT.

Calculating TFT's Fitness. In an average patch, a proportion ϕ of TFT's interactions will be with other TFT's, yielding a payoff of R. At the start of TFT's life, first-time interactions with CA begin at a frequency of $(1 - \phi)$ and then converge to a steady state frequency determined by the flux of CAs through the patch, which in turn depends on the optimal residence time of CA. Assuming a lifetime of many interactions ($L = 1000$), the initial period of disequilibrium can be ignored and TFT's fitness can be calculated as follows: The probability of a particular TFT meeting a particular CA that remains in a patch for I^* interactions is $1 - ((M - 1)/M)^{I^*}$. If $(1 - \phi)M$ is the proportion of CAs in a patch and if I^* is the residence time of each CA, then CAs arrive at the rate of $(1 - \phi)M/I^*$. Multiplying the arrival rate by the probability of meeting any particular CA at least once, we obtain the proportion of encounters with CA that yield a payoff of S .

If we let $Y = (1 - ((M - 1)/M)I^*(1 - \phi)M/1^*$, when CA is not sedentary, then

$$G(I)_{TFT} = L[\phi R + (1 - \phi)[(YS) + (1 - Y)P]] \qquad (5)$$

This function is linear because the numbers of CAs entering and leaving a patch are in steady state, such that the proportion of CAs encountered for the first time remains constant. I assume the fitness of TFT is proportional to the average payoff per unit interaction;

$$W_{TFT} = \frac{G(I)_{TFT}}{L}$$

$$= [\phi R + (1 - \phi)[(YS) + 1 - Y)P]] \qquad (6)$$

If, however, CA is sedentary, TFT's payoff is calculated using the logic of (4), only now with ROVER's being the (k) red faces on an M sided dice. If we let $\varepsilon(I)$ equal the expected number of CAs met at least once, then

$$\varepsilon(I) = (1 - \phi)M(1 - ((M - 1)/M)^L)$$

and

$$W_{TFT} = \frac{\varepsilon(I)S + L\phi R + (L - (\varepsilon(I) + L\phi))P}{L} \qquad (7)$$

The three terms of (7)'s numerator represent first encounters with CAs, all encounters with TFT individuals and subsequent encounters with CAs.

As with virtually all game theory models, a haploid genetic system is assumed, with the expectation that the results can be generalized to at least some diploid genetic systems (Maynard Smith 1982; Peck and Feldman 1986).

For every set of parameter values, I* for CA was first determined and then used to calculate the fitness of both CA and TFT.

Three Models for Cultural Transmission

Cultural transmission was incorporated into the model described above in three ways:

1) Frequency independent transmission about con artists (FITR). In this simple model, I assume that the transmission rate about CAs, labeled λ, is fixed, i.e., it is independent of the frequency of CAs. Transmission from others in a group allows some TFT to recognize a CA individual on its first encounter and play defect rather than cooperate.

To accomplish this the model is modified in the following way: If I* < L (i.e., con artist has not settled down), Eqs. (4) and (6) must be changed to:

$$W_{CA} = \frac{(e(I^*)(1-\lambda)T) + (I^* - (e(I^*)(1+\lambda))P}{\tau + I^*} \qquad (8)$$

$$W_{TFT} = \phi R + (1-\phi)((Y(1-\lambda)S) + ((1-Y) + Y\lambda)P]. \qquad (9)$$

Here λ diminishes the number of T's and S's obtained and increases the number of P's. When I* > L, Eqs. (4) (with a denominator of L) and (7) must be changed similarly.

2) The "con artist specific" model. Here I assume that a con artist can cheat one individual in a group, but that all other individuals in the group are informed of the identity of *that particular con artist* with some probability δ and therefore begin any interaction with that individual by defecting with that probability. This is analogous to assuming that group members become "inoculated" against a particular con artist. Here information regarding the characteristics of a particular individual needs to be transmitted (e.g., via posters with the description of the alleged cheater).

3) The frequency dependent model. Here, the transmission of information about con artists is a function of $(1 - \phi)$. Hence the probability that a cooperator is conned is a monotonically decreasing function of the proportion of the metapopulation that are con artists.

λ is now a function of $(1 - \phi)$, such that:

$$\lambda = a(1 - e^{(-(1 - \phi)b)}) \qquad (10)$$

where (10) is an exponential saturation equation with "a" representing the asymptotic value of λ and b controlling the rate at which this asymptotic value is reached. Note that since $\lambda = 0$ when $(1 - \phi) = 0$, the frequency dependent model does not affect the conditions for the invasion of CAs.

In all three models, *mechanisms* for cultural transmission are left unspecified, but could, for example, be such things as gossip, posters of alleged cheaters, or any other number of intragroup or intergroup communication mechanisms via both horizontal and/or vertical transmission.

RESULTS

No Cultural Transmission

For comparative purposes, it may be useful at this point to briefly review the results of Dugatkin and Wilson 1991; i.e., the case of no cultural transmission. Here we calculated the travel time (labeled τ_{crit}) below which ROVER could invade a population of TFT and then proceeded to examine the fate of ROVER at values of such that $\tau < \tau_{crit}$.

In the above case, invasion of ROVER is generally favored when the reward for mutual cooperation is low and the punishment for mutual defection is high, relative to the temptation and sucker's payoffs. In some cases there was little latitude for polymorphism, with ROVER sweeping to fixation at travel cost values only slightly lower than those that allowed ROVER to invade. The metapopulation then consisted of ROVER or TFT, with small changes in parameter values causing a flip from one to the other. In other cases a stable polymorphism existed for a wide range of between patch travel times. In general, the same factors that increased ROVER's chance of invading increased the potential for polymorphism. It should be noted that for virtually all parameter values that yielded a stable polymorphism, ROVER was the majority.

Additional insight was gained by inspecting the absolute fitness of the strategies as a function of the frequency of ROVER (Fig. 3). At first, ROVER's fitness declined as it encountered an increasing proportion of other ROVERs in the patches it entered. As a result, increasing the proportion of ROVERs in the metapopulation had the effect of flattening its gain curve and increasing the

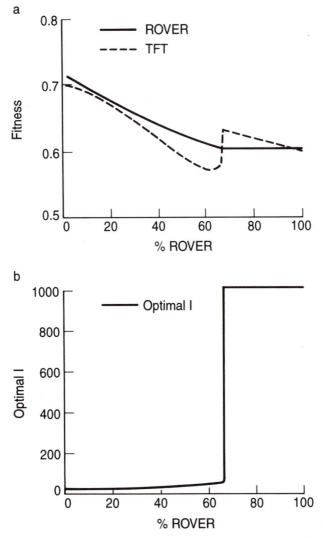

FIG. 3. No cultural transmission. (a) The fitness of ROVING defectors and TFT individuals is shown as a function of the percent of the population composed of ROVERs $(1 - \phi)$. T = 1, R = 0.7, P = 0.6, S = 0, M = 10, and $\tau = 0.9 \; \tau_{crit}$. (b) The change in I* as function of $1 - \phi$ (same parameter values as in (a)).

optimal residence time within single patches. Figure 3(b) shows that the increase in I* was gradual at first but then rose precipitously, at which point CA obtained a higher fitness by becoming sedentary.

TFT's fitness also declined as it encountered an increasing proportion of ROVERs, but then it rose, before declining again to a final value close to P. This bump coincided with the precipitous increase in the optimal number of interactions to remain in a patch as ROVER nears its settle-down point (Figs.

3(a), 3(b)). Before the rise, a substantial proportion of interactions with ROVERs resulted in the low sucker's payoff. After the rise, virtually all interactions resulted in the higher payoff of mutual defection. This shift from the sucker's payoff to the payoff for mutual defection actually increased the absolute fitness of TFT despite the fact that a slightly higher proportion of ROVERs were being encountered. After the shift, increasing the frequency of ROVERs decreased the fitness of TFT.

Frequency Independent Transmission Rate (FITR)

Table 1 shows the effect of FITR on between patch travel time and the equilibrial frequency of CA. Compared with the case of no transmission (FITR = 0), any positive FITR causes a large drop in the critical between patch travel time. That is, patches must be much closer together in order for CA to invade a population of cooperators, thus limiting the opportunity for CA to evolve above mutation frequency. When FITR is sufficiently high (for a given set of T, R, P and S) CA can never invade as the travel time needed for CA to invade is less than 0. If, however, this is not the case, CA equilibrates at a higher frequency when FITR > 0. This somewhat paradoxical result is due to the following; Initially FITR decreases the probability that CA will encounter a "naive" TFT and thus causes patches to be less profitable. This, in turn, translates into a decrease in I*, which causes a greater flow of CA in and out of patches causing a larger proportion of TFT encounters with CA to result in sucker's payoffs as opposed to mutual punishment, thereby increasing the equilibrial frequency of CA.

CON-ARTIST Specific Model

Although this model is quite different than the FITR model, the results are similar. In the FITR model all patches were the same in terms of transmission rate. In the CA specific model, however, new patches allow at least a single payoff of T, before transmission begins. As with λ, increasing δ causes the

TABLE 1

τ_{crit} and the Equilibrial Frequency of CA for Different Frequency Independent Transmission Rates

	FITR									
	0		0.2		0.4		0.6		0.8	
M	τ	%CA	τ	%CA	τ	%CAT	τ	%CAT	τ	%CA
10	2.41	66	1.57	75	0.81	82	0.22	93	<0	0
30	7.02	69	4.53	75	2.31	83	0.59	100	<0	0
50	11.63	69	7.49	75	3.81	83	0.96	100	<0	0
70	11.64	69	10.45	75	5.31	83	1.33	100	<0	0

In all cases T = 1, R = 0.7, P = 0.6, S = 0, and $\tau = 0.9\ \tau_{crit}$.

critical between patch travel time to decrease dramatically, thus reducing the possibility of invasion by CA. When δ becomes sufficiently large (the exact value is dependent on the values entered in the payoff matrix), the optimal residence time for CA when it is at very low frequency approaches 1. At this point CA can only invade if fitness lost during traveling between patches (i.e., τ translated into fitness units) is $< T - R$.

Frequency Dependent Model

While the parameter space for this model is far too large to explore in any systematic fashion a number of generalities seem to emerge from the simulations run. First, not surprisingly, increasing the asymptotic transmission rate (a) and/or the pace at which this asymptote is reached (b) causes CA to equilibrate at a lower frequency. Second, for a given payoff matrix, the equilibrium values of CA and TFT can vary dramatically as a function of a, b, and between patch travel time. For example Figures 4(a)–(d) examine: a = 0.7; $\tau = 0.75\ \tau_{crit}$ or $0.1\ \tau_{crit}$; b = 3 or 10. Even with the confines of this small parameter space, the equilibrial value of CA varies from <5% to >95% (Fig. 4). In addition, under certain conditions, the frequency dependent model produces two stable internal equilibria such that equilibrial frequency depends on starting conditions (Fig. 4(a)).

DISCUSSION

Although evolutionary game theory has had a large impact on the study of animal social behavior (Maynard Smith 1982; Axelrod and Dion 1988), rarely have particular "personality types" been examined using this technique. Normally, theoretical models of social interactions attach the somewhat amorphous terms "cooperator" and "defector" to strategies, rather than define a particular type of behavior that might qualify as cooperation or defection. While Harpending and Sobus (1987) attempt to categorize sociopathy in males and hysteria (Briquet's syndrome) in females as examples of nonreciprocators in human populations, they present only a brief mathematical model examining the evolution of such "types" and concentrate instead on the ethnography of sociopathy. Harpending and Sobus (1987) end the discussion of their model, "in a hypothetical world where there are isolated closed communities of reciprocators with perfect memory, a skilled cheater would spend a certain amount of time in a population, the time depending on payoffs to cheating and the proportion of naive reciprocators. He would then seek a new population." My previous work (Dugatkin and Wilson 1991) led me, independently, to the same conclusion.

Before proceeding any further, a number of caveats about the models presented here are in order. First, Axelrod (1986) examined the evolution of cooperation in societies that have adopted "metanorms" such as "punish

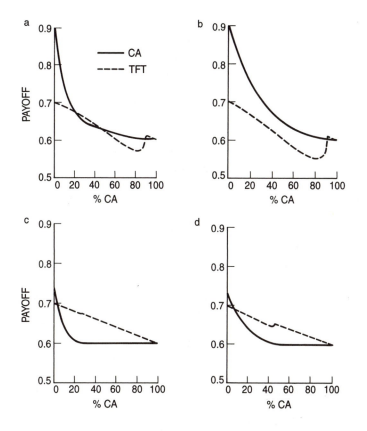

FIG. 4. The payoff to CA and TFT as a function of the frequency of CA. In all cases T = 1, R = 0.7, P = 0.6, S = 0. (a) a = 0.7, b = 10, $\tau = 0.1\tau_{crit}$; (b) a = 0.7, b = 3, $\tau = 0.1\ \tau_{crit}$; (c) a = 0.7, b = 10, $\tau = 0.75\ \tau_{crit}$; (d) a = 0.7, b = 3, $\tau = 0.75\ \tau_{crit}$.

someone who does not punish a known defector." Such metanorms, which are likely ubiquitous to human societies, are absent in the models presented here. Second, group (patch) structure in nature is itself complex and is governed by birth, death, emigration, and extinction. Such complexities are omitted from my models. Third, the mechanism of cultural transmission is unspecified (e.g., vertical vs horizontal transmission) in all models presented here. Lastly, an underlying assumption of both the frequency dependent and frequency independent models is that cooperators can identify con artists when neither they (the cooperators), nor in the extreme case any one in their group, has had any experience with a CA individual. This is equivalent to assuming that CA individuals have some sort of tag that allows them to be identified by cooperators. Dawkins (1982) refers to this problem in the context of the evolution of altruism as the "green beard" effect. In the frequency dependent and independent models, at equilibrium, the "green beard" is simply entering a patch from the outside (as it never pays for cooperators to move across groups). If we assume, however, that some TFT individuals do move between patches, perhaps as a result of "mistakes" or habitat destruction, constructing a green beard for CA becomes more problematic. In human societies, this problem may be surmounted as information transfer across groups (e.g., news, "gossip," etc.) might allow naive cooperators to identify cheaters and thus provide the needed greenbeard.

An alternative means of surmounting the green beard problem is suggested by Frank (1988). He argues that Nietzsche's proverb "One can lie with the mouth, but with the accompanying grimace one nevertheless tells the truth" is apropos to the evolution of cooperation. Frank's premise is that the benefit accrued by mutual cooperation has selected for cooperators to behave in a manner that is not subject to imitation on the part of cheaters. In other words, the best way to behave like a cooperator is to be a cooperator. Frank, however, is clear that the material benefits of cooperation do not underlie the motivational state associated with cooperation, "Trustworthiness, provided it is recognizable, creates valuable opportunities that would not otherwise be available. The fact that trustworthy persons do receive a material benefit is of course what sustains the trait within the individualistic framework. But even if the world were to end at midnight, thus eliminating all possibility of penalty for defection, the genuinely trustworthy person would not be motivated to cheat" (Frank 1988, p. 69). Such trustworthiness would also provide the necessary green beard to label cooperators. It is equally likely, however, that selection will have acted to produce cheaters that are adept at hiding their intentions. Harpending and Sobus (1987) stress this in their paper on sociopathy, "since a cheating adaptation should require, above all else, concealment of the trait, recognition and diagnosis of these traits in humans will always be difficult and ambiguous at the level of language and interpersonal interaction.''

When developing the original model of defectors moving between patches in a subdivided metapopulation (Dugatkin and Wilson 1991), it became clear that the human analog to such a strategy could be best represented by the con artist of literary fame. The original model (Dugatkin and Wilson 1991), which had no cultural transmission factors, found mobile defectors, if they could surmount invasion conditions, almost always emerged as the majority strategy. This clearly does not fit the idea of the con man, whose very talents lie tied to it being rare in the population. To attempt to create a model that more closely resembled interactions in human society and which might yield results in which con men were present, but rare, various types of cultural transmissions were incorporated. Only the frequency dependent model, however, produced an equilibrium scenario wherein con artists were rare. In the other models presented here, it is much more difficult for CAs to invade a population of cooperators, but if conditions allow invasion, CAs usually equilibrate as the majority strategy.

Even the results of the frequency dependent model may be disheartening to field researchers. Although this model may be the most "realistic" of those presented because of the explicit frequency dependent nature of transmission rates, it nonetheless indicates that the value of many parameters needs to be known accurately to predict the equilibrial frequency of CAs in a given area. In the case where the model predicts two internal stable equilibria it is also necessary to know "initial conditions" to make any predictions.

I thank D.S. Wilson for his collaboration on the original ROVER idea and his thoughts on incorporating cultural transmission into that model. I also thank T. Getty, J. Newman, H. Harpending, and two anonymous referees for helpful suggestions. G. Pollock, P.D. Taylor, and D.S. Wilson all helped in deriving the appendix. This work was supported by a National Science Foundation Dissertation Grant (No. BSR-8914333) to the author.

Appendix

I am grateful to P.D. Taylor for the following derivation.

Consider an M-sided die, with k faces red rolled I times. Let $p_0, p_1 \cdots p_k$ equal the probability that $0, 1, \ldots k$ faces have been seen after I throws. For the $(I + 1)$th throw, the probability that no red faces have been seen is:

$$p_0(M - k)/M$$

and the probability that $0 < j \leq k$ red faces have been seen is:

$$p_{j-1}[(k - j + 1)/M)] + p_j(M - k + j)/M.$$

For example, let $M = 10$ and $k = 4$. The probability that $j = 2$ red faces have been seen after $I + 1$ throws is the sum of these two terms; (a) the probability that one red face was seen after I throws (p_{j-1}) times the probability that one of the three remaining red faces was seen on the $(I + 1)$th throw $(k - j + 1)/M$, and (b) the probability that two red faces were seen after I throws (p_j) times the probability that neither of the remaining two faces were seen on the $(I + 1)$th throw $(M - k + j)/M$.

Let e_I = the expected number of red faces seen after I throws = Σjp_j

$$
\begin{aligned}
e_{I+1} &= \Sigma jp_j(M - k + j)/M + \Sigma(j + 1)p_j(k - j)/M \\
&= \Sigma jp_j(M - k)/M + \Sigma(j + 1)p_j k/M - \Sigma p_j j/M \\
&= \Sigma jp_j(1 - (1/M)) + \Sigma p_j k/M \\
&= e_I[1 - (1/M)] + k/M.
\end{aligned}
$$

Subtract k from both sides

$$e_{I+1} - k = (e_I - k)(1 - (1/M)).$$

Now let $e_0 = 0$, so $e_1 = k/M$. The general solution of the recursion is:

$$e_I = k\{1 - [(M - 1)/M]^I\}.$$

REFERENCES

Aoki, K. (1984). A quantitative genetic model of two policy games between relatives. *J. Theo. Etiol.*, *109*, 111–126.

Axelrod, R. (1980a). Effective choices in the Prisoner's Dilemma. *J. Conf Resol.*, *24*, 3–25.

Axelrod, R. (1980b). More effective choices in the Prisoner's Dilemma. *J. Conf. Resol.*, *24*, 379–403.

Axelrod, R. (1984). *The evolution of cooperation*. New York: Basic Books.

Axelrod, R. (1986). *An evolutionary approach to norms. Am. Pol. Sci. Rev.*, *80*, 1095–1111.

Axelrod, R. & Hamilton, W.D. (1981). The evolution of cooperation. *Science*, *211*, 1290–1396.

Axelrod, R. & Dion, D. (1988). More on the evolution of cooperation. *Science*, *242*, 1385–1390.

Boyd, R. (1989). Mistakes allow evolutionary stability in the repeated Prisoner's Dilemma game. *J. Theor. Biol.*, *136*, 47–56.

Boyd, R. & Richerson, P. (1985). *Culture and the evolutionary process*. Chicago: University of Chicago Press.

Boyd, R. & Lorberbaum, J. (1987). No pure strategy is evolutionarily stable in the repeated Prisoner's Dilemma game. *Nature*, *327*, 58–59.

Brown, J., Sanderson, M., & Michod, R. (1982). Evolution of social behavior by reciprocation. *J. Theor. Biol.*, *99*, 319–339.

Cavalli-Sforza, L., & Feldman, M. (1981). *Cultural transmission and evolution*. Princeton: Princeton University Press.

Chamov, E. (1976). Optimal foraging theory: the marginal value theorem. *Theor. Pop. Biol.*, *9*, 129–136.

Dawkins, R. (1982). *The Selfish Gene*. Oxford: Oxford University Press.

Dawkins, R. (1982). *The extended phenotype*. Oxford: Oxford University Press.

Dugatkin, L.A. (1990). N-person games and the evolution of cooperation: a model based on predator inspection in fish. *Jour. Theo. Biol.*, *142*, 123–135.

Dugatkin, L.A. & Wilson, D.S. (1991). ROVER: A strategy for exploiting cooperators in a patchy environment. *Am. Nat.*, in press.

Eshel, I. & Cavalli-Sforza, L.L. (1982). Assortment of encounters and the evolution of cooperativeness. *Proc. Nat. Acad. Sci.*, *79*, 1331–1335.

Fagen, R. (1980). When doves conspire: Evolution of nondamaging fighting tactics in a nonrandom encounter animal conflict model. *Am. Nat.*, *115*, 858–869.

Farrell, J., & Ware, R. (1989). Evolutionary Stability in the repeated Prisoner's Dilemma. *Theor. Pop. Bio.*, *36*, 161–168.

Feldman M., & Thomas, E. (1987). Behavior-dependent contexts for repeated plays of the Prisoner's Dilemma II: Dynamical aspects of the evolution of cooperation. *J. Theor. Biol.*, *128*, 297–315.

Frank, R. (1988). *Passions within reason*. Ontario: Penguin Books.

Getty, T. (1987). Dear enemies and the Prisoner's Dilemma: Why should territorial neighbors form defensive coalitions? *Amer. Zool.*, *27*, 327–336.

Grafen, A. (1979). The hawk–dove game played between relatives. *Anim. Behav.*, *27*, 905–907.

Harpending, H., & Sobus, J. (1987). Sociopathy as an adaptation. *Ethology and Sociobiology, 8,* 63s–72s.

Kuhlman, S. (1972). *Knave, fool and genius.* North Carolina: The University of North Carolina Press.

Linberg, G. (1982). *The confidence man in American Literature.* New York: Oxford University Press.

Maynard Smith, J. (1982). *Evolution and the theory of games.* Cambridge: Cambridge University Press.

Maynard Smith, J. & Price, G. (1973). The logic of animal conflicts. *Nature, 246,* 15–18.

Melville, H. (1857). *The Confidence Man.* The Bobbs-Merill Press.

Michod, R., & Sanderson, M.J. (1985). Behavioral structure and the evolution of cooperation. In J.J. Greenwood and M. Slatkin (Eds.), *Evolution—Essays in honour of John Maynard Smith* (pp. 95–104). Cambridge: Cambridge University Press.

Mirmirani, M., & Oster, G. (1978). Competition, kin selection and evolutionary stable strategies. *Theor. Pop. Bio., 13,* 304–349.

Nash, J. (1976). *Hustlers and con men.* New York: M. Evans.

Packer, C. (1977). Reciprocal altruism in *Papio anubis. Nature, 265,* 441–443.

Peck, J., & Feldman, M. (1986). The evolution of helping behavior in large randomly mixed populations. *Am. Nat., 127,* 209–221.

Russell, J. (1983). Altruism in coati bands: Nepotism or reciprocity? In S.K. Wasser (Ed.), *Social behavior of female vertebrates* (pp. 263–290). New York: Academic Press.

Seyfarth, R. & Cheney, D. (1984). Grooming alliances and reciprocal altruism in vervet monkeys. *Nature, 308,* 541–543.

Wilkinson, G. (1984). Reciprocal food sharing in vampire bats. *Nature, 308,* 181–4.

10 How to build a baby that can read minds: Cognitive mechanisms in mindreading

Simon Baron-Cohen
University of Cambridge

The eight central claims of the paper are that: (1) Humans have evolved to be able to attribute mental states to interpret and predict action—that is, to "mindread" (Premack's claim). (2) The neurocognitive system dedicated to this function (the Mindreading System) has 4 modular components: (a) an Intentionality Detector (ID), akin to Premack's suggestion, whose function is to represent behaviour in terms of volitional states (desire and goal); (b) an Eye Direction Detector (EDD), whose function is initially to detect the presence of eye-like stimuli, and later to represent their direction as an Agent "seeing" the Self or something else; (c) a Shared Attention Mechanism (SAM), whose function is to represent if the Self and another Agent are attending to the same object or event; and (d) a Theory of Mind Mechanism (ToMM), as Leslie outlines, whose function is to represent the full range of mental states (including the epistemic ones), and to integrate mental state knowledge into a coherent and usable theory for interpreting action. (3) ID and EDD are held to process dyadic representations, SAM processes triadic representations, and ToMM processes what Leslie calls "M-Representations". (4) Whilst SAM can build triadic representations from the output of either ID or EDD, these are more easily built in the visual modality, hence the evolution of a special relationship between EDD and SAM. (5) SAM also functions to link ID with EDD, enabling eye-direction to be read in terms of volitional states. (6) When SAM outputs its triadic representations to ToMM, this triggers the latter to function. (7) A subgroup of children with autism are postulated to be impaired in SAM, whilst congenitally blind children are not. (8) In this subgroup of autism, ToMM is therefore not activated.

Correspondence should be sent to Simon Baron-Cohen, Departments of Experimental Psychology and Psychiatry, University of Cambridge, Downing Street, Cambridge CB2 3EB, U.K. (e-mail: spjtsbc@ucl.ac.uk).
In *Cahiers de Psychologie Cognitive* (Current Psychology of Cognition), 1994, 13 (5), 513–552.

"One of the salient features of other persons in our social world is the action and focus of their eyes. The direction of another's gaze, which seems to indicate something about his or her orientation and focus of attention, may have significance for us and the organization of our own actions, particularly if we happen to be the target of these two distinctive orbs. But others are not invulnerable to the same scrutiny from us and likely will make similar adjustments depending on what they infer about our intentions, based in part on the presence or absence of our apparent attention to them."
(Fehr & Exline, 1978, p. 225).

The idea that humans have evolved an ability to interpret and predict behaviour on the basis of mental status has a relatively recent history (Jolly, 1966; Premack & Woodruff, 1978; Humphrey, 1984; Byrne & Whiten, 1988; Cheney & Seyfarth, 1990). These authors have all argued in different ways that an ability to read behaviour in terms of mental states would confer selective advantages for survival and reproduction to those organisms who possessed this ability, in making them better able to make sense of another organism's action, and predict what it might do next.

In this article, I propose the existence of a *Mindreading System* that has evolved specifically to enable attribution of mental states to agents. In its most highly evolved form, the Mindreading System is postulated to have four modular components. Two of these have been described by others (ID: *pace* Premack, 1990; ToMM: Leslie, 1991). I will have relatively little to say about these two mechanisms, as readers can go back to the original papers by these authors for a fuller account of them. The other two mechanisms (EDD and SAM) are, I think, new, though of course they build on a large body of work which I review. My suggestion is that different neurological and phylogenetic populations may lack one or more of these four modules. In the normal human case, all four are present and functioning by 4 years of age. These four modules are "special purpose computational system(s)" (Fodor, 1983, p. 47) in what Brothers (1990) calls the "social brain".

In the main section of the paper, I review the four modules in the order in which I suggest they are active in human development. The proposed relationships between them are shown in Fig. 1, to which you can refer as I describe each mechanism. Before doing this, let me briefly defend my use of the term "module".

CRITERIA FOR MODULARITY

Fodor (1983) is the person who has given most impetus and serious consideration in modern psychology to the notion that the mind and the brain have modular organization. His modularity thesis is summarized in terms of nine tenets. Modules, Fodor argued, have:

1. Domain specificity
2. Informational encapsulation
3. Obligatory firing
4. Shallow outputs
5. Rapid speed
6. Inaccessibility to consciousness
7. A characteristic ontogenetic course
8. A dedicated neural architecture, and
9. A characteristic pattern of breakdown.

As Bates (1993) points out, the first 6 of these tenets also apply to "overlearning", whereby skills acquired through experience become automatized. The last 3 tenets are more applicable to "biological" modules. This clarifies that modules may result from both innate or acquired factors

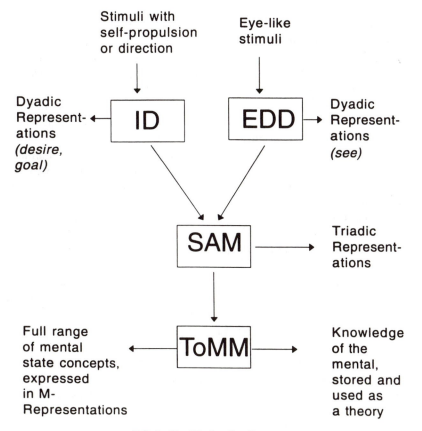

FIG. 1. The Mindreading System.

(Karmiloff-Smith, 1992). Of Fodor's 9 criteria, I reject the need for number 2 (informational encapsulation), since this seems to me to prevent the quite useful possibility that modules interact with one another in the way that I will suggest some of those in the Mindreading System do. Number 4 (shallow outputs) also seems to me to be both unnecessary and somewhat premature to include in the list, since it is an empirical question—in the case of each proposed module—as to what the output is. Number 6 (inaccessibility to consciousness) is also likely to be too strong a criterion, since different modules may vary in the extent to which their contents are accessible to introspection.

This therefore leaves 6 tenets (1, 3, 5, 7, 8, and 9). To each of the four components in the human Mindreading System, I will apply these 6 criteria, in order to see how each one stands up to this definition of a module.

FOUR COGNITIVE MECHANISMS
1. ID

ID stands for the *Intentionality Detector*. It is a primitive perceptual mechanism that I suggest is amodal, and that interprets stimuli in terms of that stimulus' goal or desire. That is, it reads stimuli as volitional. In this system, "goal" is defined as the target an action is directed towards, and "desire" is defined as a movement towards or away from a target. I intend this module to be very similar to—or coterminous with—Premack's (1990, 1991) notion of a module that is hard-wired into the human infant's visual system to detect intentionality. However, because I have modified slightly how I propose this system works, I have renamed it as ID. The suggestion is that human infants (by at least 6 months) read mental states of goal and desire into a wide range of stimuli with *direction* (e.g., a touch, a push, a jump, a shout, an arrow) or that manifest *self-propulsion* (i.e., an object that moves without an apparent external cause). This is basically what Premack also argues, although he implies a smaller set of stimuli triggers an interpretation of goal.

Applying the 6 criteria for modularity to ID, what do we find?

1.1. Domain specificity. Stimuli with direction, and self-propelling stimuli, appear to be a reasonably well-defined domain. Thus, a static circle or square has no direction, whilst a tree-branch does. Similarly, an object moving by apparent self-propulsion differs in key respects from an object that moves as a result of an external force (Mandler, 1992; Leslie, 1994).

A second approach to assessing domain specificity is to ask if the proposed system employs a unique class of representation. I will be using this approach for each of the four mechanisms I discuss in this paper. I suggest that ID builds *dyadic* representations. These specify the relation (in this case, a desire or a goal) between an Agent and something (or someone) else. They are dyadic because they code two entities in a volitional relationship. Dyadic representations can therefore take forms:

a. [Agent-Relation-Self].   Here, the relation term is bidirectional, because both elements are Agents and thus capable of an active relation with something. Examples of this form are:
> [Mummy-wants-me], or
> [I-want-Mummy].

b. [Agent-Relation-Object].   Here, the relation term is unidirectional, since one of the elements is not an Agent. An example of this form is:
> [Mummy-wants-the cup].

c. [Agent$_1$-Relation-Agent$_2$].   Here, again, the relation term is bidirectional, since both elements are Agents. Examples of this are:
> [Mummy-has goal-Daddy], or
> [Daddy-wants-Mummy].

d. [Self-Relation-Object].   Here, the relation term is unidirectional. So an example of this form is:
> [I-have goal-the toy].

Dyadic representations are not unique to ID, however, since I will argue that EDD (see below) also employs them. In this respect, the domain-specificity criterion is only partly fulfilled in the case of ID.

1.2. Obligatory firing.   ID probably meets this criterion, since Heider and Simmel (1944) report that only one out of their whole sample of normal adult subjects did not attribute agency, goal and desire terms to moving geometric shapes in a silent film sequence, when asked to describe what they saw.

1.3. Rapid speed.   No data related to speed are reported by Heider and Simmel, but the impression we have is that we do attribute desires and goals very fast. We don't need to ponder in any laboured fashion in order to compute that a stimulus might "want" something. We see the bee flying towards a colourful flower, and we 'instantly' compute that the bee *wants* to go to the flower.

1.4. Characteristic ontogenesis.   The relevant human infancy studies have not progressed very far, with which to test if ID has a characteristic ontogenesis. However, these studies are underway in several centres (Gergely, Nádasdy, Csibra, & Bíró, in press; Premack, 1993). Certainly older children (Dasser, Ullbaek, & Premack, 1989) readily interpret such minimal stimuli as moving geometric shapes as having goals and desires. And almost as soon as children start to speak, they refer to goals and desires (Wellman, 1990; Bartsch & Wellman, 1994).

1.5. Dedicated neural architecture. Perrett et al. (1992) report that specific cells in the Superior Temporal Sulcus of the monkey brain (the STS) fire in response to perceiving the *direction* of an Agent's head, or body-posture, or directed action (e.g., a hand opening a jar) suggesting that these cells may be detecting "goal" or "desire". However, since other cells in the STS respond to other features, the question of whether ID has a dedicated neural architecture needs more specific investigation.

1.6. Characteristic pattern of breakdown. There are reports that some forms of brain damage in human adult patients can lead to specific deficits in the recognition of agency or animacy (Farah, McMullen, & Meyer, 1991; Warrington & Shallice, 1984; Goodglass, Klein, Carey & Jones, 1966). This suggests that ID may have its own unique neurobiological basis that can be selectively damaged. Again, this needs more careful investigation, in order to establish if neurological patients have specific impairments in recognizing volitional states, versus agency, versus animacy.

In sum, ID fits some (but not all) of the criteria for modularity. I turn now to the other module that I propose is active in the human infant's Mindreading System.

2. EDD

EDD is the *Eye Direction Detector.* I suggest this system has two functions: first, to detect the presence of eyes (or eye-like stimuli). This function appears to be present in a large range of species (see below). Secondly, in the higher primates, EDD also represents eye-behaviour. Tantam (1992) hints that there must be such a mechanism, given the evidence for a primitive "social gaze response". Here I extend this important notion.

Applying the criteria for modularity to EDD, what do we find?

2.1. Domain specificity. Eye-like stimuli certainly constitute a well-defined domain. They typically occur in pairs, and often (though not always) comprise a dark, circular pattern. Human eyes also have contrast, as well as being able to move[1]. Their contrast is of both colour and luminescence, and is between the darker (iris/pupil—or d) region, and the white (sclera—or w) region. EDD in humans, I will argue, is sensitive to both the contrast and movement properties of eyes—it tracks and codes the spatial position of the d region relative to the w region. For convenience, I call these $d{:}w$ representations, three examples of which are depicted in Fig. 2. Naturally, these

---

[1]Another observable property of the eyes is change in pupil size, independent of illumination. People clearly respond to this and are influenced by this in their judgement about attractiveness, etc. Indeed, the use of "belladonna" or atropine to dilate the pupils is correlated with judgements of beauty. See Hess and Petrovich (1978) for a review. I do not discuss pupillometry here.

illustrations only capture the static features of *d:w* representations, and not the dynamic, movement information that must also be specified in these. Whether such representations are unique to EDD, or simply make use of more general properties of the visual system, remains to be tested.

I suggest that, in the human infant, probably from about 4 months of age (Johnson and Vicera, 1993), and possibly in some of the other higher primates, EDD not only detects eye-like stimuli in an "obligatory" fashion, but goes on to build dyadic representations of their behaviour. These dyadic representations have an identical structure to those processed by ID, but whereas for ID the relation slot is filled with a term like "goal" or "desire", in the case of EDD the relation slot is filled with a term like "see". As in the case of ID, EDD's representations are dyadic because there are only two entities, connected by a relation term. And as before, EDD's dyadic representations must thus have one of four forms:

a. [Agent-Relation-Self].   Here,   the   relation   term   is   bidirectional. Examples of this form are:
   [Mummy-sees-me], or
   [I-see-Mummy].

b. [Agent-Relation-Object].   Here, the relation term is unidirectional. An example of this form is:
   [Mummy-sees-the bus].

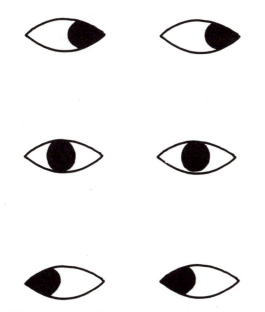

FIG. 2. Schematic illustration of some *d:w* representations.

c. *[Agent₁-Relation-Agent₂].* Here, again, the relation term is bidirectional. Examples of this are:

    [Mummy-sees-Daddy], or
    [Daddy-sees-Mummy].

d. *[Self-Relation-Object].* Here, the relation term is unidirectional. So an example of this form is:

    [I-see-the house].

I have presented the dyadic representations in a 'sentence' form, but for clarity, some dyadic representations that EDD builds are also shown in Fig. 3.

In EDD, the relation term in dyadic representations is *the* crucial advance over *d:w* representations. It specifies that eyes belonging to Agent (or Self) stand in a relation to an object (or person). As with the relation term in ID's dyadic representations, I suggest that this allows the infant to represent some basic properties of intentionality (Brentano, 1984/1970), since intentionality (or "aboutness") is essentially relational[2].

2.2. Obligatory firing.   It is hard not to notice people's eyes, especially when they are pointed at us (see Baron-Cohen, 1995). In this section, I consider the obligatory criterion by reviewing phylogenetic evidence for a special sensitivity to eyes and eye-direction.

Regarding eye-like stimuli, Blest (1957) reports that "eye-spots" are found on peacock tail feathers, on certain moth and butterfly wings (see Fig. 4), on some fish (e.g., Cichlid), on cobras, on some grasshoppers (e.g., *Ommatolampis perspicillata*), on some wasps (e.g., Mutillid) and beetles (e.g., Carabid), and on some pheasants, to name just a few. These eye-spots resemble vertebrate eyes. Evidence that such eye-spots are indeed readily detected comes, for example, from the finding that eye-spots have a deterrent effect on the predator. For example, certain species of moth flash the eye-spots on their wings, and this deters predators (Scaife, 1976). Similarly, Yellow Bunting birds retreat from butterflies with eye-spots, but eat the ones without eye-spots (Blest, 1957).

---

[2]The Self term in dyadic representations implies that the infant already has a localizable concept of self, distinct from another person. I assume infants already have a primitive self-concept, this having been derived from the perceptual distinction between single and dual sensations (Gallup, 1982; Perrett et al., 1990).

The relation slot in EDD's dyadic representations is filled by the term like *see*. I assume EDD can obtain knowledge about eyes seeing from the simple contingencies of closing and opening its own eyes (eyes closed produces the experience of darkness; eyes open produces the experience of light). Whilst this is initially based on its own experience, this knowledge could be generalized to an Agent by analogy with the Self.

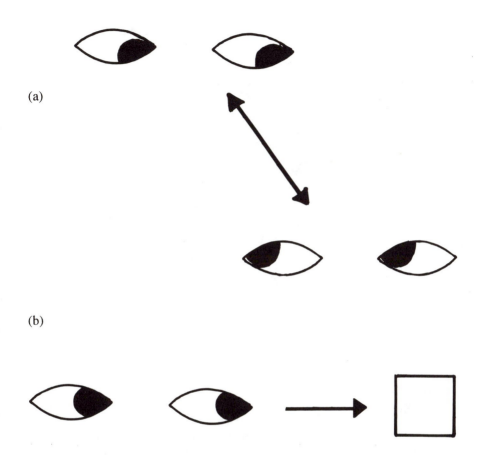

FIG. 3. Schematic illustration of some dyadic representations:
(a) [Agent-Relation-Self]; (b) [Agent-Relation-Object].

All of this probably reflects natural selection taking advantage of the effect of "eyes". According to mimicry theory (Poulton, 1890), such signals may have evolved because eye-spots as stimuli cause the predator to hesitate, thus giving the moth valuable time to escape (Arduino & Gould, 1984). Whether the predator interprets the eye-spots as *eyes looking at them* is not clear: the predator's response could simply be a hard-wired response to a stimulus of this particular shape and colour. For example, Scaife (1976) found that 37 day old white leghorn chicks show most avoidance to two tracking, eye-like shapes[3].

---

[3]Note that eye-spots are not always responded to as dangerous. For example, in the male guppy fish, the eye-spot appears during *courtship*— the male turns his body sideways to present this display to the female (Argyle & Cook, 1916, p. 6).

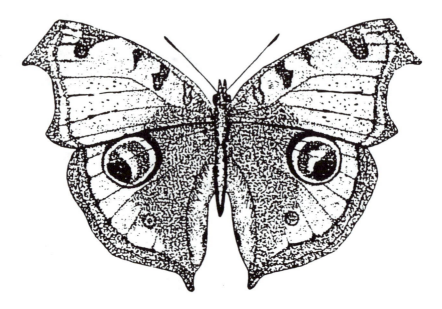

FIG. 4. Eye spots on a moth, adapted from Blest (1957).

As mentioned earlier, EDD is not solely for detecting the *presence* of eyes (though this is part of its job) but also for detecting the *direction* of eyes, since real eyes are directed at different targets in the environment. One likely primitive function of EDD is that it allows an organism to detect if another animal is aiming to attack it. Under this interpretation, eye-direction detection could be construed as a form of threat-detection.

Ristau (1990, 1991) carried out some elegant experiments with plovers, to test if these birds were sensitive to eye-direction, and whether they reacted to eyes directed at them as a threat. The birds were observed in the dunes on the beaches of Long Island, New York, where they nest. Ristau used two human intruders, one of whom looked towards the dunes, the other of whom looked towards the ocean. Each intruder walked up and down the same path, along the coastline, about 15–25 metres from the dunes. Trials began when an incubating parent plover was on her nest. Ristau found that the birds moved off and stayed off their nests for longer periods when the intruder was gazing towards the dunes than when the intruder was gazing towards the ocean. Moving away from the nest was interpreted as a sign of the parent-bird attempting to lead the intruder *away* from the nest. Ristau interpreted this as evidence that these birds are capable of detecting if an intruder is looking at their nest, and that the birds react to gaze so directed as a threat. One should note that in this study the birds had both eye-direction and head-direction available as cues.

Snakes have also been reported to be sensitive specifically to eye-direction as a cue to a potential threat (Burghardt, 1990). For example, if an intruder is about one metre from a hog-nosed snake, and looks directly at the snake, the snake will "feign death" for longer than if the intruder averts its eyes. The same is true of chickens, who also engage in *tonic immobility* for longer in the presence of a human who is staring at them than one who is not looking at them (Gallup, Cummings, & Nash, 1972). The phenomenon of tonic immobility has been documented in a range of other species, such as the lizard (*Anolis carolinensis*: Hennig, 1977), the blue crab (*Callinectes sapidus*: O'Brien & Dunlap, 1975), and ducks (Sargeant & Eberhardt, 1975). [See Arduino & Gould, 1984, for a review.]

Many animals do not react to the eyes with tonic immobility, but nevertheless react with avoidance and fear. For example, macaque monkeys look less at photographic slides of faces with eye-contact than with no eye-contact (Keating & Keating, 1982), and infant macaque monkeys show more emotional disturbance when confronted by a picture of a full face with eye-contact, compared with a picture of a face turned away to profile, with gaze averted (Mendelson, Haith, & Goldman-Rakic, 1982). Perrett and Mistlin (1990) further demonstrated that appeasement behaviours (lip-smacking and teeth-chattering) by macaque monkeys are controlled by gaze angle and head posture, in that they occur more often to a human face looking directly at the animal (from a distance of 1.5m, whether full-face or half-profile), than to a human face tilted backward (see Fig. 5).

Mutual gaze, particularly in the form of a stare, is a well-documented component of threatening displays in many non-human primates, e.g., adult male baboons (Hall & Devore, 1964), gorillas (Schaller, 1964), macaques (Altmann, 1967), and a number of other old-world monkeys and apes (van Hooff, 1962). Chance (1962) describes how struggles for dominance are often only ended with one animal averting its gaze—what he calls a "visual cut-off', possibly as a mechanism for reducing the physiological arousal produced by direct gaze (Wada, 1961; Nichols & Champness, 1971).

This array of studies might suggest the evolution of a "fear" response to eye-direction. However, in the higher primates gaze also occurs as part of grooming, greeting, and play facial expressions in old-world monkeys and apes (van Hooff, 1962). Argyle and Cook (1976), in their review of the literature, conclude that it is only in primates that gaze functions as an affiliative as well as an aggressive cue[4].

---

[4] It is of interest that in non-human primates, the sclera becomes pigmented by adulthood. Perrett and Mistlin (1990) have speculated that this itself may reflect an evolutionary adaptation. Their argument is that since (as we have seen) most primates respond to direct eye-contact as a threat, pigmentation of the sclera may allow one animal to watch another 'out of the corner of its eye" without risking overt staring eye-contact. This is because pigmentation of the sclera makes it more difficult for an animal to discern another animal's eye-direction, at least in profile direction. It may be however that in the human case it was evolutionarily adaptive to *maximize* the possibility of eye-direction being detected—in order to optimize the prosocial signal that eye-direction can convey. This would account for why in the human case, the sclera remains white throughout life.

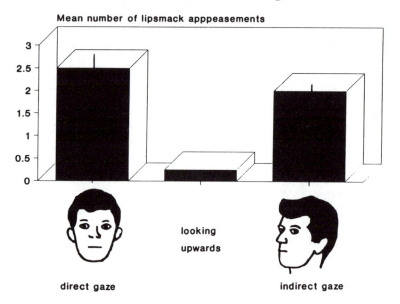

FIG. 5. Evidence of the fear response (measured in lip-smack appeasement) to eye-contact, by macaques (adapted from Perrett & Mistlin, 1990).

2.3. Rapid speed. As with ID, no specific reaction time data are available, but our impression is that "eyes looking at me" have a 'pop-out' effect—among a crowd of faces, we rapidly detect the face that is "looking at me".

2.4. Characteristic ontogenesis. If we focus on the human case, it is useful to think in terms of other people's eyes triggering EDD to fire, much like an Innate Releasing Mechanism (Tinbergen, 1951; Spitz, 1965). The idea is that when EDD detects eye-like stimuli, it fixates on these for relatively long bursts. We can infer the presence of EDD in the human neonate from Maurer's (1985) studies. For example, these report that 2 month old infants look almost as long at the eyes as at a whole face, whilst significantly less at other parts of the face[5]. These data are shown in Fig. 6. Haith, Bergman, and Moore (1977), and Hainline (1978) also found this, and Papousek and Papousek (1979) showed that 6 month olds look 2 to 3 times longer at a face looking at them than

---

[5]Johnson and Morton (1991) suggest that a logically prior mechanism (CONSPEC) initially directs the newborn infant to look at faces. CONSPEC may thus locate the right "stimulus ball-park" for EDD to be triggered.

at a face looking away. At the very least, this shows a natural preference for looking at the eyes over and above other parts of the face.

Argyle and Cook (1976) note that during breast-feeding the infant is in an optimum position to see the mother's eyes, and that mothers use very long gaze durations (more than 30 secs) towards their infants, making them akin to "supernormal" stimuli (Stern, 1977). In addition, infant's control over their visual system appears precociously mature, enabling the infant to make or break eye-contact, and thus regulate the degree of eye-contact (Stern, 1977; Schaffer, 1977). Vine (1973) suggests it is the *contrast* of the mother's eyes which makes them salient within the face.

Developmental changes in the psychophysics of EDD merit further experimentation. Lasky and Klein (1979) found that 5 month old human infants look longer at a face showing direct eye-contact than one with averted gaze, and Johnson and Vecera (1993) report 4 month olds show a similar capacity to distinguish these. Butterworth's (1991) experiments reveal that 6 month olds can judge if an Agent's eyes are looking left or right, but not at which of two objects on one side the Agent is looking. By 12 months old, they can make these discriminations. Our own studies have shown that 3 year old normal children are perfect at distinguishing "Which one is looking at you?" (Baron-Cohen & Cross, 1992: see Fig. 7). Lord (1974) found 6 year olds' judgements

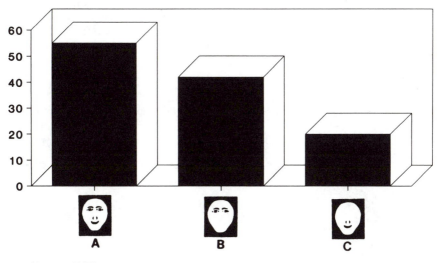

from Maurer, 1985

FIG. 6. Mean length of fixation by 2 month olds to face-like drawings (adapted from Maurer, 1985).

about gaze to different parts of the face were less accurate than adults', though Thayer (1977), using an on- versus off-face discrimination task, found that 6 year olds were as good as adults in detecting when another person was making eye-contact with them. However, they made more false positive errors by judging instances of off-face gazes as eye-contact.

Jaspars et al. (1973) found that human adults could discriminate eye-shifts of 1 cm at a distance of 100 cm, which corresponds to a change of 5 degrees, and Gibson and Pick (1963) also reported that human adults could detect an angular displacement of the eyeball of less than 3 degrees at 2 metres. Perrett

(a)   (b)

FIG. 7. "Which one is looking at you?": Photographic stimuli with (a) only eye-cues available, and (b) nose and eye-cues available (from Baron-Cohen & Coss, 1992).

and Milders (1992) found that adults were above chance in identifying a gaze shift of 2 degrees. Cline (1967) reports that human adults can detect even smaller deviations (1.4 degrees) of the eye, at a distance of 122 cm. It is not yet clear precisely how EDD distinguishes eye-contact from non-eye-contact—for example, is the relevant stimulus property the symmetry of the d region, as Anstis, Mayhew, and Morley (1969) suggest?[6]

2.5. Dedicated neural architecture. Some single-cell recording studies have found specific cells in the Superior Temporal Sulcus (STS) of the monkey brain respond selectively to direction of gaze (Perrett et al., 1985; Perrett et al., 1990; see Fig. 8). For example, Perrett et al. (1985) found that 64% of cells in the STS that are responsive to face or profile views of the head are also selective for the direction of gaze.

There is clear evidence of physiological arousal produced by mutual eye-contact. For example, galvanic skin responses increase with mutual eye-contact (Nichols & Champness, 1971). Wada (1961) also found brainstem activation in response to eye-stimuli in monkeys. These measures of arousal might of course be linked to either positive or negative emotions. In the case of human infancy, the evidence suggests it is linked with positive emotions[7], since eye-contact reliably triggers the infant to smile (Wolff, 1963; Stern, 1977; Schaffer, 1977). The neurobiology of EDD is considered in more detail elsewhere (see Baron-Cohen & Ring, 1994).

2.6. Characteristic pattern of breakdown. Lesions in the STS produce an impairment in the ability to discriminate gaze direction by monkeys (Campbell, Heywood, Cowey, Regard, & Landis, 1990). Some patients with prosopagnosia are also impaired in this ability (Campbell et al., 1990; Heywood & Cowey, 1992).

In sum, EDD fits most of the criteria for modularity.

3. SAM

SAM is the *Shared Attention Mechanism.* Its function is to identify if you and another organism are both attending to the same thing. This is a problem that it is important to be able to solve, but ID and EDD just cannot solve it. This is because the two earlier mechanisms are limited to building dyadic representations. SAM is held to be necessary for the development and production of

---

[6]I am grateful to Dave Perrett for directing me to this possibility.

[7]It is not only in infancy that eye-contact triggers pleasurable emotions. Rubin (1970) found that those couples rated as strongly in love gazed at each other more than those rated as weakly in love. Thayer and Schiff (1977) also found that judges rated reciprocated long gaze between mixed sex couples as a sign of greater sexual interest. See Kleinke (1986) for a review.

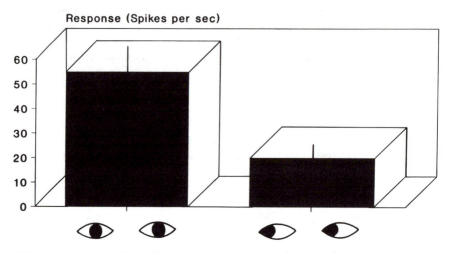

FIG. 8. Responsivity of cell M047 in the 575 to "pure" eye-direction (adapted from Perrett et al., 1990).

joint-attention behaviours[8]. In the human case, I suggest that SAM has two other key functions. First, to connect ID to EDD. Secondly, to trigger the last mechanism in the Mindreading System (ToMM).

Let us apply the 6 criteria for modularity to SAM.

3.1. Domain specificity. The conditions under which you and another person could be engaged in a mutually shared focus of attention are well-defined: there needs to be another Agent (let us call this Agent$_1$), and an additional object or Agent (if the latter, let us call this Agent$_2$). In addition, I suggest that, unlike the two earlier mechanisms, SAM codes these conditions using a unique representation, which I call a *triadic* representation[9]. Triadic representations differ in structure to dyadic representations in that they include an embedded element which specifies that Agent and Self are both attending to the *same* object. To capture this, they have one of two forms:

a. [Self-Relation-(Agent-Relation-Object)]. Here, the first relation term is bidirectional, so examples of this form are:
    [I-see-(Mummy-sees-the bus)], and
    [Mummy-sees-(I-see-the bus)].

---

[8]This mechanism could equally have been called a Joint Attention Mechanism, but the acronymn was obviously less desirable. Hence the name SAM.

[9]This term, like the term dyadic representation, is derived from Bakeman and Adamson (1984), and Trevarthen (1979). Hobson (1993) also refers to triadic relations. Note however that in my account, these are a class of *representation*.

Because this representation specifies that both I and Mummy are seeing the same bus at the same time, this fulfils the function of the triadic representation, namely, to identify shared attention.

   b. [Self-Relation-(Agent₁-Relation-Agent₂)]. Here, both relation terms are bidirectional. So examples of this form are:
   [I-see-(Mummy-sees-Daddy)], or
   [I-see-(Daddy-sees-mummy)], or
   [Mummy-sees-(I-see-Daddy)], or
   [Mummy-sees-(Daddy-sees-me)], etc.
These sentence-like expressions are my attempt at specifying what triadic representations represent. However, it is questionable whether one can fully capture the complexity of the relations with such formal descriptions. The alternative spatial description, depicted in Fig. 9, may be both more comprehensive, and simpler to "read".

As mentioned earlier, the capacity to construct triadic representations is held to be necessary for joint-attention, and I suggest that in the first instance, SAM builds these representations using the dyadic representations that it obtains from EDD's output. This is because triadic representations can be built more easily in the visual modality than they can be in other modalities. However, in principle, SAM can build triadic representations from ID's output, in order to establish joint tactile or joint auditory attention.

3.2. Obligatory firing. Infants from the end of the first year of life begin to turn spontaneously to look in the same direction as another person, when that person's eye-direction suddenly changes (Scaife & Bruner, 1975). This is a response we continue to have as adults (Tantam, 1992). If we are told to suppress it, we can—but a short exercise in self-observation will prove to you that you monitor direction of gaze all the time. It is obligatory to that extent.

3.3. Rapid speed. Again, no reaction time data exist on the gaze-following response, but by any standards it would seem to be very rapid.

3.4. Characteristic ontogenesis. From about 9 months of age, normal infants begin to engage in a range of joint visual attention behaviours (Bruner, 1983). The clearest of these are gaze-monitoring (mentioned above), and the "protodeclarative" pointing gesture (Bates, Benigni, Bretherton, Camaioni, & Volterra, 1979). In these behaviours, the infant alternates his or her own gaze between the adult's eyes and the object at which they are both attending, or at which the infant is directing the adult to look. Both of these behaviours are universally present by 9–14 months of age (Scaife & Bruner, 1975; Butterworth, 1991). Both continue to be present in older human children (Leekam, Baron-Cohen, Perrett, Milders, & Brown, 1993) and adults (Argyle

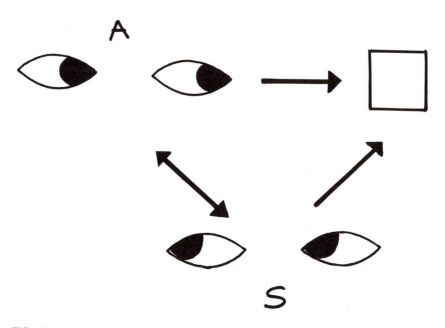

FIG. 9. Schematic illustration of a triadic representation: [Self-Relation-(Agent-Relation-Object)]. (S = Self; A = Agent).

& Cook, 1976), in whom they retain important communicative functions. There is some anecdotal evidence that chimpanzees and baboons may look in the same direction as another animal is looking, but this remains to be systematically investigated (Cheney & Seyfarth, 1990).

Regarding SAM's function of linking ID to EDD, this should result in volitional terms being imported into the relation slot of triadic representations, such that a person's *goal* or *desire* can be read from their eye-direction. Phillips, Baron-Cohen and Rutter (1992) investigated this with normal infants ranging from 9–18 months. The child was presented either with an ambiguous or an unambiguous action. One ambiguous action comprised *blocking* the child's hands during manual activity, by the adult cupping her hands over the child's. A second ambiguous action comprised offering an object to the child, but then at the last minute *teasingly* withdrawing it, just as the child began to reach for it. The unambiguous action simply comprised *giving* or presenting an object to the child.

This study found that, on at least half of the trials, 100% of the infants responded to the ambiguous actions by instantly looking at the adult's eyes (within the first 5 seconds after the tease or the block), whilst only 39% of them did so following the unambiguous action. This suggests that under conditions in which the goal of an action is uncertain, the first place young children (and indeed adults) look for information to disambiguate the goal is the eyes.

In a further study, we demonstrated that it is indeed eye-*direction* that children use to infer a person's goal (Baron-Cohen, Campbell, Karmiloff-Smith, Grant, & Walker, in press). Thus, when 3 year olds are asked "Which chocolate will Charlie take?", after being shown a display of 4 chocolates and Charlie's face looking at one of these, they tend to pick the one he is *looking at* as the goal of his next action (see Fig. 10).

Regarding inferring a person's *desire* from eye-direction, Baron-Cohen et al.'s (in press) study presented normal 3–4 year olds with the display of the 4 chocolates, and placed the cartoon face of Charlie in the centre of the display. Again, Charlie's eyes were depicted as pointing towards one of the 4 sweets, randomly selected (see Fig. 10). The subject was asked "Which one does Charlie *want?*". (In another, the subject was asked "Which one does Charlie *say* is the (x)?", in order to see if they used eye-direction to infer a person's intended referent.) Children of this age had no difficulty at all in inferring Charlie's desire (or his intended referent), from his eye-direction. Note that Baldwin (1991, 1995) has also reported 18 month olds' ability to use eye-direction to infer a person's intended referent.

3.5. Dedicated neural architecture.   We currently have no clues at all as to any possible neural localization of SAM. One should note that because SAM is

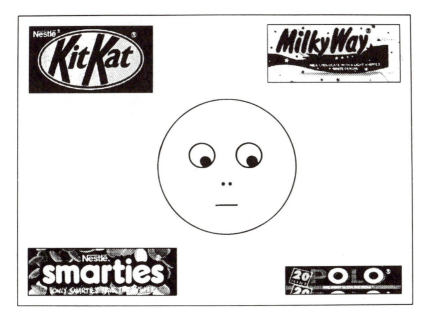

FIG. 10. The 4 Sweets display (From Baron-Cohen et al., in press).

amodal, the studies showing eye-direction sensitive cells in the STS can only be linked to EDD, and not necessarily to SAM.

3.6. Characteristic pattern of breakdown.   SAM appears to be impaired in most cases of autism, whilst both ID and EDD appear to be intact. Evidence for ID being intact in autism includes the following: These children use words referring to goal-directed action and desire in their spontaneous speech (Baron-Cohen, Leslie, & Frith, 1986; Tager-Flusberg, 1992, 1993), and they can predict emotions on the basis of a person's desire (Baron-Cohen, 1991a). Evidence for EDD being intact is that they can detect when the eyes of another person are directed at them (Baron-Cohen et al., in press). Evidence that SAM is impaired in autism is that they show few if any joint-attention behaviours (Sigman, Mundy, Ungerer, & Sherman, 1986; Leekam et al., 1993; Baron-Cohen, 1989a; Phillips et al., 1992).

Phillips et al. (1992) tested very young children with autism for their ability to use SAM to detect a person's goals from their eye-direction, using the ambiguous and unambiguous actions described earlier. However, these children did not seem to use eye-contact to disambiguate the ambiguous actions, looking as little in both conditions (less than 11% looking, in each). Baron-Cohen et al. (in press) also tested children with autism on the 4 Sweets Task and found significant impairments in the use of eye-direction in inferring want, goal, or intended referent.

If children with autism are not capable of processing triadic representations, how are they able to pass visual perspective-taking tasks, which a number of experiments show that they do (Hobson, 1984; Baron-Cohen, 1989a, 1991b; Tan & Harris, 1991)? According to this theory, they must do this by employing dyadic representations, of the form [Agent-Relation-Object].

I will defer discussion of my earlier claim about the precursor relation between SAM and ToMM, until I have introduced this final mechanism. To summarize this section, SAM fits many of the criteria for modularity.

4. ToMM

ToMM is the *Theory of Mind Mechanism*. This is the name Leslie (1991) gives to the system underpinning our everyday ability to make sense of behaviour in terms of mental states, and predict an Agent's behaviour on the basis of such states[10]. I take the liberty of slightly elaborating Leslie's proposal, to clarify that ToMM has two principal functions: (1) To represent the full range of mental state concepts, including the epistemic ones; and (2) to integrate mental state knowledge into a coherent and usable "theory" for the human child and adult to employ.

---

[10]Unless I explicitly state otherwise, the reader can assume that I am using the term ToMM to refer to what Leslie (1994) also calls ToMM System$_2$.

Applying the 6 criteria for modularity to ToMM, what do we find?

4.1. Domain specificity.   Certainly, the domain of application for ToMM appears highly specific: something either is a mental state, or it is not (Brentano, 1874/1970). Understanding the full range of mental states also requires the processing of a unique kind of representation. Leslie and Roth (1993) call these *M-Representations*[11], and suggest they have the following structure:

> *[Agent-Attitude-"Proposition"].*

An example of what could fill these three slots is shown here:

> [John-thinks-"The money is in the biscuit tin"]

In the above example, the whole M-Representation can be true even if the proposition is false. For example, the M-Representation can be true if John indeed *thinks* the money is in the biscuit tin, even if the money is in fact in the teapot. The usefulness of M-Representations is that they allow sensitive prediction of an Agent's future action. For example, they lead us to predict that John will go to the biscuit tin if he wants the money, despite the money in reality being in the teapot. M-Representations also allow one to make sense of an Agent's behaviour. For example, they help make sense of why John might look disappointed when he opens the biscuit tin[12].

4.2. Obligatory firing.   ToMM also seems to meet this criterion. As adults, it takes enormous effort for us *not* to interpret behaviour in mentalistic ways. Students of behaviourism will recall having to be specially taught to suppress the urge to refer to mental states in their descriptions—it does not come naturally to us to refer to behaviour exclusively. Rather, reference to mental states seems to be our involuntary and spontaneous way of "reading" behaviour (Dennett, 1978).

4.3. Rapid speed.   Whilst no one has attempted to time our ability to compute actions in terms of mental states, our impression is that this is not only effortless (to most of us), but indeed rapid.

4.4. Characteristic ontogenesis.   ToMM appears to have a very charac- teristic timetable (Astington, Harris, & Olson, 1988). Let me sketch this here: According to Leslie (1987, 1991), ToMM comes on line in the middle of the second year of life, and its arrival is marked by the production and

---

[11]They adopt this term in order to avoid the confusions arising from the earlier term "metarepresentations" (Perner, 1993).

[12]In recent writings, Leslie suggests M-Representations have a 4th term, to express an anchor in reality (e.g., see Leslie, German, & Happé, 1993).

comprehension of pretence, around 18–24 months of age (Harris & Kavanaugh, 1993). By 3 years of age, preschoolers are able to understand aspects of what people know (Pratt & Bryant, 1990), and by 4 years of age they can distinguish true and false beliefs (Wimmer & Perner, 1983). Their mental-state knowledge is also highly organised into a coherent "theory" which the child uses for both explanation and prediction of action (Wellman, 1990). Preliminary cross-cultural studies support the universality of this developmental timetable (Avis & Harris, 1990; Riviere, personal communication; Jolly, 1966).

4.5. Dedicated neural architecture. So far, there is little evidence regarding the specific neurobiological basis of ToMM. However, since non-human primates do not show any convincing evidence of possessing ToMM, if one judges this by whether they understand epistemic mental states (Premack, 1988; Whiten, 1993; Hayes, in press), this suggests it may have appeared only with the evolution of the *Homo sapiens* brain. A recent functional imaging study that we have carried out using SPECT (Single Photon Emission Computed Tomography) suggests that the right orbito-frontal cortex may play a specific role in supporting ToMM in normal human adults (Baron-Cohen, Ring, Moriarty, Schmidt, Costa, & Ell, 1994). This would be consistent with the neurological evidence that damage to this area can produce "loss of social judgement" (Eslinger & Damasio, 1985) and a breakdown in the pragmatics of language (Kaczmarek, 1984). (See Baron-Cohen & Ring [1994] for a review of the possible neurobiology of ToMM.)

4.6. Characteristic pattern of breakdown. Children with autism are impaired in their understanding of epistemic mental states, such as knowing and believing (Baron-Cohen, Leslie, & Frith, 1985; Baron-Cohen, 1989b & c, 1991a & b, 1992; Leslie & Frith, 1989; Perner, Frith, Leslie, & Leekam, 1989; Sodian & Frith 1992; Goodhart & Baron-Cohen, 1994). However they are un-impaired in their understanding of non-mental representations (such as photographs, drawings, maps, and models: Leslie & Thaiss, 1992; Leekam & Perner, 1991; Charman & Baron-Cohen, 1992, 1993)[13]. They also lack spontaneous pretend play (Wing & Gould, 1979; Baron-Cohen, 1987). Finally, their spontaneous speech also lacks terms referring to epistemic mental states (Baron-Cohen et al., 1986; Tager-Flusberg, 1993). This specific deficit in ToMM is thought to relate to the abnormalities in social and communicative behaviour that are key symptoms of autism (Baron-Cohen, 1988, 1990; Frith, 1989).

In sum, ToMM fits the criteria for modularity fairly well.

---

[13]See Baron-Cohen, Tager-Flusberg, and Cohen (1993), where the relevant evidence is brought together and debated.

5. The Relationship Between the Four Mechanisms

There is a big difference between the first three mechanisms and ToMM, in that the small set of mental states that the first three are able to represent possess only two of the properties of Intentionality: aboutness, and aspectuality (Dennett, 1978; Perner, 1991). By contrast, the attitude concepts that ToMM can represent progressively include *pretend*, *know*, *think*, and *believe*, amongst others. These possess a third property of Intentionality: the possibility for misrepresentation (Leslie, 1987; Perner, 1991). ToMM is therefore both more versatile than the other three, and has a larger set of mental state terms that it can represent.

A second important relationship to bring out is the earlier claim that SAM stands in a causal relationship to ToMM: that the key way ToMM is activated is by taking as input SAM's triadic representations. Elsewhere, I have referred to this special relationship in terms of SAM *facilitating* the development of ToMM (Baron-Cohen and Cross, 1992; Baron-Cohen, 1995). Focusing on the disorders of autism and congenital blindness, as Hobson (1990, 1993) recommends we do, brings out the reasons for suggesting this causal relationship.

6. Autism and Congenital Blindness

The claim is that SAM is a necessary (though not sufficient) condition for the development of ToMM. This is a testable claim about a certain kind of pre-cursor relationship between the two systems in development. Note that whilst SAM usually builds triadic representations using EDD's dyadic represen-tations, this need not be the case. For example, since children with congenital blindness lack EDD, SAM must be restricted to building triadic representations specifying joint-attention via touch or audition (e.g., [I-touch-(Mummy-touches-the cup)]). That is, SAM, in their case, must build triadic represen-tations using ID's dyadic representations. These kinds of triadic representations are likely to be considerably more difficult to build than those derived from EDD (see Baron-Cohen & Cross, 1992).

Given the evidence presented earlier that most children with autism fail to develop a fully functioning SAM, it follows from the theory outlined here that in these children this would have the knock-on effect of not activating ToMM. The theory thus predicts two subgroups of autism:

Subgroup A: both SAM and ToMM are impaired, as explained by the knock-on hypothesis. There is considerable evidence suggesting that many subjects with autism fall into this group (see Baron-Cohen, Tager-Flusberg, & Cohen, 1993; Baron-Cohen, 1991d and 1993, for reviews). In addition, absence of SAM is one predictor of autism at 18 months of age (Baron-Cohen, Allen, & Gillberg, 1992).

Subgroup B: SAM is intact, whilst ToMM is impaired in its own right. These children might correspond to those children with autism who are reported to have a period of normal development up to the age of 18 months (Volkmar & Cohen, 1989; Derek Ricks, personal communication, 1987), and then show clear signs of autism. This group remains to be fully investigated.

Finally, it follows that in children with congenital blindness, since SAM is intact, ToMM should develop, although a slight delay in this would not be surprising given the need for SAM to use ID instead of EDD.

ALTERNATIVE ACCOUNTS

Alan Leslie's Account

Leslie (1994) suggests two further mechanisms: ToBy (the *Theory of Bodies Mechanism*) detects if an object moved as a result of external causes, or is an Agent capable of self-propulsion, whilst ToMM System$_1$ detects an Agent's action as goal-directed. In effect, Leslie proposes two mechanisms to cover the functions that Premack (1990) and I suggest can be covered by one (ID). It remains to be shown that Leslie's division is justified by neuropsychological or neurological dissociation. An additional difference between ToBy and ID is that the former is a "mechanics module" (Leslie, 1994)—it processes information about physical causality as well as Agency. Patients who 'dissociate' in these two skills would pose a problem for Leslie's account of ToBy, whilst they would not for Premack or my account, since ID is not a mechanics module[14].

Furthermore, neither ToBy nor ToMM System$_1$ would be sufficient to account for why in the normal case we attend disproportionately to an Agent's eyes, nor why children with autism may attend to other aspects of Agents (such as their hands), but not especially to their eyes (Phillips, Laa, Gomez, Baron-Cohen, & Riviere, 1994). For this, I think you need EDD and SAM. Leslie's two systems would predict that the aspect of an Agent to which we might attend could be entirely arbitrary—it could be their shoulders, their hands, or even their feet! In my account, it is no coincidence that these aspects of people are passed over relatively quickly when we engage in "person perception": It is because we have two specific mechanisms (EDD and SAM) which drive us to attend to the eye-region, first and foremost.

Johnson and Morton's Account

Johnson and Morton (1991) suggest that CONLERN is a mechanism that comes on line in human development around 2 months of age, and that is sufficient for

---

[14]Indeed, I would prefer to see a separation between a mechanism (like ToBy) that processes the mechanics of objects, and a mechanism (like ID) that identifies Agency and interprets this in terms of volition.

learning about all aspects of faces and conspecifics (facial identity, expression, etc.). On their account, EDD and SAM would not be necessary. In my view, the data that I have reviewed suggest that we orient disproportionately to the eye-region, over and above other regions of a conspecific. EDD (and later, SAM) are my suggestions to account for this bias in information processing. Moreover, it is not an arbitrary bias. Rather, I suggest that this bias is highly adaptive, in that eye-direction is a reliable source of information about an Agent's goals, desires, and focus of attention. A further problem for Johnson and Morton's account is to explain why many aspects of CONLERN-processing—such as identity recognition, relationship perception, and perceptual role-taking—are intact in autism (Baron-Cohen, 1991c), whilst joint-attention is impaired. SAM is my way of overcoming this difficulty.

Digby Tantam's Account

In an important recent article, Tantam (1992) argues that (1) there is "an innate and involuntary orientation to social stimuli" (p.84); (2) "this *social attention response is* . . . absent or impaired in autism and . . . is the primary social abnormality" (p.84); (3) In the normal child there is a "second gaze response, in which gaze is drawn from a person's eyes to the object at which they are looking" (p.85); (4) "This second gaze response presupposes the first" (p.85); (5) The second gaze response is therefore also impaired in autism; and (6) "Weakness or absence of the social gaze response is enough . . . to account for many of the typical symptoms of autism, including the failure to acquire a theory of mind" (p.83).

Tantam's thesis is interesting. Effectively, he has renamed eye-contact as the "first gaze response" and joint-attention as the "second gaze response". If we equate what he calls the "first gaze response" with EDD, and the second gaze response with SAM, then his claim would presumably be that the primary deficit in autism is in EDD. However, my earlier review of the data suggests that EDD is largely intact in autism. It may be that Tantam is right, but as yet the evidence for this is insufficient.

The theory I have presented here differs from Tantam's thesis in describing the two mechanisms driving eye-contact and joint-attention (EDD and SAM); and in suggesting that whilst SAM is necessary for the development of ToMM, it is *not sufficient* for this—since ToMM is held to be independent of SAM. I would therefore take issue with Tantam's suggestion that absence of the "first social gaze response" (here taken to be equivalent to EDD) is enough to account for the failure to acquire a theory of mind. Indeed, the prediction from Tantam's theory is that the blind should also be impaired in ToMM, which, as far as we know, they are not.

Other Accounts

Some authors have argued that the origins of ToMM lie in (a) the capacity for neonatal imitation (Meltzoff & Gopnik, 1993), or (b) the capacity for social-mirroring (Gergely et al., in press), or (c) the capacity for affective responsivity (Hobson, 1990). Part of my reason for highlighting SAM in the precursor role is that the evidence for autism-specific deficits in these other domains is less robust than it is in the domain of joint-(visual)-attention. However, a plausible case has been made for all of these as candidate precursors to ToMM, and the real test will be to examine which of these (either singly, or in combination) is predictive of ToMM. Such longitudinal studies are time-consuming, but ultimately will be the only way to choose between these hypotheses.

CONCLUSIONS

I close this paper by drawing the reader's attention to the 8 claims in the Abstract, in order to summarize the arguments. In addition to these, I hope it is clear that as well as suggesting a model of the human Mindreading System, each component mechanism in this system has been evaluated in terms of the degree to which it meets criteria for modularity. In Table 1 below, I summarize the neuropsychological dissociations among the four mechanisms both in normally developing populations, and in some developmentally abnormal populations (all human). Future work will need to address the extent to which the four proposed mechanisms are present in different species. In terms of normal development, this model implies that there are at least two distinct

TABLE 1
Summary of the neuropsychological dissociations between
the 4 mechanisms.

	ID	EDD	SAM	ToMM
Normal children				
6 month olds	+	+	−	−
14 month olds	+	+	+	−
48 month olds	+	+	+	+
Abnormal children*				
Autism (A)	+	+	−	−
Autism (B)	+	+	+	−
Blind#	+	−	+	+
AB type prosopagnosia@	+	−	+	+

*	=	given a mental age above 48 months approximately;
+	=	mechanism is functioning;
−	=	mechanism is not functioning;
#	=	congenitally blind;
@	=	see Campbell et al. (1990).

theories of mind that exist at different ages: 14 month olds have what I have elsewhere called an "attention-goal" psychology (Baron-Cohen, 1993), whilst 4 year olds (and older people) have what is usually referred to as a "belief-desire" psychology (Wellman, 1990).

ACKNOWLEDGEMENTS

During the preparation of this work, I was at the Institute of Psychiatry, London, and received support from the Mental Health Foundation and the Medical Research Council. This paper evolved through presentations at the Society for Philosophy and Psychology, Montreal, June 1992, the European Conference of Developmental Psychology, Seville, September 1992, the Society for Research in Child Development, New Orleans, March 1993, and the European Society for Philosophy and Psychology, Sheffield, June 1993.

I am grateful to Annette Karmiloff-Smith, Ruth Campbell, Dave Perrett, Sue Leekam, Helen Tager-Flusberg, Pierre Jacob, and Donald Cohen for their comments on earlier drafts of this paper, and to Leslie Brothers, Juan Carlos Gómez, Digby Tantam, John Swettenham, and Ami Klin for discussions. Finally, the title of this paper owes a lot to Mandler (1992).

REFERENCES

Altmann, S. (Ed.) (1967). *Social communication among primates.* Chicago, IL: University of Chicago Press.

Anstis, S., Mayhew, J., & Morley, T. (1969). The perception of where a face or a television 'portrait' is looking. *American Journal of Psychology, 82,* 474–489.

Arduino, P., & Gould, J. (1984). Is tonic immobility adaptive? *Animal Behaviour, 32,* 921–922.

Argyle, M., & Cook, M. (1976). *Gaze and mutual gaze.* Cambridge, MA: Cambridge University Press.

Astington, J., Harris, P., & Olson, D. (1988). *Developing theories of mind.* New York: Cambridge University Press.

Avis, J., & Harris, P. (1991). Belief-desire reasoning among Baka children: evidence for a universal conception of mind. *Child Development, 62,* 460–467.

Bakeman, R., & Adamson, L. (1984). Coordinating attention to people and objects in mother–infant and peer–infant interaction. *Child Development, 55,* 1278–1289.

Baldwin, D. (1991). Infants' contribution to the achievement of joint reference. *Child Development, 62,* 875–890.

Baldwin, D. (1995). Understanding the link between joint attention and language acquisition. In C. Moore & P. Dunham (Eds.), *Joint attention: its origins and role in development.* Hillsdale, NJ: Lawrence Erlbaum Associates.

Baron-Cohen, S. (1987). Autism and symbolic play. *British Journal of Developmental Psychology, 5,* 139–148.

Baron-Cohen, S. (1988). Social and pragmatic deficits in autism: cognitive or affective? *Journal of Autism and Developmental Disorders, 18,* 379–402.

Baron-Cohen, S. (1989a). Perceptual role-taking and protodeclarative pointing in autism. *British Journal of Developmental Psychology, 7,* 113–127.

Baron-Cohen, S. (1989b). Are autistic children behaviourists? An examination of their mental–physical and appearance–reality distinctions. *Journal of Autism and Developmental Disorders, 19,* 579–600.

Baron-Cohen, S. (1989c). The autistic child's theory of mind: a case of specific developmental delay. *Journal of Child Psychology and Psychiatry, 30,* 285–298.

Baron-Cohen, S. (1990). Autism: a specific cognitive disorder of "mindblindness". *International Review of Psychiatry, 2,* 19–88.

Baron-Cohen, S. (1991a). Do people with autism understand what causes emotion? *Child Development, 62,* 385–395.

Baron-Cohen, S. (1991b). The development of a theory of mind in autism: deviance and delay? *Psychiatric Clinics of North America, 14,* 33–51.

Baron-Cohen, S. (1991c). The theory of mind deficit in autism: how specific is it? *British Journal of Developmental Psychology, 9,* 301–314.

Baron-Cohen, S. (1991d). Precursors to a theory of mind: Understanding attention in others. In A. Whiten (Ed.), *Natural theories of mind.* Oxford: Basil Blackwell.

Baron-Cohen, S. (1992). Out of sight or out of mind: another look at deception in autism. *Journal of Child Psychology and Psychiatry, 33,* 1141–1155.

Baron-Cohen, S. (1993). From attention-goal psychology to belief-desire psychology: the development of a theory of mind, and its dysfunction. In S. Baron-Cohen, H. Tager-Flusberg, & D. J. Cohen (Eds.), *Understanding other minds: perspectives from autism.* Oxford: Oxford University Press.

Baron-Cohen, S. (1995). The Eye-Direction Detector (EDD) and the Shared Attention Mechanism (SAM): two cases for evolutionary psychology. In C. Moore & P. Dunham (Eds.), *The role of joint attention in development.* Hillsdale, NJ: Lawrence Erlbaum Associates.

Baron-Cohen, S., Allen, J., & Gillberg, C. (1992). Can autism be detected at 18 months? The needle, the haystack, and the CHAT. *British Journal of Psychiatry, 161,* 839–843.

Baron-Cohen, S., Campbell, R., Karmiloff-Smith, A., Grant, J., & Walker, J. (in press). Are children with autism blind to the mentalistic significance of the eyes? *British Journal of Developmental Psychology.*

Baron-Cohen, S., & Cross, P. (1992). Reading the eyes: evidence for the role of perception in the development of a theory of mind. *Mind and Language, 6,* 166–180.

Baron-Cohen, S., & Goodhart, F. (1994). The "seeing leads to knowing" deficit in autism: the Pratt and Bryant probe. *British Journal of Development Psychology* (in press).

Baron-Cohen, S., Leslie, A. M., & Frith, U. (1985). Does the autistic child have a 'theory of mind'? *Cognition, 21,* 37–46.

Baron-Cohen, S., Leslie, A. M., & Frith, U. (1986). Mechanical, behavioural and intentional understanding of picture stories in autistic children. *British Journal of Developmental Psychology, 4,* 113–125.

Baron-Cohen, S., & Ring, H. (1994). A model of the Mindreading System: neuropsychological and neurobiological perspectives. In P. Mitchell & C. Lewis (Eds.), *Origins of an understanding of mind.* Hillsdale, NJ: Lawrence Erlbaum Associates.

Baron-Cohen, S., Ring, H., Moriarty, J., Schmidt, P., Costa, D., & Ell, P. (1994). Recognition of mental state terms: a clinical study of children with autism, and a functional neuroimaging study of normal adults. *British Journal of Psychiatry* (in press).

Baron-Cohen, S., Tager-Flusberg, H., and Cohen, D. I. (Eds.) (1993). *Understanding other minds: perspectives from autism.* Oxford: Oxford University Press.

Bartsch, K., & Wellman, H. (1994). *Talk about the mind.* Oxford: Oxford University Press.

Bates, E. (1993). Invited lecture to the MRC Cognitive Development Unit, London.

Bates, E., Benigni, L., Bretherton, I., Camaioni, L., & Volterra, V. (1979). Cognition and communication from 9–13 months: correlational findings. In E. Bates (Ed.) *The emergence of symbols: cognition and communication in infancy.* New York: Academic Press.

Blest, A. (1957). The function of eyespot patterns in the Lepidoptera. *Behaviour, 11,* 209–256.

Brentano, F., von (1874/1970). *Psychology from an empirical standpoint.* [O. Kraus (Ed.), translated by L. MacAllister]. London: Routledge and Kegan Paul.

Brothers, L. (1990). The social brain: a project for integrating primate behaviour and neurophysiology in a new domain. *Concepts in Neuroscience, 1*, 27–51.

Bruner, J. (1983). *Child's talk: learning to use language*. Oxford: Oxford University Press.

Burghardt, G. (1990). Cognitive ethology and critical anthropomorphism: a snake with two heads and hog-nosed snakes that play dead. In C. Ristau (Ed.), *Cognitive ethology: the minds of other animals*. Hillsdale, NJ: Lawrence Erlbaum Associates.

Butterworth, G. (1991). The ontogeny and phylogeny of joint visual attention. In A. Whiten (Ed.), *Natural theories of mind*. Oxford: Basil Blackwell.

Butterworth, G., & Jarrett, N. (1991). What minds have in common is space: spatial mechanisms serving joint visual attention in infancy. *British Journal of Developmental Psychology, 9*, 55–72.

Byrne, R., & Whiten, A. (1988). *Machiavellian intelligence: social expertise and the evolution of intellect in monkeys, apes, and humans*. Oxford: Oxford University Press.

Campbell, R., Heywood, C., Cowey, A., Regard, M., & Landis, T. (1990). Sensitivity to eye gaze in prosopagnosic patients and monkeys with superior temporal sulcus ablation. *Neuropsychologia, 28*, 1123–1142.

Campbell, R., Walker, J., & Baron-Cohen, S. (1993). Aspects of part-of face processing in children with autism: A discriminant function analysis. Unpublished manuscript, Goldsmiths College, University of London.

Chance, M. (1967). The interpretation of some agonistic postures: the role of "cut-off" acts and postures. *Symposium of the Zoological Society of London, 8*, 71–89.

Cheney, D., & Seyfarth, R. (1990). *How monkeys see the world*. Chicago, IL: University of Chicago Press.

Charman, T., and Baron-Cohen, S. (1992). Understanding beliefs and drawings: a further test of the metarepresentation theory of autism. *Journal of Child Psychology and Psychiatry, 33*, 1105–1112.

Charman, T., & Baron-Cohen, S. (1993). Understanding models, photos, and beliefs: a further test of the modularity thesis of misrepresentation. Unpublished manuscript, University College London, Psychology Department.

Cline, M. (1967). Unpublished manuscript, Cornell University.

Dasser, V., Ulbaek, I., & Premack, D. (1989). The perception of intention. *Science, 243*, 365–367.

Dennett, D. (1978). *Brainstorms: philosophical essays on mind and psychology*. Brighton: Harvester Press.

Eslinger, P., & Damasio, A. (1985). Severe disturbance of higher cognition after bilateral frontal lobe ablation: Patient EVR. *Neurology, 35*, 1731–41.

Farah, M., McMullen, P., & Meyer, M. (1991). Can recognition of living things be selectively impaired? *Neuropsychologia, 29*, 185–193.

Fehr, B., & Exline, R. (1978). Social visual interaction: a conceptual and literature review. In A. Siegman & S. Feldstein (Eds.), *Nonverbal behaviour and communication* (2nd edition). Hillsdale, NJ: Lawrence Erlbaum Associates.

Fodor, J, (1983). *The modularity of mind: an essay on faculty psychology*. Cambridge, MA: MIT Press.

Frith, U. (1989). *Autism: explaining the enigma*. Oxford: Basil Blackwell.

Gallup, G. (1982). Self-awareness and the emergence of mind in primates. *American Journal of Primatology, 2*, 237–248.

Gallup, G., Cummings, W., & Nash, R. (1972). The experimenter as an independent variable in studies of animal hypnosis in chickens (*Gallus gallus*). *Animal Behaviour, 20*, 166–169.

Gergely, G., Nádasdy, Z., Csibra, G., & Biró, S. (in press). Taking the intentional stance at 12 months of age. *Cognition*.

Gibson, J. & Pick, A. (1962). Perception of another person's looking behaviour. *American Journal of Psychology, 76*, 386–394.

Goodglass, H., Klein, H., Carey, P., & Jones, K. (1966). Specific semantic word categories in aphasia. *Cortex, 2*, 74–89.

Hainline, L. (1978). Developmental changes in visual scanning of face and non-face patterns by infants. *Journal of Experimental Child Psychology, 25*, 90–115.

Haith, M., Bergman, T., & Moore, M. (1977). Eye contact and face scanning in early infancy. *Science, 198*, 865–855.

Hall, K., & Devore, I. (1965). Baboon social behaviour. In I. Devore (Ed.), *Primate behaviour*. New York: Holt, Rinehart and Winston.

Harris, P., & Kavanaugh, R. (1993). Young children's comprehension of pretence. *Monographs of the Society for Research in Child Development, 58* (1).

Heyes, C., (in press). Social cognition in primates. In N. Mackintosh (Ed.), *Handbook of perception and cognition: Volume 9: Animal learning and cognition*. New York: Academic Press.

Heider, F., & Simmel, M. (1944). An experimental study of apparent behaviour. *American Journal of Psychology, 57*, 243–259.

Heit, G., Smith, M., & Halgren, E. (1988). Neural encoding of individual words and faces by the human hippocampus and amygdala. *Nature, 333*, 773– 175.

Hennig, C. (1977). Effects of simulated predation on tonic immobility in *Anolis carolinensis*: The role of eye contact. *Bulletin of the Psychonomic Society, 9*, 239–242.

Hess, E., & Petrovich, S. (1978). Pupillary behaviour in communication. In A. Siegman & S. Feldstein (Eds.), *Nonverbal behaviour and communication* (2nd edition). Hillsdale, NJ: Lawrence Erlbaum Associates.

Heywood, C., & Cowey, A. (1992). The role of the 'face cell' area in the discrimination and recognition of faces in monkeys. In V. Bruce, A. Cowey, A. Ellis, & D. Perrett (Eds.), Processing the facial image. *Philosophical Transactions of the Royal Society of London, B 335*, 1–128.

Hobson, R. P. (1984). Early childhood autism and the question of egocentrism. *Journal of Autism and Developmental Disorders, 14*, 85–104.

Hobson, R. P. (1990). On acquiring knowledge about people and the capacity to pretend: response to Leslie (1987). *Psychological Review, 97*, 114–121.

Hobson, R. P. (1993). *Autism and the development of mind*. Hillsdale, NJ: Lawrence Erlbaum Associates.

Humphrey, N. (1984). *Consciousness regained*. Oxford: Oxford University Press.

Jaspars, J., et al. (1973). Het observen van ogencontact. *Nederlands Tijdschrijt voor de Psychologie, 28*, 67–81. [Cited in Argyle and Cook (1976)]

Johnson, M., & Morton, J. (1991). *Biology and cognitive development*. Oxford: Basil Blackwell.

Johnson, M., & Vicera, S. (1993). Cortical parcellation and the development of face processing. In M. de Boysson-Hardies, S. de Schonen, P. Jusczyk, P. MacNeilage, & J. Morton (Eds.), *Developmental neurocognition: speech and face-processing in the first year of life*. Dordrecht: Kluwer Academic Press, NATO ASI Series.

Jolly, A. (1966). Lemur social behaviour and primate intelligence. *Science, 153*, 501–506.

Kaczmarek, B. (1984). Neurolinguistic analysis of verbal utterances in patients with focal lesions of frontal lobes. *Brain and Language, 21*, 52–58.

Kanner, L. (1943). Autistic disturbance of affective contact. *Nervous Child, 2*, 217–250. [Reprinted in L. Kanner (1973), *Childhood psychosis: Initial studies and new insights*. New York: John Wiley and Sons]

Karmiloff-Smith, A. (1992). *Beyond modularity*. MTT Press/Bradford Books.

Keating, C., & Keating, E. (1982). Visual scan patterns of rhesus monkeys viewing faces. *Perception, 11*, 211–219.

Kendrick, K., & Baldwin, B. (1981). Cells in the temporal cortex of conscious sheep can respond preferably to the sight of faces. *Science, 236*, 448–450.

Kleinke, C. (1986). Gaze and eye-contact: a research review. *Psychological Bulletin, 100*, 78–100.

Langdell, T. (1978). Recognition of faces: an approach to the study of autism. *Journal of Child Psychology and Psychiatry, 19*, 225–238.

Leekam, S., Baron-Cohen, S., Perrett, D., Milders, M., & Brown, S. (1993). Eye direction detection: a dissociation of geometric and joint-attention skills in autism. Unpublished manuscript, Institute of Social and Applied Psychology, University of Kent, Canterbury.

Leekam, S., & Perner, J. (1991). Does the autistic child have a metarepresentational deficit? *Cognition, 40*, 203–218.

Lempers, J., Flavell, E., & Flavell, J. (1977). The development in very young children of tacit knowledge concerning visual perception. *Genetic Psychology Monographs, 95*, 3–53.

Leslie, A. M. (1987). Pretence and representation: the origins of "theory of mind". *Psychological Review, 94*, 412–426.

Leslie, A. M. (1991). The theory of mind impairment in autism: evidence for a modular mechanism of development? In A. Whiten (Ed.), *Natural theories of mind*. Oxford: Basil Blackwell.

Leslie, A. M. (1994). ToMM, ToBy, and Agency: Core architecture and domain specificity. In L. Hirschfeld & S. Gelman (Eds.), *Mapping the mind: Domain specificity in cognition and culture*. Cambridge, MA: Cambridge University Press.

Leslie, A. M., German, T. P., & Happé, F. G. (1993). Even a theory-theory needs information processing: ToMM, an alternative theory-theory of the child's theory of mind. *Behavioral and Brain Sciences, 16*, 56–57.

Leslie, A. M., & Thaiss, L. (1992). Domain specifcity in conceptual development: Neuropsychological evidence from autism. *Cognition, 43*, 225– 251.

Leslie, A. M., & Roth, D. (1993). What autism teaches us about metarepresentation. In S. Baron-Cohen, H. Tager-Flusberg, & D. J. Cohen (Ed.), *Understanding other minds: perspectives from autism*. Oxford: Oxford University Press.

Lord, C. (1974). The perception of eye contact in children and adults. *Child Development, 45*, 1113–1117.

Mandler, J. (1992). How to build a baby, II: Prelinguistic primitives. *Psychological Review, 99*, 587–604.

Maurer, D. (1985). Infants' perception of facedness. In T. Field & M. Fox (Eds.), *Social perception in infants*. Norwood, NJ: Ablex.

Meltzoff, A., & Gopnik, A. (1993). The role of imitation in understanding persons and developing a theory of mind. In S. Baron-Cohen, H. Tager-Flusberg, & D. J. Cohen (Eds.), *Understanding other minds: perspectives from autism*. Oxford: Oxford University Press.

Mendelsohn, M., Haith, M., & Goldman-Rakic, P. (1982). Face scanning and responsiveness to social cues in infant monkeys. *Developmental Psychology, 18*, 222–228.

Nichols, K., & Champness, B. (1971). Eye gaze and the GSR. *Journal of Experimental Social Psychology, 7*, 623–626.

O'Brien, T., & Dunlap, W. (1975). Tonic immobility in the blue crab (*Callinectes sapidus*): Its relation to threat of predation. *Journal of Comparative and Physiological Psychology, 89*, 86–94.

Papousek, H., & Papousek, M. (1979). Early ontogeny of human social interaction: Its biological roots and social dimensions. In M. von Cranach, K. Foppa, W. Lepenies, & D. Ploog (Eds.), *Human ethology: claims and limits of a new discipline*. Cambridge, MA: Cambridge University Press.

Perner, J. (1991). *Understanding the representational mind*. Cambridge, MA: Bradford Books, MIT Press.

Perner, J. (1993). The theory of mind deficit in autism: rethinking the metarepresentation theory. In S. Baron-Cohen, H. Tager-Flusberg, & D. J. Cohen (Eds.), *Understanding other minds: perspectives from autism*. Oxford: Oxford University Press.

Perner, J., Frith, U., Leslie, A. M., & Leekam, S. (1989). Exploration of the autistic child's theory of mind: knowledge, belief, and communication. *Child Development, 60*, 689–700.

Perrett, D., Hietanen, M., Oram, W., & Benson, P. (1992). Organization and function of cells responsive to faces in the temporal cortex. In V. Bruce, A. Cowey, A. Ellis, & Perrett, D. (Eds.), Processing the facial image. *Philosophical Transactions of the Royal Society of London, B 335*, 1–128.

Perrett, D., Harries, M., Mistlin, A., Hietanen, J., Benson, P., Bevan, R., Thomas, S., Oram, M., Ortega, J., & Brierley, K. (1990). Social signals analyzed at the single cell level: someone is looking at me, something touched me, something moved! *International Journal of Comparative Psychology, 4*, 25–55.

Perrett, D., & Milders, M. (1992). Unpublished data, Department of Psychology, University of St Andrews, Scotland.

Perrett, D., & Mistlin, A. (1990). Perception of facial characteristics by monkeys. In W. Stebbins & M. Berkley (Eds.), *Comparative perception, Vol II: Complex signals*. New York: John Wiley and Son.

Perrett, D., Smith, P., Potter, D., Mistlin, A., Head, A., Milner, A., & Jeeves, M. (1985). Visual cells in the temporal cortex sensitive to face view and gaze direction. *Proceedings of the Royal Society of London, B223*, 293–317.

Phillips, W., Baron-Cohen, S., & Rutter, M. (1992). The role of eye-contact in goal detection: evidence from normal infants, and children with mental handicap or autism. *Development and Psychopathology, 4*, 375–383.

Phillips, W., Laa, V., Gomez, J.-C., Baron-Cohen, S., & Riviere, A. (1994). Treating people as objects, agents, or subjects. Unpublished manuscript, Institute of Psychiatry, London.

Pratt, C., & Bryant, P. (1990). Young children understand that looking leads to knowing (so long as they are looking into a single barrel). *Child Development, 61*, 973–983.

Premack, D. (1988). 'Does the chimpanzee have a theory of mind?' revisited. In R. Byrne & A. Whiten (Eds.), *Machiavellian intelligence: Social expertise and the evolution of intellect in monkeys, apes, and humans*. Oxford: Oxford University Press.

Premack, D. (1990). The infant's theory of self-propelled objects. *Cognition, 36*, 1–16.

Premack, D. (1991). The infant's theory of self-propelled objects. In D. Frye & C. Moore (Eds.), *Children's theories of mind*. Hillsdale, NJ: Lawrence Erlbaum Associates.

Premack, D. (1993). Invited address, MRC Cognitive Development Unit, University College London, November.

Premack, D., & Woodruff, G. (1978). Does the chimpanzee have a 'theory of mind'? *Behavioral and Brain Sciences, 1*, 515–526.

Poulton, E. (1890). *The colours of animals*. London. [Cited in Blest (1957)]

Ristau, C. (1990). Aspects of the cognitive ethology of an injury feigning plover. In C. Ristau (Ed.), *Cognitive ethology: the minds of other animals*. Hillsdale, NJ: Lawrence Erlbaum Associates.

Ristau, C. (1991). Attention, purposes, and deception in birds. In A. Whiten (Ed.), *Natural theories of mind*. Oxford: Basil Blackwell.

Rubin, A. (1970). Measurement of romantic love. *Journal of Personal and Social Psychology, 16*, 265–273.

Sargent, A., & Eberhardt, L. (1975). Death feigning by ducks in response to predation by red foxes (*Vulpes fulva*). *American Midland Naturalist, 94*, 108–119.

Scaife, M. (1976). The response to eye-like shapes by birds. II: The importance of staring, pairedness, and shape. *Animal Behaviour, 24*, 200–206.

Scaife, M., & Bruner, J. (1975). The capacity for joint visual attention in the human infant. *Nature, 253*, 265.

Schaffer, H. (1977). Early interactive development. In H. Schaffer (Ed.), *Studies in mother–infant interaction*. New York: Academic Press.

Schaffer, G. (1964). *The mountain gorilla*. Chicago, IL: Chicago University Press.

Sigman, M., Mundy, P., Ungerer, J., & Sherman, T. (1986). Social interactions of autistic, mentally retarded, and normal children and their caregivers. *Journal of Child Psychology and Psychiatry, 27*, 647–656.

Spitz, R. (1946). The smiling response: a contribution to the ontogenesis of social relations. *Genetic Psychology Monographs, 34*, 57–125.

Stern, D. (1977). *The first relationship: infant and mother*. Cambridge, MA: Harvard University Press.

Tager-Flusberg, H. (1992). Autistic children's talk about psychological states: deficits in the early acquisition of a theory of mind. *Child Development, 63*, 161–172.

Tager-Flusberg, H. (1993). What language reveals about the understanding of minds in children with autism. In S. Baron-Cohen, H. Tager-Flusberg, & D. J. Cohen (Eds.), *Understanding other minds: perspectives from autism*. Oxford: Oxford University Press.

Tan, J. & Harris, P. (1991). Autistic children understand seeing and wanting. *Development and Psychopathology, 3*, 163–174.

Tantam, D. (1992). Characterizing the fundamental social handicap in autism. *Acta Paedopsychiatrica, 55*, 88–91.

Thayer, S. (1971). Children's detection of on-face and off-face gazes. *Developmental Psychology, 13*, 673–674.

Thayer, S., & Schiff, W. (1977). Gazing patterns and attribution of sexual involvement. *The Journal of Social Psychology, 101*, 235–246.

Tinbergen, N. (1951). *The study of instinct*. Oxford: Oxford University Press.

Trevarthen, C. (1979). Communication and cooperation in early infancy: a description of primary intersubjectivity. In M. Bullowa (Ed.), *Before speech*. Cambridge: Cambridge University Press.

Van Hooff, J. (1962). Facial expressions in higher primates. *Symposium of the Zoological Society of London, 8*, 97–125.

Vine, I. (1973). The role of facial signalling in early social development. In M. von Cranach & I. Vine (Eds.), *Social communication and movement: Studies of men and chimpanzees*. London: Academic Press.

Volkmar, F., & Cohen, D. (1989). Disintegrative disorder or 'late onset' autism? *Journal of Child Psychology and Psychiatry, 30*, 717–724.

Wada, J. (1961). Modification of cortically induced responses in brainstem by shift of attention in monkeys. *Science, 133*, 40–42.

Warrington, E., & Shallice, T. (1984). Category specific semantic impairments. *Brain, 107*, 829–854.

Wellman, H. (1990). *Children's theories of mind*. Bradford, MIT Press.

Whiten, A. (1993). Evolving a theory of mind: the nature of non-verbal mentalism in other primates. In S. Baron-Cohen, H. Tager-Flusberg, & D. J. Cohen (Eds.), *Understanding other minds: perspectives from autism*. Oxford: Oxford University Press.

Wimmer, H., & Perner, J. (1983). Beliefs about beliefs: Representation and constraining function of wrong beliefs in young children's understanding of deception. *Cognition, 13*, 103–128.

Wolff, P. (1963). Observations on the early development of smiling. In B. Foss (Ed.), *Determinants of infant behaviour* (Vol 2). New York: Wiley.

Yamane, S., Kaji, S., & Kawano, K. (1988). What facial features activate face neurons in the inferior temporal cortex? *Experimental Brain Research, 73*, 209–214.

Submitted May 11, 1993
Accepted November 10, 1993

11 The Social Competition Hypothesis of Depression

John Price[a], Leon Sloman[b], Russell Gardner Jr[c], Paul Gilbert[d] and Peter Rohde[e]

[a]*Sussex;* [b]*Clarke Institute of Psychiatry, Toronto;* [c]*University of Texas Medical Branch, Galveston;* [d]*Derby University;* [e]*Harley Street, London.*

Depressive personality and depressive illness are examined from an evolutionary adaptationist standpoint. It is postulated that the depressive state evolved in relation to social competition, as an unconscious, involuntary losing strategy, enabling the individual to accept defeat in ritual agonistic encounters and to accommodate to what would otherwise be unacceptably low social rank.

There is some agreement that depressive states represent 'a psycho-biological response pattern' which is part of the inherited behavioural repertory of the human organism (Lewis, 1934; Hill, 1968; Beck, 1987; Nesse, 1990; Gilbert, 1992; Powles, 1992). This means that depression performed some function over the course of our evolution and that those of our ancestors who had the capacity to become depressed survived at the expense of those who did not. However, it is easier to agree that there was a function than to agree on what that function was. To ignore the problem would be to limit our understanding of the biology of depression and possibly forgo pointers to research into aetiology, classification and treatment.

Performance is limited in depression. There is impairment of perception, of execution and of the central processes which mediate between perception and execution, experienced as difficulty in making decisions (Radford et al., 1986). Even in mild depressions there is some impairment, particularly for tasks requiring initiative.

Impairment of performance is not incompatible with a biological function. Performance is impaired in sleep and hibernation; viewed out of the context of circadian and circannual change we might be sceptical of their adaptive value.

It is in relation to social competition that depression can be seen to exercise a function (Price, 1967; Sloman, 1976; Gardner; 1982; Sloman et al., 1989; Gilbert, 1992). The result of competition is that winners and losers behave differently, and it may be that mood change is the mechanism that mediates this variation in behaviour.

Identification of depression as a component of a behavioural system which we share with other animals anchors our subject firmly to the basic disciplines of comparative ethology (the study of behaviour as it occurs in nature) and behavioural ecology (the analysis of behaviour in terms of function), thus supplementing the pioneering work of John Bowlby on attachment behaviour (Goldberg, 1991).

Recent work in behavioural ecology has been concerned with situations in which an animal utilises only one from a set of two or more alternative behavioural strategies (Krebs & Davies, 1987). Depression may be identified as a losing or de-escalating strategy and elevation of mood as a winning or escalating strategy.

Since adopting a losing strategy often implies forgoing resources which may contribute to reproduction, depression might also fall into the category of altruistic behaviour, which has been of interest in recent evolutionary theory (Hamilton, 1963; Krebs, 1987).

Finally, the mathematical analysis of animal contest behaviour requires a variable to express the animal's knowledge of its own fighting capacity. This animal self-concept has been termed "resource-holding potential' (RHP) and may be the evolutionary primordium of human self-esteem (Parker, 1974; Wenegrat, 1984; Archer, 1988). RHP determines whether an animal escalates a confrontation and attacks, or de-escalates and adopts the 'involuntary subordinate strategy', which we think may be the primordium of depressive states. Thus we are able to use the tools of behavioural ecology in the analysis of the mutual interaction of self-esteem and mood change, which permeates much of psychiatric practice.

STATEMENT OF THE HYPOTHESIS

The social competition hypothesis of depression is that human beings share with their more primitive ancestors a mechanism for yielding in competitive situations. This 'involuntary subordinate strategy' has three main functions: (a) an executive function which prevents the individual from attempting to make a 'come-back' by inhibiting aggressive behaviour to rivals and superiors (but not to dependants) and by creating a subjective sense of incapacity; (b) a communicative function which signals 'no threat' to rivals and 'out of action' to any kin or supporters who might wish to push the individual back into the arena to fight on their behalf; and (c) a facilitative function which puts the individual into a 'giving up' state of mind which encourages acceptance of the outcome of competition and promotes behaviour which expresses voluntary yielding. This leads to reconciliation and the termination of whatever conflict triggered the 'involuntary subordinate strategy'. But if voluntary yielding is blocked for any reason, the involuntary subordinate strategy may become intense and prolonged and may be recognised as depressive illness.

Social competition can be described at a number of different levels and the hypothesis relating depression to social competition can be expressed in terms of each level, as follows.

Sexual Selection

Darwin (1871) pointed out that alongside natural selection, a social process operates in animal species to determine which individuals in each generation reproduce (Ryan, 1985; Harvey & Bradbury, 1991). He called this phenomenon sexual selection and subdivided it into *inter-sexual* selection (in which one sex chooses another for mating), and *intra-sexual* selection in which each sex competes with members of the same sex for access to the other sex (Sloman & Sloman, 1988). The implication of this hypothesis is that in each generation one or more social processes divide the population into those who are successful and those who are either unsuccessful or unable to maintain the success that they have achieved. Clearly, the successful and unsuccessful must show a major difference in behaviour; for instance, the unsuccessful must suffer a relative inhibition of reproductive behaviour. Recognisable states of inhibition include:

(a) death; rare in vertebrates, common in invertebrates, e.g. spiders (Huntingford & Turner, 1987)
(b) physiological suppression of sexual development, as occurs, for example, in the naked mole rat and in some New World monkeys (Abbott et al., 1989)
(c) inhibition of sex change, so that the subordinate individual is maintained in the opposite sex by the signals of the dominant individual, as occurs in some fish (Keenleyside, 1979)
(d) some psychiatric syndromes, including the phenomena we recognise clinically as depression; this depression could occur as a lifelong phenomenon, in the form of depressive personality, in the case of those who are never successful, or as an episode of depressive 'illness' in those who achieve success and then lose it.

Social Hierarchy

The social roles of successful and unsuccessful animals are represented in two different but related ways. In some species the two contrasting roles are 'territory owner' and 'non-territory owner'. In other species they are high ranking and low ranking within a social hierarchy.

We suggest that depression is a component of the behavioural strategy evolved for the role of non territory owner and low ranker.

We would expect to find depression manifesting in the form of both illness and personality, reflecting the fact that some individuals achieve ownership and/or high rank and then lose it, whereas others have never achieved these objectives in the first place.

A social hierarchy performs two different functions. First, it regulates the transfer of power and of breeding opportunities from one generation to the next. Second, it stratifies each generation in terms of power and breeding opportunities, and it is this second function which mediates sexual selection.

The simplest hierarchy is the asymmetrical two-person relationship. There are many ways of negotiating the one-down position in such a relationship (Price, 1988, 1992a) and these may be associated with perceptual and cognitive distortion in the one-down member. There may be adulation in which the status of the one-up member is magnified, and there is depression in which the status of the one-down member is diminished. Both ensure a stable complementarity of the relationship and avoid the disruptive 'arms race' of symmetrical schismogenesis (Bateson, 1972). Unlike adulation, the depressive mechanism allows for a switch in one-upness, when chronic depression in the formerly one-down member may be replaced by an acute depression in the formerly one-up member (Price, 1991). The association of depression with loss of social rank in animals has been discussed for birds (Price & Sloman, 1987), monkeys (Price, 1989) and lizards (Price, 1992b).

Ritual Agonistic Behaviour

Ritual agonistic behaviour is the social interaction which produces these role asymmetries in the majority of vertebrate species. An encounter between competitors is followed by ritualised fighting. The ritualisation reduces the physical risk to both parties. The losing behaviour is as ritualised as the fighting. Depression can be seen as a ritual form of losing behaviour producing temporary psychological incapacity which signals submission to the winner but preserves the loser without physical damage. It performs the function which death performs in unritualised fighting, and which the referee performs in culturally ritualised competition.

Resource-Holding Potential (RHP)

Agonistic behaviour can be described in terms of a self-concept called resource-holding potential (RHP) (Parker, 1974, 1984). RHP is an estimate of fighting capacity by both the individual and others. Size, strength, skill, previous success, weapons and allies all indicate increased fighting capacity. The output from a high self-perception of RHP is threat or attack.

All the phenomena of ritual agonistic behaviour can be described in terms of signals of either absolute or relative RHP (Price, 1988). Ritual agonistic behaviour can then be conceptualised as an RHP management system which produces a rank order of individuals according to differences in RHP.

Self-esteem is the nearest we can get to RHP in human terms, and our hypothesis is that self-esteem evolved out of RHP. This would explain two aspects of self-esteem which would seem to be puzzling: its global nature and the great variation in self-esteem in the population (*Lancet*, 1988); both these features are essential to the function of RHP. Re-phrasing our hypothesis in terms of RHP, we can state that depression in its chronic form is a function of low RHP, and in its acute form a function of falling RHP. If we now substitute self-esteem for RHP, and also adopt the current ethological practice of regarding behavioural variation as alternative strategies, we can formulate depression as a low self-esteem strategy.

It may be asked how such a system can evolve, when all the advantage seems to be on the side of the high self-esteem strategy. In fact the advantages of the two strategies are likely to be equalised by negative frequency-dependent selection, as has been shown by Maynard-Smith (1982), using what is known as evolutionary game theory. He calls the high self-esteem strategy a 'hawk' strategy, which is characterised by escalation of agonistic encounters, and the low self-esteem strategy a 'dove' strategy, which is characterised by de-escalation. He has demonstrated in his evolutionary model that, given certain conditions, a pure hawk strategy is not 'evolutionarily stable', in that it can be infiltrated by a mixed hawk/dove strategy. In this model it is assumed that in encounters between hawk and dove the hawk has the higher pay-off, in terms of survival and reproduction; but when hawk meets hawk, the pay-off is lower because of the risk of escalation to unritualised combat with consequent serious injury or death. Yielding ensures the loser survives.

The low self-esteem strategy can be seen as a form of altruistic behaviour which promotes the survival and reproduction of close relatives and so raises 'inclusive fitness' (Hamilton, 1963; Krebs, 1987). In fact, an alternative term for the low self-esteem strategy might be 'kin-helper strategy', contrasting with the 'self-helper' high-esteem strategy.

HUMAN SOCIAL COMPETITION

We have presented the yielding hypothesis in terms of ritual agonistic behaviour, suggesting that the mechanisms of depression evolved when ritual agonistic behaviour was the principal form of social competition underlying sexual selection, as it is in most vertebrate species today. However, ritual agonistic behaviour is not the main form of human social competition. As pointed out by Barkow (1989) and by Gilbert (1992), competition by attraction has largely replaced competition by intimidation, and is the main form of competition seen in primitive tribes by anthropologists. In order to achieve the prestige which guarantees reproductive success (usually the possession of more than one wife in the case of males, and marriage of children to high-ranking partners in the case of females), individuals have to make themselves attractive to others, either to their peers or to particular patrons, and it is the latter who make the decisions which determine the differential allocation of rank.

If it were not for the findings of ethology, it would be doubtful whether we would recognise ritual agonistic behaviour as occurring in human beings. Agonistic behaviour and social asymmetries have been ascribed to cultural factors, or to the carry-over into adult life of the parent–child asymmetry and the punishment which is a common component of child-rearing. Such was the view of Freud, who did not have the benefit of the ethological descriptions of agonistic behaviour and social asymmetry in such a wide variety of vertebrate species, including many reptiles who have no parent–offspring contact at all. Thus it was natural for him to conceptualise the neuroses associated with adult power struggles in terms of unresolved nursery conflicts, a view which was corrected by neo-Freudians such as Sullivan and Horney (Birnbach, 1962); but even the latter saw adult conflict in cultural terms, and did not conceive that mankind might share with animals a phylogenetically old mechanism for creating social asymmetry between previously equal adults.

ACCOUNTING FOR THE FEATURES OF DEPRESSION

Our hypothesis is concerned with 'ultimate' causes (the function of the 'involuntary subordinate strategy' during evolution) and is therefore to some extent independent of proximal causes. However, it is compatible with what is known about the social origins of depression (Brown et al., 1986; Powles, 1992; Kendler et al., 1993), and it is only the constraint of space which prevents us from pursuing at length this interesting topic.

Proponents of an evolutionary hypothesis of any psychiatric condition also have a duty to show that it is consistent with the known features of the condition and that these features can perform the postulated function. In fact, the social competition hypothesis is the only evolutionary hypothesis which accounts for the incapacity of depression; indeed, we see the incapacity as the main functional feature of depression, which is hypothesised to be a ritual (psychological) substitute for the physical damage which is suffered by the loser of an unritualised contest.

The social competition hypothesis also accounts for the cognitive distortions of depression. Beck (1967) described a triad of distortions in which there are negative views of the self, the world and the future. These distortions are compatible with a 'de-escalating' state of mind. The depressed self is not a strong 'favourite' for successful competition; the world of the depressive is not a favourable arena for competing; and the pessimism of the depressive is in stark contrast to that optimism which seems to be required for successful competition. The depressive is not only pessimistic about the future, but has a distorted view of the past in which former rank, ownership and success seem to the patient like a sham, and, therefore, not to be regained.

Apart from ownership and RHP, the only variable which is important in the mathematical analysis of agonistic behaviour is 'resource value', which expresses the value of whatever is being fought about (Parker, 1984). The lower the resource value to a contestant, the more likely he is to yield (flee or submit) rather than to attack. In depression there is a generalised reduction in the perceived value and significance of all goals and incentives, which is usually described as loss of interest. The depressive loss of interest favours de-escalation of conflict. If the resource under consideration is the general one of social rank and success, then reduction in resource value is synonymous with loss of pride and ambition.

We feel that our hypothesis accounts for most of the features of depressive states. In particular, it accounts for the incapacity suffered by depressed patients and for the distortions in their thinking, features which are not explained by theories which see the function of depression to be the conservation of resources (Beck, 1987; Powles, 1992), the management of investment in the environment (Nesse, 1990), the relinquishing of unrealisable goals (Klinger, 1975; Hamburg et al., 1975) or the redressing of imbalance in reciprocal exchange (Glantz & Pearce, 1989).

Our hypothesis is consistent with subjective heterogeneity in depression. It does not matter whether yielders refrain from fighting back because they are too tired, or too frightened, or feel too physically ill, or think they will not win, or that they do not deserve to win, or that their allies will not come to their support.

Ethological observations of depressed patients show that active (spontaneous, person-oriented) submission such as flattery is reduced, but passive submission such as looking down is increased (T. Schelde, personal communication, 1993), which highlights the difference between the 'involuntary subordinate strategy' underlying depression and the voluntary subordinate behaviour which may pre-empt or replace it.

Epidemiological Features

Our hypothesis is consistent with the fact that depression is more common, more severe and more prolonged in later life, for the most important acts of yielding are required when one generation is giving way to the next. We have dealt elsewhere with the fact that depression tends to follow 'exit' events such as bereavement, whereas it might be expected that yielding would more often be required following the entry of new members to the group (Price, 1988). We argue that social rank is so dependent on the support of others that loss of significant others has become the main predictor of loss of rank. The dependence of rank on support from kin and other allies is a widespread characteristic of non-human primates (De Waal & Harcourt, 1992), suggesting that it may have applied to the simian and human common ancestor some 40 million years ago, allowing sufficient evolutionary time for close interconnections to develop between the brain mechanisms subserving agonistic and affiliative behaviour.

We have also (Price, 1988) dealt with the problem that depression is commoner in women than men, whereas agonistic behaviour is thought to be more common in males. Our argument is that agonistic behaviour is more conspicuous but not more common in males, and, in any case, there is evidence that when women have equal opportunities, the female excess of depression disappears (Wilhelm & Parker, 1989).

IMPLICATIONS FOR RESEARCH

Animals

Our hypothesis suggests a wide choice of animal models for research into depression. Low rank and falling rank in animals have been used as models for human physical disease, such as heart disease (Henry et al., 1986) and renal disease (von Holst, 1986) and it would be surprising if social stress intense enough to produce these physical pathologies did not also induce psychopathology. In his work on social stress in tree shrews, von Holst (1986) has observed two distinct forms of reaction to subjugation, one associated with increased adrenomedullary activity and one with adrenocortical activity, the latter showing extreme social withdrawal ending in death; these reactions in tree shrews bear a resemblance to the contrasting fight/flight and conservation/withdrawal clinical syndromes described by Powles (1992).

In equally promising work on guinea pigs, Sachser & Lick (1991) have shown that being brought up in a colony (as opposed to with a single female) abolishes the aggression which occurs when two strange males are put together in the presence of a female. This suggests that the experience of living with other males during adolescence may create the variation in resource-holding potential (RHP) which is required to avoid pairwise contests among adults. They also made the observation that the loser of a contest could be predicted from changes in the status of his adrenal and other hormones before there was any detectable change in his fighting behaviour; this supports Leshner's (1983) hypothesis that the switch from escalation to de-escalation involves a positive feedback loop which includes the adrenal cortex.

Some animals are promising for research because they show physical effects of rank change. Some reptiles and fish and at least one monkey change colour following rank change (Price, 1989); some fish change sex (Keenleyside, 1979). These might not only be possible markers for mood change, but they offer a path by which the mechanism responsible for the physical changes might lead to the central mechanism. Both low rank and depression are associated with increased activity of the hypothalamic-pituitary-adrenocortical axis, and there is an interesting association between rank and indolamine metabolism in both monkeys (McGuire; 1988) and fish (Winberg & Nilsson, 1993). A project currently under way in the Department of Psychiatry of the University of Tasmania is using low rank in a marsupial called the sugar glider as a model for depression (I.H. Jones & J. Mallick, personal communication, 1992).

Human Beings

Our hypothesis that depression evolved out of mechanisms mediating ranking behaviour throws a new light on the extensive work which has been carried out on the expression of hostility in depression, and which has produced very conflicting results (Riley et al., 1989). Some workers have found that depressed patients express more anger than controls (Fava et al., 1993), and this might seem to conflict with our idea that depression functions to inhibit aggression.

In fact, our hypothesis states that only hostility to equal- and higher-ranking people is inhibited, whereas hostility expressed to lower-ranking people is often increased; and it is our clinical impression that hostility in depression is usually unexpressed or 'taken out on' the furniture, or expressed to subordinate spouses or children. No published study to date has considered whether the hostility is felt or expressed to a higher-ranking or a lower-ranking person. Yet from an ethological perspective, expressing hostility up a hierarchy is a very different matter from expressing it downwards. Our hypothesis predicts that, if depression occurs in one partner in a complementary relationship, hostility expressed by the patient to the other will be increased if it is the dominant partner who gets depressed, but will be reduced if it is the subordinate partner who gets depressed.

IMPLICATIONS FOR TREATMENT

Analysis of the Patient's Situation

The 'yielding' hypothesis helps the physician to explore the patient's situation, identify any conflictual relationships and assess the reasons for nonresolution of any agonistic interaction. There are five options:

(a) The conflict may be resolved by negotiation and compromise. Here we are talking in terms of reconciliation, which implies penitence, atonement, forgiveness and other forms of negotiation.
(b) The patient may be helped to win the conflict. This applies particularly to patients who are insufficiently self-assertive.
(c) The patient may be assisted to substitute voluntary yielding in the form of conscious submission for the involuntary and unconscious yielding of depression.

(d) The patient may be enabled to leave the arena. This may involve physical separation from the adversarial person and certainly involves mental detachment.

(e) Help may come from reducing the patient's assessment of the value of the resource being competed for. Aspirations may be excessive or too narrow, the patient having 'all his eggs in one basket'. These are concerns common to psychotherapy, philosophy and religion.

Sharing with the Patient

It may or may not be desirable to share the yielding hypothesis with the patient; for instance, the therapist might say: "Your depression is serving an important function in your marriage, it is enabling you to submit to your husband's demands without rebellion, and is therefore saving your relationship from probable rupture". This is a form of 'positive connotation' of the symptom, a technique widely used in family therapy; and it is also a re-framing from the patient's previous formulations which may have been in terms of hormones or physical illness. It is also something of a challenge, suggesting to her that she need not submit to her husband's demands, puts in her mind the idea that there may be alternative ways of dealing with those of her husband's demands which she finds unacceptable.

To patients of a more scientific frame of mind, it may help simply to explain what is going on, since lack of meaning adds yet another morbid dimension to the experience of depression. We sometimes use the analogy of hibernation, explaining that while hibernation is nature's way of helping certain animals to survive unfavourable weather conditions, depression is nature's way of helping certain humans to survive unfavourable social conditions. This is often acceptable to depressed patients, who may themselves feel like curling up into a ball in a hole in the ground and staying there for a long time. And the seasonal recovery from hibernation helps the patient to believe in the likelihood of remission.

On the other hand, often the situation can be resolved without the patient being aware of conflict. Haley (1963), for instance, advocates the resolution of agonistic situations in marriage by means of nonagonistic interpretations, such as parent–child interaction, and we would endorse this view.

Relation to Other Psychotherapies

Our evolutionary perspective supports those therapies aimed at resolving interpersonal conflict (Karasu, 1990; Stravynski & Greenberg, 1992) and the various schools of family therapy which are sensitive to deviations of hierarchy such as cross-generational coalitions (Haley, 1963).

Cognitive behaviour therapy appears to us to be a means for raising RHP and other components of self-esteem and of rendering the basis for these self-appraisals realistic. Both these aims are supported by our approach. We think our main contribution is the conceptualisation of depression as a failsafe strategy to which there are alternatives at higher levels of mental organisation. Whereas psychoanalysis aims to render unconscious thoughts conscious, therapy based on evolutionary principles aims to replace unconscious behavioural strategies with conscious ones.

ACKNOWLEDGEMENT

This paper is dedicated to Dr M.R.A. Chance whose insight into the relation between agonistic behaviour and psychopathology stimulated the train of thought summarised above.

REFERENCES

Abbott, D.H., Barrett, J., Faulkes, C.G., et al. (1989). Social contraception in naked mole-rats and marmoset monkeys. *Journal of Zoology, London, 219,* 703–710.

Archer, J. (1988). *The Behavioural Biology of Aggression.* Cambridge: Cambridge University Press.

Barkow, J.H. (1989). *Darwin, Sex and Status: Biological Approaches to Mind and Culture.* Toronto: University of Toronto Press.

Bateson, G. (1972). *Steps to an Ecology of Mind.* New York: Ballantine Books.

Beck, A.T. (1967). *Depression: Clinical, Experimental and Theoretical Aspects.* New York: Hoeber.

Beck, A.T. (1987). Cognitive models of depression. *Journal of Cognitive Psychotherapy, 1,* 5–37.

Birnbach, M. (1962). *Non-Freudian Social Philosophy.* Stanford: Stanford University Press.

Brown, G.W., Andrews, B., Harris, T., et al. (1986). Social support, self-esteem and depression. *Psychological Medicine, 16,* 813–831.

Darwin, C. (1871). *The Descent of Man and Selection in Relation to Sex.* London: John Murray.

De Waal, F.B.M. & Harcourt, A.H. (1992). Coalitions and alliances: a history of ethological research. In A.H. Harcourt & F.B.M. De Waal (Eds.), *Coalitions and Alliances in Humans and Other Animals* (pp. 1–19). Oxford: Oxford University Press.

Fava, M., Rosenbaum, J.F., Pava, J.A., et al. (1993). Anger attacks in unipolar depression. Part I: clinical correlates and response to fluoxetine treatment. *American Journal of Psychiatry, 150,* 1158–1163.

Gardner, R.J., Jr. (1982). Mechanisms in major depressive disorder: an evolutionary model. *Archives of General Psychiatry, 390,* 1436–1441.

Gilbert, P. (1992). *Depression: The Evolution of Powerlessness.* Hove: Erlbaum. New York: Guilford.

Glantz, K. & Pearce, J.K. (1989). *Exiles from Eden: Psychotherapy from an Evolutionary Perspective.* London: W.W. Norton.

Goldberg, S. (1991). Recent developments in attachment theory and research. *Canadian Journal of Psychiatry, 36,* 393–400.

Haley, J. (1963). Marriage therapy. *Archives of General Psychiatry, 8,* 213–234.

Hamburg, D.A., Hamburg, B.A. & Barchas, J.D. (1975). Anger and depression in the perspective of behavioral biology. In L. Levi (Ed.), *Emotions: their parameters and measurement* (pp. 235–278). New York: Raven Press.

Hamilton, W.D. (1963). The evolution of altruistic behaviour. *The American Naturalist, 97,* 354–356.

Harvey, P.H. & Bradbury, J.W. (1991). Sexual Selection. In J.R. Krebs & N.B. Davies (Eds.), *Behavioural Ecology: An Evolutionary Approach* (pp. 203–233). Oxford: Blackwell.

Henry, J.P., Stephens, P.M. & Ely, D.L. (1986). Psychosocial hypertension and the defence and defeat reactions. *Journal of Hypertension, 4*, 687–697.

Hill, D. (1968). Depression: disease, reaction or posture? *American Journal of Psychiatry, 125*, 445–456.

Holst, D. Von (1986). Vegetative and somatic components of tree shrews' behaviour. *Journal of the Autonomic Nervous System*, (suppl.), 657–670.

Huntingford, F. & Turner, A. (1987). *Animal Conflict*. London: Chapman & Hall.

Karasu, T.B. (1990). Toward a clinical model of psychotherapy for depression. I: Systematic comparison of three psychotherapies. *American Journal of Psychiatry, 147*, 133–147.

Keenleyside, M.H.A. (1979). *Diversity and Adaptation in Fish Behaviour*. Berlin: Springer.

Kendler, K.S., Kessler, R.C., Neale, M.C., et al. (1993). The prediction of major depression in women: toward an integrated etiologic model. *American Journal of Psychiatry, 150*, 1139–1148.

Klinger, E. (1975). Consequences of commitment to and dis-engagement from incentives. *Psychological Review, 82*, 1–25.

Krebs, D. (1987). The challenge of altruism in biology and psychology. In C. Crawford, M. Smith & D. Krebs (Eds.), *Sociobiology and Psychology* (pp. 81–118). Hillsdale: Erlbaum.

Krebs, J.R. & Davies, N.B. (1987). *An Introduction to Behavioural Ecology*, 2nd edn. Oxford: Blackwell.

Lancet (1988). Editorial: self-esteem. *Lancet, ii*, 943–944.

Leshner, A.I. (1983). The hormonal responses to competition and their behavioral significance. In B.B. Svare (Ed.), *Hormones and Aggressive Behavior* (pp. 393–404). New York: Plenum.

Lewis, A.J. (1934). Melancholia: a clinical survey of depressive states. *Journal of Mental Science, 80*, 277–378.

McGuire, M.T. (1988). On the possibility of ethological explanations of psychiatric disorders. *Acta Psychiatrica Scandinavica, 77*, suppl. 341, pp. 7–22.

Maynard-Smith, J. (1982). *Evolution and the Theory of Games*. Cambridge: Cambridge University Press.

Nesse, R.M. (1990). Evolutionary explanations of emotions. *Human Nature, 1*, 261–289.

Parker, G.A. (1974). Assessment strategy and the evolution of fighting behaviour. *Journal of Theoretical Biology, 47*, 223–243.

Parker, G.A. (1984). Evolutionarily stable strategies. In J.R. Krebs & N.B. Davies (Eds.), *Behavioural Ecology: An Evolutionary Approach*, 2nd edn (pp. 30–61). Oxford: Blackwell.

Powles, W.E. (1992). *Human Development and Homeostasis: The Science of Psychiatry*. Madison CT: International Universities Press.

Price, J.S. (1967). Hypothesis: the dominance hierarchy and the evolution of mental illness. *Lancet, ii*, 243–246.

Price, J.S. (1988). Alternative channels for negotiating asymmetry in social relationships. In M.R.A. Chance (Ed.), *Social Fabrics of the Mind* (pp. 157–195). Hove: Erlbaum.

Price, J.S. (1989). The effect of social stress on the behaviour and physiology of monkeys. In K. Davison & A. Kerr (Eds.), *Contemporary Themes in Psychiatry* (pp. 459–466). London: Gaskell Press.

Price, J.S. (1991). Homeostasis or change: a systems theory approach to depression. *Journal of Medical Psychology, 64*, 331–344.

Price, J.S. (1992a). The agonic and hedonic modes: definition, usage, and the promotion of mental health. *World Futures, 34*, 234–269.

Price, J.S. (1992b). Accentuate the positive, eliminate the negative: the role of boosting and putting-down signals in mental health. In D. Trent (Ed.), *Promotion of Mental Health, Vol. 1, 1991* (pp. 89–101). Aldershot: Avebury.

Price, J.S. & Sloman, L. (1987). Depression as yielding behavior: an animal model based on Schjelderup-Ebbe's pecking order. *Ethology and Sociobiology, 8* (suppl.), 85–98.

Radford, M.H.B., Mann, L. & Kalucy, R.S. (1986). Psychiatric disturbance and decision-making. *Australian and New Zealand Journal of Psychiatry, 20,* 210–217.

Riley, W.T., Treiber, F.A. & Woods, M.G. (1989). Anger and hostility in depression. *Journal of Nervous and Mental Disease, 177,* 668–674.

Ryan, M.J. (1985). *The Tungara Frog: a Study in Sexual Selection and Communication.* Chicago: University of Chicago Press.

Sachser, N. & Lick, C. (1991). Social experience, behavior and stress in guinea pigs. *Physiology and Behavior, 50,* 83–90.

Sloman, L. (1976). The role of neurosis in phylogenetic adaptation with particular reference to early man. *American Journal of Psychiatry, 133,* 543–547.

Sloman, S. & Sloman, L. (1988). Mate selection in the service of human evolution. *Journal of Social and Biological Structures, 11,* 457–468.

Sloman, L., Gardner, R. & Price, J.S. (1989). Biology of family systems and mood disorders. *Family Process, 28,* 387–398.

Stravynski, A. & Greenberg, D. (1992). The psychological management of depression. *Acta Psychiatrica Scandinavica, 85,* 407–414.

Wenegrat, B. (1984). *Sociobiology and Mental Disorder.* California: Addison-Wesley.

Wilhelm, K. & Parker, G. (1989). Is sex necessarily a risk factor to depression? *Psychological Medicine, 19,* 401–403.

Winberg, S. & Nilsson, G.E. (1993). Time course of changes in brain serotonergic activity and brain tryptophan levels in dominant and subordinate juvenile arctic char. *Journal of Experimental Biology, 179,* 181–195.

*John Price, DM, MRCP, FRCPsych, *Odintune Place, Plumpton, E. Sussex, BN7 3AN*; Leon Sloman, FRCP(C), *Associate Professor, Clarke Institute of Psychiatry, Toronto, Canada*; Russell Gardner, Jr, MD, *Professor of Psychiatry, University of Texas Medical Branch, Galveston, Texas, USA*: Paul Gilbert, PhD, FBPsS, *Professor of Clinical Psychology, Derby University*; Peter Rohde, MB, BCh, FRCP(E), FRCPsych, *53 Harley Street, London W1N 1DD.*

*Correspondence: *Department of Psychiatry, Wellington School of Medicine, Wellington, New Zealand*

(First received May 1993, final revision September 1993, accepted September 1993)

12 Depression in evolutionary context

Michael T. McGuire
University of California at Los Angeles and Sepulveda Veterans Administration Medical Center, USA
Alfonso Troisi
Università Tor Vergata Rome, ITALY
Michael M. Raleigh
University of California at Los Angeles and Sepulveda Veterans Administration Medical Center, USA

INTRODUCTION

Depression is a common human affliction. For major depression (severe, debilitating depression) and dysthymia (chronic, mild–moderate depression) the combined male–female life-prevalence estimate in the United States is 24.5%, with a 29.3%–17.5% female–male differential. The 12-month prevalence estimate is 13.8%, with a 15.9%–9.8% female–male differential (Kessler et al., 1994). Major depression and dysthymia are the two most frequently diagnosed mood disorders in which depression is a primary feature. Disorders in which mania is either a primary or secondary feature are also classified as mood disorders. Mania will only be discussed briefly. Our focus is on depression.

Disorders that appear with the frequencies noted deserve consideration as possible adaptations. It is relatively easy to construct an adaptive scenario for externally elicited, mild–moderate, time-limited, spontaneously resolving depression: the symptoms of depression may warn a person that past or ongoing strategies have failed; physiological slowing and social withdrawal may remove a person from high-cost, low-benefit social environments; and signalling one's emotional state to others may initiate others' help without incurring long-term payback requirements. Variants of this type of depression are seen in response to personal losses (e.g. death of one's child), destruction of personal property (e.g.

earthquakes), and discontinuation of essential employment. Although epidemiological estimates are not available, perhaps 15–20% of depressions fit into this category (many of which are unlikely to find their way into life-prevalence estimates).

At another extreme, there are individuals who become severely depressed and exhibit signs and symptoms associated with what is classified as major depression (American Psychiatric Association, 1994). Markedly diminished interest or pleasure, weight loss, psychomotor agitation or retardation, chronic insomnia or hypersomnia, fatigue, the inability to concentrate, social withdrawal, feelings of worthlessness, and striking reductions in functional capacities comprise the most common cluster of indices for this disorder. External precipitants are often absent. Some individuals experience only a single episode whereas others have recurrent episodes. For yet others the disorder may become chronic despite all available medical and social interventions. Compared to instances of mild–moderate, time-limited depression, major depression is less easily interpreted as an adaptation.

In between these extremes are a number of conditions in which the signs and symptoms of depression are readily apparent but not the only clinical manifestations. Dysthymia, or dysthymic disorder, is an example. Chronic moderate depression, usually coupled with functional capacity limitations, failed social strategies, and varying degrees of social isolation are typical features of this disorder (Essock-Vitale and McGuire, 1990; American Psychiatric Association, 1994). Both dimensional and quantitative differences distinguish dysthymia from time-limited depression and major depression. Although symptom intensity may vary across social environments, persons are seldom symptom-free, and functional capacity limitations are more often enduring than not (Essock-Vitale and McGuire, 1990; McGuire and Essock-Vitale, 1982). Dysthymia may or may not qualify as an adaptation.

In what ways can evolutionary theory inform our understanding of major depression and dysthymia? Answers to this question would be less difficult if clinical cases of depression were confined to only those signs and symptoms that are most readily explained by adaptive models. Such cases are rare. By far the more common clinical finding is one in which clear indices of depression are accompanied by signs and symptoms associated primarily with other disorders or no specific disorder (e.g. memory dysfunction, somatic pain, anxiety, parathesia) (McGuire, Raleigh, Fawzy, Spar, & Troisi, in press), as well as a history of pre-disorder functional limitations and inflexible personality features (McGuire et al., in press).

Answers are further complicated by the fact that there are many findings that do not fit easily into existing adaptationist interpretations. For example, over a thousand medical diseases and disorders are known to reflect atypical genetic information (e.g. Huntington's disease) (Nesse & Williams, 1994). There is little about the majority of these conditions to suggest that they are adaptations.

Given the broad range of these conditions, there is no a priori reason to discount the possibility that many instances of depression not only reflect atypical genetic information, but are also maladaptive. Indeed, this possibility has fuelled the search for biological markers of depression for over three decades.

Another set of potentially complicating factors has to do with common final pathway phenomena, which is a shorthand way of saying that multiple causes can lead to similar phenotypes because of constraints on phenotypic expression. For a significant percentage of depressions, available historical and physiological data are consistent with common final pathway explanations: e.g. some persons who develop depression grow up and/or live in adverse social environments whereas others do not; and significant individual differences in putative depression-causing physiological systems (e.g. norepinephrine, serotonin) are frequently reported (see Kaplan & Sadock, 1995, for a review). Further, some instances of depression remit spontaneously; some respond to one type of anti-depression medication but not to another; some do not respond to any type of medication but do respond to electroconvulsive treatment; and some do not respond to any known intervention. This array of individually different outcomes is expected if similar phenotypes have different causes. Although multiple causes and constraints on phenotypic expression do not obviate adaptive-response interpretations, their inclusion into disorder explanations can either complicate or simplify adaptationist hypotheses. We return to this point later.

The possibility that many cases of depression do not easily fit adaptationist models can lead to different evolutionary approaches to explaining depression. One is to disregard individual differences, identify the "core" features of depression, and assess their potential adaptiveness. This approach has two obvious advantages: it minimises the need to explain the diversity of clinical findings, and it facilitates the development of unitary causal hypotheses. Thus far, the majority of evolutionary interpretations of depression have employed this approach (e.g. Nesse, 1991a; Price, 1967; Price, Sloman, Gardner, Gilbert, & Rohde, 1994; Sloman, Price, Gilbert, & Gardner, 1994). Although these interpretations offer important insights into possible core features, on balance they remain distant from what one encounters clinically. An alternative approach is to take the clinical data as they are and use more than one evolutionary concept to explain both core features and individual differences.

We employ both approaches. We view individuals as mosaics of traits, many of which vary independently in terms of their optimality relative to some established measure (e.g. McGuire & Essock-Vitale, 1982) as well as their probability of acting in concert. Trait clusters and multiple causes, rather than unitary traits and single causes, are assumed to be responsible for the majority of depressions. This view is consistent with reports from pedigree studies, personality assessments, and behavioural genetics research, which show, respectively, strong familial trends for depression (e.g. Goodwin & Jamison,

1990; Kendler, Pedersen, Johnson, Neale, & Mathe, 1993); different cross-person enduring behavioural and physiological profiles (e.g. Cloninger, 1986; Cloninger, Svrakic, & Przybeck, 1993); and heritability for specific traits (e.g. Plomin, Owen, & McGuffin, 1994; McGuffin, Owen, O'Donovan, Thapou, & Gottesman, 1994). The net effect of these and other influences is a significant degree of cross-person variability. To cite but one finding from the study of stress, when normal healthy male volunteers are exposed to stress tests (e.g. quiz, arithmetic task, etc.) and peripheral cortisol concentrations are used to measure stress responses, results show a continuum between "complete reactors and nonreactors" (Berger et al., 1987). Among clinical populations, persons who are depressed (as well as those who, by clinical criteria, are successfully treated for depression) often differ significantly from controls in their capacity to develop and enact social strategies, in their ability to discontinue or compartmentalise emotions that negatively influence function, and in their response to stressful environments and personal failures (Essock-Vitale & McGuire, 1990; McGuire & Essock-Vitale, 1982; McGuire & Troisi, in press). When several of these capacities are simultaneously suboptimal (a trait condition) and/or dysfunctional (a state condition), individuals are not only at risk for depression, but the cross-person manifestations of depression will also differ. Viewed this way, some instances of depression turn out to be adaptive (e.g. instances of depression that have minimal functional consequences and spontaneously resolve); some represent attempts to adapt; and some turn out to be minimally adaptive or maladaptive.

From an evolutionary perspective, one might argue that the preceding view confounds more than it clarifies, and that evolutionary interpretations of disorders should focus primarily on core adaptations and disregard "noise", e.g. the manifestations of suboptimal capacities not specific to depression. But to take this position is to miss the implications of the preceding discussion in a several ways. First, different types of depression may develop in response to different adaptive problems; e.g. depression associated with the loss of an important other may differ from depression associated with the loss of employment. Second, suboptimal traits may contribute to the onset of depression, as well as influence its subsequent course, as is often the case in repeated instances of personal failure. Conversely, optimal traits, such as the capacity to signal one's mood state accurately to others, may increase the probability that others will provide assistance and thereby improve clinical outcome. Even traits that are usually considered adaptive, such as a mother's care for an ill child, may increase the chance of depression. Third, and most important for this paper, competing evolutionary concepts may explain much of the supposed clinical noise, that is, viewing depression as a unitary adaptive strategy may serve the aesthetics of theorising yet delay attempts to develop comprehensive evolutionary explanations of depression.

In our view, evolutionary explanations can not exclude either disorder-associated traits or trait variation. These are as much a part of clinical phenotypes as core features. Trait variation is both an obvious and undisputed evolutionary outcome. Moreover, there is little reason to suppose that selection has favoured cross-person similarity for a variety of traits ranging from sickle-cell trait to responses to stressors. As Nesse and Williams (1995) have emphasised, traits that may have been valuable in the past lead to a directional bias in subsequent selection; and selection is characterised by "trade-offs". Biases and trade-offs not only render many current traits far from optimal (e.g. bone strength) but they can also increase susceptibility to diseases or disorders (Nesse & Williams, 1995; Nesse, in press). Genetic recombination can serve as an example. There are evolutionary advantages to recombination (e.g. variations in traits that correlate with differential reproductive outcomes across environments) but it is far from an error-free process, hence occasional genetic mistakes and their phenotypic consequences. A related, although perhaps a more controversial point, is that selection for psychological capacities may have been secondary to selection for other traits, such as immunological competence and reproduction (Hamilton & Zuk, 1982). This hypothesis is developed in detail elsewhere (McGuire & Troisi, in press). Here, we will only note that it is consistent with the wide distribution of measurements for IQ, reading speed, and comprehension, as well as numerous social navigation skills (Bouchard, Lykken, McGuire, Segal, & Tellegen, 1990; McGuire and Essock-Vitale, 1982; Plomin et al., 1994;).

The preceding views conflict with hypotheses developed by evolutionary psychologists (e.g. Tooby & Cosmides, 1990), which emphasise phenotypic plasticity, cross-person similarity in adaptive capacities, and selection favouring the development of psychological mechanisms or rules (traits) that mediate behaviour largely in response to environmental contingencies. Although this view may characterise some persons, persons with disorders provide an exception. If they are nothing else, most disorders are examples of compromised plasticity, rule use, and functionality; and within disorder categories, individual differences are often as striking as attribute similarity. Disorder classification systems (e.g. DSM—IV, American Psychiatric Assocation, 1994) accommodate the preceding point by requiring only a subset of disorder-related indices to establish a diagnosis. Further, the plasticity view is not easily reconciled with findings showing that a significant percentage of depressed persons have chronic information-processing limitations (McGuire & Essock-Vitale, 1982; McGuire et al., in press; Silberg et al., 1990; Silberman, Weingartner, Laraia, Byrnes, & Post, 1983), that there are significant sex differences in life-prevalence estimates for depression, and that when all psychiatric disorders are lumped together the life-prevalence estimate is 48% (Kessler et al., 1994).

Those favouring the phenotypic plasticity view often point out that trait differences fail to predict reproductive outcome consistently, thus such differences should be viewed as selectively neutral. On this point, studies of the reproductive success of persons with psychiatric disorders yield mixed results. For the most severe disorders, findings range from significant to nonsignificant reductions in reproductive rates (e.g. Erlenmeyer-Kimling & Paradowski, 1977; Odegard, 1960, 1980), although all of the studies suffer from one or more methodological limitations (e.g. duration of studies, use of secondary sources, study populations limited to hospitalised patients, salutary drug effects). To our knowledge, no replicated studies have shown increased reproductive rates among persons with disorders, although studies consistently reveal strong assortative mating effects (e.g. Guze, Goodwin, & Crane, 1970; Merikangas, 1982; Merikangas, Bromet, & Spiker, 1983). When persons with dysthymic disorders have been studied in detail and reproductive histories confirmed with knowledgeable kin (rather than through secondary sources), findings show a significant reduction in reproductive rates (Essock-Vitale & McGuire, 1990). Thus, disorder–reproduction relationships remain to be clarified, and part of the clarification may require consideration of an earlier-mentioned hypothesis: Namely, to the degree that selection has favoured the strategy of offsetting parasite effects through genetic recombination, in which case selection for reproduction is likely to take precedence over selection for psychological capacities, reproductive rates may vary minimally among populations with and without disorders. In effect, psychological traits may be selectively neutral by default, which is not to say that trait differences lack consequences or that they do not influence the probability of disorders.

Traits and trait variations notwithstanding, most depressed persons respond to environmental change; and over the last three decades hypotheses tying specific contingencies (e.g. others' competitive behaviour) to depression have been given evolutionary interpretations primarily by Price (Price et al., 1994), Sloman (Sloman et al., 1994), Gardner (1982), Gilbert (1995), and Birtchnell (1993). However, significant cross-person response differences to similar contingencies are observed, a point suggesting that additional research is essential if person–environment interactions are to be characterised precisely. That more research is needed is not surprising. Even the most unambiguous social encounter usually has multiple features; for example, persons send mixed signals; and motivational states and cognitive capacities influence how signals are interpreted.

From another perspective, attempts to develop comprehensive explanations of depression invite an enquiry into possible contributions from disciplines studying depression using nonevolutionary models. Depression has been investigated as much, if not more, than any other disorder by psychiatry and related disciplines. There are well formulated psychological, learning, genetical, and physiological causal hypotheses often coupled with impressive bodies of empirical evidence (e.g. see Kaplan & Sadock, 1995, for a review). Although these hypotheses may omit insights offered by evolutionary interpretations (e.g. ultimate causation, sexual selection), it is unlikely that much of the empirical data are wrong or that many of the hypotheses are groundless. It is the relevance of selected data and hypotheses that needs to be assessed, explained, and, where warranted, integrated into evolutionary thinking.

The preceding discussion not only suggests that the next generation of evolutionary explanations of depression will result in more complex models than heretofore, but also that future models may serve as signposts for what needs to be accomplished if evolutionary thinking is going to inform clinical findings. To realise these ends, four points come to mind: to explicate further ultimate and proximate cause contributions to depression; to specify further possible adaptive features of depression; to identify disorder-related features that compromise or facilitate the potential adaptiveness of depression; and, where applicable, to integrate nonevolutionary hypotheses and findings with evolutionary explanations.

Obviously, accomplishing all of these is more than we can hope for in this paper. Thus, only selected points will be addressed. We begin with a brief discussion of sexual selection theory with the aim of identifying possible contributing factors to sex-related differences in the prevalence of depression—these differences are too striking to ignore. We will then discuss several evolutionary models of depression (e.g. common final pathway and core hypotheses) and attempt to integrate the models with selected hypotheses and findings developed from nonevolutionary disciplines. We conclude with a review of an ecological model of disorder-triggering and disorder-worsening person–environment interactions (regulation–disregulation theory) and its potential evolutionary relevance. Clinical vignettes are used to illustrate key points.

Sex Differences in Depression

Sexual selection

Evolutionary theory permits the development of predictions about the sex-related probability of disorders. Sexual selection theory (see Trivers, 1985 for a review), which, in part, views male and female physiology, anatomy, and reproductive strategies as outcomes of dissimilar past adaptive problems, can serve as a point of departure for this discussion.

To review findings that are well covered in the literature quickly: Compared to males, females allocate more time and energy to producing and caring for offspring, and to developing and maintaining social support networks; whereas males allocate more time and energy to male–male status competition and resource acquisition (Buss, 1994). In selecting mates, females tend to prefer males who are older, have high social status, have or give indications that they can acquire resources, and who signal their interest in long-term relationships (Buss, 1985, 1988, 1994; Cashden, 1993; Sloman & Sloman, 1988). Males tend to value females who are younger, attractive, and submissive; and males more than females are interested in multiple short-term relationships (Brown & Kenrick, 1995; Buss, 1994; Grammar, 1995). The consistency of these and related findings across numerous cultures (see Buss, 1994, for a review) suggests that mate-selection and reproductive strategies are most parsimoniously explained as predisposed traits, refined and constrained by culture and experience.

Not unexpectedly, differences in mate-selection and reproductive strategies lead to within- and cross-sex conflict. Competition among males for females, in part, clarifies why males more than females attempt to conceal mates. And, because of paternity uncertainty, males are more inclined to try and possess females, as well as to dominate them physically (Daly, Wilson, & Weghorst, 1982). On the other hand, females have greater control over sexual access and often engage in infidelity threats rather than physical coercion during disagreements (Buss, 1988).

Given the preceding characterisations, disorder frequencies and responsiveness to environmental variables can be expected to show sex-related differences. For example, disorders associated with failed attempts to attract mates with specific qualities, failure to reproduce or to develop social-support networks, and intrusions into one's "somatic territory" (one's sense of the boundaries of one's body) should have a greater prevalence among females, whereas disorders associated with losses in male–male competition, failure to gain sexual access to females, failure to acquire resources, and declining social status should be more frequent among males. Epidemiological data are consistent with these predictions.

Histrionic personality and erotomania have mate attraction components; anorexia nervosa and depression due to infertility have reproductive components; and agoraphobia and hypochondriasis have somatic territory components. Each of these disorders occurs significantly more often among females than among males (Kessler et al., 1994; American Psychiatric Association, 1994). For example, 37% of females experience psychological disruptions in association with marital infertility whereas only 1% of males show such disturbances (McEwan, Costello, & Taylor, 1987). Turning to males, impulse-related disorders, depression and/or suicide following competitive losses, and alcoholism have both male–male competition and resource acquisition components; and many types of sexual deviance have female access components. These disorders are more common among males than females (Kessler et al., 1994; American Psychiatric Association, 1994). An obvious implication of this line of reasoning is that sex differences should be integrated into disorder explanations.

Applying the preceding points to depression, the finding that males tend to prefer submissive females is expected to increase the probability that females who are excessively submissive will be victims of depression triggered by interpersonal conflict and oppressive or dominating male tactics. Greater male possessiveness and the hiding of females may also contribute to the increased incidence of depression among females via their constraints on females' social options. Failure to develop social-support networks should also be a factor, e.g. studies of females with dysthymic disorder show that they have significantly smaller social-support networks compared to controls (Essock-Vitale &

McGuire, 1990). Also, male proclivities for short-term relationships, combined with female preferences for more enduring relationships, may result in a higher percentage of disappointing and high-cost relationships for females. On the other hand, males should be particularly vulnerable to status declines and female tactics that suggest infidelity or involve cuckoldry (Buss, 1994; Trivers, 1985). When the preceding points are summed, depression-contributing events are likely to occur more frequently among females than among males, and frequency differences may explain part of the reported prevalence differences.

EVOLUTIONARY MODELS OF DEPRESSION

The models discussed next incorporate many of the ideas and findings from the work of Price (1967, 1969; Price & Gardner, 1995; Price & Sloman, 1987; Price et al., 1994), Sloman (1976; Sloman & Price, 1987; Sloman et al., 1994; Sloman & Sloman, 1988), Henderson (Henderson, Byrne, Duncan-Jones, Scott, & Adcock, 1980), Gardner (1982), Nesse (1990a,b, 1991a,b), Gilbert (1989, 1993, 1995; Gilbert & Allen, 1994), Gut (1989), and their colleagues. Individual differences are not emphasised in this section, but return to the discussion in the final part of the paper. Consistently with these authors, as well as other investigators using evolutionary models (e.g. Plutchik, 1980; Salzan, 1991), we assume that persons are goal-directed and that depression is an evolved emotion that influences thought and behaviour.

Although all of the evolutionary models of depression have ultimate and proximate cause features, for discussion they can be conveniently subdivided into three, not necessarily mutually exclusive, groups that emphasise ultimate causes; developmental disruptions; and ultimate–proximate cause interactions.

Models of Depression Emphasising Ultimate Causes

Three possible ultimate cause models of depression are considered.

Depression-is-an-adaptive-trait

The possibility that depression can be an adaptive response to adverse external conditions has at least a five-decade history. In 1936 Lewis suggested that depression is a way of eliciting help from others. The idea that depression is an alternative response to the intolerability of low social status has been a central theme in the work of Price (1967), Sloman (1976), and their colleagues. Engle and Schmale (1972; Engle, 1980) postulated that depression conserves energy and functions as a homeostatic regulatory process. Klerman (1974) identified several possible adaptive functions of depression, including its often positive social communication effects. Also, Gut (1989) has argued that coping with depression often results in individuals becoming more psychologically healthy and self-aware. Much of this history has been reviewed by Gilbert (1989).

The depression-is-an-adaptive-trait model is primarily an ultimate cause explanation that requires a proximate trigger. The model builds from the idea that depression is an evolved trait (or strategy) responding to an actual or potential reduction in goal achievement (negative cost:benefit balance), such as a fall in status or a loss in resource-holding power (Price, 1967; Price & Sloman, 1987). Pathogenic events are usually external, although internal precipitants are not precluded. The emotion provides information about one's negative cost:benefit state and physiological slowing constrains further costly behaviour. Affects inform others about one's condition. Co-evolution has favoured the capacity to recognise and to respond to persons who are depressed, although care provided by others is contingent upon the presence of established social-support networks. If the precipitating factors abate, depression may also abate. The model is not limited to depression; and it does not assume or require that depression is shaped by common final-pathway constraints.

For this model, information processing and signalling capacities are assumed to be functional; and disorder-triggering events are expected to differ between males and females, e.g. loss of status versus infertility.

In instances in which precipitating events can be identified (e.g. failing to achieve an important goal), and where there is *no* evidence of previous periods of depression, this model is an obvious explanatory candidate. Persons who have experienced a loss or an important competitive defeat frequently become depressed. Members of kin and nonkin social networks often provide help without requiring paybacks, thereby easing the requirements for continuing group membership for individuals who are depressed. Although exact percentages are not known, a reasonable estimate is that half of the mild-to-moderate, time-limited depressions that are responses to adverse events resolve satisfactorily, without professional intervention, and are adaptive.

In what ways can nonevolutionary hypotheses be integrated into the depression-is-an-adaptive-trait model? Depression-triggering environmental events, such as a significant loss or living in a stressful and depriving social environment, are consistent with both the sociocultural and psychoanalytic views that the social environment can have pathogenic properties. Thus these hypotheses can be integrated. Other hypotheses are less easily included. For example, neurochemical and hormonal explanations of depression are usually framed such that physiological contributions are discussed independently of possible adverse social events. If physiological changes are viewed as secondary, they may be integrated; if they are viewed as primary, they do not easily qualify. Developmental disruption explanations are also not easily integrated, at least in the narrow interpretation of the model. As they are usually understood, disruptive events increase disorder vulnerability, which is not a requirement of the model, although undoubtedly combinations of developmental disruptions and adverse environmental contingencies are implicated in many instances of depression. Similar reasoning applies to pedigree and inadequate learning models, both of which place importance on the presence of compromised capacities prior to the onset of a disorder. These conditions are not required.

Ms. E—A clinical vignette.   After having spent 3 years in a near full-time effort to write a book, Ms. E was unable to obtain a publisher. Following her eleventh rejection, she became depressed, refused to leave her home, and avoided social interactions with friends and family. Friends and family continued to provide support; and a close friend took it upon herself to contact other publishers, one of whom took an interest in Ms. E's book. Book negotiations followed, and eventually a contract for the book was signed. Within a month, the signs and symptoms of depression began to resolve. After 3 months, Ms. E was functioning normally and was actively involved in the final editing of her book. In this vignette, Ms. E's depression is a consequence of failing to achieve a high-priority goal.

The pleiotropy-model-of-depression

Pleiotropy is also an ultimate cause explanation, and it references a type of selection in which a gene or set of genes control one or more phenotypes. It is the possibility of more than one phenotype that makes this model attractive, especially if the nondisorder phenotype is highly adaptive, e.g. high fecundity, above-average mate attractiveness. The model is not limited to depression, and it provides a potential explanation for how disorder-related genes can remain in a population and avoid strong selection effects. It does not require either that persons become depressed or the presence of common final pathway constraints, although constraints are not precluded. The possibility that persons who become depressed will attempt to act adaptively, or that others will provide help, are also not precluded. Further, the model does not specify at what stage of life depression is most probable, although a reasonable assumption is that severe depression would be less likely among females during prime reproductive years because of the negative effects on mate choice and offspring rearing.

The model has been used to explain senescence (Williams, 1957), and it may apply to the first-time occurrence of depression among post-menopausal women. External precipitating events are not required in this explanation: changes in central nervous system anatomy or physiology associated with ageing could be the pleiotropic trait, and thus a major contributing factor to disorder onset. It is also a potentially attractive explanation for both pre-menopausal major depression and bipolar illness, which are often associated with superior intelligence and/or creative capacities (Goodwin & Jamison, 1990), attributes that are likely to increase one's attractiveness as a potential mate. Information processing capacities need not be suboptimal in this model, although periods of dysfunctionality are assumed to occur.

In the pleiotropy model, female and male differences in the prevalence of depression should be influenced by the advantages conferred by the associated adaptive trait(s). For example, if the associated trait is an above-average capacity to read others' behaviour rules (i.e. others' minds), the cross-sex frequencies of depression should be about equal because reading other's rules is important to both sexes. However, if the associated trait is above-average fecundity, a greater prevalence of depression among females would be predicted because the adaptive trait is likely to be sex-linked.

Several nonevolutionary hypotheses can be integrated into this model. Those emphasising neurochemical or physiological dysfunctionality qualify if the pleiotropic trait is neurochemical (e.g. dysfunctionality of the norepinephrine system). Chronic low self-esteem, intrapsychic conflicts, and constrained functional capacities could represent phenotypic expressions of a pleiotropic trait. However, they are not required by the model. Hypotheses dealing with maturational disruptions and environmental perturbations also are not required.

Mrs. N—A clinical vignette.   Mrs. N was a 64-year-old female in good physical health who lived with her husband. She was an active member of a close and supportive family; and her 3 daughters and 2 sons lived nearby, as did her 14 grandchildren. She had no prior history of depression. Without any precipitating incident, Mrs. N developed signs and symptoms of depression. Withdrawal from her family and friends followed. An array of anti-depression medications minimally altered her condition. Eventually, she received electroconvulsive treatment, which resulted in a return to her pre-depression state. In this vignette, the onset of a first-time bout of depression in a woman with above-average fecundity, and without obvious external or internal provocations, is consistent with the pleiotropy model.

Mr. P—A clinical vignette.   Mr. P was a 42-year-old, successful, physically attractive, male writer who had been married numerous times. Beginning in his early twenties, he experienced intermittent periods of hypomania and depression. Females found him most attractive during his hypomanic periods, and it was at these times that he married. Subsequent periods of depression ended in divorce. He had seven children. In this vignette, the presence of superior creative capacities associated with a form of bipolar illness is consistent with the pleiotropy model.

The trait-variation model of depression

This model assumes that cross-person differences in trait clusters and differential within-cluster trait optimality influence the probability of depression. Trait profiles may be due to the chance effects of genetic mixing at conception, biased genetic information, or reflect incomplete trait refinement: as noted, pedigree data strongly suggest that genetic information influences the probability of depression, and assortative mating among persons with disorders is a well-documented finding. Different trait clusters should result in different types, intensities, and clinical courses of depression, e.g. short-term versus chronic depression. Common final pathway constraints are assumed to apply in this model. A large percentage of chronic, treatment-refractive depressions are consistent with this model, whereas the once-only bouts of depression associated with clear precipitating incidents and rapid resolution are more parsimoniously explained by other models.

The model requires evidence of either functional capacity limitations or disorder vulnerability prior to disorder onset. In the narrow interpretation of the model, biomedical hypotheses are potentially applicable, e.g. suboptimal traits may be physiological. Sexual selection also may be a factor. For example, because (on average) the requirements for social interaction skills are likely to be greater among females than among males, suboptimal social skills should contribute to a higher incidence of depression in females. The model does not assume that depression is adaptive; but as with the two preceding models, it does not preclude the possibility that help will be provided by others or that persons who are depressed will attempt to act adaptively.

Mr. A and Mr. B—A clinical vignette.   Mr. A and Mr. B were monozygotic twins who were separated at birth and who did not know of each other's existence until they met in their late twenties. One had grown up in a warm and supportive family, the other in a stern and often verbally abusive family. Both graduated from college; both had jobs in which they were successful; and both were married and had children. Each had suffered from periods of moderate to severe depression beginning when they were teenagers. Psychotherapy (Mr. A) and multiple trials of anti-depression medications (Mr. B) did not alter their clinical conditions significantly. In this vignette, similarities in clinical histories in two persons with the same genotypes, but with different upbringing histories, favours a genetically-influenced trait variation interpretation.

Developmental Disruption Model of Depression

One evolutionary model is considered in this category.

The disrupted-maturation-programmes model of depression

The assumptions underlying the narrow interpretation of this model include the following: infants have normal genetic information for maturation programmes; maturation programmes are disrupted; and disruptions lead either to depression or increased vulnerability for depression. Put another way, an individual who otherwise would have grown up normally becomes vulnerable to depression because of disruptive events during development.

This model is similar to psychoanalytic, behavioural, and psychosocial models that postulate the presence of developmental insults or atypical upbringing environments as associated with an increased probability of disorders. Ultimate cause explanations provide a framework that informs these hypotheses. In condensed form, one such explanation runs as follows: mothers have been selected to bond with and care for their infants (e.g. provide nutrients and protection); and infants have been selected to bond with caretakers and to engage in behaviour that facilitates bonding on the part of caretakers. However, selection has not favoured a high degree of self-sufficiency among infants during the early months of life, presumably because, in the past, successful bonding between mother and infant occurred with a great enough frequency that alternative selection paths were not favoured. One outcome of these events is infant dependency, e.g. slowly unfolding maturational programmes that are vulnerable to adverse social conditions.

The causes of maturational disruptions vary in timing, type, intensity, and consequence, e.g. the effects of excessive maternal alcohol use will differ from the effects of maternal rejection. As infants grow, they become increasingly capable of managing adverse events (e.g. social tension, periods of caretaker absence), although periods of increased susceptibility may occur during critical transition periods. Although the model does not assume that depression is adaptive, it does not preclude either attempts to act adaptively by those who become depressed or the possibility that others will provide help.

In this model, suboptimal information processing is implicated. Male–female differences in disorder prevalence could be influenced by disruption type. A number of prevailing model hypotheses can be incorporated into the narrow interpretation of the model, e.g. explanations dealing with the effects of toxins on DNA encoding and, in turn, physiological suboptimality. If the constraints on the hypothesis are relaxed so that almost any developmental disruption is admissible (e.g. excessive sensitivity to rejection due to disorder pre-dispositions), the hypothesis loses power, as it does when studies point to nonshared environmental factors and their interaction with disorder probabilities (e.g. Silberg et al., 1990).

Mr. P—A clinical vignette.   For reasons unrelated to his health or behaviour, Mr. P was placed in 4 different foster homes before he was 15 months old. Reports by step-parents indicated that his pleasant, outgoing nature changed when he was switched from the third to the fourth home. There was no history of depression among first-degree relatives. Signs of depression first appeared when Mr. P was 8 years old, and chronic symptoms of depression coupled with intermittent bouts of more debilitating depression continued into adulthood. Despite numerous interventions, no satisfactory treatment was found. In this vignette, it is the disruptive effect on bonding due to multiple placements that is the key postulated contributing factor leading to maturational disruption and depression.

Models of Depression Emphasizing Ultimate–Proximate Cause Interactions

Three variations of ultimate–proximate interaction models of depression will be discussed. Each requires the occurrence of an external event (proximate cause) that compromises goal achievement. Because depressed persons often identify themselves as having failed in their efforts to achieve goals, and because they often believe that environmental events are the basis of their failures, clinical histories compatible with these models are frequently provided by parents. Both ultimate and proximate mechanism explanations interact in these models. Ultimate causation explains why persons are "locked-in" to their social environment (even adverse environments) to achieve goals (McGuire & Troisi, in press), as well as their response strategies. Proximate events explain how disorders are triggered. Depression may be adaptive in these models, and the models do not preclude others providing help.

Variation 1: The-competitive-loss-or-decline-in-social-status model

In this variation, one's perception of a fall in status and/or communication by others that such a fall has occurred results in changes in psychological and physiological systems. The model builds on the evolutionary concepts of competitive interactions and hierarchical relationships. It assumes that both the symptoms and signalling features of depression are ultimately caused, and it is consistent with the findings from regulation–disregulation theory discussed later. Clinical data are compatible with this model in that social-status decline or competitive losses often go hand-in-hand with depression. Males, more than females, would be expected to develop depression in this model.

Variation 2: Failure-to-resolve-interpersonal-conflict model

The key feature of this variation is that interpersonal conflict can result in either a dominant or a ritualised submissive response towards the person with whom one is in conflict, with the ritualised submissive response manifesting as depression (Price et al., 1994). In their words (1994, p. 309): "It is postulated that the depressive state evolved in relationship to social competition, as an unconscious, involuntary losing strategy, enabling the individual to accept defeat in ritual agonistic encounters and to accommodate to what would otherwise be unacceptably low social rank." The model offers a proximate triggering explanation of depression, although capacities to engage in ritualised agonistic behaviour are ultimately caused. A reasonable assumption is that many persons who are unable to resolve interpersonal conflicts also have compromised functional capacities that enhance the probability of unresolved conflicts. This assumption is not required by the model, however.

The model has clinical utility in that depression is often associated with unresolved interpersonal conflicts, particularly when interacting parties are interdependent. Cost:benefit interpretations are also relevant. For example, ritualised submissive behaviour may be more costly than discontinuing a relationship unless depression reduces both conflict intensity and duration. If depression results in a decline in costs and resolves a conflict, the model may qualify as a variant of the depression-is-adaptive model applied to situations of interpersonal conflict. Relationship type should determine whether males or females are more likely to be depressed, with females having a greater disorder probability than males due to male tendencies to dominate and guard females.

Variation 3: Response-to-loss model

This is perhaps the most familiar of the models of depression, and it is similar to models developed by psychoanalytic and psychosocial theorists. Losses can be real, anticipated, or imagined. This model differs from the competitive loss model because competitive losses may be reversed whereas interpersonal losses (e.g. death of a crucial other) often cannot. A relaxation of the model's constraints allows for other types of losses, such as the loss of a capacity (e.g. a decline in technical skills associated with ageing). The model has clinical utility in that loss frequently correlates with depression. An associated factor is the potential cost involved in attempting to replace a critical other. Such costs can be considerable.

Of the nonevolutionary models of depression, the sociocultural (e.g. excessive stress, poverty) and the psychoanalytic (e.g. response to loss) are most easily integrated into ultimate–proximate interaction models. Biomedical models dealing with neurochemical disregulation remain secondary. Variations in responses to triggering conditions point to the presence of common final pathway constraints.

To summarise this section, the preceding review of evolutionary models of depression accomplishes a number of things. It considers potential disorder-related consequences of sexual selection. It underscores the fact that evolutionary models are not necessarily mutually exclusive and that depression is as likely to have multiple causes as a single cause. It identifies possible genetic, physiological, psychological, and environmental conditions that are associated with an increased probability of depression. It specifies the conditions under which features of nonevolutionary models can be integrated with evolutionary interpretations. In turn, the explanatory power and therapeutic options of both evolutionary and nonevolutionary models are increased: e.g. a framework that facilitates the use of evolutionary explanations in clinical settings is developed. For example, if some instances of depression are adaptive, and if depression is accompanied by physiological system changes, interventions designed to alter physiological states may compromise the adaptation.

REGULATION–DISREGULATION THEORY AND RELATED FINDINGS

A central theme of the first part of this paper was that comprehensive evolutionary explanations of depression need to accommodate individual differences in both disorder severity and cause. A central theme of the evolutionary model section was that environmental contingencies can trigger depression or increase vulnerability to depression. Regulation–disregulation theory, which is discussed in detail elsewhere (McGuire and Troisi, 1987; McGuire & Troisi, in press; McGuire et al., in press), integrates these themes by addressing the bidirectional effects of social interactions and physiological and psychological system functionality. The theory offers insights into how events in the social environment influence behavioural change and trigger the onset of disorders among persons vulnerable to disorders. In extremely adverse social environments, the theory can explain the onset of disorders among persons who are not predisposed or vulnerable to disorders.

The term regulation references a state in which psychological and physiological systems are functioning optimally, e.g. homeostatically. One feels well, has the energy to do what one wants to do, thinks clearly, goes about achieving goals efficiently, and is asymptomatic. For many reasons (e.g. trait variation, maturational disruptions), individuals differ with respect to both their degree of optimal functionality (their set point), and the usual range of psychological and physiological change that can be tolerated without symptoms. The term disregulation references dysfunctional states. Moderate infrastructural dysfunctionality is associated with symptoms such as mild depression, anxiety anger, boredom, and limited capacities to think clearly and act efficiently. This state is not considered a disorder, but rather a "somatic warning" that disregulation is underway. Severe dysfunctionality is associated with more debilitating symptoms and signs and the onset or worsening of disorders.

The theory builds from the following findings. (1) Humans are social animals and strongly predisposed to live in close proximity to, and to interact with, one another. (2) Information recognition systems have evolved that are highly sensitive to others' signals. (3) The behaviour of others influences recogisers' physiological and psychological systems. (4) Specific types and frequencies of social interactions are essential for maintaining regulation. (5) Persons seek out social environments and interactions that regulate. (6) Disregulated states are associated with undesirable feelings and thoughts, and an increased probability of disorders and features of disorders, as well as a worsening of disorders among persons already suffering from them (McGuire & Troisi, 1987, in press).

The idea that different types of social interactions can have psychological, physiological, and functional consequences is based on evidence from psychiatry, psychology (e.g. Bowlby, 1969, 1973; Hofer, 1984; Schultz, 1965; Spitz, 1945), and primatology (e.g. Harlow & Harlow, 1962; McGuire, Raleigh, & Johnson, 1983; McGuire, Raleigh, & Pollack, 1994; Raleigh, Brammer, McGuire, & Yuwiler, 1985; Raleigh & McGuire, 1989, 1993; Raleigh, McGuire, Brammer, Pollack, & Yuwiler, 1991; Raleigh, McGuire, Brammer, & Yuwiler, 1984; Rosenblum et al., 1994; Sapolsky, 1989, 1990). What is involved can be modelled by studies of vervet monkeys, self–other separateness, and positron emission tomography (PET).

Vervet monkey studies

Among vervet monkeys (*Cercopithecus aethiops sabeaus*), high-status or dominant males have peripheral serotonin levels averaging almost twice as high as low-status or subordinate males, as well as significantly elevated measures of central nervous system (CNS) serotonin sensitivity (i.e., significantly greater responsiveness to drugs influencing CNS serotonin activity). When CNS serotonin sensitivity is high, the frequency of initiated aggressive behaviour is low; animals are more relaxed socially, more tolerant of the behaviour of other animals, and they more frequently initiate and respond to affiliative gestures by other group members. Essentially the opposite set of findings applies to animals with low CNS serotonin sensitivity, a condition that is associated with low social status, fewer initiated and received affiliative behaviours, a higher frequency of received threats, and high levels of inter-animal vigilance. Said differently, high-status animals are more regulated than low-status animals, and degree of regulation is context-dependent (McGuire et al., 1983, 1994; Raleigh et al., 1984, 1985, 1991).

Although the advantages of high status (e.g. preferential access to females) no doubt contribute to male–male competition for high status, findings also permit the interpretation that animals compete because of the desirable effects associated with elevated CNS serotonin sensitivity, such as being more relaxed and more responsive to others' affiliative behaviour (McGuire & Troisi, 1987). Such behaviour is analogous to humans competing with each other to achieve desired feeling states (e.g. high status) or seeking out specific social environments (e.g. rock concerts) in which they feel comfortable and relaxed.

A number of findings from vervet monkeys extend to humans. For example, among high-status, relatively aggressive competitors, sometimes called "Machiavellians", the relationship between peripheral serotonin concentrations and social rank is strongly positive. For more deferent individuals, sometimes called "moralists", who are also high status, the relationship is negative (Madsen, 1985, 1986; Madsen & McGuire, 1984). Among reported studies, the ratio between high-status Machiavellians and high-status moralists is 7:1. Although peripheral–central serotonin relationships still need to be clarified in humans, the similarity between peripheral serotonin levels and status in nonhuman primates and humans remains striking.

Serotonin, of course, is only one of many systems influencing behaviour. For example, correlations between ratios of different neurotransmitters (e.g. serotonin, norepinephrine, and dopamine) and both normal personalities and features of personality disorders are thought to exist (Cloninger, 1986; Cloninger et al., 1993); and hormones, such as thyroid, oestrogen, and testosterone interact with behaviour (Nyborg, 1994). From the perspective of this paper, different personalities and physiological profiles are associated with different enduring trait features, and different cross-person physiological set points are postulated to correlate with different neurotransmitter and hormone ratios, as well as different degrees of risk for depression.

Self–other separateness

Physical self–other separateness is a biological fact, and most of the time persons recognise that they are physically distinct from others. When they do, others are perceived as leading their own lives and having their own values and aspirations. Yet there are moments in which separateness is less clear. For example, there is often a blurring of physical boundaries during sexual orgasm, periods of intense infatuation, moments of empathy and dependence, intoxication, and periods of group excitement. Blurring is associated with an increased receptivity to others' signals and influence (McGuire & Troisi, in press). Conversely, when separateness is intensified, as when one is preoccupied with one's thoughts, one's receptivity to others' signals declines. In between these extremes is the modal state that most persons experience most of the time: basic separateness, with greater or lesser degrees of blurring across different social interactions. The capacity to move back and forth within what can be called "a window of separateness" differs across persons. For example, in terms of the personality distinctions discussed earlier, moralists usually stand back, evaluate, and judge; that is, windows of separateness are narrow and self–other distinctions are intensified. In contrast, Machiavellians are more inclined to manipulate others in face-to-face interactions, which presupposes an openness to others' signals not characteristic of moralists. The reasons for such differences are multiple and include trait variation and degree of regulation.

Both pre-disorder and depressed states are frequently associated with windows of separateness that can be characterised as either too-narrow-and-too-rigid, or too-wide-and-too-labile. In both states atypical information processing occurs. When windows are too-narrow-and-too-rigid, as is observed among persons who are socially distant and reticent to interact during nondepressed and depressed states, physiological disregulation is likely because of the reduced frequency of received regulating signals. When windows are too-wide-and-too-labile, which is often observed among persons who are highly dependent on others and/or who are unusually sensitive to negative social information, others' signals are often misinterpreted, and disregulation may follow. (Self–other separateness is a likely explanation for the earlier mentioned differences in cortisol responses to stress tests.) In short, both extremes of self–other separateness increase the probability of disregulation; and both extremes are observed among persons who become depressed.

PET findings

Findings from PET studies of both normal populations and persons with depression inform a number of the preceding points. For example, studies demonstrate that both regional cerebral blood flow and glucose metabolism differ among persons with depression and normal controls (e.g. Baxter et al., 1985; Bench et al., 1992; Biver et al., 1994; Dolan, Bench, Brown, Scott, & Frackowiak, 1994; George, Ketter, & Post, 1993). In principle, these findings are not surprising: CNS changes are expected with depression. Other studies have shown that depression-characteristic glucose metabolism findings normalise following successful treatment (Martinot et al., 1990). This finding is also expected; and it is consistent with many cases of depression that are clinically reversible. However, among a subset of depressed persons, both frontal cortex and whole-cortex hypometabolism persist following successful treatment (Martinot et al., 1990) and regional blood flow studies show an anatomical dissociation between the effects of depressed mood and depression-related cognitive impairment (Bench et al., 1992; Dolan et al., 1992). Such findings may in part explain differences in disorder vulnerability, and also, perhaps, instances of chronic cognitive suboptimality observed among many persons with dysthymia (Essock-Vitale & McGuire, 1990; McGuire et al., in press). Yet other findings show regional blood flow differences among normal males and females when they have experimentally induced dysphoric thoughts (George et al., 1995; Pardo, Pardo, & Rauchle, 1993). This finding opens the door to the possibility that different parts of the male and female brain are active during depression. If so, such differences may partially account for sex-related prevalence differences (see McGuire et al., in press). Further, should (on average) windows of separateness be more open in females, females would be more vulnerable to the influences of negative external information.

Figure 12.1 extends the preceding points in ways that are consistent with clinical findings. It shows changing physiological and psychological states for Persons A and B in social environments X and Y. The horizontal axis depicts time. The vertical axis shows areas depicting regulated and disregulated states. Zero (0) on the horizontal axis references physiological regulation. In Environment X, others are supportive, minimally competitive and demanding, and there are numerous social options. Environment X represents a low-stress environment in which social interactions are rewarding and psychologically and physiologically regulating. In Environment Y, others are not supportive but are highly competitive and socially demanding, and there are few social options. Environment Y is a high-stress environment, one that can easily contribute to

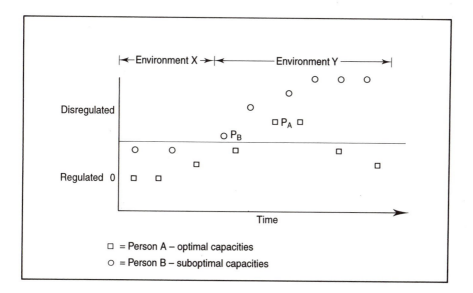

FIG. 12.1. Relationships between physiological disregulation, two social environments, and the probability of disorders. (Adapted from McGuire et al., in press).

disregulation. Person A has optimal functional capacities, modal self–other separateness, and normal CNS glucose metabolism. Person B has suboptimal functional capacities, atypical self–other separateness, and CNS glucose hypometabolism.

In Environment X, Persons A and B are maximally physiologically and psychologically regulated. Person A is not symptomatic, and Person B is mildly symptomatic. When Persons A and B enter Environment Y, they become disregulated and symptomatic (e.g. tense, anxious, depressed) because of increased competition and social demands, limited social options, and the low frequency of others' behaviour that facilitates disregulation.

Critical differences in Person A and Person B's responses to Environment Y occur at points P_A and P_B where Persons A and B first experience unpleasant emotions. Person B becomes disregulated and symptomatic (Point P_B) sooner than Person A. For persons with different functional capacities and set points, the timing of point P_B will differ. At Point P_A, Person A has two options to avoid further disregulation: he may change behavioural strategies and engage persons in Environment Y in ways that lead to regulation (e.g. become socially dominant); or he may leave Environment Y and return to Environment X, where less competitive and less stressful social interactions will facilitate regulation.

The first alternative is shown in the figure: Person A changes behavioural strategies and regulates. Hypothetically, the same options are available to Person B. However, because of limited functional capacities, Person B lacks the capacity to change behaviour to the degree required to attain dominance status and to regulate in Environment Y. Should Person B remain in Environment Y for an extended period, he will become further disregulated, symptoms will appear, and a disorder may be triggered. In principle, Person B could regulate by returning to Environment X, but clinical experience suggests that a large percentage of persons with suboptimal capacities fail to locate themselves in environments that are optimal for regulation. (The opposite picture may also occur. Person B may avoid entering Environment Y as a self-protective strategy.)

Mr. L—A clinical vignette.   Mr. L was a 47-year-old married male with 3 grown children. He sought therapy because of depression.

His history revealed that he was physically healthy and had not previously suffered from a mental disorder. He had been president of his high school class, and captain of his high school football team. He was a member of a close-knit and supportive family, enjoyed recreational activities, and was an active participant in community projects. His history also revealed that he was very selective in his choice of friends, and that he was unusually competitive with other males. At work, he frequently spent extra hours in order to finish tasks before others were able to do so; and when others were prematurely or unfairly promoted, he suffered from periods of intense anger. He lacked psychological insight.

Five months prior to seeking therapy, he was informed that he had failed in his active attempt to gain the presidency of a large manufacturing firm for which he had worked for 15 years. A younger, and in his view a less competent, male had been appointed president. His anger was so intense that he resigned from the firm and took a lower-status job with a competing company. Within a month symptoms of depression appeared. Over the ensuing months his symptoms became worse, although he was able to continue work.

Interventions involved both medications and psychotherapy. Medications were moderately effective in relieving his symptoms. However, undesirable side-effects reduced his compliance. Psychotherapy was unproductive. Then, the sudden departure of the president of the company for which Mr. L was working led to his appointment as Acting President. Two months later he was appointed President. These changes were followed by a dramatic decline in his symptoms.

The case illustrates two points: the importance of competitive victories and high social status among males; and interactions between status and psychological and physiological states.

DISCUSSION

We have explored a comprehensive evolutionary approach to interpreting depression. Rather than limiting the discussion to putative core features, the evolutionary concepts of trait variation, sexual selection, and bi-directional behaviour–physiology interactions have been introduced in an attempt to identify some of the factors contributing to both individual differences in depression and vulnerability to depression. In addition, we have attempted to reconcile evolutionary explanations of depression with clinical findings and features of nonevolutionary hypotheses. We have assumed that common final pathway constraints are compatible with evolutionary interpretations of depression, although the implications of this assumption still need to be worked out.

In the three types of depression discussed earlier, externally precipitated, mild–moderate, time-limited, spontaneously-resolving depression qualifies as an adaptation. Dysthymic disorder is viewed as a combination of an adaptive response (depression) and traits that compromise adaptation. Compromised traits and their consequences (e.g. decreased reproduction) make dysthymic disorder marginally adaptive. Except for the possibility of pleiotropy, major depression is viewed as a consequence of common final pathway constraints associated with significant suboptimal and dysfunctional psychological and physiological traits. Certain features of major depression may reflect core adaptations, but in most instances they are obscured by other factors. For example, responses to salutary environmental change is observed among most persons with major depression. Thus, capacities for plasticity are present. However, responses are usually minimal, and rarely do environmental alterations result in significant clinical improvement.

What are the treatment implications of the preceding analysis? Not treating an adaptive response (e.g. moderate, time-limited depression) has already been mentioned. A second possibility is to treat those features of disorders that interfere with adaptive responses. In part, this is the rationale for pharmacological interventions in instances of major depression and dysthymia: In effect, if signs and symptoms become debilitating and compromise attempts to adapt, most clinicians are likely to intervene with drugs. That there may be sex differences in response to specific drugs is one implication from the preceding discussion of PET findings. A third possibility is to attempt to optimise adaptive responses, for example, by increasing or consolidating social-support networks, or reducing the impact of others' negative behaviour through environmental change.

Finally, it is worth returning to the prevalence estimates with which this paper began. If approximately 75% of persons will *not* become depressed during their lives, and 25% will, there are likely to be important differences between these two populations. Persons who do not suffer from depression are not free of trait variation. For example, within wide ranges, IQ scores do not correlate with depression. Thus, trait variation per se does not correlate with the probability of depression. Rather, it is the types of traits and their combinations that are critical in influencing disorder probability.

ACKNOWLEDGMENTS

The authors wish to thank the Giles and Elise Mead Foundation, the Harry Frank Guggenheim Foundation, the University of California, and the Veterans Administration for their support, and N. Brown for help in the preparation of the manuscript.

REFERENCES

American Psychiatric Association (1994). *DSM–IV. Diagnostic and statistical manual of mental disorders (4th Edn.)*. Washington, DC: American Psychiatric Association Press.

Baxter, L.R., Phelps, M.E., Mazziotta, J.C., Schwartz, J.M., Gerner, R.H., Selin, C.E. & Sumida, R.M. (1985). Cerebral metabolic rates for glucose in mood disorders. *Archives of General Psychiatry, 42*, 441–447.

Bench, C.J., Friston, K.J., Brown, R.G., Scott, L.C., Frackowiak, R.S.J. & Dolan, R.J. (1992). The anatomy of melancholia—focal abnormalities of cerebral blood flow in major depression. *Psychological Medicine, 22*, 607–615.

Berger, M., Bossert, S., Krieg, J-C., Dirlich, G., Ettmeier, W., Schreiber, W. & von Zerssen, D. (1987). Interindividual differences in the susceptibility of the cortisol system: An important factor for the degree of hypercortisolism in stress situations. *Biological Psychiatry, 22*, 1327–1339.

Birtchnell, J. (1993). *How humans relate*. Westport, CT: Praeger.

Biver, F., Goldman, S., Delvenne, V., Luxen, A., DeMaertelaer, V., Hubain, P., Mendlewicz, J. & Lotstra, F. (1994). Frontal and parietal metabolic disturbances in unipolar depression. *Biological Psychiatry, 36*, 381–388.

Bouchard, T.J. Jr., Lykken, D.T., McGuire, M., Segal, N.L. & Tellegen, A. (1990). Sources of human psychological differences: The Minnesota study of twins reared apart. *Science, 250*, 223–228.

Bowlby, J. (1969). *Attachment and loss Vol. I. Attachment*. London: Hogarth Press.

Bowlby, J. (1973). *Attachment and loss Vol. II. Separation: Anxiety and anger*. London: Hogarth Press.

Brown, S.L. & Kenrick, D.T. (1995). *Paternity certainty and female dominance: Should males prefer submissive females?* Paper given at the Human Behavior and Evolution Society meeting, June 28–July 2, 1995, Santa Barbara, CA.

Buss, D.M. (1985). Human mate selection. *American Scientist, 73*, 47–51.

Buss, D.M. (1988). From vigilance to violence: Tactics of mate retention in American undergraduates. *Ethology Sociobiology, 9*, 291–317.

Buss, D.M. (1994). *The evolution of desire*. New York: Basic Books.

Cashden, E. (1993). Attracting mates: Effects of paternal investment on mate attraction strategies. *Ethology Sociobiology, 14*, 1–24.

Cloninger, C.R. (1986). A unified biosocial theory of personality and its role in the development of anxiety states. *Psychiatric Developments, 3*, 167–226.

Cloninger, C.R., Svrakic, D.M. & Przybeck, T.R. (1993). A psychobiological model of temperament and character. *Archives of General Psychiatry, 50*, 975–990.

Daly, M., Wilson, M. & Weghorst, S.J. (1982). Male sexual jealousy. *Ethology Sociobiology, 3*, 11–27.

Dolan, R.J., Bench, C.J., Brown, R.G., Scott, L.C. & Frackowiak, R.S. (1994). Neuropsychological dysfunction in depression: The relationship to regional blood flow. *Psychological Medicine, 24,* 849–857.

Dolan, R.I., Bench, C.J., Brown, R.G., Scott, L.C., Friston, K.J. & Frackowiak, R.S. (1992). Regional cerebral blood flow abnormalities in depressed patients with cognitive impairment. *Journal of Neurology, Neurosurgery and Psychiatry, 55,* 768–773.

Engle, G.L. (1980). The clinical application of the biopsychosocial model. *American Journal of Psychiatry, 137,* 535–544.

Engle, G.L. & Schmale, A.H. (1972). Conservation-withdrawal: A primary regulatory process for organismic homeostasis. In R. Porter & J.K. Night (Eds.), *Physiology, emotion, and psychosomatic illness* (pp. 57–85). Amsterdam. CIBA.

Erlenmeyer-Kimling, I. & Paradowski, W. (1977). Selection and schizophrenia. In C.J. Bajema (Ed.), *Natural selection in human populations* (pp. 259–275). Huntington, NY: Krieger.

Essock-Vitale, S.M. & McGuire, M.T. (1990). Social and reproductive histories of depressed and anxious women. In R.W. Bell & N.J. Bell (Eds.), *Sociobiology and the social sciences* (pp. 105–118). Lubbock, TX: Texas Technical University Press.

Gardner, R. (1982). Mechanisms of manic-depressive disorder, an evolutionary model. *Archives of General Psychiatry, 39,* 1436–1441.

George, M.S., Ketter, T.A., Parekh, P.I., Horwitz, B., Herscovitch, P. & Post, R.M. (1995). Brain activity during transient sadness and happiness in healthy women. *American Journal of Psychiatry, 152,* 341–351.

George, M.S., Ketter, R.A. & Post, R.M. (1993). SPECT and PET imaging in mood disorders. *Journal Clinical Psychiatry, 54*(Suppl), 6–13.

Gilbert, P. (1989). *Human nature and suffering.* Hove, UK: Lawrence Erlbaum Associates Ltd.

Gilbert, P. (1993). Defence and safety: Their function in social behaviour and psychopathology. *British Journal Clinical Psychology, 32,* 131–153.

Gilbert, P. (1995). Biopsychosocial approaches and evolutionary theory as aids to integration in clinical psychology and psychotherapy. *Clinical Psychology Psychotherapy, 2,* 135–156.

Gilbert, P. & Allan, S. (1994). Assertiveness, submissive behaviour and social comparison. *British Journal of Clinical Psychology, 33,* 295–306.

Goodwin, F.K. & Jamison, K.R. (1990). *Manic depressive illness.* New York: Oxford University Press.

Grammar, K. (1995). *Age and facial features influencing mate choice.* Paper given at the Gruter Institute Meeting, April 24–26, 1995, Munich, Germany.

Gut, E. (1989). *Productive and unproductive depression.* New York: Basic Books.

Guze, S.B., Goodwin, D.W. & Crane, J.B. (1970). A psychiatric study of wives of convicted felons: An example of assortative mating. *American Journal of Psychiatry, 126,* 1773–1776.

Hamilton, W.D. & Zuk, M. (1982). Heritable true fitness and bright birds: A role for parasites? *Science, 218,* 384–387.

Harlow, H.F. & Harlow, M.K. (1962). Social deprivation in monkeys. *Scientific American, 207,* 136–146.

Henderson, S., Byrne, D.G., Duncan-Jones, P., Scott, R. & Adcock, S. (1980). Social relationships, adversity and neurosis: A study of associations in a general population sample. *British Journal of Psychiatry, 136,* 574–583.

Hofer, M.A. (1984). Relationships as regulators: A psychobiologic perspective on bereavement. *Psychosomatic Medicine, 46,* 183–197.

Kaplan, H.I. & Sadock, B.J. (1995). *Comprehensive testbook of psychiatry/VI.* Baltimore, MD: Williams & Wilkins.

Kendler, K.S., Pedersen, N., Johnson, L., Neale, M.C. & Mathe, A.A. (1993). A pilot Swedish twin study of affective illness, including hospital- and population- ascertained subsamples. *Archives of General Psychiatry*, *50*, 699–706.

Kessler, R.C., McGonagle, K.A., Zhao, S., Nelson, C.B., Hughes, M., Eshelman S., Wittchen, H.U. & Kendler, K.S. (1994). Lifetime and 12-month prevalence of DSM–III–R psychiatric disorders in the United States: Results from the national comorbidity survey. *Archives of General Psychiatry*, *51*, 8–19.

Klerman, G.L. (1974). Depression and adaptation. In J.R. Friedman & M.M. Katz (Eds.), *Psychology of depression: Contemporary theory and research* (pp. 127–144). New York: Wiley.

Lewis, A.J. (1936). Melancholia: A clinical survey of depressive states. *Journal of Mental Science*, *80*, 1–43.

Madsen, D. (1985). A biochemical property relating to power seeking in humans. *American Political Science Review*, *79*, 448–457.

Madsen, D. (1986). Power seekers are biochemically different: Further biochemical evidence. *American Political Science Review*, *80*, 261–269.

Madsen, D. & McGuire, M.T. (1984). Whole blood 5-HT and the Type A behaviour pattern. *Psychosomatic Medicine*, *45*, 546–548.

Martinot, J-L., Hardy, P., Feline, A., Huret, J-D., Mazoyer, B., Attar-Levy, D., Pappata, S. & Syrota, A. (1990). Left prefrontal glucose hypometabolism in the depressed state: A confirmation. *American Journal of Psychiatry*, *147*, 1313–1317.

McEwan, K.L., Costello, C.G. & Taylor, P.J. (1987). Adjustment to infertility. *Journal of Abnormal Psychology*, *96*, 108–116.

McGuffin, P., Owen, M.J., O'Donova, M.C., Thapar, A. & Gottesman, I.I. (1994). *Seminars in Psychiatric Genetics*. London: Gaskell.

McGuire, M.T. & Essock-Vitale, S. (1982). Psychiatric disorders in the context of evolutionary biology: The impairment of adaptive behaviours during the exacerbation and remission of psychiatric illnesses. *Journal of Nervous Mental Disease*, *170*, 9–20.

McGuire, M.T., Fawzy, F.I., Spar, J.E., Weigel, R.W. & Troisi, A. (1995). Altruism and mental disorders. *Ethology Sociobiology*, *15*, 299–322.

McGuire, M.T., Raleigh, M.J., Fawzy, F.I., Spar, J. & Troisi, A. (in press). Dysthymic disorder, regulation–disregulation theory, CNS blood flow, and CNS metabolism. In L. Sloman (Ed.), *Dominance and depression: The link between Darwin and Prozac*.

McGuire, M.T., Raleigh, M.J. & Johnson, C. (1983). Social dominance in adult male vervet monkeys: General considerations. *Social Science Information*, *22*, 106–117.

McGuire, M.T., Raleigh, M.J. & Pollack, D. (1994). Personality features in vervet monkeys: The effects of sex, age, social status, and group composition. *American Journal of Primatology*, *33*, 1–13.

McGuire, M.T. & Troisi, A. (1987). Physiological regulation–disregulation and psychiatric disorders. *Ethology Sociobiology*, *8*, 9S–12S.

McGuire, M.T. & Troisi, A. (forthcoming) *Darwinian Psychiatry*. New York: Oxford University Press.

Merikangas, K.R. (1982). Assortative mating for psychiatric disorders and psychological traits. *Archives of General Psychiatry*, *39*, 1173–1180.

Merikangas, K.R., Bromet, E.J. & Spiker, D.G. (1983). Assortative mating, social adjustment, and course of illness in primary affective disorder. *Archives of General Psychiatry*, *40*, 795–800.

Nesse, R.M. (1990a). The evolutionary functions of repression and the ego defenses. *Journal of the American Academy of Psychoanalysis*, *18*, 260–285.

Nesse, R.M. (1990b). Evolutionary explanations of emotions. *Human Nature*, *1*, 261–289.

Nesse, R.M. (1991a). What good is feeling bad? The evolutionary benefits of psychic pain. *The Sciences, Nov/Dec*, 30–37.

Nesse, R.M. (1991b). Psychiatry. In M. Maxwell (Ed.), *The sociobiological imagination* (pp. 23–45). New York: State University of New York Press.

Nesse, R.M. (in press). *What Darwinian medicine offers psychiatry.* In W.R. Trethan, J.J. McKenna, & E.O. Smith (Eds.). New York: Oxford University Press.

Nesse, R.M. & Williams, G.C. (1995). *Why we get sick.* New York: Times Books.

Nyborg, H. (1994). *Hormones, sex, and society.* Westport, CT: Praeger.

Odegard, O. (1960). Marital rate and fertility in psychotic patients before hospital admissions and after discharge. *International Journal of Social Psychiatry, 6,* 25–33.

Odegard, O. (1980). Fertility of psychiatric first admissions in Norway, 1936–1975. *Acta Psychiatrica Scandinavica, 62,* 212–220.

Pardo, J.V., Pardo, P.J. & Raichle, M.E. (1993). Neural correlates of self-induced dysphoria. *American Journal of Psychiatry, 150,* 713–719.

Plomin, R., Owen, M.J. & McGuffin, P. (1994). The genetic basis of complex human behaviours. *Science, 264,* 1733–1739.

Plutchik, R. (1980). *Emotion. A psychoevolutionary synthesis.* New York: Harper & Row.

Price, J.S. (1967). The dominance hierarchy and the evolution of mental illness. *Lancet, 7502,* 243–246.

Price, J.S. (1969). Neurotic and endogenous depression: A phylogenetic view. *British Journal of Psychiatry, 114,* 119–120.

Price, J.S. & Gardner, R. Jr., (1995). The paradoxical power of the depressed patient: A problem with the ranking theory of depression. *British Journal of Medical Psychology, 68,* 193–206.

Price, J.S. & Sloman, L. (1987). Depression as yielding behaviour: An animal model based on Schyelderup-Ebbe's pecking order. *Ethology Sociobiology, 8,* 85S–98S.

Price, J., Sloman, L., Gardner R. Jr., Gilbert, P. & Rohde, P. (1994). The social competition hypothesis of depression. *British Journal of Psychiatry, 164,* 309–315

Raleigh, M.J., Brammer, G.L., McGuire, M.T. & Yuwiler, A. (1985). Dominant social status facilitates the behavioural effects of serotonergic agonists. *Brain Research, 348,* 274–282.

Raleigh, M.J., McGuire, M.T., Brammer, G.L., Pollack, D.B. & Yuwiler, A. (1991). Serotonergic mechanisms promote dominance acquisition in adult male vervet monkeys. *Brain Research, 559,* 181–190.

Raleigh, M.J., McGuire, M.T., Brammer, G.L., and Yuwiler, A. (1984). Social and environmental influences on blood 5-HT concentrations in monkeys. *Archives of General Psychiatry, 41,* 405–410.

Raleigh, M.J. & McGuire, M.T. (1989). Female influences on male dominance acquisition in captive vervet monkeys, *Cercopithecus aethiops sabaeus. Animal Behavior, 38,* 59–67.

Raleigh, M.J. & McGuire, M.T. (1993). Environmental constraints, serotonin, aggression, and violence in vervet monkeys. In R. Masters & M. McGuire (Eds.), *The neurotransmitter revolution.* (pp. 129–145). Carbondale, IL: Southern Illinois University Press.

Reite, M., Short, R., Seiler, C. & Pauley, J.D. (1981). Attachment, loss, and depression. *Journal of Child Psychology and Psychiatry, 22,* 221–227.

Rosenblum, L.A., Coplan, J.D., Friedman, S., Bassoff, T., Gorman, J.M. & Andrews, M.W. (1994). Adverse early experiences affect noradrenergic and serotonergic functioning in adult primates. *Biological Psychiatry, 35,* 221–227.

Salzan, E.A. (1991). On the nature of emotion. *International Journal of Comparative Psychology, 5,* 47–88.

Sapolsky, R.M. (1989). Hypercortisolism among socially subordinate wild baboons originates at the CNS level. *Archives of General Psychiatry, 46,* 1047–1051.

Sapolsky, R.M. (1990). Adrenocortical function, social rank, and personality among wild baboons. *Biological Psychiatry, 28*, 862–878.

Schultz, D.P. (1965). *Sensory deprivation*. New York: Academic Press.

Silberg, J.L., Heath, A.C., Kessler, R., Neale, M.C., Meyer, J.M., Eaves, L.J. & Kendler, K.S. (1990). Genetic and environmental effects on self-reported depressive symptoms in a general population twin sample. *Journal of Psychiatric Research, 24*, 197–212.

Silberman, E.K., Weingartner, H., Laraia, M., Byrnes, S. & Post, R.M. (1983). Processing of emotional properties of stimuli by depressed and normal subjects. *Journal of Nervous Mental Disease, 171*, 10–14.

Sloman, L. (1976). The role of neurosis in phylogenetic adaptation, with particular reference to early man. *American Journal of Psychiatry, 133*, 543–547.

Sloman, L. & Price, S.J. (1987). Losing behaviour (yielding subroutine) and human depression: Proximate and selective mechanisms. *Ethology Sociobiology, 8*, 99S–109S.

Sloman, L., Price, J., Gilbert, P. & Gardner, R. (1994). Adaptive functions of depression: Psychotherapeutic implications. *American Journal of Psychotherapy, 48*, 1–16.

Sloman, S. & Sloman, L. (1988). Male selection in the service of human evolution. *Journal of Social Biological Structures, 11*, 457–468.

Spitz, R. (1945). Hospitalism. *The psychoanalytic study of the child, Vol. 1* (pp. 53–74). New York: International Universities Press.

Tooby, J. & Cosmides, L. (1990). On the universality of human nature and the uniqueness of the individual: The role of genetics in adaptation. *Journal of Personality, 58*, 17–67.

Trivers, R. (1985). *Social evolution*. Menlo Park, CA: Benjamin/Cummings.

Williams, G.C. (1957). Pleiotropy, natural selection, and the evolution of senescence. *Evolution, 11*, 398–411.

Subject & Author Index